PSYCHOLOGY OF ADJUSTMENT

THE DORSEY SERIES IN PSYCHOLOGY

PSYCHOLOGY OF ADJUSTMENT

AUDREY HABER
Garden State Rehabilitation Hospital

RICHARD P. RUNYON

1984

THE DORSEY PRESS
Homewood, Illinois 60430

ISBN 0-256-02859-1

Library of Congress Catalog Card No. 83–72620

Printed in the United States of America

1 2 3 4 5 6 7 8 9 0 K 1 0 9 8 7 6 5 4

PREFACE

The different ways people react have always intrigued us. Some seem so self-confident and able to overcome any and all adversity. Others seem to fall apart at the slightest provocation. Psychology as a science has made tremendous strides in helping us understand some of these diversities in human functioning.

What does it mean when we refer to someone as "well-adjusted"? How can we learn to understand and cope with the stresses of life? What role do our emotions and motivations play in our daily functioning? These are but a few of the questions this book addresses.

We have tried to communicate what psychologists have learned about those issues that affect our daily lives. We have integrated this scientific knowledge with a more practical approach that gives insight into how we as individuals can deal with these issues. We have utilized real-life scenarios to illustrate many of the ideas presented in each chapter. We felt that these glimpses into the lives of real people will make the concepts and theories more real for you.

As we wrote this book, we learned a great deal about psychology and adjustment. We hope you, too, will benefit from this book as well.

ACKNOWLEDGMENTS

Any textbook is the result of the collaborative effort by many people. We would like to give thanks to a number of our colleagues who contributed many useful suggestions and insights at various points along the way. Specifically, we would like to thank the consulting editors, Dr. Wendell Jeffrey of the University of California–Los Angeles and Dr. Salvatore R. Maddi of the University of Chicago. We would also like to express our appreciation to our reviewers: Professor James Daley, Diablo Valley College; Professor Nancy Bowers, Pikes Peak Community College; Professor Lynn D. Zager, University of Tennessee–Chattanooga; Professor Joseph P. Cangemi, Western Kentucky University; Professor Luciano L'Abate, Georgia State University; Professor Richard Hirschman, Kent State University; Professor David G. Weight, Brigham Young University; Professor James O. Davis, Southwest Missouri State University; and Professor Charles W. Johnson, University of Evansville.

Audrey Haber
Richard P. Runyon

CONTENTS

PSYCHOLOGY OF ADJUSTMENT

C H A P T E R 1

OVERVIEW OF ADJUSTMENT

Dear Mom and Dad:

Since I left for college, I have been bad about writing. Please excuse my thoughtlessness. I promise to do better in the future. I'm going to fill you in on what has been going on. Please do not read further until you grab a chair. OK?

I'm getting along pretty well right now. The skull fracture and the concussion I got when jumping out of the dormitory window are almost healed. The fire wasn't too bad, but I count myself lucky to be alive. I spent only two weeks in the hospital, and I am getting my hearing back. I am learning to live with the constant headaches. Fortunately, the fire was witnessed by a gasoline station attendant. He called the fire department and saved my life. He visited me at the hospital daily. Since I had no where to go after getting out of the hospital (the dormitory will take months to be repaired), Mike was good enough to offer to share his apartment with me. He's a beautiful boy and I know you will love him just as I do. We're planning to get married.

We're not sure when, but I promise you it will be before my pregnancy starts to show. Yes, dear parents, your little girl is pregnant. I know how much you look forward to being grandparents, and I am sure you will give the baby plenty of love. The only thing preventing us from getting married is a little infection we picked up that prevents us from passing our blood test. It's one of those resistant strains, so we're not sure when it will be cleared up.

Now that I have brought you up to date, I want to tell you there was no dormitory fire, no skull fracture, no live-in roommate, no pregnancy, and no infection. However, I am getting a D in History and an F in Biology. I want you to see these marks in their proper perspective.

Your loving daughter,[1]

This letter was probably never written. It has been going the rounds for a number of years now. But it contains a message you'll be reading often throughout this book. One of the most important principles of effective adjustment is putting things into perspective. The perspective may involve evaluation of the significance of present events in your life, or it may place these events in a time frame. For example, at times, everyone feels overwhelmed with problems, conflicts, and emotional turmoil. You wonder if you'll ever breathe freely again. In those silent conversations you carry on with yourself throughout many of your waking hours,

[1] Based on *Fortune* (1970).

it is wise to pause and ask, How will I feel about the present situation in a week? A year? Ten years from now? Often the answer will put your present situation into perspective. You'll realize that a failing grade, loss of employment, a speeding ticket, or a love affair gone sour are not the end of the world. Somehow, you'll even survive events that seem catastrophic at the time they occur—bereavement over the loss of a loved one, a serious health problem, and so forth. How will you survive? Will you emerge from minor setbacks, major disappointments, and even life-shattering experiences as a "better," stronger, and more flexible person? Or will adversity leave in its wake a tired memory of what was once a vibrant human being? Finding the answers to these questions and applying them to your own life are really the subject matter of this book . . . adjustment.

WHAT IS ADJUSTMENT?

LuAnn could not believe what the obstetrician had said. "Your child is normal and healthy in the physical sense of the word, but I fear that there is a problem with his mental development." That was all the doctor said. LuAnn's mind screamed out in anguish. Her first impulse was to tell the doctor to get out of her sight and say no more. She refused to hear the words *mentally retarded.* This could not possibly be happening to her. It was all a bad dream. But with the pain of the delivery still fresh in her mind and body, the reality of the moment was inescapable. A child, her child, had been born. Normal but not normal? What did the doctor mean? Did he mean she would lose her child? Would her baby have to be institutionalized? She shuddered at the thought. What could she do? Her mind reeled under the assault of so many questions.

Suppose we asked you to make a judgment: Is LuAnn's behavior maladjusted? You might say yes. She wished to deny the reality of the situation, dismiss the doctor's words, and run away from the inevitable. Moreover, her emotions were not under complete control. She appeared unable to gather together her resources and cope with the circumstances of her child's birth.

On the other hand, what more can we expect? LuAnn has just undergone a mentally and physically exhausting experience in which all her resources were taxed to the utmost. And then she learned that all was not right with the child whose birth she had eagerly anticipated. She even had sufficient composure to ask herself what she could do. Given the extreme stress of the situation, you could argue convincingly that LuAnn acted in a "normal" fashion under the circumstances.

It is not easy to distinguish between good and poor adjustment. One of the reasons is that the term *adjustment* is used in so many different ways. Consider the following:

Five out of six people want to see a particular film. Rosemary does not. Nevertheless, she decides to go along with the majority. Rosemary has adjusted her behavior by conforming to the wishes of the group.

Gene is recovering from a major heart attack. Under his doctor's orders, he has had to make many adjustments in his daily routines, including time spent

In spite of the loss of an arm, this man shows extreme self-sufficiency. Would you say he adjusted well to his disability? How is the term *adjustment* used in this example?

Susan Lapides 1981/Design Conceptions

at work, type and amount of exercise, and choice of foods. Here, adjustment is used in the sense of regulating daily schedules.

Mark has a bad knee that causes him almost constant pain. But he does not let it interfere with his daily activities. You may say Mark had adjusted to the pain. Here, adjustment means *growing accustomed to* or *learning to live with*. Growing accustomed to circumstances can be an effective adjustment when the situation is not amenable to change. In this context, the concept of adjustment refers to the notion that a person must accept things over which he or she has no control. Since Mark can do nothing about his pain, he avoids situations in which the pain would be aggravated. For example, he swims instead of jogs. He makes reservations at restaurants and waits a few weeks to see a new "hot" movie so that he doesn't subject himself to long periods of standing in line. Thus, he has made certain adjustments in his lifestyle to accommodate a situation that cannot be changed. But, while he makes certain accommodations in areas that are of little importance to him, he refuses to allow the pain to dominate his life. He accepts the pain but continues to engage in productive living.

Let's take another look at LuAnn. Following the initial shocked reaction, LuAnn learned to adjust to the inescapable fact that her child was mentally retarded and would remain so. If she had merely passively accepted what she could not change and attempted to do no more, her adjustment would not be considered satisfactory. Instead, she reached out to various community resources for guidance and assistance. Specifically, she asked what she could do to maximize her child's potential for growth. In other words, effective adjustment consists of accepting limitations that cannot be changed while actively modifying those that can. This approach is beautifully stated in the serenity prayer of Alcoholics Anonymous:

> God grant me the serenity to accept the things I cannot change, the courage to change the things I can, and the wisdom to know the difference.

You might expect that great confusion arises from the numerous ways in which the term "adjustment" is used. Fortunately, this is not often the case. For the most part, we rely on the context to communicate subtle nuances in the meaning of the word. It is when we are speaking about psychological adjustment that difficulties present themselves. We may speak in terms of good and poor adjust- ment, adaptive and **maladaptive behavior,** normal and abnormal reactions, and so forth.

maladaptive behavior: behavior that fails to conform to the requirements of the situation.

We shall not attempt a comprehensive definition of adjustment since there are so many elements that comprise this concept. Some of the facets of "good" adjustment will be examined in a later section of this chapter: Characteristics of Effective Adjustment. Before doing so, let us attempt to clarify some of the more common problems associated with this concept.

Adjustment and Normality

Frank is worried. The big exam in his major is coming up tomorrow. For some reason, he has been unable to hit the books for the past few weeks. Instead of studying, he goes to the local bar for a drink or two and then winds up at the neighborhood movie house for the late feature. Red-eyed and disheveled the next day, he makes an abortive attempt to take the exam.

Contrast Frank's behavior with that of Nora in the following scenario.

Nora's world is coming apart at the seams or at least it appears that way to her. The apartment she just moved to permits the tenants to keep pets. The only problem is that she is terrified of dogs. Ever since she can remember, the mere sight of a dog causes an inexplicable fear and panic to well up inside of her. Her heart races, her face flushes, and beads of perspiration form on her forehead. It has become so bad that she is unable to leave the confines of her apartment. All social contacts have, of necessity, been terminated.

Is Frank maladjusted? What about Nora? Are their behaviors abnormal? These two examples show that maladjustment and abnormality are related but not necessarily the same. Let's take a closer look at Frank.

Clearly, Frank's behavior is maladaptive and nonproductive. He stands little or no chance of passing the exam. He has done no studying. He has gotten little rest and the alcohol has probably fogged his mind and reflexes. But is he abnormal in the sense that he displays bizarre behavior, shows disordered thought processes, and has a distorted perception of realtiy? Probably not. Failure to adjust satisfactorily to the demands of one's environment is not sufficient in itself to be labeled abnormal.

Nora's dilemma is different. Not only is her behavior maladapative and nonproductive, but it also contains elements of the bizarre. So crippling is her irrational fear of dogs that she has become a virtual prisoner of her own fears. Her entire emotional, social, and occupational life seems to revolve around this debilitating **phobia.**

phobia: an irrational and intense fear of people, objects, or events in which the danger is exaggerated.

In these two examples, you see that it is possible to be maladjusted but not abnormal (Frank) or maladjusted and abnormal (Nora). Is it also possible to be abnormal but not maladjusted? Strange as it may seem, it is. For example, Rodney has a compulsive need to wash his hands. He experiences extreme anxiety if he suspects his hands are even moderately soiled. Thus, he spends an unusual amount of time keeping his hands clean. His co-workers may even have noticed that

Which of these behaviors is abnormal? Why? Can you conclude that either individual is maladusted?

John Thoeming

John Thoeming

there is something a bit strange in Rodney's behavior. He seems to spend an awful lot of time in the washroom. But, in spite of all this hand-washing activity, Rodney is able to perform his work-related activities in an effective manner.

Psychologists and psychiatrists have labored long and hard to come up with diagnostic categories of abnormal behavior. These categories are defined in terms of certain specific symptoms or clusters of symptoms. Thus, an individual may display certain symptoms that cause us to label his or her behavior as abnormal. However, the same individual may be able to adapt to the demands of the environment and perform everyday functions in a satisfactory manner.

In summary, the concepts of adjustment-maladjustment and normality-abnormality overlap but are not one and the same. The criteria for judging abnormal behavior have been more clearly spelled out. The chances are that if you are dealing with an individual displaying abnormal symptoms, that individual is also maladjusted. On the other side of the coin, a maladjusted individual is not necessarily abnormal. However, you should not overlook the possibility that some abnormal process may underlie poor adjustments to life's demands. We will explore abnormal behavior in Chapter 12.

Adjustment: State or Process?

At one time or another, you have probably heard a friend or acquaintance described in such terms as: "Billy is extremely maladjusted, and I think he's going to be that way the rest of his life." Or "Suzy is so well adjusted, I just hope I can be like her some day." In both of these observations, the underlying assumption is that effective adjustment is a state that you will achieve if you are lucky and you work hard enough at becoming adjusted. Thus, you might say, "I may not be well adjusted right now, but if I work hard at it I will someday become a well-adjusted individual." In this conception of adjustment, the *state* of well adjusted is like some distant and desired geographical location where you hope to live someday. When you have arrived at that adjustment Shangri-la, you will be able to proclaim, "At last, I am well adjusted." At this point in time, you may sit back, relax, and bask in the glory of your accomplishment.

At first blush, there is much to commend the conception of adjustment as a state toward which everyone strives. As is repeated throughout this book, one of the most important principles of effective adjustment is setting realistic goals and then striving to achieve them. But is the state of "well adjusted" a realistic goal? Is it reasonable to expect to someday be always happy, free from fears and stress, and with no problems to mar a blissful existence? The *state* conception of adjustment implies that the person as a whole is either adjusted or maladjusted. If you think about this for a moment, you'll realize that this is a rather simplistic view of adjustment. Even the most well-adjusted people sometimes fall short of their goals or ideals. At some time or another, everyone acts in ways they later regret. On occasion, they disappoint themselves and others. They feel guilt and are rarely completely free of fear and worry. These observations are nicely expressed in the following excerpt from *Notes to Myself* by Hugh Prather:

There are occasions when I talk to a man who is riding high on some recent insight or triumph, and for the moment life probably seems to him to have no problems. But I just don't believe that most people are living the smooth, controlled, trouble-free existence that their careful countenances and bland words suggest. Today never hands me the same thing twice and I believe that for most everyone else life is also a mixture of unsolved problems, ambiguous victories, and vague defeats—with very few moments of clear peace. I never do seem to quite get on top of it. My struggle with today is worthwhile, but it is a struggle nonetheless and one I will never finish. (Prather, 1970)

Life situations and goals sometimes undergo major changes. In 1968 Jerry Rubin was one of the leaders of the anti-establishment movement. Ten years later he was a research analyst on Wall Street.

United Press International Photos

In truth, adjustment is an ongoing process that will continue throughout your life. Life situations are always changing. Everyone experiences setbacks in the quest to achieve desired goals. People are continually changing their goals as life circumstances change. What was regarded as the most pressing and urgent need yesterday may now have faded into the background and be remembered with only a smile. According to the *process* conception of adjustment, the effectiveness of adjustment is measured in terms of how well a person copes with ever-changing circumstances.

Life is dynamic and filled with a continuous interplay between internal and external forces. To some extent, you are a product of your environment and your unique experiences, and are subject to circumstances over which you do not always exercise complete control. Consequently, it is inevitable that the quality of your adjustments will vary from time to time and from situation to situation. As a result, you will occasionally fall flat on your face. You will sometimes experience moments of unhappiness and even despair. On the other hand, if you display the resiliency that is inherent in all of us, you will cope effectively with stress and conflict either by meeting life's challenges head-on or by changing the circumstances to fit your needs. This book focuses on the view that adjustment is not a state but rather an ongoing, life-long process. All of us are capable of learning skills that enable us to cope with the everyday demands of living.

CHARACTERISTICS OF EFFECTIVE ADJUSTMENT

Historically, professionals in the mental- and emotional-health fields have tended to conceptualize adjustment in a negative sort of way. The *absence* of characteristics that define abnormality was taken as evidence of effective adjustment. Thus, a person free of pathological symptoms was thought to be "healthy." Over the years, the emphasis has shifted. We now say, in effect, it's not what you *don't* have that constitutes effective adjustment but, rather, what you *do* have. In other words, adjustment is regarded in terms of the positive characteristics an individual displays. Implicit in this positive approach is the view that strengths rather than lack of weaknesses underlie good adjustment.

There are no simple and easy prescriptions for dealing with life. Since you are totally unique, you must make your own way based on your own resources and environmental circumstances. Nevertheless, there are guideposts along the route to satisfactory adjustments. In the following sections, we examine some of these guideposts.

Accurate Perception of Reality

Almost everyone would agree that an accurate perception of reality is a prerequisite to good adjustment. But what is reality? Is my reality the same as yours? It is easy to get bogged down in philosophical discourses on the nature of reality. There is really no way of knowing in any absolute or ultimate sense of the word whether or not any two of us are experiencing reality in precisely the same manner. However, all is not as hopeless as it may seem. Psychologists have developed standards for ascertaining agreement among individuals. To illustrate, if the majority of Neil's acquaintances see him as warm, accepting, and outgoing, we will assume that this is a valid description of Neil. If only one person finds him cold, aloof, and withdrawn, we may suspect the accuracy of this person's perception of reality. However, this would not be a definite conclusion. We should acknowledge the possibility that Neil is, indeed, cold, aloof, and withdrawn in his interactions with this individual.

How can you be sure that you are seeing reality accurately? How many of us know ourselves well enough to recognize when our personal motives and biases distort reality? Have you ever admitted, "I heard what I wanted to hear" or "I saw what I wanted to see"? How often do fans applaud a decision by a referee when it goes against the home team? More often than not, they accuse the referee of being blind as a bat. We have to constantly keep in mind the fact that we are all prone to color our perceptions with the unique paint of our own desires and motivations. There are times when people want to see or hear something so much that they actually believe they have heard or seen it.

We are often cautioned to be realistic about setting our goals. Certainly the "well-adjusted" individual sets realistic goals that he or she actively pursues. But again, we are faced with a question: what is realistic? If Jay is obtaining low grades on all the courses in the science curriculum, how realistic is his pursuit of a premedical program? Unless Jay adjusts either his approach to study or his end goal, he is destined to experience frustration and considerable anguish in his choice of vocational field. From the adjustment point of view, Jay would be well-advised to seek guidance, direction, and clarification of his goals. Indeed, many people would profit from professional guidance when faced with career and/or educational choices. Once you are assured that your end goals are realistic, you are much more likely to experience success in their pursuit.

Sometimes, because of environmental constraints and opportunities, you find that you must either change or modify your goals. In fact, setting goals and modifying them is a continuous process throughout life. To illustrate, Ruth is in love with Martin and looks forward to marrying him. Unfortunately, she learns that Martin is already married. He informs Ruth in no uncertain terms that he has no intention of obtaining a divorce. Ruth considers a number of different alternatives. She can continue the relationship with Martin on his terms—temporary and part-time. Or she can seek relationships where there is hope of permanency. The choice is hers. From the point of view of adjustment, it can only be hoped that she will make a realistic appraisal of the consequences of each course of action. Indeed, one of the most important aspects of an accurate perception of reality is the ability to recognize the consequences of your actions and to guide your behavior accordingly. It is possible that Ruth will find the part-time relationship proposed by Martin both acceptable and fulfilling. However, if she engages in self-deception in this matter, she may be sentencing herself to many moments of loneliness, grief, and unhappiness.

Ability to Cope with Stress and Anxiety

Let us pose one of the great riddles of our time. Why is it that, amidst the highest material standard of living that any nation has ever enjoyed, there is so much stress, anxiety, and unhappiness? Think back to your study of history. A mere few generations ago, the workday often started before dawn and continued well into the hours of darkness. This went on day after day for six or more days a week. There were no paid vacations, no child labor laws, limited educational opportunities, and little legal protection for the average person in the streets. Entertainment was largely limited to what the family or neighborhood could provide for itself.

Contrast this picture with the one you see today. A mere flick of a switch and light fills the dark corners of a room. Foods are available in a variety that was unimaginable to our forebears. You adjust a dial and there is instant entertainment emanating from virtually anywhere on the globe. Why even the very poor among us enjoy a higher material standard of living than the affluent of past generations. Yet problems of stress, anxiety, unhappiness, and violence continue to gnaw at us, like a canker sore. Why is this so?

The answer, in part, appears to be that we humans are exquisitely well tuned to making comparisons. We do not judge our present circumstances in terms of absolutes but, rather, in terms of relatives. In other words, we appraise the significance of ourselves and events in terms of where we stand in relationship to other people and other circumstances. For example, if you find yourself "low on the totem pole," you may respond with a mixed bag of emotions—anxiety, guilt, and hostility, to name a few. The precise emotion you feel depends in large part on where you place the blame for your low position. If you feel inadequate, you experience anxiety. If you blame yourself for not having tried enough, you may find your mind racked with guilt. However, if you attribute your circumstances to others or to "the system," you may seethe with hostile feelings.

Of course, there is more. Often the "tube" equates the possession of material goods with happiness. Even your breakfast foods and candies promise to make you happy. You may think, "If only I had the latest Walkman, I would be truly happy." When you acquire it, you experience momentary elation, which is only to be followed by the pangs of new desires. You soon learn that more is involved in happiness than the immediate satisfaction of your material needs.

The following quote from *Notes to Myself* expresses the short-lived satisfaction gained from material acquisitions:

> The number of things just outside the perimeter of my financial reach remains constant no matter how much my financial condition improves. With each increase in my income a new perimeter forms and I experience the same relative sense of lack. I believe that I would be happy if only my earnings were increased by so much and then I could have or do these few things I can't quite afford, but when my income does increase I find I am still unhappy because from my new financial position I can now see a whole new set of things I don't have. The problem will be solved when

I realize that happiness is a present attitude and not a future condition. (Prather, 1970)

The media reinforce the tendency to expect immediate gratification of your every desire. We are encouraged to think, "I want what I want when I want it." They even provide toll-free phone numbers that permit us to order things we want without delay. In fact, the salesperson tells us, "Stop what you are doing. Don't delay. Order right now."

These enticements run contrary to one of the inescapable realities of life. We cannot obtain instant satisfaction of our every need. We cannot hope to reach distant goals in a moment of time. We must learn to tolerate the delays necessitated by the nature of the goal. We don't become educated overnight. We don't jump from assistant clerk on Monday to president of the company on Tuesday. We may have to save our pennies before we can get credit toward the purchase of the latest dream machine.

But pursuit of long-term goals is not easy (see Box 1.1). There are immediate needs that are crying for satisfaction. Delaying gratification of these needs often leads to feelings of discomfort and stress. You may resent the sacrifices you are forced to make to reach these long-range goals. Long-range goals appear to be so distant that it is often difficult to see how they are relevant to your present life.

BOX 1.1: CONTROLLING YOUR OWN BEHAVIOR

Throughout recorded history, thinking people have been deeply concerned over the question of determinism versus free will. The determinists have argued that all things in the world behave according to natural laws. No exceptions are made for any species. Thus, human beings are as much controlled by events outside and within themselves as the lowliest insect and the most exalted tree. Our behavior is, in a word, the inevitable consequence of external forces operating on our biological machinery. In contemporary psychology, behaviorists take the determinist view.

Advocates of free will, on the other hand, argue that we do make judgments and choices on our own. These are not completely determined by external forces and our biological makeup. We can screen our environment, select stimuli to which we will attend and exclude others. Humanists occupy the free-will camp in this ongoing battle.

But whether we are behaviorists or humanists, few will deny that people act *as if* they possess a free will. They process information selectively, make judgments about it, and then make choices based on these judgments. So, without attempting to resolve a philosophical dilemma that has generated as much heat as light over the millenia, we will assume that people do have a measure of control over their own lives. For some, self-control comes easily; for others, it is an almost endless series of opposing contests that are waged on many different battlegrounds. Let us look at ways to gain greater control over our own impulses and behavior.

To begin with, it is important to note that we often (or, as some believe, always) operate on the pleasure/pain principle. We engage in those activities that will bring us gratification and avoid those that lead to pain or displeasure. Our tendency is to seek this gratification immediately since delay of pleasure often entails discomfort and effort. However, many of our goals are remote in time. To illustrate, the goal of becoming a professional—a lawyer, physician, or psychologist—requires years of study and preparation, often accompanied by emotional, physical, and economic hardships. Self-control is concerned with learning to forestall or delay immediate gratification so

BOX 1.1 *(concluded)*

that more remote goals can be reached. Self-control is not easy since it operates against the pleasure/pain principle.

Here are a few of the principles involved in self-control:

1. Clearly specify your goals. Many people express their goals in such vague and general terms that they are unable to say that they have achieved their goals. When you don't know whether or not you have reached a goal, you deprive yourself of the satisfactions that allow you to continue in the face of adversity. To illustrate, when asked to specify one of his goals in life, Manuel answered, "I want to be happy." When queried further, "What makes you happy?" he replied, "I don't know." Manuel might have much greater prospects of success if he specified as his goal, "To find a career that challenges me and allows me to develop my capabilities." He can now begin a search that will bring about a happy marriage of his abilities and interests with some career goal.

2. Monitor the behavior of interest to establish a baseline for comparison. We often pay little attention to many of our daily behaviors. How accurately do you think you could answer such questions as: How many minutes a day do you spend in recreational activities? How much time do you spend on studies? How many glasses of water do you drink each day? How often do you daydream? If you are a smoker, how many cigarettes do you smoke daily? If you want to bring some behavior under greater self-control— e.g., smoking, eating, studying—it is important that you have a handle on your current practices. Only

then can you later say with assurance, "I have reduced my caloric input by 10 percent and increased my exercise by 5 percent," or "I am spending 25 percent less time watching television and 15 percent more time studying."

3. Make a plan. The plan should represent a realistic appraisal of your assets, liabilities, sources of support, and environmental obstacles. To illustrate, the person who decides to give up smoking should consider such factors as: the severity of the habit. (Am I a one-pack-a-day or a three-pack-a-day person?) If the habit is deeply ingrained, a more gradual approach to giving up the weed might be considered. Efforts should be made to remove all sources of temptation. Do not keep cigarettes in your desk drawer just in case. Indeed, get rid of other stimuli that might provoke the urge to smoke, e.g., book of matches in a pocket or purse, ashtrays strewn about the room, etc. Also enlist the support of others. "Jan, I am determined to stop smoking. I want you to help me. I also ask you to be understanding if I become a bit edgy and irritable for a few days." If you are lucky, Jan might decide to join you. One plus one might add up to more than two if others joined you, as well.

4. Implement the plan, keeping records of your efforts. This step is vital for you to be able to detect change. When the change is in the desired direction, lavish praise and other forms of self-reinforcement on yourself. "That a way. You went from 40 cigarettes a day during the first week down to 35 cigarettes a day during the second week. Now let's aim for 30 a day for the coming week."

But they are relevant. If they are realistic, they give a sense of purpose to your life and provide both a direction and focus for your present energies. Sally derives great pleasure from working with young children. A realistic appraisal of her capabilities, interests, and opportunities leads her to pursue the long-term goal of a career in elementary education. This goal gives direction to some of her present activities. By organizing several aspects of her life around her future career objectives, Sally is better able to tolerate the inescapable stresses that she will encounter along the way. For example, she takes summer jobs as a camp counselor and volunteers for after-school work in day-care centers. She even makes friends with individuals who share her interests. Thus, her future career goal has actually enhanced her adjustment by making her present life more enjoyable.

Moreover, the goal-related jobs help her maintain contact with her future profession.

This does not mean that Sally's ventures will always be on calm seas. One of the inevitable realities of life is that things rarely go smoothly and without a hitch. Even the best-laid plans "oft go awry." At these times, even well-adjusted individuals experience their share of stress and anxiety. One measure of adjustment is how well you cope with these setbacks, problems, and conflicts. Chapter 7 addresses this very issue.

A Positive Self-Image

> Whenever Richard Cory went downtown,
> We people on the pavement looked at him:
> He was a gentleman from sole to crown,
> Clean favored, and imperially slim.
>
> And he was always quietly arrayed,
> And he was always human when he talked:
> But still he fluttered pulses when he said,
> "Good morning," and he glittered when he walked.
>
> And he was rich—yes, richer than a king—
> And admirably schooled in every grace:
> In fine, we thought that he was everything
> To make us wish that we were in his place.
>
> So on we worked, and waited for the light,
> And went without the meat, and cursed the bread:
> And Richard Cory, one calm summer night,
> Went home and put a bullet through his head.
>
> *Edwin Arlington Robinson*

This poem reminds us that each of us is not one self but many selves. You are the "self" you carry in your head as well as the "self" as others perceive you. Who was Richard Cory? Was he the self-assured and confident person whom the townspeople viewed in such a positive light that they even wished to take his place? Richard Cory's final act contradicted this public perception. From this final act, we can infer that Richard Cory did not regard himself as favorably as others did. There were two different views of Richard Cory. They were obviously not in accord.

Many psychologists view the various perceptions of the self as indicators of the quality of adjustment. When these perceptions are not in agreement, the individual is more likely to be maladjusted. On the other hand, when the different perceptions are harmonious, the probability is higher that the individual's adjustment is satisfactory.

How do you develop self-perceptions? How do you answer the question. "Who am I?" To a large extent, you base your self-perceptions on the labels that others have attached to you and the ways they have behaved toward you. Joey's parents constantly tell him, "You are bad: You are rotten to the core!" and heap other

It has been said that we must first love ourselves before we can learn to love another.

© Joel Gordon 1982

types of mental and physical abuse upon him. Is it so surprising that Joey will also use the same abusive descriptions of himself? Is he likely to grow up with a positive self-image?

One of the hallmarks of effective adjustment is to view oneself in a positive manner. What hope is there for the Joeys of this world if all they hear are negative evaluations? The field of psychology heralds this hope. To the extent that self-perceptions are learned, they may also be modified. Given proper encouragement and a realistic assessment of his capabilities, even Joey may someday look upon himself with favor.

Although effective adjustment requires that you have a positive self-image, it is important not to lose sight of the realities of yourself. You should be aware of and acknowledge your weaknesses as well as your strengths. If you see yourself as someone worthy of esteem, you must also acknowledge that part of yourself in which you do not take pride. Capabilities as well as shortcomings should be recognized. If you are able to know and understand yourself in a truly realistic way, you are on the road to realizing the full potential of your personal resources. Chapter 3 pursues in greater detail the role of the self in adjustment.

Ability to Express Feelings

"I don't understand it. Peter was such a gentle boy. He wouldn't hurt a fly. It's true, he was quieter than most people. I never once saw him become the least bit annoyed or angry at anyone. Come to think of it, I never saw him laugh much either. He was just a good quiet boy. I still can't believe the things they are saying about him."

How often have you heard such a description applied to someone who recently made the headlines for committing an act of violence? Using the negative approach to adjustment—the absence of behavioral characteristics that are readily recognizable as either maladjustive or abnormal—many people may have concluded that Peter was as good as gold.

blunted affect: the feeling or experience of emotion is dulled or deadened.

Subsequent investigations of the loner who commits a violent act usually reveal a person with a **blunted affect.** Such individuals appear to be incapable of expressing the full range of emotions. This is not to say that they do not feel such emotions as rage, jealousy, envy, and love. They may or they may not. Some people are so frightened by the emotional turmoil within their mental life that they successfully suppress it even from their own self-knowledge. Others fear what they see in themselves and expend much energy to conceal the richness of their inner lives from outside observers. In either case, what the world sees is a person who rarely betrays his or her feeling and emotions. Observations of such people gave rise to the folk wisdom, "still waters run deep."

On the other side of the coin are individuals who are unable to inhibit expression of the affective sides of their lives. They react to minor provocations with excessive anger or they become moody and depressed at the slightest hint of criticism, the slightest setback in their plans. Healthy adjustment requires that a balance be struck between over- and undercontrol. We often have difficulty expressing our emotions openly and honestly. Perhaps we have been trained to withhold our true feelings. For example, you may have been taught that it is wrong to express anger to a loved one. Consequently, you find yourself bottling up your true reactions, allowing them to seethe inside.

You may feel anxious and tense and unable to identify the source of your feelings. Try to get in touch with them. Are you feeling anger? fear? hostility? Stop and think of the event that immediately preceded the feeling you are experiencing. For example, were you just insulted by someone close to you? Were you put down by someone you respect? Were you caught in a lie? If you can label the emotion you are feeling, you have taken a giant step forward in making an adequate adjustment to emotional expression.

Once you have identified the emotion, consider your options in how that emotion should be expressed. Your best friend has just insulted you. You feel angry. Consider the most constructive ways you can express this emotion. Try and think in terms of long-range effects rather than immediate gratifications. For example, responding with a bitter retort may make you feel momentarily satisfied. But what will it do to your overall relationship with the other person? Take your time before responding. A cool appraisal of the situation may suggest a response more in proportion to the experience.

Emotionally healthy people are able to feel and express the full spectrum of emotions and feelings. However, their displays of emotion are both realistic and generally under their own control. They cry at a funeral, laugh at a well-performed comedy act, and take joy in their own accomplishments as well as those of their loved ones. When they feel anger, they are able to express it in ways that do not inflict injury on others, either psychological or physical. Moreover, emotionally healthy individuals are able to establish and maintain meaningful **interpersonal relations.** We return to the topic of emotions in Chapter 5.

interpersonal relations: relationships involving two or more people.

Good Interpersonal Relations

You might imagine that, in addition to being unable to feel and express the richness of emotions and feelings, Peter experienced difficulties in his relations with others. Indeed, the most crucial aspect of satisfactory interpersonal relationships involves sharing emotions and feelings A person with a blunted emotional life has little to give to others and will often resist accepting what others have to offer. Barriers are constructed that block those interchanges that most of us find so satisfying and fulfilling. The result is the loner.

But most of us do not want to be alone. We need and seek the satisfactions that come with one-to-one relationships with others. We spend most of our lives in the company of other people. Our degree of involvement with them varies from casual acquaintances (neighbors, co-workers, and shopkeepers) to close personal friends to intimate love relationships. Well-adjusted people are able to achieve appropriate degrees of intimacy in their social relationships. They are both competent and comfortable in their interactions with others. They enjoy being liked and respected by them. In turn, they enjoy and respect other people. They derive pleasure from making others comfortable in their presence. They recognize that even the best of relationships can, at times, be frustrating and occasionally painful. They develop a sense of perspective in which they allow for the fact that life is not always smooth sailing on a calm body of water. To illustrate:

> Vicki has just landed the job of her dreams. It is an exciting opportunity with excellent chances for advancement. In fact, she has been promised the top position at a new branch office as soon as her six-month orientation period has been satisfactorily completed. However, a problem develops. From her initial contacts with her immediate supervisor, she forsees a clash in personalities. There are disagreements about how various tasks should be done and by whom. Moreover, the supervisor seems to be very rigid and out of touch with the latest developments in the field. Vicki is faced with an immediate dilemma. Should she go along with the supervisor's way of

doing things? In this way she would be more likely to win the approval necessary for her promotion. Or should she argue for what she believes is right? By doing so, she might alienate the supervisor and kill her chances of obtaining the promotion. Thus, she could "win the battle but lose the war."

It is one thing to agree that satisfying and rewarding interpersonal relationships play an important role in your lives; it is yet another matter to understand how they may be achieved. Chapters 9 through 11 explore various aspects of interpersonal relations such as attraction, friendships, love, and sexuality.

The 10 Hallmarks of Well-Being

What is the healthy, well-adjusted person really like? Based on four-and-a-half years of research and surveys of more than 60,000 adults of all ages, Gail Sheehy (1981) examined the characteristics of people who feel exceptionally good about themselves and their lives. She developed a Life History Questionnaire (see Box 1.2) for measuring well-being. What emerged from the surveys was an outline of the person who enjoys optimum well-being. She called these people pathfinders and believed that the following 10 self-descriptive statements best characterizes these people (pp. 14–20).

1. "My life has meaning and direction."
Sheehy found that people who were highly satisfied with their lives were committed to something beyond themselves (work, an idea, a future vision) that gave their lives meaning and direction.

2. "I have experienced one or more important transitions in my adult years, and I have handled these transitions in an unusual, personal, or creative way."

BOX 1.2: LIFE HISTORY QUESTIONNAIRE

In case you are curious about how you would rate in terms of well-being, the following is an abbreviated version of the well-being scale.

Check to see whether your answer falls above or below the arrow shown here. If your answer is above the arrow, you fall above average for that item on the well-being scale. If your answer is below the arrow, you fall below the average.

Follow this procedure with each of the questions. Then count how many of your 24 answers were above average.

If you scored above average on 11 or 12 of the questions, you probably are of medium well-being. If you answered more than 17 of the questions in the above-average range, you are likely to be enjoying especially high well-being.

11. How often do you feel bored?
    1. Almost never
    2. Rarely
Average →
    3. Occasionally
    4. Fairly often
    5. Most of the time
    6. Almost all the time

13. How often do you enjoy the work that you do?
    1. Almost all the time

BOX 1.2 *(continued)*

Average →
  2. Most of the time
  3. Fairly often
  4. Occasionally
  5. Rarely
  6. Almost never

14. Do you feel that your major work activity makes a contribution to society?
  1. Definitely yes

Average →
  2. Most of the time
  3. Some of the time
  4. Almost none of the time
  5. Definitely no
  6. Not applicable

19. Looking back at the goals, aspirations, or "dreams" you had as you entered adulthood, how do you feel at this point in your life?
  1. I am just beginning to shape my dream.
  2. I am on my way to achieving my dream.
  3. I have achieved my original dream and have generated a new one.
  4. I have achieved a great deal but it's quite different from my original dream.

Average →
  5. I have never had a clear dream or aspiration.
  6. I am not sure whether I am on my way to achieving my dream.
  7. I will probably never achieve my original dream.
  8. I have achieved my original dream and haven't generated a new one.

21. How have you been feeling about:
  a. My work or primary activity
    1. Delighted
    2. Pleased

Average →
    3. Mostly satisfied
    4. Mixed (about equally satisfied and dissatisfied)
    5. Mostly dissatisfied
    6. Unhappy

  7. Terrible
  8. Not applicable

21b. My love relationship or marriage
    1. Delighted
    2. Pleased

Average →
    3. Mostly satisfied
    4. Mixed (about equally satisfied and dissatisfied)
    5. Mostly dissatisfied
    6. Unhappy
    7. Terrible
    8. Not applicable

21c. Children and being a parent
    1. Delighted
    2. Pleased

Average →
    3. Mostly satisfied
    4. Mixed (about equally satisfied and dissatisfied)
    5. Mostly dissatisfied
    6. Unhappy
    7. Terrible
    8. Not applicable

21d. Degree of recognition, success
    1. Delighted
    2. Pleased

Average →
    3. Mostly satisfied
    4. Mixed (about equally satisfied and dissatisfied)
    5. Mostly dissatisfied
    6. Unhappy
    7. Terrible
    8. Not applicable

21e. My financial situation
    1. Delighted
    2. Pleased
    3. Mostly satisfied

Average →
    4. Mixed (about equally satisfied and dissatisfied)
    5. Mostly dissatisfied
    6. Unhappy
    7. Terrible
    8. Not applicable

BOX 1.2 *(continued)*

21f. My health
1. Delighted
2. Pleased

Average →

3. Mostly satisfied
4. Mixed (about equally satisfied and dissatisfied)
5. Mostly dissatisfied
6. Unhappy
7. Terrible
8. Not applicable

21g. Personal growth and development
1. Delighted
2. Pleased

Average →

3. Mostly satisfied
4. Mixed (about equally satisfied and dissatisfied)
5. Mostly dissatisfied
6. Unhappy
7. Terrible
8. Not applicable

21h. Exercise and physical recreation
1. Delighted
2. Pleased
3. Mostly satisfied

Average →

4. Mixed (about equally satisfied and dissatisfied)
5. Mostly dissatisfied
6. Unhappy
7. Terrible
8. Not applicable

21i. Religion, spiritual life
1. Delighted
2. Pleased
3. Mostly satisfied

Average →

4. Mixed (about equally satisfied and dissatisfied)
5. Mostly dissatisfied
6. Unhappy
7. Terrible
8. Not applicable

21j. My sex life
1. Delighted
2. Pleased

3. Mostly satisfied

Average →

4. Mixed (about equally satisfied and dissatisfied)
5. Mostly dissatisfied
6. Unhappy
7. Terrible
8. Not applicable

21k. The way my spouse or lover's life is going
1. Delighted
2. Pleased

Average →

3. Mostly satisfied
4. Mixed (about equally satisfied and dissatisfied)
5. Mostly dissatisfied
6. Unhappy
7. Terrible
8. Not applicable

21l. Friends and social life
1. Delighted
2. Pleased

Average →

3. Mostly satisfied
4. Mixed (about equally satisfied and dissatisfied)
5. Mostly dissatisfied
6. Unhappy
7. Terrible
8. Not applicable

21m. My physical attractiveness
1. Delighted
2. Pleased
3. Mostly satisfied

Average →

4. Mixed (about equally satisfied and dissatisfied)
5. Mostly dissatisfied
6. Unhappy
7. Terrible
8. Not applicable

21n. The degree to which I make a contribution to others
1. Delighted
2. Pleased

Average →

3. Mostly satisfied

BOX 1.2 *(concluded)*

4. Mixed (about equally satisfied and dissatisfied)
5. Mostly dissatisfied
6. Unhappy
7. Terrible
8. Not applicable

21o. Balance of time between work, family, leisure, home responsibilities, etc.
1. Delighted
2. Pleased
3. Mostly satisfied

Average →

4. Mixed (about equally satisfied and dissatisfied)
5. Mostly dissatisfied
6. Unhappy
7. Terrible
8. Not applicable

21p. My life as a whole
1. Delighted
2. Pleased

Average →

3. Mostly satisfied
4. Mixed (about equally satisfied and dissatisfied)
5. Mostly dissatisfied
6. Unhappy
7. Terrible
8. Not applicable

25. In general, how would you describe your life?
1. It's a very unusual life.

2. It's a fairly unusual life.

Average →

3. It's a fairly ordinary life.
4. It's a very ordinary life.

27. How much control do you have over the important events in your life?
1. Almost total control
2. Mostly under my control

Average →

3. About half the time I can control the important events
4. Mostly not under my control
5. Almost no control

28. Looking back over your adult life, how responsible do you feel for the way it has turned out?
1. Totally responsible
2. Very responsible

Average →

3. Somewhat responsible
4. Slightly responsible
5. Not at all responsible

42. Are you currently in love?
1. Yes, for the first time.
2. Yes, but not for the first time.

Average →

3. No, but I have been.
4. I have never been in love.

Source: "The Well-Being Scale," in *Pathfinders* by Gail Sheehy. Copyright © 1981 by Gail Sheehy. By permission of William Morrow & Company.

People with high well-being were most likely to have encountered important life transitions and to have made dramatic changes in some aspect of their lives. What distinguished the person with optimum well-being was the way in which he or she handled the normal, predictable crises of life. In Sheehy's words:

> Coming up with creative solutions to common life crises registered clearly in every sample as characteristic of adults who enjoy optimum satisfaction. Not that these people tend toward having exotic life-styles. They are, simply, a little more courageous in facing reality and a lot more resourceful in thinking up ways to extend their capacities than people who wait for life's events to happen to them by chance or who sit around and complain about them.

People of low satisfaction often become obsessed or depressed about roads not taken in the past. Toward the future these people may adopt a "this or nothing" attitude and as a result feel cheated if they do not get what they want. Unable to make satisfactory compromises with their weaknesses or desires or to dare to take other avenues, they may become soured, believing that life is unfair to them, that they have been singled out for an injustice, or that they are simply no good. Instead of turning their energies toward handling the transition at hand, or anticipating the future, they often become relentlessly negative and mired in the past. They look backward for scapegoats or flaws in themselves to blame for their current trap or dilemma.

And these are usually there to find.

It was surprising to learn that frequent introspection is not correlated closely with high satisfaction. The happiest people do plan ahead, but they seem to take time for critical self-reflection only when approaching a tough transition or after making one. Otherwise (except for creative people) they do not spend much time contemplating their inner thoughts and feelings.[2]

3. "I rarely feel cheated or disappointed by life."

Although the most contented people are less likely to fail in the first place, what distinguishes them is the way in which they respond to failure. People of high satisfaction see failure as a constructive experience that has enhanced lives and left them better off than they were before. Low-satisfaction people view failure as a confirmation of their own inadequacies or as another bitter pill to be swallowed along the shaky road of their lives.

4. "I have already attained several goals that are important to me."

Sheehy found the same long-range goals at all levels of satisfaction: a comfortable life, family security, and a sense of accomplishment. However, more than half of the high-satisfaction people reported that they had already attained these goals.

One of the most interesting findings that emerged from this study was the different things high- and low-satisfaction people are willing to do to attain professional success. Those people who were the most discontent were the most willing to sacrifice their love relationships or families in their quest for success.

5. "I am pleased with my personal growth and development."

Although most everyone in the sample aspired to the same personal characteristics—being honest, loving, and responsible—highly content people were most likely to describe themselves in terms of these qualities.

6. "I am in love: my partner and I love mutually."

People of high well-being are rarely involved in one-sided love relationships. They not only spend more time with the person they love, they would also like more time to spend.

---

[2] In *Pathfinders* by Gail Sheehy, p. 15. Copyright © 1981 by Gail Sheehy. By permission of William Morrow & Company.

Is sexual pleasure an important element of overall life satisfaction? Sheehy reports:

> Among one group of young, highly successful professional women I sur-veyed, there was a ripple of amused acknowledgment when the greatest contributor to their satisfaction with life was revealed—and it wasn't career promotions. The more contented these women were with the quality of their sex lives, the happier they were with their entire existence. (p. 18)

7. "I have many friends."

The most satisfied people have the most friends. Thus, in time of need, they have more people they can turn to for comfort and support.

8. "I am a cheerful person."

The most contented people not only have the most optimistic outlook on life, they rarely report a time of chronic depression in their lives. On the other hand, the least contented people describe themselves as being seriously depressed and discontented at almost every stage of their lives.

According to Sheehy,

> Being cheerful not only makes it more pleasant to live with oneself; a person with a positive outlook is more likely to attract friendship and love, which promise in turn the richer intimacy and emotional supports that characterize overall life satisfaction.
>
> People who allow themselves to become soured on life often set in motion a self-reinforcing cycle. Their anger or self-pity becomes so off-putting that it deprives them of the friends and help they otherwise would deserve and that might restore their buoyancy. (p. 19)

9. "I am not thin-skinned or sensitive to criticism."

The person of high well-being does not react to criticism as a personal attack on his or her sense of worth.

10. "I have no major fears."

The most common fears reported by the least satisfied people are of being lonely, messing up their personal lives, and being "locked in," unable to freely change their way of life. For those over 45, the most common fears were of "no longer being physically attractive," "being abandoned by spouse or lover," or "declining physical capabilities, illness."

Sheehy's outlook is very optimistic. She feels that the qualities that characterize pathfinders are qualities that each of us has. Moreover she finds that the happiest Americans are in their mid-50s and older. She believes that her research indicates that today's youths can look forward to a satisfying middle age and beyond.

SUMMARY

- In commenting on "A Letter Home," it was noted that some events or life situa-tions overwhelm us at the time they occur. It is often useful at these times to try to project your evaluation of present circumstances in terms of the perspective of time. How will I regard the current event in 5 or 10 years? Looking at life's circumstances in such a way may permit you to deal more objectively and less emotionally with present crises.

- Effective psychological adjustment is not easy to define. It is not synonymous with the absence of abnormal symptoms since individuals who appear symptom-free may have severe adjustment problems, whereas others who exhibit abnormal symptoms may be satisfactorily adjusted in most areas of life.

- Adjustment may be regarded as a state to which we aspire as the result of the conscientious application of principles of effective adjustment in our own lives. However, since goals and life circumstances are in continual flux, it is helpful to regard adjustment as a process that continues throughout life. According to this view, you may expect the quality of adjustment to vary from time to time.

- Some of the factors that signal a healthy adjustment are:

  a. Accurate perception of reality. This includes your acknowledgment of a tendency to distort your perception of reality and your interpretation of events. By seeing things as they are, your adjustments are more likely to be appropriate to the realities of the situation.

  b. Ability to cope with stress and anxiety. Successful coping includes your acknowledging that pursuit of long-term goals gives direction to life and makes you better able to withstand the inevitable reversals, frustrations, and stresses that occur along the way.

  c. A positive self-image. Your self-appraisal should include the positive as well as the negative. Moreover, you should not dwell on those aspects of yourself that you find undesirable. Rather, you should attempt to modify them to the extent that they are changeable.

  d. Ability to express the full range of emotions. Problems of emotional expression include overcontrol and undercontrol. Overcontrol leads to a blunted affect; undercontrol to excessive emotional expression. Either may signal potential adjustment problems.

  e. Good interpersonal relationships. Humans are preeminently social beings. From the moment of conception on, we are dependent on others to fill our needs—physical, social, and emotional. Well-adjusted individuals are capable of relating to others in productive and mutually beneficial ways.

- Ten hallmarks of well-being were presented and discussed.

TERMS TO REMEMBER

Maladaptive behavior	**Blunted affect**
Phobia	**Interpersonal relations**

PSYCHOANALYTIC AND BEHAVIORISTIC THEORIES OF PERSONALITY

Jerry is happy; Arlene is feeling blue.

Larry exudes self-confidence; David wallows in self-doubt.

Mindy sets and achieves her goals; Tracy engages in self-defeating behaviors.

Bill is generous, outgoing, and gives freely of himself; Nelson is withdrawn and rarely goes out of his way for anyone

How do we explain these differences? Most of us have our own personal ideas about the "whys" of human behavior. Or, at the very least, we feel we can explain the behavior of those close to us. It is probably safe to say that these private theories differ from each other as much as the differences in the behaviors they attempt to explain. These personal theories usually have no formal structure. Indeed, we may never have verbalized them as such. We may have left unstated our assumptions about underlying causes of behavior as well as the steps by which we move from assumptions to explanations. Nevertheless, our interactions with people are governed by the implicit views we hold. For example, if our successful goal-achiever, Mindy, proposes a plan, we are more inclined to go along with her because of her track record.

These personal views are, in turn, colored by our own motives, needs, and personal experiences. For example, a child who has had largely positive interactions and experiences with others is likely to develop a "theory" that people are essentially good. In contrast, another child who has been exploited and badly treated most of the time, is likely to "theorize" that most people are mean and untrustworthy. It wouldn't be surprising if the first child responded toward people in a warm and trusting fashion, the second with hostility and suspicion.

It has been suggested that the private theories we hold may shed more light on *us* than on the behavior we are attempting to understand. For this reason, we may often gain insights into our own feelings, motivations, and behavior by examining our own private theories.

hypotheses: proposed explanations of the relationships between events or variables. The explanations can be examined in the light of relevant evidence.

Professional students of behavior have proposed various formal theories to help us understand the basic characteristics of people and why they behave as they do. In contrast to our private theories, the professional theories have explicitly stated assumptions and formulated **hypotheses** which can be supported or rejected on the basis of evidence. In this chapter and the next, we explore three schools of thought—psychoanalysis, behaviorism, and humanism—that provide theoretical bases for understanding human behavior.

PSYCHOANALYTIC THEORIES: FREUD

History has given us few figures as provocative, incisive, and controversial as the Viennese physician, Sigmund Freud (1856–1939). During his lifetime, he developed a theory of personality that profoundly influenced almost every aspect of the human experience—literature and the fine arts as well as behavioral theory. Among other things, Freud is recognized as the founder of psychoanalysis. In staid Victorian society, he proposed that sexual matters constitute a source of conflict from the cradle to old age. Because he touched on areas that were so "hush-hush" in his day, it was inevitable that a heavy fire of criticism was leveled against him. Nevertheless, Freud inspired a whole new way of looking at human behavior. Specifically, he saw human development as a sort of battleground in which the individual's biological urgings wage constant warfare against the realities of life.

Poised on this battleground are three different forces that operate simultaneously within the individual—the id, the ego, and the superego. The *id* represents the basic biological urgings of the individual. It is unconscious, extremely demanding, and has no regard for the consequences of its actions. Unless it is satisfied, tensions build up in the body which become transformed into psychic energy. This psychic energy causes unpleasant states of tension and irritability. The *id* operates on the **pleasure principle:** it demands immediate gratification of its every desire. Relief of tension is its only goal. The operation of the pleasure principle is seen most clearly in the very young infant where the demand for satisfaction of its biological urgings operates with no constraints. "He wants what he wants when he wants it." But the child is not developing in a vacuum. He soon begins to learn that his demands do not always receive or warrant instant attention. Continued development of the child ushers in a shift from behavior at the level of the pleasure principle to behavior at the higher level of the **reality principle.**

pleasure principle: the tendency to seek immediate gratification of basic needs.

reality principle: adapting the demands of the id (self-gratification) to the realities of the environment.

internalize: to incorporate the norms and values of society into one's internal system of values.

The *ego*, or self is functioning on the reality principle when the child is able to control the demands of the id, when the child is able to delay eating until "mealtime" and will wait until placed on the toilet seat before voiding. Finally, as the child begins to incorporate the beliefs and values of the adult society, the *superego*, or conscience begins to emerge as a dominant force. The superego represents the **internalized** values of the society to which the individual belongs. It opposes unacceptable impulses that arise from the id, including aggressive tendencies and prohibited sexual activity. In a sense, then, the ego is the battleground in which the id and superego engage in continual combat. In another sense, it is the referee—it attempts to reconcile the differences between the two contending forces.

Imagine the following situation in which the three "characters" show their true colors.

Id, Ego, and Superego have 7:30 reservations. They arrive at the restaurant at 7:40 P.M. The hostess tells them that there will be a 30-minute wait for seating. Id balks at this outrageous situation. "We have reservations and I demand to be seated right away." Ego tries to calm Id down by the subtle reminder, "After

In which individual is the superego likely to be a dominant force?

George W. Gardner   George W. Gardner

all, we did arrive 10 minutes late." Superego reprimands Id for the display of such juvenile behavior. "I'll never take you to a restaurant again if you persist in these childish outbursts."

The well-adjusted personality achieves a stable relationship among these three opposing forces. What happens if we are unable to strike a balance? Suppose the ego and superego never develop sufficiently to quash the demands of the id? What emerges is an immature adult—an intolerant, impatient, and impulsive individual. We have all been victimized by these rude, inconsiderate, and unrestrained people. They push their way into lines; they pass us on the road even though we're doing the speed limit; they honk their horns and heap verbal abuse on us if we're not moving fast enough for their satisfaction. We may feel like responding in kind, but we bow to the demands of our own superego.

What happens if the superego is the dominant force? We find a frightened, highly cautious, and extremely uptight person who would never dream of committing even the most minor of infractions. This individual would be racked by guilt at the mere suggestion that he or she had not done the "right" thing.

Levels of Consciousness

It is interesting to explore Freud's distinction between levels of the mind's consciousness. This helps us understand Freud's ideas about why we act the way we do. Earlier we noted that the id works in the unconscious realms of the mind. Many of the biological instincts and impulses that comprise the id are unacceptable at the conscious level. In contrast, the ego operates primarily at the conscious level. Thus, awareness of social pressures to behave according to prescribed laws, rules, and moral values brings it into inevitable conflict with the id. The ego may be forced to resort to psychological defenses to prevent the surfacing of the id's unacceptable impulses. You may already be familiar with several of these mechanisms—rationalization, repression, compensation, and regression. We shall have more to say about defense mechanisms in Chapter 7.

Like the id, the superego operates mainly at the unconscious level. This is largely due to the fact that the conscience is built into us before we are old enough to know what is going on. Can you recall the circumstances under which you were taught to distinguish between right and wrong? It was such a continuous process that the specific memories have faded away from the conscious level and now reside in the great unconscious. Many of us would have difficulty putting into words how we *really* feel about various ethical concerns.

Let's face it. The conscience is a bit of a drag. We don't often wish to pay attention to the demands of our superegos. Most of us seek greater and sometimes "forbidden" pleasures and attempt to avoid the self-sacrifices and limitations imposed by the unconscious, absolute, and irrational demands of the superego. It is relatively easy to consciously relax our social standards. We tell ourselves, "One more for the road won't hurt anybody," or "I'm suffering student burnout. I'll be better off if I don't study tonight," or "I'm really not in the mood for another boring dinner party. I think I'll cancel out on the Lustigs tonight."

Make no mistake about it. It may be comparatively easy to ignore the dictates of our conscience when it spoils our immediate pleasures. However, it is not easy to rid ourselves of our early moral training. At the conscious level, we may feel free to defy old-fashioned social standards; at the unconscious level there may be hell to pay. Our only clue that the conscience is uneasy may be uncomfortable feelings of guilt and depression.

In Chapter 13 we examine some of the techniques Freud proposed as a path to the unconscious—free association, slips of the tongue, and interpretation of dreams.

Psychosexual Stages of Development

In the course of his investigations, Freud found himself in the position of dealing with a subject heavily laden with taboos. The traditional view held that sexual life began with puberty and that any manifestations of sexuality in children were rare and abnormal. But Freud uncovered a wealth of phenomena suggesting that sexuality in children dated back almost to birth. Initially, the first hints of sexuality in children came from adult reports and thus were shrouded with the usual doubts associated with old and, possibly, distorted memories. But as Freud began to analyze children themselves, he felt he had factual bases for his unprecedented views.

Sexuality in children differed in many ways from the sexuality of adults and,

erogenous zones: sensitive areas of the body that become the centers of sexual pleasures

in many cases, manifested itself in ways that were denounced as depraved. Freud broadened the concept of sexuality to include all the energies that go into survival. Thus, more than sexual intercourse and genital stimulation were included in the concept. Pleasurable sensations accompanying the stimulation of sensitive areas of the body, known as **erogenous zones,** are included in Freud's concept of sexuality. At differing times in the development of the individual, the focus of these pleasure zones shifts. Different parts of the body—the mouth, the anus, and the genitals—become the source of gratification.

In recent years, stage theories of development have come into prominence. It is interesting to note that Freud was among the first to conceptualize development as proceeding in an orderly and predetermined sequence. Since Freud emphasized the motivational and sexual aspects of development, the various phases he proposed have been referred to as *psychosexual stages.* Generally, we pass through these stages rapidly and without fanfare. Occasionally, however, frustrations and traumas are encountered that have lasting significance for later development. Freud considered the first few years of a child's life crucial to the development of the adult personality. He felt that the adult is greatly affected by what happens during each stage and by the way traumas, frustrations, and conflicts are resolved before passing on to the next stage. He proposed that various character traits observed in later years are associated with failure to move in an orderly fashion from one stage of psychosexual development to the next. Freud referred

fixation: arrested development at a particular psychosexual stage.

to these failures to progress as **fixations.**

Consider the following analogy. The stages of development can be likened to different floors of a building. Each floor serves as a foundation for all the floors above it. If one of these floors is structurally unsound, it is unable to support the excess weight or stress that is imposed on it by the floors above. If one floor collapses, the other floors will fall to its level.

Oral Stage. The first developmental stage to be identified is the oral stage, which starts at birth and continues through the first year of life. During this stage, the mouth is the primary source of pleasure and potential stress. Sucking and biting are the predominant oral activities manifested by the infant. Unusual frustrations encountered during this stage (e.g., early and abrupt weaning, punishment associated with thumb sucking) may lead to fixations that crop up in later life. During this stage, the infant is completely dependent on others for nourishment and maintenance. Thus it is not surprising that feelings of dependency first arise during this period. To illustrate, suppose an adult named Linus is encountering great stress and emotional turmoil at a particular junction in life. Suppose also that he had developed a weak psychological "structure" during the oral

regress: returning to behaviors characteristic of an earlier stage of development.

stage of development. He might **regress** to the oral behaviors characteristic of the fixated stage. He might smoke or drink to excess, talk too much, or even heap verbal abuse on the sources of his frustrations. Moreover, he may show excessive dependence on others and be blindly trusting and naive in his relations with others.

In Freud's oral stage (A), pleasure is focused on the mouth area. In the anal stage (B), the child develops control over a basic bodily function, thereby developing control over other things in life as well. During the phallic stage (C), the child feels attraction toward the opposite-sex parent, while during the latency period (D), sexual energy is focused away from erogenous zones and the child's attention is turned to school and play. Sexuality resurfaces in the genital stage (E), when the adolescent becomes interested in heterosexual relationships.

A   B   C   D   E

© Joel Gordon 1976   © Susan Lapides 1981   © Joel Gordon 1982   Jean-Claude LeJeune   George W. Gardner
                      /Design Conceptions

Anal Stage.   After about the first year of life, the focus of the child's pleasures shifts to the anal area. Either withholding or expelling feces may provide pleasureable sensations. Indeed, children even derive pleasure from playing with their waste products, much to the chagrin of their parents. Such play substances as molding clay and Silly Putty have been recommended as suitable substitutes.

The primary conflict at this stage centers around the parents' desire to regulate the eliminative functions, thus interfering with involuntary anal gratifications. This battle over toilet training is probably the child's first real squabble with the adult world. It may be the first time the child is prevented from doing what he or she wants. The act of defecation provides an opportunity for the child to make a "decision." Baby Nelson can either part obediently with his feces ("good boy") or else he can hold back. Holding back can initially be a means of experiencing anal gratification; later, it can act as a way of asserting his own will. So much importance is attached to defecation that the child may begin to feel like the goose that lays the golden eggs.

Much has been made of the view that fixation at the anal stage may strongly influence the development of adult personalities. Children who derive their pleasure from expelling body wastes may become outgoing and generous as adults. In contrast, those who received gratification by withholding waste may become stingy and miserly adults. From this view, Scrooge was a classic case of an anal-retentive throughout most of his adult years. There is evidence to suggest that children who have had demanding and strict toilet-training experiences are more likely to be rigid and uncompromising, whereas those who have been more gently treated tend to be more relaxed and easygoing (Deci, 1980).

Phallic Stage. When does a child first "discover" the differences between the sexes? Freud proposed that, between the ages of three and six, the focus of sexual gratification shifts to the genital area. Children at this age are usually intensely curious but do not always understand the answers to the many questions they ask. They fantasize a lot (usually more fiction than fact), they examine and play with their own and, sometimes, their friends' bodies, and they find masturbation (i.e., fondling their genitals) pleasurable. However, during the phallic stage, the frequency of masturbation is increased and, for the first time, fantasies are introduced. The pleasures of masturbation combined with the *nature* of the accompanying fantasies led Freud to postulate what he considered one of the cornerstones of his theory—the **Oedipus complex.** By now, the young boy has already formed a strong attachment to his mother. During the phallic stage, this attachment unconsciously becomes tinged with sexual impulses that come forth. This is the core of the oedipal conflict—the child desires the mother yet must inhibit these impulses because of fear of the father. These feelings create guilt and anxiety, and the child may find it extremely difficult to deal on a conscious level with the **ambivalent** feelings aroused. The father is seen as a rival—an obstacle to be removed. At the same time, the father is bigger and stronger and can get back at the child for these shameful feelings and desires. A boy's sexual curiosity leads him to discover the absence of a penis in women. He may conclude that the penis is a detachable part of the body. Thus, he may fear that his father will physically retaliate by doing some harm or damage to his penis. This special fear in the phallic stage is known as **castration anxiety.**

A similar conflict occurs with little girls at this stage. The Oedipus complex (sometimes called the **Electra complex** in girls) means the sexual urgings are directed toward the father. The little girl hates and feels jealous of her mother. Moreover, she may feel resentful because she fantasizes that she once had a penis that her mother took away from her (as punishment for her shameful desires?) The disappointment and shame that arises as a little girl views the male penis may lead to feelings of jealousy known as **penis envy.** Freud has suggested that penis envy is at the core of a female's sense of inferiority.

To build a strong "foundation" at this stage of development, the young child must successfully resolve his or her oedipal strivings. An inadequate resolution of the conflicts at this stage will deeply affect the development of the superego which is occurring at this time. By adopting the moral codes, standards, and values of the parents, the child is better equipped to deal with unconscious and forbidden impulses.

Some parents have worried so much about Freud's ideas on sexual attraction between small children and their opposite-sex parents that these parents have been afraid to touch and cuddle their children. They may unrealistically fear that holding their children or taking preschool children who have nightmares into bed with them will lead to incest. There is no evidence to indicate that

---

Oedipus complex: in Freudian theory, a young boy's unconscious sexual desires for his mother.

ambivalent: mixed feelings, both positive and negative, toward a person, an object, or a situation.

castration anxiety: in Freudian theory, a boy's fear that his father will castrate him in retaliation for his oedipal desires.

Electra complex: in Freudian theory, a young girl's unconscious sexual desires for her father.

penis envy: In Freudian theory, the female's unconscious feelings of jealousy because she doesn't have a penis.

taking small children into bed when they are frightened leads to incest or other difficulties.

Latency Period.   Freud believed that, once the turbulent affairs of the phallic stage have settled, sexual feelings lie dormant and the sexual drive goes undercover for a few years. Self-control is built up and unacceptable impulses are held in check. Because the sexual drive is dormant, this period is not considered a *stage* of psychosexual development. Rather, it is referred to as the latency *period.* Nonsexual activities assume greater importance during these early school years. Energies are channeled into socially accepted activities such as school, sports, and peer relations.

The latency period is a critical time for the child. It is a time for learning about one's abilities and strengths and for developing a realistic appraisal of one's self. The things learned early in life are now tested in the real world. Interactions are with real people and objects rather than with those fantasized. Two possible reasons for the decrease of fantasy thinking have been proposed (Freud, 1946):

1. Children in the latency period do not dare to engage in fantasy thinking because of the danger of sexual conflicts resurfacing.
2. There is no longer a need to do so because the ego is now relatively strong and can ease up in its efforts to subdue the instinctual processes of the id.

There are some critics who doubt the presumption that sexual interests are latent during this period. Rather, they suggest that children simply learn to hide unacceptable desires and behaviors from disapproving adults (Engler, 1979).

Genital Stage.   The onset of puberty brings to a sudden and abrupt halt the relative calm and tranquility of the latency period. The beginning of puberty signals a whole series of dramatic changes in the child. The child starts to mature physically and sexual energies are once again focused in the genital area. We now have a fully matured body governed by an inexperienced mind.

According to Freud, the adolescent, assaulted by those "forbidden" and unacceptable impulses once again popping up, must marshal the protective powers of the ego as he or she tries to deal successfully with the oncoming invasion. But sexual changes are only a part of the total picture. Numerous external forces are pressing on the adolescent—peer pressures, the need to formulate life goals, and societal codes and standards. In the wake of the greatest sexual revolution of all time, the adolescent is still restricted (too young) from engaging freely and without guilt in normal heterosexual outlets. Thus, it is not surprising that masturbation and homosexual outlets play significant roles in the acquisition of fears and anxieties during this period. The adolescent is required to exercise increased ego control to reconcile undesirable impulses with the external pressures of society.

In contrast to the genital stage, the pregenital phases are mostly self-centered. Young children are concerned only with their own growth. Once they have learned to master their physical and mental environments, they are then able to turn their love fully from themselves to others in the genital stage. The path to sexual achievement ushers in a trail of turmoil, not restricted to the sexual area. Later, we will discuss the disorders created in the social realms of behavior.

Freud considered the genital stage to be the final stage of development, the summit of a long and arduous journey from the early years of self-directed sexual activity to the final destination of normal heterosexual pleasures. According to Freud, the genital stage begins at puberty and lasts through adulthood until the onset of senescence. Clearly, much is happening during the 50 or so years of adult life; however, Freud held to the belief that the first five years of life are crucial to the development of adult behavior. Thus, he had little to say about adulthood.

PSYCHOANALYTIC THEORIES: ERIKSON

Erik Erikson is in the psychoanalytic camp and, like Freud, is an advocate of a stage theory of development. However, rather than emphasizing biological and sexual factors in development, Erikson emphasizes the importance of social, cultural, and historical influences. Moreover, many of the most critical and formative experiences occur after the individual has achieved adulthood. Thus, unlike Freud, who telescoped all the years from adolescence through adulthood into a single stage (the genital stage), Erikson proposes that developmental stages are encountered throughout the life cycle. Where Freud saw four stages, Erikson finds eight. Four of these stages occur from adolescence through the adult years.

Erikson regards each stage in terms of a specific emotional crisis that surfaces during the course of development. However, rather than regarding these crises negatively, he looks at them as challenges or opportunities to grow emotionally. Let's look at the eight psychosocial stages of development.

Trust versus Mistrust

In the first year of life (Freud's oral stage), the crisis involves *trust versus mistrust.* The types of experiences the child has—how he or she is treated and the quality of care received—will determine whether the child develops a sense of trust or mistrust. If treated in a warm, loving manner during this stage, the child will grow up trusting others. Since development is an ongoing lifelong process, personality is not fixed at any given time. Events, circumstances, and social relationships are dynamic and changing. Thus, even a child who emerged from the first stage of life with a strong sense of trust may become mistrustful and cynical if betrayed in later social relationships. Hence, personality is not viewed as fixed by the fifth year of life, as Freud believed, but remains fluid throughout the life span.

Autonomy versus Shame and Doubt

Between the ages of one and three (Freud's anal stage), children are developing a growing sense of control over their own lives. They can now walk, run, climb,

Each individual grows up with a unique set of life experiences; therefore, when two individuals are confronted with the same situation, they may each display completely different reactions.

United Press International Photo

and get into all sorts of mischief. A sense of autonomy develops as they learn new skills and achieve a feeling of control over their environment. Some parents, out of concern or impatience with their children's progress, may intervene and do things that the children should be doing by themselves. Other parents may demand a level of competence of which their children are not yet physically and/or emotionally capable. In either case, these children begin to doubt their own abilities and feel ashamed when they fail to live up to parental expectations.

Initiative versus Guilt

Preschool children evidence an explosion in their competencies. In addition to markedly improved motor skills, they have made enormous progress in their language and communication skills. For the first time, they are truly capable of initiating independent action. Successful experiences leave them with feelings of confidence in their own initiative. However, if they are belittled or humiliated for their efforts, they may develop feelings of guilt.

Industry versus Inferiority

By the age of six, the child is in elementary school. During the ensuing five years, the most important events in the child's life revolve around setting and accomplishing goals related to the school situation. When children are successful in mastering the many behaviors expected of them during these years, they develop feelings of competency and a sense of industry. They may express such feelings as: "I can do anything if I work hard enough." In contrast, children who see themselves as less capable than their peers develop feelings of inferiority.

Identity versus Role Confusion

The adolescent years are celebrated in both prose and song as the days of the identity crisis. Are adolescents adults or are they not? They are sexually prepared for parenthood, but most are not emotionally or financially ready. They enjoy the playground, but know they should be thinking of careers. They are told they are adults or are approaching adulthood, but they are denied adult privileges. Indeed, there are pushes and pulls in so many different directions, it is not surprising that role confusion develops.

Typically, adolescents feel they are on center stage and everyone is looking at them. They are often highly critical of themselves and feel that others are equally critical. Their thoughts turn inward. They look at themselves and question whether or not they measure up to their peers. "Am I good-looking or ugly? What sort of an impression do I make on others?" They also begin thinking about lifelong goals and careers, wondering whether they will make it in the world of the adult. Their ruthless self-appraisal is often beneficial. It results in the development of values, social attitudes, and standards. This inward focus appears to be necessary for the development of a firm sense of self and of broader roles in the social order. Resolution of the identity crisis is essential if one is to harbor any hopes of proceeding in an orderly fashion through the remaining psychosocial stages of development.

Intimacy versus Isolation

Adolescence is now behind the individual and the early adult years loom ahead. Energies are focused on building careers, establishing lasting social ties, and achieving and maintaining intimate relationships. Marriage or cohabitation makes many demands on the individual—sharing, compromising, and relinquishing social mobility to some degree. Also, many young adults begin having children and raising families. Those who were unsuccessful in resolving their identity crisis may find themselves isolated from the mainstream of society and be unable to maintain satisfactory intimate relationships.

Generativity versus Stagnation

We are now in the middle years. By this time, most people are firmly established in their careers; perhaps they have been married and even divorced; their children have left the nest or will soon be doing so. They may become disgruntled with the yawning sameness of their daily routines and wish to add a little spice to life. Long-standing marriages are at risk during this period. Perhaps a new partner will break the monotony of day-to-day existence and add that sought after dash of spice. Others become workaholics, so enmeshed in their occupational web that they have no time to reflect on where they are going or where they have been. Still others reject stagnation and a loss of interest in the world about them. They strive to remain productive, generate new ideas, and make a contribution to society.

Integrity of the Self versus Despair

These are the years of maturity. During youth, people almost believe in their immortality, so distant do the later years appear to be. But no longer can they engage in the delusions of their early years. Time is a merciless taskmaster. It reminds us of our mortality and that we must come to grips with the inevitability of death. If we have resolved all of the earlier crises in our lives, we can look back with satisfaction at the path we took. We are able to maintain our sense of worth and of personal integrity during our final years. Those who have not resolved earlier crises will look upon the prospects of old age and death with a deep sense of dread and despair.

THE BEHAVIORISTIC APPROACH

Josh couldn't believe what was happening to him. If anybody had asked him a few short months ago whether he was satisfied with his achievements on the job, his marriage, and his prospects for the future, he would have given a broad smile and rendered the A-OK sign with his hand. But with the suddenness of a summer rain squall, his life had turned topsy-turvy. First there were troubles at the office. The new senior vice president came in with a bunch of untested and untried ideas and he expected Josh to implement them like a good soldier. Josh, who never could knuckle under to raw authority, resisted in every way possible. The resulting clashes left him emotionally drained and fearing for the security of his job. To compound the problem, he had carried his troubles home with him. All of a sudden, he was short-tempered with Anne and the children. He always felt pangs of remorse and wrenching guilt afterwards, but that did nothing to alleviate the situation. He knew his behavior was inexcusable but he felt powerless to do anything about it. Things had gotten so bad that Anne was beginning to talk seriously about a trial separation. He was drinking too much. In fact, that little belt before lunch seemed to be the one ingredient necessary to carry him through the day. To make matters worse, he was also eating too much and smoking too much. He couldn't get a good night's sleep,

Ronald Reagan is an outstanding example of an older person who has maintained his sense of worth.

Michael Evans/The White House

and his nerves seemed to be constantly rasping on the edge of a steel file. He finally spoke words to himself that he never expected to hear, "Josh you're becoming a nervous wreck."

As we can see, Josh is in trouble. But what ails him? Psychoanalysts of a Freudian persuasion would urge us to search into Josh's early experiences for evidence of trauma and fixation at one of the psychosexual stages in his development. The belief is that only when we have uncovered the root causes of his present difficulties can we begin the necessary repair work. The Freudian approach to personality development is primarily biological. The psychosexual stages are facets of our biological makeup. It is when life experiences disrupt the normal flow of biologically determined stages that adjustment disorders arise.

In contrast, behavioristic psychologists would direct us to look at the learning history and the available repertory of learned behaviors if we want to understand why Josh is experiencing adjustment problems. They would point to a number of basic principles of learning and say that all learning, adaptive or maladaptive, involves precisely the same set of principles. In short, we learn to adjust well; we also learn to make poor adjustments. We learn to be happy, sad, frivolous, inconsiderate, moody, and obstinate. We learn to successfully pursue goals, but we also learn those irritating and self-defeating behaviors that keep some of us in chronic states of dissatisfaction. We learn to succeed; we learn to fail.

The behavioral approach provides a new way of conceptualizing, diagnosing, and changing behavior. This approach makes few, if any, assumptions about internal processes. Rather, it views personality as a complex of learned behaviors which are elicited by stimulus events.

The behavioristic approach is optimistic—it asserts that, if we can learn to be maladjusted, so also can we learn to adjust well to the demands of life. Indeed, in contrast to the traditional psychoanalytic approach, behaviorist theory contends that we need not necessarily dig deeply into root causes to improve a person's adjustment. All we need do is identify and modify those behaviors that are interfering with satisfactory adjustment. And since all behavior follows the same basic principles of learning, it is as easy to learn adaptive behaviors as maladaptive responses. Furthermore, environmental conditions or situations have a greater impact on influencing behavior than do internal personality traits (Mischel, 1968). Thus, the thrust of the behavioral approach is training behaviors rather than changing aspects of the person that may underlie these behaviors. Let us examine some of the things we know about the learning process. We'll look at three forms of learning: classical conditioning, operant conditioning, and observational learning.

Classical Conditioning

classical conditioning: a form of learning in which a formerly neutral stimulus, through repeated pairings with a stimulus that elicits a response, acquires the capacity to elicit the response made to the original stimulus.

At about the turn of the century, a Russian physiologist by name of Ivan Pavlov made a series of observations that were to transform the ways we look at the learning process, particularly learning involving emotions and the **autonomic nervous system (ANS).** Prior to this time, the autonomic nervous system was also known as the involuntary nervous system—it seemed to be under the complete control of biological systems and structures within us. Few scientists had suspected that the ANS could "learn" to respond to external stimuli or that it could be brought under voluntary control.

autonomic nervous system (ANS): the part of the nervous system which regulates the heart, stomach, intestines, genitals, blood vessels, and other internal organs. The ANS controls

Pavlov's initial observations had hardly seemed earth shattering. While investigating the physiology of digestion, for which he earned the Nobel prize, Pavlov noted that a "neutral" stimulus, such as the rattling of a food tray, appeared to acquire the capacity to cause laboratory animals to salivate. This was a result of the rattling being associated with the delivery of food. Since salivation was considered an involuntary function, the observation ran counter to the wisdom of the times. It appeared that an external, nonphysiological stimulus had gained "con-

conditioned response: in classical conditioning, the learned response to a previously neutral stimulus.

conditioned stimulus: in classical conditioning, the neutral stimulus after it has acquired the capacity to elicit the conditioned response.

unconditioned stimulus: in classical conditioning, an unrelated stimulus that automatically elicits a particular response.

unconditioned response: in classical conditioning, any response that is elicited automatically by the unconditioned stimulus.

such reactions as trembling, pulse rate, blood pressure, and perspiration.

trol'' over an automatic response. Although fellow physiologists understated the significance of this observation, Pavlov was obsessed by the idea that he had stumbled on the most basic form of learning—conditioning. He devoted the remainder of an extremely productive life to exploring conditioning and its many ramifications.

The basic model for classical or *Pavlovian* conditioning is quite straightforward. A neutral stimulus that has no initial capacity to bring about a given autonomic response, such as salivation, is introduced moments before the presentation of a stimulus that can elicit salivation, such as food. After many pairings of the two stimuli, the neutral stimulus acquires the capacity to elicit the response by itself. Thus, if prior to conditioning, a tone (the neutral stimulus) is presented alone, no salivation will occur. If, however, the tone is paired with food in the mouth, the tone will, in time, lead to salivation. The "learned" salivation is called the **conditioned response,** and the tone is now referred to as the **conditioned stimulus.** The original stimulus (food) that naturally elicits salivation is called the **unconditioned stimulus.** The naturally occurring response (salivation) to this unconditioned stimulus is called the **unconditioned response.** The conditioning process is outlined in Figure 2.1.

Interest in classical conditioning is not restricted to the laboratory and salivation. Conditioning is a real and powerful force in everyday life. Since it typically involves the autonomic nervous system, it is intimately associated with our emotions and feelings. When we experience strong emotions like anger and fear, the ANS is activated, causing widespread physical changes. The heart beats faster, blood pressure shoots up, digestive processes slow down, blood flows to the "fight

FIGURE 2.1

PARADIGM OF CLASSICAL CONDITIONING: Initially the neutral stimulus (tone) has no capacity to elicit salivation. After several pairings of the tone with meat in mouth, the tone acquires the capacity to elicit salivation. Therefore, we say that the tone is the conditioned stimulus for salivation.

Prior to conditioning	(Neutral stimulus) Tone ———————→	Attending, pricking of ears, etc. No. salivation.
	(Unconditioned stimulus) Meat in ————→ mouth	(Unconditioned response) Salivation, other autonomic responses, emotions and feelings.
During conditioning	Tone ———————→ Meat ——→ Salivation, etc.	
After conditioning	Tone ———————→ Salivation, etc.	
	(Conditioned stimulus)	(Conditioned response)

or flight'' muscles, and perspiration increases. These responses can become conditioned to any neutral stimulus. It is quite possible that many emotional reactions have been inadvertently conditioned to various stimuli through accidental pairings of these stimuli with emotionally arousing events or situations. To illustrate, suppose that you experience pain (the unconditioned stimulus) in the dentist's chair (initially the neutral stimulus). All of the components of the emotion, fear, are unconditioned responses to the pain. Through classical conditioning, the mere sight of the dentist's chair acquires the capacity to elicit these fear responses. Moreover, even making a dental appointment may set off a frenzy of emotional reactions. The same principles also operate in the conditioning of pleasant emotional states. Your physical presence in a restaurant where you have enjoyed good food is sufficient to elicit feelings of contentment and well-being.

In the years since Pavlov's initial accounts of the conditioned response, numerous investigators have extended and built upon his discoveries. Three important principles have emerged: *experimental extinction, spontaneous recovery*, and *stimulus generalization*.

experimental extinction. the reduction in response strength that occurs in classical conditioning when the conditioned stimulus is repeatedly presented *without* the unconditioned stimulus.

Experimental Extinction.   Once a response has been conditioned to a given stimulus, the connection between the two is not engraved in stone. Indeed, the relationship is tenous. If the conditioned stimulus is repeatedly presented without the unconditioned stimulus, the conditioned response will undergo extinction. In other words, unless the tone is at least occasionally followed by meat in the mouth, the salivation response to the tone will gradually taper off until it disappears entirely. This principle is extremely important since it represents one method for breaking undesirable habits and/or eliminating unwanted emotions. For example, what do you suppose would happen if you experienced no pain during subsequent visits to the dentist? Do you think you would still cringe at the sight of the dentist and/or the chair? With repeated extinction trials (presentation of the conditioned stimulus alone—no pain), the conditioned fear response would gradually decrease in strength. Eventually, you would be able to sit in the chair with no visible feelings of discomfort. The use of experimental extinction techniques is the cornerstone of desensitization therapy (See the section on Observational Learning and Chapter 13).

spontaneous recovery: the rebound of a previously extinguished learned response following a rest period.

Spontaneous Recovery.   Suppose you visited the dentist many times after the initial distressing experience. All of these visits were painless. Does the extinction process cancel out the conditioned response? Can you now confront the dentist's chair with no hint of fear?

One of the most interesting observations to emerge from Pavlov's work is that extinction of the conditioned response is *not* permanent. If we allow some time to pass after extinction, we find that the conditioned response will reappear if the conditioned stimulus is presented again. So you're really not out of the woods. If an aching tooth sends you scurrying back to the dentist, you may find yourself subjected to another ''dose'' of agony and discomfort. Once again, you relive the misery and agony that have become associated with the dentist, the chair, and possibly even the amiable receptionist. This recurrence of the previously extinguished conditioned response after a time interval is called spontaneous recovery.

stimulus generalization: when we have learned to make a response to one stimulus, we tend to make the same response to similar stimuli.

Stimulus Generalization. It is often difficult to trace the origins of learned emotional responses. One of the reasons is that the initial learning may no longer be accessible to recall—it may have occurred at an age when little detail is remembered or the experience may not have been sufficiently vivid to produce a lasting memory. Why is it, then, that people still respond emotionally to situations and stimuli with origins that have been submerged in the dim past? Moreover, why is it that emotional reactions are not restricted to the *original*

Without stimulus generalization, an infant would have to learn to recognize her mother every time she wore a new outfit or changed her hairstyle.

Charles Gatewood

stimulus situations? For example, somewhere along the way, you may have learned to fear one creepy, crawly creature. Why do you now recoil at the sight of a multitude of bugs?

The key to our retention of any learned experience is stimulus generalization. When we have learned to respond to a specific situation or stimulus in one way, we tend to make the same response to all similar situations and stimuli. We are truly fortunate that learning can be generalized, since no two situations are ever identical. Without generalization, we would be forced to learn over and over again the responses that are appropriate to every new situation. Otherwise, a child who learned to trust one person would not transfer this trust to any other person. Trust would have to be earned anew by every individual encountered during the course of everyday living.

discrimination:
learning to respond in a different manner to similar stimuli.

Adequate adjustments to life also require that we learn to make appropriate **discriminations,** as well. We cannot always respond in the same way to all similar stimuli. For example, our trusting child must not transfer trust indiscriminately to everyone he or she meets. The child must learn to distinguish between those who merit trust and those who pose a potential threat. Indeed, discrimination among stimuli is a continuing and necessary process throughout life.

operant conditioning:
a form of learning that occurs whenever behaviors are reinforced or punished.

Operant Conditioning

As we have just seen, the principles of classical conditioning are involved in learning to like, love, hate, fear, and trust. All of these reactions involve the autonomic nervous system, our emotions, and our feelings. However, much learning in life requires that we operate in some way on our environment to reach goals. For example, we learn to drive a car to get from one place to another; we learn to talk, read, and write so that we may communicate; and we learn to operate a washer and dryer to do our laundry. In each of these examples, we learn to do something to get something. This is the crux of operant conditioning.

Imagine the following situation. Wendi has recently become hooked on crossword puzzles. You buy her a crossword dictionary in the hope that she will learn how to use this important reference book. Nevertheless, she continues to ask you the definitions of words. You remind her that she can find the answers in the crossword dictionary. When she uses the dictionary and finds the answer, a smile spreads across her face. She is obviously delighted. As a matter of fact, you both are pleased. You have used her interest in crossword puzzles as a means of motivating her to learn a skill that will serve her well for many years to come.

Let's take a moment to compare classical conditioning with operant learning:

1. In classical conditioning, there is a specific conditioned stimulus that elicits a response (e.g., meat in the mouth elicits salivation). There is no comparable situation in operant conditioning. The crossword puzzle does not automatically elicit the behavior of consulting the crossword dictionary. In fact, this is precisely what we wish the child to learn: When I want to know a word, I can use a dictionary.

2. In classical conditioning, the motivation of the individual is irrelevant. Meat in the mouth will elicit salivation whether or not we are hungry. In operant conditioning, however, motivation is of paramount importance. Unless Wendi is motivated to use the dictionary, it will sit on the library shelf and gather dust.

3. The response in classical conditioning is fixed and automatic. We do not "volunteer" to salivate when meat is placed in our mouths. Just the opposite is true in operant conditioning. The response to be learned is voluntary and purposeful. Wendi learns to use the dictionary *because* she wants to achieve some goal.

4. In operant conditioning, the tendency to make the operant response is influenced by the consequences of the response. If the response leads to **reinforcement,** the tendency to make that response in a given situation is increased. There are, however, two types of reinforcers. A **positive reinforcer** is usually a pleasant event that follows a response and increases the probability that the response will occur again. Thus, if Wendi is rewarded for consulting the crossword dictionary (e.g., she finds the answer), she is more likely to refer to it in the future. A **negative reinforcer,** on the other hand, occurs in unpleasant situations—ones we would like to escape. The removal of a negative stimulus is desired. Thus, any behavior will be strengthened if it leads to the termination of undesirable or noxious stimulation. For example, if we find public speaking unpleasant, we will learn to avoid situations where we may be required to give a speech. Avoidance behavior will be negatively reinforced (strenghtened) by the consequent removal of the unpleasant posibility of giving a speech.

reinforcement: a stimulus that increases the strength of a response that precedes it.

positive reinforcer: an event whose presentation increases the probability of the response preceding it.

negative reinforcer: An event whose removal increases the probability of the response preceding it.

Although classical and operant conditioning differ in several ways, the principles of experimental extinction, spontaneous recovery, and stimulus generalization apply to both types of learning. Thus, if reinforcement is terminated or suspended, a learned operant response will gradually extinguish (see Box 2.1). Following an interval of time, the behavior will recover spontaneously. Finally, when we have learned to make a response in one situation, we will tend to make the same response in similar situations. To illustrate, Shari is an exemplary employee. She always arrives a bit early and never complains if she must stay late. Her work is always done neatly and efficiently. She is extremely well organized. Everyone knows they can count on Shari to get the job done. She is rewarded with annual pay increases, bonuses, and lots of praise. Then one day her company is taken over by a large conglomerate. Somehow Shari is lost in the shuffle. No one seems to notice or even pay attention to her work habits. Since no one else seems to care, Shari starts to lose interest. She begins arriving late and her work becomes slovenly and undisciplined. Thus, due to the withdrawal of positive reinforcement, Shari's superior work habits have gradually been extinguished. When she returns from her annual two-week vacation, there is a brief interlude during which the old Shari reappears. However, this is short-lived and Shari decides to change jobs. She is offered a job with a small company, much like her company

BOX 2.1: BREAKING BAD HABITS

We learn undesirable habits or responses such as smoking or binge eating in much the same way as we learn desirable ones. How do we unlearn them? We have already seen that extinction occurs when reinforcement is withheld following a learned response. Many of the methods of habit breaking rely on extinction to some degree. Let us look at a number of different techniques to see how we can use the principles of conditioning to weaken or break a bad habit.

1. *Keep score.* Keep track of the number of times you engage in the behavior you wish to change. For example, write down on a piece of paper the number of cigarettes you smoke daily, the number of times you say "you know" in conversation, or the number of trips you make to the refrigerator.

2. *Set goals.* Make sure the goals you set are realistic. To avoid frustation, it is best to set intermediate goals as well as end goals. Suppose you have to write a 10-page term paper. Set aside a block of time during which you resolve to complete at least three pages. Promise yourself a reward each time you succeed in meeting your goal.

3. *Identify the reinforcement for the undesirable habit.* Once you have discovered what is reinforcing a habit, try to avoid or delay the reinforcement. For instance, suppose every time you sit down to study or write a paper, you find yourself taking a break every few minutes to call a friend. These phone conversations are reinforcing your desire to avoid studying. You should do your studying at school, the library, or some other place where no telephone is available. Or else you should resolve to put in an hour of study for each 10 minutes you spend on the telephone.

4. *Try to discover what cues are eliciting the bad habit.* See whether you can remove or change the stimuli that normally evoke the undesired behavior. Perhaps you wish to cut down on the number of cigarettes you smoke daily. If you find you smoke more when you are with other smokers, try to avoid being in their company. Sit in nonsmoking sections of restaurants or other public places. Confine your smoking to certain limited areas such as your car or only one room in your house.

5. *Make a new, incompatible response in the presence of cues that normally elicit the original undesired behavior.* This technique involves preventing an undesirable response and simultaneously replacing it with a new response. The new response should be incompatible with the original one; that is, the two responses cannot occur at the same time. Suppose you are a very fast eater—you eat so rapidly that your plate is usually clean before anyone else has even made a dent in their food. Assuming you do not like to talk and eat at the same time, try substituting talking for eating. Before each meal, think out a number of different topics on which to converse. Then when you sit down, start talking for a while before you even take your first mouthful. Make a concerted effort to intersperse conversation throughout your meal. You might also try putting your utensils down between each mouthful.

6. *Make the undesired response so often that it becomes boring or painful.* This technique will increase your awareness of the bad habit and will tend to discourage its recurrence. This technique, which has been called *negative practice,* has been effective in eliminating repetitive typing errors (Dunlap, 1932). A person who repeatedly typed *hte* instead of *the* was instructed to deliberately type *hte* over and over again. In this case, negative practice helped to eliminate the undesirable habit by exaggerating the difference between it and the correct habit. Thus, the subject became more aware of the discrimination between the two responses.

used to be. In this new but similar environment, Shari generalizes her original work habits and once again becomes the "ideal" employee.

Observational Learning

Francis was delighted. That strange dog he had seen jogging down the road was headed directly for him. He loved dogs and he wondered why his parents wouldn't let him have one. As the dog approached, he started to run toward it, arms outstretched. Suddenly another child appeared and ran toward the same dog. The dog growled first and then snapped at the child. The child screamed, "It bit me," and fled, crying bitterly. Francis stopped dead in his tracks and retreated in fear.

Sharon loved Saturday mornings. Nothing to do but loll about in her pajamas and watch the cartoons on TV. One of the cartoon characters seemed to be having a great time pummeling its teddy bear. It looked like loads of fun. Sharon began delivering karate chops to her Jimmy doll. She was right. It was fun.

Dora had just spent her last dollar buying a personal computer for use in her business and for managing her numerous household affairs. Her problem was that she didn't know beans about computers or how to run them. She sought help from the salesperson who had sold her the computer. He said, "Well, the first thing you do is to place the diskette in the disk drive. Then you close the door, like this. . . ."

These examples all have elements in common. Not all emotions are learned as a result of classical conditioning and learning adaptive behavior does not require that operant procedures be followed. We learn much from others by observing their emotions in various situations and by imitating their behaviors in other circumstances. For example, Francis will probably learn to fear dogs as a result of observing the fear expressed by another child. The cartoon characters may be providing a model of aggressive behavior which Sharon is learning to imitate. Has anyone ever said to you, "Why you sound exactly like your mother (your father)?" To what extent have you acquired mannerisms in your speech as a result of imitating one or both of your parents?

Prior to the past several decades, few psychologist paid much attention to the process of learning through observing others. We have now come to appreciate how pervasive this form of learning is. You may learn to be aggressive by observing the aggression of others; you may learn to be afraid by observing the fears of others; you may learn to overcome fears of various situations by observing models who are unafraid; surprisingly, you may even improve creative talents by observing creative people in action. Let's look at a few examples.

Imagine that Billy is engaging in a prohibited act, such as eating crackers in front of the TV set and getting crumbs all over the carpet. His mother is annoyed. "How many times have I told you not to eat in the living room. Go to the kitchen immediately," she commands. Billy does not budge. Her annoyance is transformed into momentary fury by Billy's act of defiance. His mother lashes

We learn many of our behaviors by imitating actions of our parents.

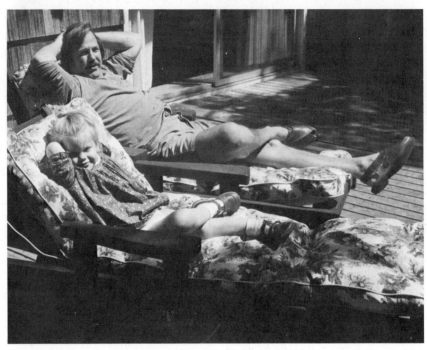

George W. Gardner

out at him and strikes him full on the side of the face. Billy whimpers but now obeys the command. His mother thinks, "I wish I didn't have to hit him all the time, but that's the only way I can get him to listen. It works."

social learning: a form of learning that occurs as a result of observing models.

A leading **social learning** theorist, Albert Bandura, argues that more is learned by Billy in these encounters than to obey his mother. His mother is also serving as a model for aggression. In Bandura's words:

> When a parent punishes a child physically for having aggressed toward peers, for example, the intended outcome of this training is that the child should refrain from hitting others. The child, however, is also learning from parental demonstration how to aggress physically. And the imitative learning may provide the direction for the child's behavior when he is similarly frustrated in subsequent social interactions. (Bandura, 1967)

This learning is more than a mere copy of the behavior of the model. The child sorts out this information, stores it and files it in memory, evaluates it, adds it to other similar experiences, and then applies it "creatively" to a wide variety of situations. Thus, Billy may take a swing at his little sister when she annoys him, and pummel his playmates when frustrated.

If observational learning techniques can inadvertently provide models of undesirable behaviors so also can they, by design, serve as models of desired responses. In one study, people with a disabling fear of snakes were used as subjects (Bandura, Blanchard, & Ritter, 1969). They wished to overcome their fear because it was interfering with their recreation and even their choice of a homesite. They were unable to go hiking, camping, or hunting and they had to live in the city rather than in the country.

The subjects were assigned to one of four different conditions: (1) In the *symbolic modeling* condition, the subjects viewed films in which the models interacted· with plastic and then with live snakes. The scenes went from mild to threatening. The subjects were instructed to maintain a relaxed state while viewing the film. (2) The *systematic desensitization* condition combined relaxation with experimental extinction. The subjects constructed a scale of 34 scenes from the film that varied from most to least fearful. The mildest scenes were presented until the fear had been extinguished and the subjects were able to relax. Then more frightening scenes were introduced until, gradually, the anxiety was extinguished. (3) In the *live modeling* condition, the subjects watched a model in a series of increasingly threatening interactions with live snakes. The model then conducted the subjects in interactions with snakes—touching, stroking, and eventually holding them. (4) Finally, the control subjects were tested before and after "treatment," but they were not given any training. However, so as not to deny them the benefits of the treatment, they were given symbolic modeling after the study had been completed. All of the treatment procedures were effective. However, live modeling with participation by the subjects produced the greatest gains.

The fascinating thing about observational learning is that the individual does not merely mimic the model. In fact, it has been shown that children can learn to imitate creativity as long as the model exhibits creativity (Zimmerman & Dialessi, 1973). After watching a model name various uses for a cardboard box, the children were asked to suggest uses for a tin can. Their scores improved, even though the children rarely repeated the model's words. They seemed to learn: use your imagination (Navarick, 1979).

COGNITIVE BEHAVIOR MODIFICATION— "STRESS INOCULATION"

Are you plagued by headaches that assault you whenever you feel under great tension and stress? Do you experience difficulty controlling aggression whenever your anger is provoked? Use of a technique known as *stress inoculation training* promises to help individuals cope with stressful circumstances better. (Meichenbaum, 1977; Novaco, 1977a).

We are all familiar with inoculation against some dreaded viral disease. A dead or weakened strain of a dangerous virus is administered to individuals who may be or have recently been exposed to the virus. The body erects defenses against this virus in the form of antibodies. The body is then able to resist damaging effects in the event that the full-strength virus invades the individual. But what is stress inoculation training?

In a word, it involves preparing an individual in advance to resist the damaging effects of stress. The technique is cognitive rather than behavioral in nature. That is, the emphasis is placed on bringing about cognitive changes in the individual rather than focusing upon changing the person's behavior directly. It might be helpful to look at the procedures developed by one team of researchers to help individuals resist stress-related headaches (Holroyd, Andrasik, & Westbrook, 1977).

Three groups of headache sufferers were compared—those receiving stress-inoculation training, those undergoing biofeedback training, and control subjects who were awaiting treatment. There were three phases in the stress-inoculation training:

1. Providing an explanation for the headaches in terms of some behavioral or cognitive deficiency in the individual. Thus the clients learn to attribute the headaches to conditions that are correctable rather than to those that they are likely to regard as incurable (e.g., "I didn't inherit it from my mother, rather, "I immerse myself in thoughts that only multiply the tension.")

FIGURE 2.2   MEAN WEEKLY HEADACHE SCORES IN TWO-WEEK BLOCKS

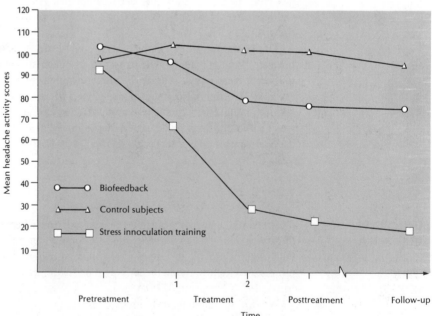

Source: From K. A. Holroyd, in *Behavioral Approaches in Medicine,* ed. J. R. McNamara (New York: Plenum Press, 1979).

2. Teaching the clients to monitor their responses to stressful circumstances. Specifically, they learn to identify and recognize: the events that trigger the stress; the thoughts accompanying the stress; and the behavioral responses that typically occur under stress.

3. Training the individual to interrupt the thought sequences that preceded the emotional reactions. This may involve: *(a)* Reinterpreting the threatening situation (e.g., "Whenever my boss appears to be angry, I assume the anger is directed at me. This is almost never actually the case. Usually, the anger has been provoked by circumstances over which I have no control.") *(b)* Directing the individual's attention to other, nonthreatening aspects of the environment (e.g., "The work must get done in spite of the boss' temper tantrum.") *(c)* Engaging in fantasy to divert the individual from engaging in tension-increasing thoughts (e.g., "TGIF. This weekend I'm going to spoil myself rotten. First, I'll stay in bed until some outrageous hour. Then, I'll . . .")

The results of the study are summarized in Figure 2.2. Note that there was a dramatic reduction in headache scores among the clients undergoing stress inoculation training during treatment, after treatment, and over a later follow-up period. The improvement following biofeedback training was less impressive. Finally, the headache scores of the nontreated controls remained relatively stable throughout the period.

Stress inoculation techniques have also been used successfully to treat community clients and law enforcement officers with anger problems (Novaco, 1975, 1977b) and hospitalized patients suffering from depression (Novaco, 1977a).

SUMMARY

- Most of us hold private theories concerning underlying causes of behavior. These views are colored by our own motives, needs, and personal experiences.

- Two schools of thought—psychoanalysis and behaviorism—were explored in this chapter.

- Freud, the founder of psychoanalytic theory, saw three basic forces as being at war within the individual: the id, consisting of basic biological urgings that operate on the pleasure principle; the superego, representing the internalized values of a society and opposing the unacceptable impulses of the id; and the ego or self, which attempts to reconcile the differences between the id and the superego.

- Developing a stable balance between these three forces is essential for making mature life adjustments.

- The id works in the realm of the unconscious; the ego, primarily at the conscious level; and the superego, mainly at the unconscious level.

- The cornerstone of Freud's theory of personality are the psychosexual stages of development. During life, the erogenous zones shift from the mouth to the anus, and then to the genitals.

- Fixations may occur at any stage due to trauma or other circumstances. These fixations may become the focus of conflicts experienced in later life.

- The psychosexual stages are: oral, anal, phallic, and genital. The latency period occurs after the phallic stage.

- Erikson also proposed a stage theory of development. Unlike Freud's, Erikson's theory does not emphasize biological and sexual factors but focuses on social influences.

- The eight stages proposed by Erikson include: trust versus mistrust, autonomy versus shame and doubt, initiative versus guilt, industry versus inferiorty, identity versus role confusion, intimacy versus isolation, generativity versus stagnation, and integrity of the self versus despair.

- Behaviorists direct us to look at the learning history and the available repertory of learned behaviors if we wish to understand adjustment. They view personality as a complex of learned behaviors which are elicited by stimulus events.

- The thrust of the behavioral approach is to train behaviors rather than to change aspects of the person.

- Three forms of learning have been described: classical conditioning, operant conditioning, and observational learning.

- Classical conditioning, which involves the autonomic nervous system, underlies much of our emotional learning. If neutral stimuli are paired with stimuli that naturally elicit specific responses, the neutral stimuli will acquire the capacity to elicit the response.

- Operant responses are learned in a given situation when these responses are followed by reinforcement.

- We learn much behavior by observing others. However, the behavior acquired in this way does not merely mimic the model but adds characteristics of its own.

- In all of these forms of learning, the principles of extinction, spontaneous recovery, and generalization apply.

- Stress inoculation training is a behavioral approach to managing stressful circumstance which focuses on changing the cognitive reaction to the circumstances. Individuals are taught to identify the cues that set off a stress reaction and to monitor their thoughts. They are then trained to actively stop disruptive thoughts.

TERMS TO REMEMBER

Hypotheses	Conditioned response
Pleasure principle	Conditioned stimulus
Reality principle	Unconditioned stimulus
Internalize	Unconditioned response
Erogenous zones	Experimental extinction
Fixation	Spontaneous recovery
Regression	Stimulus generalization
Oedipus complex	Discrimination
Ambivalent	Operant conditioning
Castration anxiety	Reinforcement
Electra complex	Positive reinforcer
Penis envy	Negative reinforcer
Classical conditioning	Social learning
Autonomic nervous system	

C H A P T E R 3

HUMANISTIC THEORIES
OF THE SELF

Larry is very creative. He loves to paint, sculpt, and build things. Everyone agrees that he is very talented. However, for years, Larry has been trying to "find himself." His various ventures into the world of business have all produced disappointment and failure. He takes jobs that he finds tedious and boring and which offer no prospects for growth and excitement. Larry makes a realistic appraisal of his situation and realizes that he will only find fulfillment if he can harness his creative talents in a productive manner. After researching all potential opportunities, he finds that designing and dressing windows and displays is the "perfect" career. Initially, things are very tight for him. First he must learn a new vocation and then build a business. This involves a period of sacrifice—he cannot buy that stereo he's been coveting or eke out the pennies necessary to subscribe to cable TV. Indeed, all of his recreational activities have been curtailed.

Finally, his efforts begin to pay off. His business flourishes, he enjoys his work, and he is beginning to reap the harvest of his labors. As Larry continues to grow, he expands his horizons to include redecorating apartments and condominiums. For the first time in many years, he feels fulfilled.

THE HUMANISTIC VIEW

The psychoanalytic and behavioral approaches tend to concentrate on what can go wrong with adjustment. In contrast, the humanistic approach is more positive, emphasizing characteristics of the fully functioning human being. Humanists believe that we are basically good—unquestionably an optimistic view of human nature. We have the potential for kindness as well as selfishness, for greatness as well as mediocrity.

Such leading humanistic theorists as Carl Rogers and Abraham Maslow believe that our dominant tendency is to sustain, actualize, and elevate ourselves. They assert that we are capable of maintaining and improving ourselves so that we can strive for a better life. They contend that we are not simply victims of our environment, as behaviorists would say. We are ingenious, imaginative, and versatile, capable of determining, changing, and controlling our own destinies. If we are displeased with our circumstances, we have the ability to change them. If there is confusion and disorder in our lives, we are capable of restoring balance and harmony. We are constantly changing, and there is a continuing process of learning from ongoing experiences. Maslow, in particular, restricted his theories to positive, healthy aspects of the individual. He believed that every person has an enormous potential for growth toward complete fulfillment and **self-actualization.** This process of actualizing is not spontaneous or easy. Rather, it involves a great deal of effort and even some sacrifices and suffering. However, it is the profound desire to grow that keeps a person going. Larry is an example of personal growth.

self-actualization: Maslow's name for the individual's need to strive toward realizing his or her fullest potential in accord with the highest ideals of humanity.

Since so much of humanistic theory centers on the key concept of the self, we will continue to explore the self in subsequent sections.

THE DIMENSIONS OF THE SELF

Imagine the following:

> You are on a summer vacation. As a change of pace, you decide to get close to nature. You plan to spend several weeks in the backlands of our country, camping in open fields and reducing to a bare minimum your dependence on material luxuries. Early one evening, however, you discover that your provisions are getting low. You had better stop at that town down in the valley to stock up for the next few days.
>
> First you'll stop at the general store. Afterwards, if you're up to it, you'll seek out some human companionship. As you enter the store, you are slightly surprised and a little peeved that nobody seems to pay any attention to you. No greeting, no nod, no indication that you have even been noticed. You take out your shopping list and approach the storekeeper. You say hi, but she doesn't return your greeting. In fact, she seems not to be looking at you but through you. Your skin begins to crawl just a bit. The experience is eerie. You have never before encountered such coldness, such indifference. You are unable to conceal your annoyance and you say a few harsh words. The storekeeper continues what she is doing without any sign that she has acknowledged your presence. Irately, you turn to one of the customers and shout, "What's the matter with her. Is she deaf or something?" The customer pays you no attention, but looks right through you, just like the storekeeper. Annoyed, confused, and beginning to doubt your own sanity, you quickly leave the store, being sure to slam the door on your way out. You try to stop a passerby for directions to another store. He does not stop, shows no sign of seeing or hearing you, and moves on. This scene is repeated over and over again with identical results. When another pedestrian walks by, you don't even make an attempt to stop her. During the brief interval that you have been in the town, your annoyance has turned to anxiety, your anger to fear, and your confidence to disbelief. Why is this so?

self (self-concept): an internal perception of one's competencies, virtues, and feelings of value.

social self: the self as defined by the ways in which others react to us.

This scenario reminds us that there is more to the **self** than our physical body, our home, family, and all the material things that define us. There is also the **social self,** the self that is delineated by the recognition that others give us. Withdraw this recognition, and we are left with a gaping void in our self.

Another dimension of the self is the *valuing self.* Carl Rogers believes that there is an inborn process that permits us to value positively those experiences we perceive as sustaining and improving the quality of our lives. This valuing self also causes us to place less value on those experiences that diminish our growth. As one psychologist has noted:

> The criterion for values is the actualizing tendency—does this action or experience enhance or maintain the organism? Full trust is placed in the

How do you suppose this man's social self is affected by the fact that no one is paying attention to him?

United Press International Photo

developing individual to value what is best for growth, whether it be a particular diet, a schedule for sleep, a choice of intellectual activities, or special relationships. The fact that so few individuals seem to select activities that are most enhancing is not evidence against a centered valuing process but rather a reflection of how few people are raised to trust in their own natural valuing process. (Prochaska, 1979, p. 128)

THE DEVELOPMENT OF SELF

How do we develop a concept of ourselves, who we are, our values, beliefs, attitudes? Carl Rogers, who uses the terms self and self-concept interchangeably, believes, "At bottom, each person is asking, 'Who am I, *really?* How can I get in touch with this real self, underlying all my surface behavior? How can I become myself?'" (Rogers, 1961, p. 108). These are questions we have all posed at one time or another.

The infant starts life with an unclear distinction between "me" and "not me." Indeed, many psychologists have described infancy as a period of **egocentrism.** Children have not yet learned the borders that separate them from other objects and other people. As the infant develops and starts to explore his or her environment, he or she begins to suspect that there are other individuals who have independent and separate existences of their own. The child has begun to differentiate his or her body from people and objects that are not part of

egocentrism: the inability to see things from any perspective other than one's own.

Because of the rigid regimentation and uniformity of the military environment, soldiers soon lose their sense of individuality.

© Joel Gordon 1976

him- or herself. The child becomes aware that he or she is a distinct being, similar but different from others.

This differentiation or sense of personal identity is aided by the explosive growth of language during this period. Words such as "I," "me," "you," and "they" provide labels that highlight and accentuate the distinction between self and others. In addition, significant people in the child's life apply labels. "You are a bad boy." or "Get out of my sight. You make me sick." or "You're such a good child. I love to have you around." The child begins to apply these labels to him- or herself. "Good boy," says Jimmy as he hugs his teddy bear. "Naughty girl," murmurs Carla as she spanks her doll.

Labels become a part of children's self-images as they attach personal values to these descriptions. Rogers believes that there is an important distinction between values that are acquired directly from one's own experiences and those that are internalized or acquired from others. When children learn directly from their own experiences, they will realistically label their feelings and not become maladjusted. When children mislabel experiences because of a need to please others, they may internalize parental viewpoints of their own experiences and the stage is then set for maladjusted behavior. To illustrate, when an adult tells a child it is wrong to be frightened, the child learns to avoid labeling his feelings as fear because he doesn't want to think himself as bad in the eyes of the parent. Children learn to misrepresent their actual feelings to please their parents. When the experience (fear) is out of tune with the labeled self, the conditions are ripe for maladjustment. The lack of consistency leads to anxiety and tension. Also, certain perceptions become unacceptable and the child is forced to misrepresent reality and resort to exaggerated psychological defenses.

Childhood is a crucial time for the lasting effects of early social relationships and for the development of the concept of self (see Box 3.1). So much depends on the environment and the quality of the experiences. If these experiences are largely negative, the concept of self will be negative. To develop a positive self-image, we all need warmth, acceptance, and positive self-regard from others. Children will do almost anything to satisfy this need. To gain parental approval, children may distort or deny their own perceptions, feelings, and emotions. In the long run, this may lead to problems. Denial or distortion of important aspects

The way we regard ourselves is, in large part, a reflection of the way others respond to us.

Jim Whitmer/Nawrocki Stock Photo

BOX 3.1: "MOMMY, NOBODY LIKES ME"

Finding a pal to share secrets or giggle with isn't just a matter of fun and games. Friendship is serious business to school-aged youngsters. "When you don't have a friend, it's terrible," explains Jenny, aged seven. "It makes you feel mad and sad." Psychologist Willard Hartup puts it another way: "Friends aren't a luxury for children—they're a necessity."

Being able to form relationships with others is a vital part of the growing-up process, says Dr. Hartup, a professor of psychology at the University of Minnesota. Sadly, studies show that grade schoolers who are shut out by their peers are more apt to develop emotional or behavioral problems as teenagers.

Clearly, no one manages to grow up without ever experiencing some social rejection. As parents we've all had the experience of consoling a child who wasn't invited to someone's birthday party. But for a surprising number of youngsters—as many as one out of five or six in every class—being "left out" doesn't just mean missing a few parties or not being chosen for the team. It means being chronically excluded.

To help these isolated children, a number of psychologists have been trying to penetrate the mysteries of what makes some youngsters more popular than others. Is there some key quality that gives well-liked children the edge? And if so, can we help their less-popular peers acquire it? The answer to both these questions seems to be yes, according to recent studies.

Researching the behavior of a group of nursery schoolers, psychologist Hartup documented clear-cut differences in the way popular and unpopular children behave toward their classmates. A large number of friendless children do tend to be aggressive, his findings indicate. They pick fights, insult and generally bully their classmates. Not surprisingly, well-liked children behave in more positive ways. As companions, they listen well and are helpful and sympathetic to others. They know how to share and compromise. In short, they have better friendship-making expertise.

FRIENDSHIP LESSONS

Impressed by research showing that unpopular children lack the social tools they need to be "nice guys," Sherri Oden, a professor of psychology at Wheelock College in Boston, and psychologist Stephen Asher, who teaches at the University of Illinois, experimented with giving friendship-making "lessons" to unpopular school-aged children. They found that they could markedly improve youngsters' social skills. And as a result, classmates started liking these children better.

For their project, the research team asked the children in third and fourth grade classes to rate their peers' popularity. Oden and Asher identified the three least popular children in every class. The psychologists then invited one of these rejected youngsters to attend five once-a-week play periods. In each session, the unpopular child was paired with a more well-liked classmate. Before the activities began, either Oden or Asher coached the unpopular child on ways to make the play time "more fun." Social strategies that were stressed included how to be cooperative, how to communicate well, and how to show interest in others. After the session, the researcher and child talked about what had happened during the game and what the youngster might have done to improve his or her participation.

Five days after the coaching program ended, the children's popularity ratings by their classmates rose impressively. A year later they showed even more gains. Also striking is the fate of the unpopular ones who hadn't received friendship lessons. Not only did their social standing not improve, but over the year, they actually lost ground slightly.

Why was this short course in friendship making so effective? Stephen Asher thinks the sessions provided a consciousness-raising experience, making the youngsters more aware of how they interact with other children. Some did not seem to behave with an instinctive understanding of how relationships work. During one meeting, for example, third grader Laurie turned to Asher with amazement and said, "You mean what I do affects whether the other kids like me or not?" Says Asher, "It was like a light bulb going on for her."

So far no one has developed a packaged program to help "turn on the light bulb" for friendless children like Laurie. But psychologists Asher and Oden believe there is an important message for parents in their research. "Adults don't always realize how important

BOX 3.1 *(continued)*

learning social skills is for a child," says Oden. Parents who worry about whether their preschoolers can recognize the letters of the alphabet or count to 10, she says, should be equally concerned about whether their four-year-old is learning to get along with other children.

Youngsters without playmates, experts feel, miss an important aspect of the growing-up process. As children play together, they pick up key lessons in survival from their peers. "They learn the kind of give-and-take necessary to cope as adults," says Dr. Susan Fisher, a Chicago psychiatrist. "They also help teach one another society's values, sometimes more effectively than adults can. Children are merciless when they catch each other cheating at a game, telling a fib, or 'showing off.' ".

But to set the stage for healthy interaction with schoolmates, it's crucial that children learn basic social skills at home. As with other behavioral patterns, parents teach by example, psychologist Oden explains. For instance, mothers and fathers who take the time to listen to what their children have to say are more likely to rear good listeners than are those parents who consistently tune youngsters out. Conversely, parents who yell at their children a lot are teaching them that people deal with each other with angry words.

NURTURE SOCIAL SKILLS

In addition to indirect lessons, Oden suggests ways parents can actively nurture social skills at various ages:

Infants and Toddlers. Conventional wisdom says that babies are much too self-centered to be really interested in one another. New studies, however, show that even infants and toddlers enjoy and benefit from having friends. Infants should be given opportunities to play together and to practice ways of getting along as early as six months of age. Little more is required at this stage than what most parents do naturally, she says—refereeing when squabbles break out and trying to teach Susie and Billy how to share the shovel.

Preschoolers. Children between the age of three and five teach each other about sharing, taking turns,

and being nice. Strike a balance between letting youngsters work out problems themselves and being available to step in when play sessions get seriously out of control. Help them see that there are options in social situations. "Why don't you let Jimmy play with the truck now and you play with the train" teaches youngsters that there are alternatives to fighting. Also, encourage children to put themselves in another child's shoes. ("Did you hurt Cindy's feelings?") Begin to teach them, too, about the consequences of their actions. ("If you grab that crayon from Mark, what do you think he'll do?")

WHEN SHOULD YOU STEP IN?

In grade school, friendships become of paramount importance to youngsters and most can manage relationships fairly well on their own at this stage. But when a child does run into serious social troubles, it's time for an adult to step in and offer help and support. What can parents do when a child comes home from school and says, "Mommy, nobody likes me"? Psychologist Oden offers some ideas:

Above all, don't dismiss your child's feelings. Draw him or her out and try to ascertain whether the fears are real. Often children worry because they think that everyone has to like them. Some need simple reassurance that it's normal to be liked by some people and not others.

When social problems persist, it's a good idea to set up a conference with your child's teacher. Ask if he or she can find ways to help integrate your child into classroom activities.

The teacher will probably be able to provide some insight as to the source of your child's trouble. It's important to know whether he or she is being actively rejected by classmates or is simply not sought out by other kids as a playmate. The social rejects—usually the ones who bully their playmates in the school yard—are the ones that especially worry experts. They're youngsters who haven't learned to master their aggressive impulses and may eventually need a consultation with a child psychologist.

Realize that some children truly enjoy playing alone, a predilection parents should respect. Not everyone has to be a social butterfly, but sometimes a

BOX 3.1 *(concluded)*

natural "loner" may need to be reminded, at least occasionally, to socialize and seek out playmates.

Offer your child some positive suggestions about ways he or she might improve social life. Are there any group activities he or she could join in class? Is there a classmate the child would like to know better and perhaps invite home to play?

You might suggest your child invite another youngster to join with you on a family outing when there will be an adult around to keep things running smoothly. Plan some noncompetitive activity as opposed to a game of football or tennis that can spark tensions between the players.

As painful as it is for parents to see a child experience rejection, try to be supportive without becoming overly involved. To some extent youngsters have to learn to negotiate on their own. Avoid making your youngster feel as if the object is to win a popularity contest. All children really need to learn is how to make and keep a friend. They don't have to be invited to every birthday party.

Source: Geraldine Carro, *Ladies Home Journal,* April 1982, pp. 118, 120. © 1982, Family Media Inc. Reprinted with permission of the author and *Ladies Home Journal.*

of ourselves may result in incomplete and unrealistic self-images. We may feel threatened by experiences that disagree with our self-concepts. Conflicting experiences are likely to be prevented from entering conscious awareness and are usually perceived inaccurately. To close out these disturbing events, maladjusted human beings tend to build inflexible defenses. Since they avoid many potential experiences that may be threatening to their self-concepts, they never learn the limits of their own potential. Thus, they fail to set goals that would provide the opportunity to actualize their potential. Let us look at an example.

Eddie really doesn't like his new sister Karen. She seems to be getting all the attention. Everyone makes a big fuss over her. One day he gets really annoyed and pushes her out of her carriage. His mother yells at him, "You bad boy!" Eddie starts to believe that his mother will not love him unless she thinks he cares for and will be nice to his baby sister. Eddie's need for acceptance and love may cause him to engage in self-deception. In spite of the fact that he still feels jealous and resentful toward his sister, he hides these feelings behind a mask of love and concern to gain approval and acceptance. Thus, he learns to reject or deny his own true feelings because they are threatening and may lead to intense anxiety if he senses loss of his mother's love. If he learns that it is wrong to *feel* angry, he may begin to perceive these feelings as dangerous. To feel worthy, he may be unable to accurately perceive feelings of anger and hostility when they do occur. He may begin to believe that any expression of aggression is bad. He may not be able to accurately perceive that sometimes its expression is satisfying. Eddie may be unable to distinguish his feelings from his actions. His feelings are important in helping him to understand his experiences. His actions may or may not be suitable.

Suppose Eddie's mother had responded in a different way. Suppose she had communicated to him that she still loved him even though his behavior was bad. Eddie learns to distinguish between "bad behavior" and "bad boy." He realizes

Children have many different feelings toward their siblings. It is important that they accept the positive and negative feelings that they experience.

George W. Gardner

that he can still be loved even though his behavior is not always so terrific. He also learns that bad behavior does not mean that *he* is necessarily bad. This is a critical distinction for Eddie, because the way he feels about himself is crucial to his future happiness and effectiveness. If Eddie can learn to accept and live with his negative feelings, he may also learn to change his behavior in constructive ways. For example, he may try playing with his sister instead of fighting with her, or sharing some of his toys instead of trying to grab all of hers. And when he does feel angry, he can accept these feelings but learn to control their expression in more appropriate ways.

Rogers maintains that the way we regard ourselves depends largely on the kinds of regard given by others. In the ideal situation, love is given freely and is not dependent on any specific behaviors. Rogers calls this facet of love **unconditional positive regard.** Unconditional acceptance leads to unimpaired growth and the development of positive characteristics. Children who have received unconditional positive regard have high **self-esteem**—they feel good about themselves, develop positive self-concepts and feelings of self-respect. Moreover, they maintain realistic self-concepts that embrace all their own significant qualities. They have accurate perceptions of their own worlds, their experiences are free and unrestricted, and they regard themselves highly. Well-adjusted people rely on their own knowledge and understanding to make decisions. Rogers believes that fully functioning individuals live totally in the present and are continually changing to make full use of their various potentialities.

Rogers contends that difficulties in functioning are caused by a lack of unconditional acceptance by others starting early in life. In other words, children may

unconditional positive regard: Rogers' term for acceptance of the value of a person regardless of their behavior.

self-esteem: the way we feel about ourselves; self-respect.

The positive regard of others builds and supports our self-esteem and satisfies our needs for love and affection.

© Joel Gordon 1982

conditional positive regard: acceptance of the value of a person based on the acceptability of that person's behavior.

see that **conditional positive regard** is given only under certain circumstances. Children may come to believe that they will not be loved unless they act and feel the way their parents except them to. If Eddie's mother says, "You are a bad boy for hurting your sister," she is, in effect, telling Eddie, "I will not love you if you hurt your sister." Thus, Eddie's mother is stipulating the conditions under which he will be loved and accepted.

THE SELF-CONCEPT

Chuck couldn't believe what was happening to him. Fifteen years of married life and Martha was calling it quits. The shock was all the greater because there were no warning signs. There had been no warfare, either physical or psychological; no indications of deep dissatisfaction; no accusations of infidelity; no financial crisis; no obvious signs that they were drifting apart emotionally.

At dinner the previous evening, she detonated the bomb, quietly and almost without feeling. "I'm going to leave you, Chuck." She paused momentarily, as if gauging his reaction. Then she continued, "It has nothing to do with you. You're a good husband and a fine person." For a moment he sat stunned, looking at Martha with disbelief. Momentarily he expected her to break into a smile and hear a confession that she had made him the victim of a bad joke. But she neither smiled nor retracted her words.

"I don't understand." he mumbled. "What have I done? No. What do you *think* I have done?"

"I told you, it has nothing to do with you."

"Well, dammit, there must be something eating at your craw." He was furious. It took all of his powers of self-control to squelch the urge to vent his anger.

"Please listen to me, darling, and try to understand. My day-to-day existence has become meaningless to me. No, even more. It has become sheer drudgery. I used to wake in the morning with a sense of anticipation. I always felt that something good and uplifting would happen to me that day. Nothing much ever did. But the feeling that something *might* happen sustained me. I no longer feel that way. Every today is a clone of yesterday. I must simply get away from this stultifying atmosphere. I must give direction to my life, set some goals beyond what I'll prepare for dinner tonight and who we'll entertain next weekend. Do you understand what I'm saying?"

"Of course. You're bored. Well, let's do something to get rid of the boredom."

"You don't understand. It has nothing to do with boredom. I feel wasted. I'm an intelligent woman. You know it. God knows, you've said it often enough. Well, I want to challenge my intelligence for the first time in years. I want to feel that tingle in the mind that comes only from intellectual stimulation."

"You're saying one thing but I'm hearing something else. If only we had been able to have kids, things would have been different."

"I honestly can't say. All I know is that when I look at myself in the mirror, I see a pretty face with a few crow's feet forming. Not bad for a gal approaching 40. The trouble is I don't like what I see behind that face—a good mind lying fallow. I sometimes despise myself, and that's not good . . . for me, for you, for anybody."

"So you're just going to up and leave? Just like that. My feelings don't count in the least. You say you've given 15 good years to me. Well, what about me? Have I given nothing?"

You have given me much and I love you for it. But I'm tired of taking. I want to earn something for myself. Let me tell you my plans. I have been offered a job as a news writer for a television station 1,000 miles from here. The job is right up my alley. I've been trained for it and I'm good at it. Or at least I hope so. Fifteen years out to pasture may have tarnished my abilities a bit, but it's nothing that a little elbow grease won't remove. I'm convinced I'll do a good job. Do you understand, Chuck? I need to do a good job. I'm going to have to live with myself for the rest of my life. I want to hear happy talk inside me. I'm tired of listening to a dirge."

A superficial reading of this scenario reveals two lives in trouble, but a deeper probe discloses some of the tremendous complexity, variety, and plasticity of the human experience. It also reveals aspects of the self which give the humanists cause for optimism.

It is clear that Martha is unhappy. She has looked deeply into herself and is troubled by what she finds—a woman in her middle years who is going nowhere fast. But then there is the other side of the coin. By rejecting a path she found intolerable and asserting her determination to blaze a new trail, Martha is proclaiming that the self is an *active agent* rather than a clump of clay that is shaped by circumstances. One of the fundamental beliefs of the humanistic position is that all individuals have the capacity to take control over their own lives. This is not to say that they will do so. It is often easier, both physically and mentally, to go along with the tides rather than to buck them. But if we are to achieve a sense of fulfillment in our lives, the self must be at the helm and guide the individual in both calm and turbulent seas. Besides being active, the self spontaneously moves toward good mental health. As expressed by Maslow:

> The more we learn about man's natural tendencies, the easier it will be to tell him how to be good, how to be happy, how to be fruitful, how to respect himself, how to love, how to fulfill his highest potential. This amounts to automatic solution of many of the personality problems of the future. The thing to do seems to be to find out what you are *really* like inside, deep down, as a member of the human species and as a particular individual. (Maslow, 1962, p. 4)

Although Martha is unhappy in her present circumstances, she is plotting out a course which will enhance her sense of worth. But nobody ever said that the path toward self fulfillment is a well-marked superhighway. She will unquestionably meet boulders and other obstructions along the way but, if her goals are clearly stated and her resolve remains high, she will continue to improve in spite of occasional setbacks along the way.

Even the emotions Martha experiences may facilitate goal-directed behavior (unless they are unreasonable or improper). Rogers views emotions in a very positive way. He believes that full appreciation and experience of emotions enhances growth. Rejection, deception, or evasion of emotions may lead to confusion and chaos. Self-actualization comes about most easily when we are fully tuned in to the sum total of our experiences. If we accept and trust our faculties and feelings, we allow the process of self-catualization to evolve and expand.

Throughout the conversation between Martha and Chuck, one feature of their perceptions dominated their thoughts and actions. Both had internal **frames of reference** in terms of which they gauged the "real world." According to humanistic psychologists, these internal states are more important in determining our actions than is external reality itself. In other words, we behave according to what we *believe* are the facts rather than what the facts actually are. Nevertheless, we usually agree that the perceptions we have in common are the correct perceptions. However, reality is basically a very personal affair. Humanists use the term **phenomenal field** to refer to this personal reality. Our phenomenal field consists of the total realm of our conscious and unconscious experiences at any given moment in time.

One of the reasons for Chuck's stunned reaction to Martha's announcement is that he believed she was happy and content in her role as housewife. This community of private thoughts determine how he interacted with Martha throughout their married life. Presumably, there is the potential for misunderstanding in human relationships to the extent that our perceptions of the inner world of others differ from the actual content of their thoughts. "There is really far less danger in travel by plane than going the same number of miles by car," we tell the person who is terrified of planes. But this observation is usually to no avail for it is not objective reality to which we repond. Rather, it is the reality within our internal world that prompts us to feel fear in one situation, joy in another, and anger in a third. Indeed, one measure of maladjustment is the disparity between these two worlds. When we feel fear where there is no danger, joy when our fortunes are bad, and anger where there is no threat, it can be presumed that we are experiencing some adjustment difficulties.

These considerations take us to the crux of the humanistic position. It is only when we can see and accept ourselves realistically that we can experience reality without distortion. As expressed by Rogers (1951), "Psychological adjustment exists when the concept of the self is such that all the sensory and visceral experiences of the organism are, or may be, assimilated at a symbolic level into a consistent relationship with the concept of the self" (p. 15). In many life situations, we erect complex structures to shield ourselves from unfavorable self-appraisals. "I am really happy in my role as a housewife," Martha must have said to herself countless times to defend her self-illusion as fulfilled and successful. The trouble is that other experiences must be arranged, modified, and distorted to protect this illusion. Before long, Martha is unable to distinguish between what she really feels and what she thinks she should feel.

frame of reference: the unique standard of beliefs and attitudes by which one evaluates events and situations.

phenomenal field: the sum total of one's experiences, both conscious and unconscious, that defines personal reality.

By taking active responsibility for certain household chores, the child develops a sense of independence as well as pride in accomplishment.

Ken Yee

Society may be of little use in promoting a degree of self-understanding necessary to achieve our highest levels of actualization. One critic expressed the difficulty as follows:

> Obstacles to realizing this potential come from everywhere. The methods used to organize social institutions frequently squelch creativity and impose mediocrity. Society seems to place a premium on relationships featuring hypocrisy and superficiality—relationships that are tolerated rather than sources of happiness. (Schutz, 1967, p. 15)

Self-actualization occurs more easily when we are completely liberated and can accept our own experiences. If we use our faculties, feelings, emotions, and sensations and trust them fully, we are allowing the process of self-actualization to grow and develop.

The growth toward self-actualization can occur only when the options and alternatives are clearly perceived and understood. If the choices are not clear, we cannot distinguish between going forward or falling back. When choices are clear, Rogers maintains that we will choose to grow rather than regress. The individual will develop in positive directions so long as there are no obstacles and anxiety is not excessive.

ADJUSTMENT AND THE SELF

Marianne was visibly shaken. She had just returned from an interview with Jimmy's school counselor. Jimmy was encountering difficulties in school. Without coming right out and saying it, the counselor left her with the impression that the fault lay in the home environment. Her first impulse was to reject everything that the counselor had said. "What can he possibly know about my home and the care we give our children? He's never even been there." But some of the things he had said still grated on her nerves. "Jinny feels he is unloved. He feels nobody cares about him or takes any interest in what he is doing." Absurd! I love Jimmy more than anything else in the world. My whole life revolves around being a good mother to my children. After all, don't I spend half my life chauffering them from place to place? And who cares for them when they are sick? Who cleans up after them, and tolerates the bedlam that breaks loose whenever their friends come to visit? I hate doing all these things, but I do them anyway. Doesn't that prove that I'm really a good mother?

That evening, in an unusually frank conversation with Jimmy, she reminded him of all the sacrifices she makes for him. His answer was very disquieting, "Yes, but you always seem so angry. I feel you don't like me when I ask you to do something for me." For the first time, she began to waver. Perhaps there was some truth in what the counselor had said.

In this brief scenario, we see an individual faced with a conflict between values she has incorporated into her self-concept and her actual experiences. Marianne sees herself as a "good mother." And yet she had to admit there was a glimmer of truth in what the counselor and Jimmy had said. She really didn't like doing all those things that go along with motherhood. Perhaps Jimmy was more perceptive than she thought. It is possible that her anger was so thinly veiled that it was showing through?

Marianne faced a type of conflict that all or most of us have experienced from time to time. Deep down under the skin, we don't like the hours we spend on tedious homework assignments; we abhor our job; we resent the time we must spend in the company of people we find boring. We strive to maintain a consistent and favorable image of ourselves. Well-adjusted individuals will do this without resorting to exaggerated defenses and self-deception. Rather, they will realistically appraise their situation and take action to reduce the discrepancy. For example, imagine that Joan perceives herself as a flexible and undemanding person. But looking realistically at her present job, she is forced to admit that even she cannot bend to the demands it makes upon her. As a well-adjusted person, she realizes that she must either modify her self-concept ("maybe I'm not as flexible and undemanding as I thought") or change her behavior. She decides to seek employment that will not make demands on her that she finds unbearable.

In contrast to the well-adjusted person, maladjusted individuals will resort to defenses that distort their perception of reality when their experiences are markedly out of tune with their self-concept. They say they love school, enjoy their work, or take pleasure in the company of others. By denying reality, these distortions interfere with the growth toward self-actualization that characterizes well-adjusted individuals. The distortions limit the freedom of maladjusted individuals to pursue alternative courses of action. Unable to realistically and truthfully look at their own feelings, perceptions, and emotions, such individuals become mired in consistent but self-delusional pathways. They continue in major fields for which they are not suited, jobs that are unchallenging, and social gatherings that produce boredom. Moreover, they feel miserable without understanding the whys and the why nots of their behavior.

The best way to gain insight into an individual is to understand the individual's behavior as he or she perceives it. We are the only ones who can fully know and interpret our experiences. As an outside observer, we can never have a thorough understanding of another person's behavior since we interpret it from our own frame of reference. For example, if you are on a diet and you see a person push aside a dessert without touching it, you may say to yourself, "Aha, another person on a diet." In truth, the other individual may simply not like the dessert. To gain any insight into the behavior of others, we must depend on their reports of their experiences. However, communication is never perfect or completely satisfactory. In many cases, it may be misleading or false.

THE FULLY FUNCTIONING SELF

Rogers (1959) suggests that there are five characteristics that describe the *fully functioning person*. He uses this phrase to describe the individual who is functioning at an optimal level.

1. Openness to Experience. Fully functioning people are open, aware, and accepting of all their experiences and feelings. They can acknowledge both positive and negative feelings and decide whether or not it is proper to do something about them. During a cocktail party, for example, a man may feel resentful and jealous of his wife's attentions toward another man. However, he resists the impulse to do something about it at the moment because he realizes it would be tasteless. However, he does not feel threatened by his feelings or by the fact that he must delay acting on them.

2. Existential Living. After months of intensive effort, Mindy has just passed the state exam for her real estate license and is now out in the field. She feels happy, fulfilled, and is enjoying her life to the fullest extent possible. All experiences are unchartered and unexplored for her. There is no rigid structure telling her how to act or feel in any given situation. She is learning and growing in a variety of circumstances. When sudden or unforseen events occur, she views them as adventures—new chances to grow and learn.

3. Organismic Trust. Larry and Gayle are developing a warm and beautiful relationship. They find they enjoy each other's company so much that they decide to share an apartment. Neither feels ready to make a permanent commitment. As fully functioning people, they trust in their own judgment. They are aware of other's opinions and societal codes, but do not feel committed to them. This doesn't mean that they don't care about other's views, but they are doing what they think is best. They are ethical and moral, but their ethics come from within themselves.

4. Experiential Freedom. Have you even been involved in a discussion and found somebody said something you didn't quite understand? What did you do? Did you stop the discussion and ask, "Could you explain that?" Or did you let it continue in spite of the fact that you didn't understand anything from that point on? Fully functioning people assume complete accountability for their own actions and decisions. They realize they have freedom of choice and do not feel bound by others' wishes or desires. They feel free to acknowledge and act on their needs and desires. Thus, the fully functioning individual would stop the discussion and ask for clarification.

5. Creativity. Sy is active, competent, and constructive in his surroundings. He welcomes novelty and variety and adapts easily to changes and transitions. His versatility and adaptability make his movement toward self-actualization smooth and effortless.

As one observer noted of Rogers' views:

> Rogers emphasizes that his is not a "Pollyanna," or naively optimistic, point of view. Terms such as "happy," "blissful," or "contented" do not necessarily describe fully functioning people; rather, such people are challenged and find life meaningful. Their experiences are "exciting," "enrich-

ing," and "rewarding." Self-actualization requires the "courage to be" and the willingness to launch oneself into the process of life. (Engler, 1979, p. 330)

SUMMARY

- The humanistic approach emphasizes healthy, well-adjusted development. The overall orientation is that people are essentially good and, given the proper circumstances, will strive for self-actualization.

- In this chapter we looked at the self—its dimensions and development, the self-concept, adjustment and the self, and the fully functioning self.

- Three dimensions of the self are the physical self, the social self, and the valuing self. The social self is the self that is delineated by the recognition that others give. The valuing self values positively those experiences we perceive as maintaining and improving the quality of our lives.

- We start life with an unclear distinction between "me" and "not me." Differentiation involves a growing awareness that others exist apart from us. The distinction is aided by language, which provides labels that highlight differences between the self and others.

- The labels become a part of the self-image. Since the labels are applied by others who do not have direct access to the content of the mind, mislabeling of experiences can occur. We may say, "I am not afraid," because we have been told that we should not be afraid.

- How we regard ourselves depends largely on the kinds of regard given by others. In the ideal situation, unconditional positive regard is given. Such regard produces high self-esteem within the individual.

- Conditional positive regard may cause us to believe that we won't be loved unless we behave according to the expectation of us.

- Humanists regard the self as an active agent that spontaneously moves toward good mental health, and perceives the world and responds to it in terms of internal frames of reference. Only when we can see and accept ourselves realistically are we able to see reality without distortion. Self-actualization occurs most readily when we are liberated and can accept our own experiences without distorting them.

- Humanists believe that we strive to maintain a consistent and favorable image of ourselves. Individuals who are maladjusted protect their self-images by resorting

to exaggerated defenses and self-deception. In contrast, well-adjusted people modify their self-concepts to bring them into line with reality, or they make appropriate
changes in their behavior.

- The fully functioning self is open to experience, living existentially, trusting, experiencing freedom of choice, and creative.

**TERMS TO
REMEMBER**

Self-actualization	Self-esteem
Self (self-concept)	Conditional positive regard
Social self	Frame of reference
Egocentrism	Phenomenal field
Unconditional positive regard	

CHAPTER 4

MOTIVATION

**Not for Her
Eyes Only**

How she loved these Saturday trips to the shopping mall with all of her friends! Jenny's whole being tingled with excitement at the very thought. Although her funds were severely limited and she could do little more than "shop with her eyes," she took great pleasure in these escapades into the realm of unreality. There, in the fertile world of her fantasies, she could don the latest fashions from 5th Avenue, apply the most exotic cosmetics and Parisienne perfumes, and master the latest gadget that promised to make a difficult task as easy as one-two-three. "Whoever said one-two-three is easy?" she asked, laughing inwardly. "I still have trouble with one plus one."

How alive she felt! How utterly free and unharnessed! Little matter that she had drifted away from the rest of her friends. She would join them later in the cafeteria, a nondescript collection of laminated tables and chairs bearing a highfallutin name, The Refectory. It was all arranged in advance. "If we become separated, we'll meet at noon at the Infectory." Another delighted inner laugh as she repeated the same pun for the umpteenth time.

Then she espied the jewelry counter. She was drawn to it like a magnet. She was particularly fascinated by the precious and semiprecious stones. How she enjoyed their brilliant colors, their shimmering aliveness, their mysterious and unplumbed depths.

She picked up a bracelet and held it up to the light. Then turning it slowly, she thrilled at the cascades of colored rays that seemed to pour out of the core of its very being. How she would love someday to own something so beautiful. As she looked around, to see if anyone else was sharing in her delight, she realized the counter was unattended. No one was anywhere in sight. Then, on an impulse, she dropped the bracelet into her purse. It was an act she would live over and over again in her mind. An act she would remember with deepest regret; an act she wished a thousand times or more that she could undo.

Her first thought was to put it back, but she was afraid she might be seen. Instead, she headed to the nearest exit and safety. She realized that her mind and body were in a state of tumult bordering on panic. She felt her heart throbbing in her chest and experienced an unaccountable shortage of breath. "Don't rush," she told herself, "act normal. Nobody will know if you don't give yourself away." The door out of the store and into the mall was a few scant feet away. Fighting the impulse to run, she stepped calmly through the door and breathed a deep sigh of relief.

Suddenly she felt a vicelike grip on her shoulder. She felt her body turn to jello. A voice, at once firm and kind, spoke to her, "If you will just come quietly with me we can avoid a scene." She turned toward the voice, pleading in her eyes. But the woman was all business. She identified herself as a security guard and told Jenny that she must accompany her to the manager's office. It was clear from her tone and her demeanor that no compromise was possible. She must follow or risk public humiliation.

The rest was largely a blur. She could remember the security guard commenting to the manager, "I don't understand it. So many of them come from good homes. What can they possibly hope to gain from such behavior?" The manager was not assailed by doubts, "They're spoiled, that's all there is to it. They're spoiled and selfish. They get everything they ask for, so why not just take it without asking?" The arresting police officer chimed in, "They have no discipline, no sense of values. A few whacks on the behind would have taken care of this problem years before it could ever come to this point." Her father was unexpectedly sympathetic. "I don't understand what got into her. Somewhere along the line we must have failed her. She didn't have to steal. All she had to do was ask." Her mother blamed her transgression on unhealthy social influences. "It's that bunch she's been hanging around with. They put that idea in her head. Certainly, she didn't learn it at home."

For her part, Jenny was totally mystified. She had never done anything like this before. If anybody had asked three hours before, she would have said, "impossible." She admitted to herself that such thoughts had previously run through her mind but she had dismissed them as harmless daydreaming, no different from her childhood fantasies about being the tight end for the Packers.

---

motivation: a general term referring to the forces that determine the arousal and direction of goal-seeking behavior.

This story illustrates many points about ***motivation.*** Motives are the forces that determine the *arousal* and *direction* of purposeful behavior. Moreover, motives *sustain* behavior. For example, if a person is hungry and looking for food, food-seeking behavior will be aroused and directed toward locating potential sources of food. These activities will be sustained until the hunger is satisfied.

We assume most behavior is motivated, that is, directed toward specific goals. But we pursue some goals more intensely than others. Moreover, the same goal may be pursued for many different reasons, or different goals for the same reason. We use the concept of motivation to explain the causes of behavior—why we do something.

When someone behaves in an unexpected fashion, we search for flawed motivations. We ask such questions as, "What got into Jenny? Why did she do it? What did she hope to accomplish? What was her goal?" On the other hand, when someone behaves as expected, we raise no such questions. We assume all is well in that person's motivational structure. In other words, we take it for granted that motivations explain behavior. When our favorite fictional detective investigates a mysterious death and sagely mumbles, "The motive is everything. If you find the motive, you find the criminal," we nod our heads in solemn agreement.

Ah, but finding the motive. There's the rub. There are so many processes underlying behavior that we do not directly observe. For example, we do not directly observe learning. We infer it from the changes that take place in some

Do you think the motivations of these athletes are the same? The same behavior may be prompted by a variety of different motives.

United Press International Photo

George W. Gardner

aspect of our behavior after an individual is exposed to learning materials or life's everyday experiences. Neither can we observe each others' thoughts. We are often forced to rely on what others tell us they are thinking, knowing full well how easy it is to think one thing and say something entirely different, "No I don't mind your smoking in this close, crowded, airless, and stuffy room. Go right ahead (cough, cough)." And so it is with motivation. We never directly witness the hunger drive in others, or the motive to succeed or the need for affiliation. But if we see people gorging themselves with food, we judge them to be hungry. If Beth strives to be the best at everything she undertakes, we infer a strong motive to succeed. If John is unhappy whenever he is alone but becomes animated when in the company of others, we suspect that the need to affiliate is strong in him.

MOTIVATION AND AWARENESS

What makes the process of inferring motivational states so difficult is that we often erect psychological barriers to conceal our motives from others and even from ourselves. Jenny is a case in point. Each person who reviewed the crime inferred different motives for her behavior—Jenny included. Why the concealment? To begin with, we may never have correctly identifed and labeled

What system of motives permits this runner to continue a task that is so painful?

United Press International Photo

some of our motivational states during our childhood years. Recall that motives are not directly observed, like objects in the physical world. When we were learning to apply labels to our motivational states, we were completely dependent on others (our parents or caregivers) to supply the labels. But since they were unable to "see" our motives, they were really attaching labels to informed guesses. If they told us we were sleepy when we were really hungry, we would mislabel hunger as sleepiness. Presumably this incorrect labeling would be corrected in time, but what about some of the motivational states that are not as clearly distinguished, e.g., self-esteem, affiliation, or the need to succeed? Some may remain rather hazy notions throughout our lives.

Add to this the fact that many motives make us uncomfortable. To illustrate, if we have been taught that sex is dirty and unhealthy, we may feel shame or guilt when forbidden thoughts enter our minds. We may eject such thoughts from consciousness, thereby hiding the fact of our own sexuality from ourselves as well as from others.

What this all boils down to is that motives are often shrouded in uncertainty. There are times that we hide our motives from ourselves, but they are visible to others. At other times, we understand our own motivations, but we effectively conceal them from others. On yet other occasions, we conceal our motives from both ourselves and from others. Finally, there are times that our motivational states are not concealed from anyone, ourselves or others. The combination of known and not known to self and known and not known to others can be represented in a diagram (Figure 4.1) that has been called a Johari Window (Luft, 1970).

Notice that the Johari Window contains four quadrants. Quadrant I represents motivational states that are known to all—others as well as the self. Many of the biological drives (e.g., hunger and thirst) as well as socially approved motives (e.g., altruism) are represented in Quadrant I. Generally, there is little reason to hide these motivational states from ourselves or from others.

The remaining three quadrants are of greater interest from the adjustment point of view since they all involve some degree of concealment of motivations. In Quadrant II there is self-deception that is not successfully concealed from others. Marcus likes to think of himself as a strong and sensible person who bases his decisions on objective facts rather than on whim or sentiment. His friends and acquaintances, however, recognize him for what he is—soft, sentimental, and an easy mark for a sob story. As a result, many people take advantage of him. He is vaguely uncomfortable after many social transactions but is at a loss to explain his feelings.

The opposite is true in Quadrant III: we know our own motivations but we hide them from others. To illustrate, Margaret has strong sexual feelings toward her closest friend, Karen. She is well aware of these feelings since she frequently has fantasies involving sexual encounters with Karen. However, the thought of such a relationship fills her with guilt and shame. She must keep these secret motivations concealed at all costs. In fact, she sometimes seems to reject Karen's friendship altogether—she refuses to see her or talk to her on the phone. For her part, Karen is mystified by Margaret's sudden shifts in mood and friendliness.

FIGURE 4.1

THE JOHARI WINDOW: When something is known to ourselves as well as to others (Quadrant I), the window is open. If known to others but not to ourselves, it is open to them and blind to us (Quadrant II). Quadrant III represents things we know about ourselves but hide from others. In Quadrant IV, the window is shuttered to all.

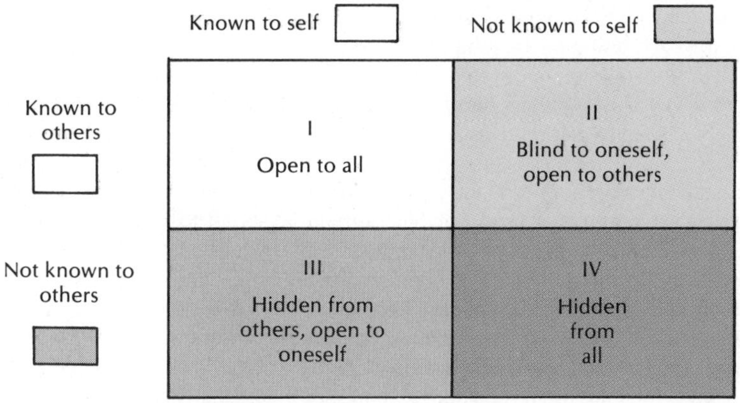

Known to self ☐   Not known to self ▥

	Known to self	Not known to self
Known to others	I Open to all	II Blind to oneself, open to others
Not known to others	III Hidden from others, open to oneself	IV Hidden from all

Source: Adapted from *Group Processes: An Introduction to Group Dynamics,* by Joseph Luft, with permission of Mayfield Publishing Company, 1970.

But she values Margaret's friendship and is willing to overlook her occasionally strange behavior and social slights.

In Quadrant IV the window to our motivations is opaque to ourselves as well as to others. Jenny as well as her friends think of her as honest to a fault. "I can't understand it," they murmured in unbelieving tones after learning of her arrest, "She wouldn't hurt a fly. To deliberately steal a bracelet . . ." Jenny was equally stunned. "I don't know what got into me," she would repeat over and over again. "I am not a dishonest person. I have never stolen anything in my life."

In a sense, Quadrants II and IV, both of which involve self-concealment and self-deception, constitute the most serious types of adjustment difficulties. When we do not understand our own motivations, we lose control over them (see Box 4.1). We are unable to deal constructively with the problems that these rogue motivational states engender in our daily lives. In many ways, it is comparable to alcoholics who steadfastly refuse to acknowledge their condition. Those involved in the treatment appear to be agreed on this one point—you cannot help an alcoholic who does not want to be helped.

MOTIVATION AND BEHAVIOR

Mr. F, the power behind the throne, so to speak, gets what he wants at the highest levels of government and business. How? He studies the people he has to deal with and tries to figure out what motivates them.

BOX 4.1:   LEARNING TO RECOGNIZE YOUR OWN MOTIVATIONAL STATES

It is axiomatic that you must know yourself to develop your capabilities and potentials to their maximum. However, the possibility of self-knowledge is both limited and impaired by the degree to which you successfully conceal your own motives from yourself. However, some of the Johari Windows are not completely opaque to a motivated and observant learner. Here are a few things you can do to gain better insight into both your motives and your behaviors.

1. Pay attention to your own inner conversations and fantasies. Have you ever thought of the amount of time you spend talking to yourself? Whenever you are awake, alone, and not involved in some competing activity, you are certain to be engaging in an inner conversation or fantasy. Take note of these private transactions. They are intimately involved in planning your daily lives, they are often recreational, and they may provide slits in the "opaque" window through which you can see yourself better.

Do you find that some themes repeat themselves over and over again? For example, do your fantasies

involve scenarios that gain you social approval? Perhaps affiliation is one of your dominant motivations. Or are they suffused with anger, hostility, sexual themes? Do you often play the conquering hero role? Have you ever fantasied harm befalling you and watched with satisfaction as loved ones wept over your lifeless body? What motive or complex of motives underlies such fantasies? By asking such questions while observing your own inner life, you may gain valuable insights into yourself.

2. Pay attention to the ways in which others respond to you. Recall that some of your motivations may be opaque to you but open to others. Friends will often respond to you in ways that reveal their own insights into aspects of your personality, including motivations. Note what they *fail* to say as well as what they say. Why did Carol—an intimate and trusted friend—not offer much sympathy when you told her how badly you had done in a course? Perhaps she never believed that you were highly motivated to do well. Perhaps she was right.

He knows that there are some people whose needs are so powerful that they can be motivated to do almost anything. For example, he needs a favor from Mr. J. He knows of Mr. J's insatiable thirst for power. By helping Mr. J attain his goal, Mr. F gets his favor granted.

As this simple example shows, in dealing with other people, one of the keys is to figure out what motivates them. However, as we saw in the previous section, it isn't so easy to guess another person's motives. Why? Remember that motives cannot be directly observed; they must be inferred from behavior and from the circumstances surrounding that behavior. But we can't always guess motivation from behavior. The same behavior may be prompted by a variety of different motives. For example, the next time you go to a restaurant, look at the people around you. Do you think they are all in the restaurant for the same reasons? Surely some are there because they are hungry. But others are there for a variety of social and business motives.

Not only is there variability in motives around the same behavior, but all people are not motivated by the same needs. Consider the following example.

E and S have 460 employees in several nursing homes. Since it is essentially a service business, it is critical that the employees do a good job and that they are happy in their work. E and S are well aware that a happy and satisfied employee does a better job than a dissatisfied and discontented one. Over the years, they have learned what motivates their employees, in general, and some key ones, in particular. They have found that some of their people will expend considerable effort for monetary rewards. Others will work long and hard for a chance at advancement. And still others will give their all for simple words of praise and recognition. They have used this knowledge to get the best out of each person.

Unquestionably, motivation plays an important part in everyday living. What we do and how we do it is largely determined by our wants, our needs, and our motivations (see Box 4.2). Whom we choose to be our friends, our style of life, and the goals we pursue are all reflections of our underlying needs and desires. We often find that several different motives are operating at the same time. Motivation helps to explain the direction our behavior takes. Generally, the strongest motive will determine our behavior in a specific situation. Moreover, the amount of effort we are willing to expend usually reveals the strength of the underlying motivation. You have probably observed instances in which a highly motivated individual will go through a great deal of trouble to attain a desired goal. Thus, the goals we select and the obstacles we are willing to overcome provide clues to our underlying motivational states.

As we saw, we are not always aware of the motives operating within ourselves. To further complicate matters, our motives change over time. What seemed critical at one point in our lives may be viewed as relatively unimportant later. For example, a desire for money and independence may prompt a student to drop out of school and take a job. Later, this same student may reevaluate his or her goals and decide to return to school.

The needs and wants of children are constantly changing as they grow. Figuring out what motivates a child is critical in shaping that child's behavior. However, as most parents have discovered, this is not an easy task. Children are notoriously fickle in their desires. At one point, a child might say, "I'd do anything for a Rubik's Cube," only to have his or her head turned by a bigger and better toy. As children approach adolescence and young adulthood, they will spend a great deal of time thinking and trying to decide among different goals. Some will choose rather easily, while others will labor long and hard trying to find the "right" direction.

As we grow older, we develop more voluntary control over our motivations and their expression. We force ourselves to stay awake at the wheel, fighting the urge to satisfy the strong pull of our sleep drive. We wait until intermission to go to the rest room, delaying satisfaction of an impelling need to eliminate. Our directions become more specific and our goals become more stable as we mature. We select career and family goals and actively pursue them. As one group of authors suggest, there are

three phases of motivation over the life span: growth, realization, and constriction. In the growth phase, we acquire direction to our arousal and

---

BOX 4.2:   CAN REWARDS UNDERMINE MOTIVATION? INTRINSIC VERSUS EXTRINSIC MOTIVATIONS

Most of us have heard the common complaint of people whose achievements fall short of what was expected of them. "My heart just wasn't in it," they say, and we nod our heads in understanding. Experiences of this sort remind us that motivations can be distinguished in terms of their source: In some cases the activity is inherently interesting and we can think of the motivation as arising from within the individual. We call such internally motivated behavior *intrinsic motivation*. Some common examples of intrinsically motivated behavior include participation in amateur athletic events, playing solitaire, or solving crossword puzzles "just for the fun of it." Intrinsically motivated behavior will continue even when there is no one else to observe the behavior and to distribute rewards when certain levels of performance are achieved.

By and large, the bulk of our motivations stems from external sources—a desire to obtain rewards (positive reinforcements) or to avoid or escape undesirable consequences (negative reinforcements). Indeed, the principles of operant conditioning are based on the effects of positive and negative reinforcements on behavior. Motivations based on external reinforcements have been termed *extrinsic motivation*. Many students attend college as a means of ultimately gaining a livelihood, to receive the approval of parents and friends, or to avoid negative evaluations from others for "not going on with their education." Others will labor many hours at an unpleasant job in return for the monetary rewards that come on payday.

Our experience with extrinsically motivated behaviors teaches us that reinforcements following specific responses increase the strength of the tendency to repeat these behaviors under similar circumstances. Thus, when first-grader Kathleen receives a gold star for reading aloud in class, it is presumed that the reward will improve her later performance. Similarly, multimillion-dollar contracts or large monetary prizes awarded to professional athletes are assumed to be worth the investment in terms of subsequent performance levels. "People will try harder for bigger rewards," is the general assumption. Is this necessarily the case?

Recent studies suggest that it is not. Indeed, it appears that intrinsically motivated behavior may be undermined by the addition of rewards and incentives. Suppose the following. Little Tony, a toddler, is utterly entranced by drawing with felt-tipped pens. He will spend long periods of time hunched over paper making various designs on it. His nursery school teacher sees this activity as desirable and wants to give Tony all the encouragement possible. The teacher tells Tony that he will receive a Good Player Award whenever he paints with the pens. During a free play period, the pens are again made available. Will Tony's motivation to play with the pens be increased by the addition of positive reinforcement? When these procedures were incorporated in actual studies involving nursery school children, it was found that they spent less time painting with the pens during free play periods after the introduction of rewards (Lepper, Greene, & Nisbett 1973; Lepper & Greene, 1978). Turning play into work apparently makes the activity less attractive. In another study, it was found that the quality of the performance was lowered by the imposition of rewards following intrinsically motivated behavior (Kelly & Michela, 1980). The moral here is clear. Perhaps we should reserve our rewards for use in situations where the motivations are extrinsic and permit intrinsically motivated behavior to follow its own course.

---

define specific goals for achievement, such as financial security, a good professional or personal reputation, having children, or enjoying social success. Such desires may be realized or gratified in middle age. Then, during the construction phase in late middle age, retirement and changes in health may bring the goal of a strategic retreat from life. (Birren, Kinney, Schaie, & Woodruff, 1981, pp. 582–3)

THE BIOLOGICAL DRIVES

biological drives. motives that arise from the physiological state of the organism, e.g., hunger.

The two functions of motivational states—to energize behavior and direct it toward goals or away from undesirable stimulation—are seen most clearly in relation to the **biological drives,** such as hunger, thirst, sleep, elimination, pain, temperature regulation, and sex. These drives function by providing strong and distinctive inner stimulation, usually uncomfortable or downright painful, that goads the individual into responding. Thus, an accumulation of urine in the bladder gradually builds up sufficient internal tension that the individual voids the bladder to gain relief. Similarly, we eat food to quiet the pangs of hunger, and withdraw our hand from a flame to avoid and/or escape the pain of a burn. As long as the basic biological drives are routinely satisfied, they play reduced roles in our everyday adjustment routines. However, if they go unsatisfied (as might well happen with the hunger drive in impoverished environments) or thwarted (as is the sex drive by social regulations), they can become dominant forces in our daily lives. Moreover, although biological drives are unlearned, the ways in which these drives are satisfied in humans are strongly influenced by learned factors.

In this section we shall direct our attention to three biological drives—hunger, sleep, and sex. We'll focus on facets of these motivations that can cause adjustment problems.

Hunger

excitatory nucleus: a group of neurons that activate the behavior for which it is responsible. For example, activation of the excitatory nucleus for eating leads to increased eating.

inhibitory nucleus: a group of neurons that suppress or curb the behavior for which it is responsible. For example, activation of the inhibitory nucleus for eating leads to decreased eating.

lipostat: a mechanism in the hypothalamus that sets the amount of fat that the organism needs.

The messages to start and stop eating are regulated by a tiny structure in the brain called the hypothalamus. The hypothalamus is sensitive to levels of sugar and fats (lipids) in the blood. When the level drops too low, the **excitatory nucleus** is activated and the organism eats. When the blood sugar level is within the normal range, the **inhibitory nucleus** of the hypothalamus is activated and eating is discontinued (Balagura, 1973). Although much more complex, it is possible that these two centers are analagous to a thermostat. When the levels of lipids drop below a certain point, a **lipostat** turns on and signals the individual to eat. When lipids approach the upper limit, the lipostat shuts off eating behavior (Sclafani & Kluge, 1974). It is also possible that the palatability of the food affects the settings on the lipostat (Sclafani, 1976). When the food is tasty and desirable, the upper setting of the lipostat is increased and we eat more. In contrast, when the food is unappetizing, the lower set point is decreased. Thus, we will undergo a greater weight loss before the lipostat is activated.

In our culture, where stout is out and thin is in, control over weight can take on considerable social significance (see Box 4.3). People who are obese are frequently regarded almost as social outcasts. As a result, dieting books are commonly found in the top 10 list of nonfiction bestsellers. Millions of dollars are spent on dieting fads, weight-reducing schemes, and diet pills. Many promise almost magical results with a minimum of effort. Most fail because they do not take into account the psychological factors and lack of exercise involved in overweight conditions. What are some of these factors?

BOX 4.3: ON LOSING WEIGHT

There is much confusion about the relationship between weight and health. For years, insurance companies have been telling us that excess weight is hazardous to your health. They have even penalized overweight individuals by increasing their premiums. The basis for this practice was a study conducted during the 1950s. This trend-setting study was seriously flawed since the sample consisted of overweight individuals who were already seriously ill (Runyon, 1981). No overweight individuals in normal health were included. The result was a distorted view of the impact of weight on physical health. This study, which seemed to prove that overweight people face severely curtailed life expectancies, spawned a national concern for weight control that put many Americans on fad diets. Many of these are more dangerous to health than overweight conditions. Indeed, a recent study came up with a startling finding—underweight individuals are in the highest risk category with respect to mortality (Sorlie, Gordon, & Kenwell, 1980). Although overweight individuals suffer a number of disorders (e.g., diabetes, gout, elevated blood pressure, and higher serum cholesterol levels), their mortality rates are quite comparable to those of persons of normal weight for their height. Why then would anyone want to lose weight?

There are several reasons, both physical and psychological. Overweight people are less mobile and less able to enjoy athletics and various other outdoor activities. They often suffer from a loss of self-esteem since they may regard themselves as unattractive. Moreover, many regard themselves as deficient in some way since they appear to be unable to control their appetites.

If you decide you want to lose weight, you should be aware that success does not depend on food intake alone. Diet determines caloric intake; physical activity regulates caloric outflow. In some cases, dramatic changes in weight can occur by instituting relatively minor adjustments in your level of physical activity. To illustrate, a useful rule of thumb is that it takes about 3,500 calories in excess of body needs to add a pound to your weight. If a person's weight is stable, the individual can remove a pound about every 12 days by burning up, through increased exercise, 200 additional calories a day. This translates into about 30 pounds a year.

The success of weight reduction procedures involves the same principles enumerated in Box 1.1 (Controlling Your Own Behavior).

1. State your objectives clearly and realistically. If your goal is to lose a certain number of pounds, do not try to reach the desired weight in too short a period of time. Your goal is not so much to lose weight as it is to change your eating and exercise habits in a way that will be comfortable to you and permit you to lose weight gradually. Half a pound a week of weight loss may not seem like much to you. However, in the course of the year, it will result in a reduction of 26 pounds. Above all, avoid crash and fad dieting. These are more often a test of your ability to take sustained punishment than they are realistic steps toward permanent weight control.

2. Make a plan. Probably the best plan from a physical and psychological health point of view would include the combination of lowered caloric intake with greater exercise. To repeat: don't try to punish yourself. No plan that keeps you chronically daydreaming about the contents of the refrigerator has any real chance of success.

3. Increase the total eating time per meal. This procedure permits sufficient time (approximately 20 minutes are required) for the brain to send the "full" message to the stomach (Musante, 1976). You may accomplish this delay by: waiting a minute before beginning to eat, slowing down the rate of chewing, and putting the eating utensils down between each bite.

4. Restrict your eating to specific times and places. Do not eat while watching TV, studying, or talking on the phone. Set a cutoff time at night after which you are not allowed to eat. Setting a precise eating schedule will help you to avoid snacks. If you feel the urge to snack at a "prohibited" time, force yourself to wait at least 15 to 20 minutes to see whether you are still hungry. Use low-calorie snacks such as carrots, celery, or bouillon to subdue your appetite.

5. Keep a daily record of your progress. Record your weight and whether or not you have achieved your stated goal. Monitor your daily caloric intake and exercise. It is easy to lose sight of the impact

of an occasional snack between meals. When you keep score, you can make adjustments. To illustrate, sometimes five minutes additional time on the trampoline jogger will compensate for another helping of a favorite food.

6. Implement your plan and administer self-reinforcements lavishly when you have demonstrated progress. However, try to avoid reinforcements that conflict with your objectives. Rewarding yourself for losing a pound by consuming a "Banana Split Supreme" with gushy chocolate syrup and whipped cream topping can have a devastating impact on both your weight loss and your resolve.

Is this person overweight because of a glandular or hormonal irregularity, or is he simply not motivated to maintain an athletic appearance?

George W. Gardner

To begin with, the eating behavior of obese individuals appears to be more influenced by external factors (time of day, palatability of the food) than by inner bodily cues, such as hunger pangs. If the food is dull and uninteresting, for example, obese individuals will eat less than usual. However, when the food is particularly attractive, obese individuals will consume large amounts whether or not they are experiencing physiological hunger. In contrast, people in the normal and underweight ranges will consume an amount more appropriate to their physiological state (Schachter, 1971). What is more, overweight individuals appear to be less willing to work for their food. Many will not eat nuts unless they are preshelled and they rarely use chopsticks when eating in a Chinese restaurant (Schacter & Rodin, 1974).

The problem of overweight individuals is not necessarily one of overeating. In one study, the caloric intake and daily exercise were recorded for overweight versus normal-weight girls. The results were surprising. The overweight girls actually consumed several hundred calories *less* than the girls of normal weight. However, the normal-weight girls put in about three times as much exercise each day (Thomas & Mayer, 1973). To summarize:

> The moral of all this research on obesity is clear. If you are overweight and wish to reduce, do not look for quick and magical solutions. Engage in plenty of exercise and try to pay more attention to what your body is telling you about its needs. Also consider the possibility of making high-calorie food less accessible, limiting the number of locations in which you eat, and cutting down on seconds by keeping the serving platters off the table. (Haber & Runyon, 1983)

Keep in mind, however, that the goal of any weight-reducing program is to improve the state of health and physical well-being of the individual.

Sleep

It may seem strange for sleep to be classified as a motivational state. Isn't the major feature of drive states the fact that they serve as goads to greater activity? When we are hungry, we look for food; when thirsty, we search for a source to quench our thirst but, when we are tired, we look for a place in which we can diminish our activity—a sleeping place. However, like thirst and hunger, the need to sleep increases as the period of sleep deprivation increases. Try going without food, water, or sleep for 24 hours and you'll see how much they are alike. With all, you'll experience progressive irritability and a compelling urge to end the deprivation.

Moreover, sleep is not "a little bit like death without all of its permanence." Rather it is a period of fitful activity. We have learned much about sleep over the past few decades, during which electronic breakthroughs have permitted the monitoring of the electrical activity using a device called an **electroencephalograph,** or EEG, for short. Using this device, several different stages of sleep have been described.

Initially, your sleep is very light—a sort of twilight zone between waking and full sleep. This is stage 1 which lasts for only a few minutes. Then, in

electroencephalograph (EEG): an instrument used to record the electrical activity of the brain.

A person participating in a sleep experiment.

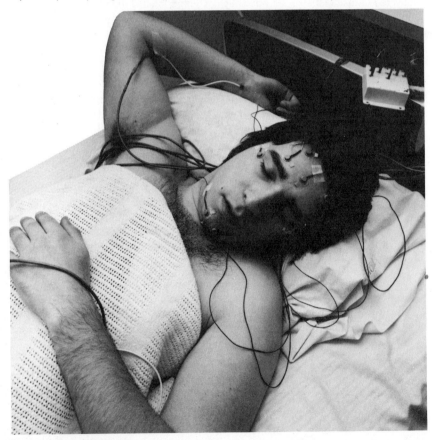

Arthur Tress

rapid order, you progressively enter deeper stages of sleep, until about a half hour later, you are in the deepest stage of sleep—stage 4. It is during stage 4 sleep that the body restores itself. The heart rate is low and regular, blood pressure decreases, and breathing is slow and deep. In children, the pituitary releases growth hormone during stage 4. It is difficult to awaken someone during this deepest stage of sleep.

About an hour later, roughly 90 minutes into sleep, a dramatic change occurs in the sleep pattern. You reenter stage 1 sleep, but with a wrinkle. Your eyes begin to move rapidly back and forth under closed lids. Furthermore, your heart rate, blood pressure, and breathing become quite variable. The physiological signs are akin to arousal. You are now in stage 1—**rapid eye movement (REM).** If you were awakened at this moment, the chances are that you would report a dream in progress—about 80 percent of the time as compared to 19 percent during non–REM awakenings (Berger, 1969). You enter state 1—REM about four or five times a night. Whether or not you remember, you probably dream between three to five times each and every night of your life. Figure 4.2 diagrams the typical sleep cycle for an adult.

rapid eye movement (REM): rapid movements of the eye that occur during sleep. When subjects are awakened during stage 1—REM, they generally report that they have been dreaming.

FIGURE 4.2

A TYPICAL NIGHT OF SLEEP FOR AN ADULT: Note that the first REM period occurs about 90 minutes into sleep. It is relatively short in duration. Each succeeding REM period is longer in duration. In this record, the individual woke up during the last REM period.

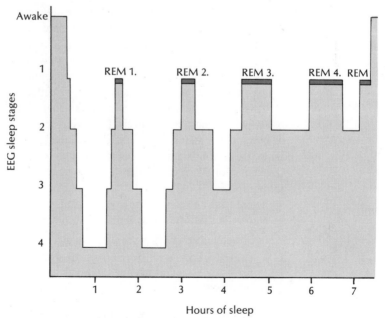

Source: R. D. Cartwright, *A Primer on Sleep and Dreaming* (Reading, Mass.: Addison-Wesley Publishing, 1978), p. 13.

There are two types of dreamlike experiences that can be upsetting to the individual—night terrors and nightmares. Night terrors occur during stage 4 sleep and often involve a single event, e.g., being attacked by a monster. They are fairly rare, experienced by approximately 3 percent of children between 5 and 12 years of age (Cartwright, 1978). The individual having a night terror might sit bolt upright in bed, shriek in apparent terror, and then return quietly to sleep within minutes. Since the individual does not usually recall the night terror, the experience may be more terrifying for an observer than for an individual undergoing the experience.

Nightmares, on the other hand, occur during REM sleep. The content may contain episodes similar to those experienced in night terrors, but the anxiety is usually better controlled in nightmares. Moreover, nightmares are usually remembered the following day. It is possible that both dreams and nightmares are safe ways of experimenting with different ways of coping with anxieties aroused by the anticipation of coming events (Cartwright, 1978).

Another disturbance of sleep involves insomnia—a difficulty in achieving and/or maintaining sleep. Many individuals misclassify themselves as insomniacs when their sleeping patterns are well within the normal range of variation. The reason for the difficulty is that sleep, in itself, is not uniform from individual to individual. It may vary in length and in depth. There are short, long, and variable sleepers. Long sleepers spend an average of about 10 hours a night in sleep, whereas short sleepers get by with an average of about 6 hours (Hartmann, Baekeland, & Zwilling, 1972). Expressed another way, by the time they are 60, long sleepers have spent about 25 years in the sack, while short sleepers have had an extra 10 years of waking time. If short sleepers are in the habit of turning in early, they may emerge from a night's sleep during the bewitching hours of the morning convinced they have insomnia. In reality, they have had a full night's sleep, as far as their needs are concerned, but their motors have been turned on at the wrong time as far as the workaday world is concerned.

In addition, there are also some individuals who are very light sleepers and others who remain asleep even if a Mac truck is driven through the bedroom. The slumber of light sleepers is easily disturbed by external stimuli. Consequently, where extraneous sound sources are common, they may awaken frequently during the course of the night. Thus, like the short sleeper, they consider themselves insomniacs.

Before treating a person for insomnia, it is important that an accurate diagnosis be made. This requires both a waking record and a sleeping EEG:

> To fill in the waking psychological picture, there needs to be a good clinical workup: a history of the disorder, a detailed inquiry into the sleep habits, a set of psychological tests, and a good evaluative mental-status interview. This is needed to discover whether the sleep problem is acute and a sign of some oncoming illness or psychiatric breakdown, a response to a severe current stress situation, a chronic problem due to long-standing physical illness which interrupts sleep, a set of poor sleep habits, a hyperactivity syndrome, or chronic depression.

A sleeping EEG will determine what kind and amount of sleep is being lost. How long is the sleep-onset period? Does the patient get enough (deep) sleep for his or her age? Is the REM onset latency too long or too short? Is there a reduced total REM time? Are there multiple awakenings throughout the night? Is it hard for the patient to regain sleep once awakened? (Cartwright, 1979, p. 100)[1]

Individuals who are clinically diagnosed as insomniac differ in a number of ways from light and short sleepers. A large proportion obtained high scores on psychological tests indicating depression (Kales & Kales, 1973). Moreover, they tend to direct stress inwardly. They do not blow off steam or express anger. Rather, they carry their problems to bed with them. The price is disturbed sleep (Kales, Caldwell, Preston, Healey, & Kales, 1976).

Numerous critics of the current American scene have observed that, in many ways, we are a society of pill poppers. If we are anxious, we take a pill; if depressed, we pop a different color. Our medicine cabinets often overflow with a stunning assortment of sizes, shapes, stripes, and hues. Almost always included in this over-the-toilet pharmacy is one or more substances promising to induce sleep. How effective are sleeping pills? Do they maintain their effectiveness indefinitely?

If we compare insomniacs not taking sleep medication with normal subjects, we find that they take a longer period of time going to sleep, lie awake for longer periods of time during the night, but have about the same amount of REM time (Kales & Kales, 1973). When the comparison is made between insomniacs who chronically take sleep medication and normal subjects, some striking differences arise. In spite of the drugs, insomniacs continue having difficulty going to sleep and maintaining sleep once it is achieved. But more important, they evidence a sharp decrease in both REM time and stage 4, or deep sleep. If REM sleep is involved in working out adjustment problems, as some scientists believe, the pill takers are possibly denying themselves a natural remedy. Moreover, we previously noted that many restorative activities take place during stage 4 sleep. In an effort to obtain some relief, most individuals resort to ever-increasing doses. But they rapidly build up a tolerance to each promotion in the dosage level taken. The result is a huge intake of medication with no improvement in sleep (Cartwright, 1978).

Since this is the case, why do insomniacs continue to ingest their favorite sleeping medication? Here is a classic case of the "cure" being worse than the disease. If they suddenly cold turkey the medication, they will experience even greater difficulty in achieving sleep. Additionally, they will experience REM-rebound, i.e., their deprivation of REM while under medication will be followed by a sudden increase in REM sleep. The dreams they have during REM are often disturbing. Thus, it is easier to choose the path of popping pills than to give them up altogether. One procedure that has a good chance of success is a gradual substitution of a less potent agent which is, in turn, slowly phased out (Cartwright, 1978).

---

[1] R. Dymond Cartwright. *A Primer on Sleep and Dreaming.* © 1978. Addison-Wesley, Reading, MA. pp. 100. Reprinted with permission.

Sexual Motivation and Arousal

The sex drive is like other biological drives in many ways. It builds up during periods of deprivation; its arousal leads to increased activity and restlessness; the individual engages in behavior that will provide a release of the sexual tension; when the sexual act is completed, the drive appears to be satiated and the restless activity will either decrease or end for a time.

In lower organisms, male sex hormones known as *androgens* are largely responsible for motivating (initiating the desire for sexual activity) and arousing (activating sexual responses to effective sexual stimuli) sexual behavior. Hormones also play an important role in human sexual behavior but, as we shall see, so also do psychosocial factors. As two authors of a book on human sexuality have noted:

> Sexual pleasure in humans is dramatically influenced by a number of factors: experiences and emotions; the level of intimacy between two people; the particular surroundings where people meet together; and a range of other influences. As evidenced by the incredible number of available sex manuals, though, many people turn to the printed word seeking foolproof methods for "how to do it." In the movie *Summer of '42*, there was a scene where young teenage boys copied steps from a sex manual to ensure success of a beach-party seduction. The episode was humorous, and yet poignant. Many of us have had similar experiences where we have learned the hard way that there simply are no guarantees—no matter how carefully one follows the steps. The processes of arousal are too complex to be captured by a formula. (Crooks & Baur, 1980, p. 189)

Perhaps the effects of hormones on behavior can most readily be understood when we examine individuals in whom certain hormones are either deficient or absent during stages of development in which they are usually present. Take the male sex hormones, the androgens, as an example. If one of several diseases of the hormonal system strikes a prepubescent male, the production of androgens may be impaired. The emergence of secondary sex characteristics (e.g., growth of facial and body hair, deepening voice) may be retarded or altogether absent. Such individuals may never become interested in sexual activities. However, if the deficiency develops after sexual maturation has occurred, the results are far less predictable. In most cases, there will be some reduction in both motivation and sexual arousal. However, the sexual behavior of some individuals seem little affected by the deficiency.

Castration (the removal of the testicles, usually for medical reasons) also produces variable results. In one Norwegian study, the majority of the subjects evidenced a marked decline in both sexual interest and activity within a period of one year (Bremer, 1959). A word of caution is in order. The operation often strikes at the male's sense of manliness. Perhaps psychological factors—embarrassment, fear of performance, or the assumption that sexual activity is no longer possible—may contribute as much to the decline as the loss of androgens. In any case, there have been instances in which individuals have continued to engage actively in sexual intercourse for decades after the loss of their testicles (Hamilton, 1943; Ford & Beach, 1951).

Surprisingly, the female hormone, *estrogen,* appears to play little role in the motivation and arousal of the female sexual response. Women who have had their ovaries removed or have gone through menopause—when estrogen production is sharply reduced—often continue an active sexual life. Indeed, in some instances, sexual activity may increase because the fear of becoming pregnant has been removed. The hormones underlying sexual motivation and arousal in females are, as in the males, the androgens (male hormones). When undergoing androgen therapy for medical reasons, increases in sexual interest and activity have been observed (Dorgman & Shipley, 1956).

As we have seen, hormones play a significant role in human sexual motivation and arousal. But the story does not stop here. Why do many individuals engage in sexual behavior even after the output of androgens has been sharply reduced? How can we account for the wide variations in the expression of the sex drive? Why do we continue our sexual activities over long spans of time? The obvious answers to these questions are that the experience "feels good" and "variety is the spice of life." However, the incentives involved in sexual behavior go beyond the reinforcing properties of orgasm itself. Following is a list of a few factors that might explain our continuing interest in sexual matters:

1. The pleasure of erotic stimulation accompanying sexual arousal.
2. The gratification ensuing from the sexual orgasm.
3. The satisfaction and pleasure that results from close physical proximity to another person. (What some might call contact comfort or affiliation.)
4. The sense of worth or self-esteem that comes from being loved or wanted.
5. Reduction of feelings of inadequacy or anxiety (sometimes this can act as a negative motivation for "sex as reassurance").

STIMULUS NEEDS

stimulus needs: the tendency to seek certain kinds of stimulation. No underlying physiological bases have been discovered for this tendency.

sensory deprivation: an extreme reduction in stimulation.

sensory overload: an extreme excess of stimulation.

We seem to have an inborn tendency to seek certain kinds of stimulation. We call this class of motivations **stimulus needs.** Although they function like biological drives, no underlying physiological bases have been found for them. They do not appear to be learned. Rather, we seem to have an innate need to be active and stimulated and to require change and variety in stimulation and experiences.

The extreme absence of stimulation is called **sensory deprivation.** Many sensory deprivation experiments have been conducted. Findings from these studies suggest that we need some kind of sensory stimulation to function normally. In the absence of meaningful and organized stimulation from the environment, we manufacture our own in the form of fantasies and hallucinations. The scientists who planned the space missions were aware of this need and made sure that the astronauts had sufficient auditory and visual stimulation.

In contrast, an extreme excess of stimulation, or **sensory overload,** is experienced as offensive. Have you ever felt overwhelmed by all the demands on you? Perhaps you delayed studying for all your finals until the last minute. Or you were pressured to deal with too many problems at once. We dislike and tend to avoid very high arousal states such as those accompanying panic, extemely strong levels of stimulation, or very high drive states. If we are in too high a state of arousal, we will take action to reduce some sources of stimulation. For example, if the stereo is blaring so loud that we can't hear ourselves think, we will either lower it or leave the room. If we have signed up for too many courses at one time, we may drop one or limit our other activities.

BOX 4.4: SENSATION-SEEKING SCALE, ARE YOU A HIGH OR A LOW?

Test your own sensation-seeking tendencies. For each of the 13 items, circle the choice, A or B, that best describes your likes or dislikes or the way you feel. Instructions for scoring appear at the end of the test.

1. a. I would like a job that requires a lot of traveling.
   b. I would prefer a job in one location.

2. a. I am invigorated by a brisk, cold day.
   b. I can't wait to get indoors on a cold day.

3. a. I get bored seeing the same old faces.
   b. I like the comfortable familiarity of everyday friends.

4. a. I would prefer living in an ideal society in which everyone is safe, secure, and happy.
   b. I would have preferred living in the unsettled days of our history.

5. a. I sometimes like to do things that are a little frightening.
   b. A sensible person avoids activities that are dangerous.

6. a. I would not like to be hypnotized.
   b. I would like to have the experience of being hypnotized.

7. a. The most important goal of life is to live it to the fullest and experience as much as possible.
   b. The most important goal of life is to find peace and happiness.

8. a. I would like to try parachute-jumping.
   b. I would never want to try jumping out of a plane, with or without a parachute.

9. a. I enter cold water gradually, giving myself time to get used to it.
   b. I like to dive or jump right into the ocean or a cold pool.

10. a. When I go on a vacation, I prefer the comfort of a good room and bed.
    b. When I go on a vacation, I prefer the change of camping out.

11. a. I prefer people who are emotionally expressive, even if they are a bit unstable.
    b. I prefer people who are calm and even tempered.

12. a. A good painting should shock or jolt the senses.
    b. A good painting should give one a feeling of peace and security.

13. a. People who ride motorcycles must have some kind of unconscious need to hurt themselves.
    b. I would like to drive or ride a motorcycle.

Scoring

Count one point for each of the following items that you have circled: 1A, 2A, 3A, 4B, 5A, 6B, 7A, 8A, 9B, 10B, 11A, 12A, 13B. Add up your total and compare it with the norms below.

1– 3 Very low on sensation seeking

4– 5 Low

6– 9 Average

10–11 High

12–13 Very high

Although the test gives some indication of a person's rating, it is not a highly reliable measure. One reason is, of course, that the test has been abbreviated. Another is that the norms are based largely on the scores of college students who have taken the test. As people get older, their scores on sensation-seeking tend to go down.

Source: Marvin Zucherman ''Search for High Sensation,'' *Psychology Today* February 1978.

Careful planning and budgeting of our time may help to reduce the anxiety associated with sensory overload. By strategically attacking one problem at a time, we may be able to reduce the pressure and feel less harassed. We all need to find our own techniques for maintaining the level of stimulation with which we are comfortable. Box 4.4 presents a test, the Sensation-Seeking Scale, which will help you determine whether you are a high-activation person—one who seeks excitement and change, or a low-activation person—one who avoids increased arousal levels.

People differ in the amount of stimulus overload they can tolerate and enjoy. High-activation people—those with a high demand for stimulation—will seek experiences which are rich in stimulation. In contrast, low activation people will try to reduce the amount of stimulation and will avoid activities with high stimulating properties. In a series of studies (Reykowski, 1982), it was found that there was a larger proportion of high-activation individuals in professions that carry the greatest amount of stimulation, such as jet pilots and defense attorneys. On the other hand, professions that typically have little stimulation (e.g., librarians) had a greater proportion of low-activation people. The same pattern was observed among people involved in dangerous sports (e.g., mountain climbing or parachute jumping) as compared to those not involved in sport activities (Strelau, 1980).

Apparently, there is an optimal level of stimulation which varies across individuals and in different situations. We not only require a certain amount of stimulation for normal functioning, but we actively search for new and different forms of stimulation.

Have you ever wanted to get someone's attention? Think about it for a moment. Were there several occasions during the past week when you wanted someone to stop and notice something you said or did? Perhaps you wanted your child or younger sibling to quit misbehaving, or your class to listen to a paper you wrote, or someone to respond to an advertisement you placed. How do we get people to attend to things we say or do in a diversity of situations? One of the best ways to attract attention is to create change in the stimulus situation (see Box 4.5).

Given a choice, we seem to show a preference for change, novelty, and complexity in our environment. Our attention is drawn to novel stimuli and away from unchanging ones. Infants will spend most of their waking hours exploring and manipulating their environment. They are attracted toward any object which makes noise, is colorful, and provides distinctive tactile stimulation. Adults will expend a great deal of time and effort to set up elaborate stereo systems that provide them with novel and different stimulation.

One aspect of stimulus variability is the *complexity* of the stimulus. Generally, we are attracted to more complex stimuli. However, there are limits on the amount of stimulus complexity with which we are comfortable. A young child will attend to a simple nursery rhyme but "turn off" if we attempt to read a great epic poem. Adults will spend many hours manipulating puzzles or playing cards and other games. We all seem to seek stimuli that are complex enough to challenge us but not so complex as to shatter our self-esteem.

BOX 4.5:   ATTRACTING ATTENTION THROUGH CHANGE

Change is important because the stimuli we create must compete with other things in the background and because change helps to overcome the problem of **sensory adaptation.** The latter concern represents a tendency to adapt to stimuli that do not change very much. Consequently, we do not notice them as much. You are experiencing sensory adaptation when a piece of chocolate tastes less sweet as you continue to eat it, a warm or cold room appears less so after a period of time, or a teacher's monotonous delivery begins to sound like a sequence of dull sounds. The following principles are suggestions for producing change that helps to attract attention. As you read them, think of one way that you could use each one in your daily affairs.

sensory adaptation: the tendency to adjust to a stimulus and stop responding after a time.

1. *Create movement or change the position or color of a stimulus that you want other people to view.* Examples: A colleague was concerned with students paying attention to his lecturing and his writing on the blackboard. Instead of standing behind his lectern, he started to pace. He also began to use colored chalk on the blackboard. A friend wanted visitors to his office building to find his office quickly. He had his office door painted green. It became the only green office door in the building.
2. *Change the size of a stimulus. Large things tend to attract attention better.* Examples: A restaurant owner had a small typed note in his window advertising for a waitress and replaced it with a sign that was three feet high. A neighbor had a small screen television. Her children showed little interest in watching some of the educational pro-

grams until she bought a set with a 25-inch screen.
3. *Vary the intensity of a stimulus. Higher-intensity stimuli are more potent than others within the same sensory modality.* Examples: Visitors to my home had a hard time finding the street number after dark. I replaced an ordinary house number sign with one that had a light in it. A student was concerned that people seldom noticed her at dances. She wore a bright, multicolored dress the next time she went. It became a great conversation piece and was an excellent "ice-breaker."
4. *Repeat the stimulation—within limits. Too much repetition may have just the opposite effect.* Examples: I once asked a hotel manager to give me a larger room. He acted as if he had not heard me. I repeated my request four times until he acknowledged it. A friend was concerned that his bosses were not aware of who wrote the memos he sent up the chain of command. He had his name typed in the upper left-hand corner of every page.
5. *Change stimuli that do not meet someone's needs and interests to those that do.* Examples: My nephew was not interested in reading until his mother bought him books on fishing and baseball, which were topics of interest to him. People were not purchasing one of the four brands of sausage a supermarket manager stocked. He cooked a batch and passed them out as free samples to customers while they shopped during the lunch hour. His sales increased.

Source: From Anthony F. Grasha, *Practical Applications of Psychology.* Copyright © 1978 by Little, Brown and Company (Inc.). Reprinted by permission.

The need for varied stimulation plays a practical role for the organism. Changes in stimulation provide important information about the environment which is often useful for adjustment and, at times, for survival. By exploring the environment, organisms find sources of food and learn which areas are dangerous and should be avoided.

If the businessperson does not explore new techniques for manufacturing and marketing, how can he or she hope to increase production? If medical doctors are willing to experiment with new and different treatments in hopeless situations, they will be better prepared the next time they are confronted with a similar situation. Our need for stimulus variability exposes us to experiences that increase our knowledge of the world around us and make us better equipped to adapt to rapidly changing events. Some of our greatest achievements have resulted from our endless desire to explore and know our environment.

SOCIAL MOTIVES

Day in melting purple dying,
Blossoms all around me sighing,
Fragrance from the lilies straying,
Zephyrs with my ringlets playing,
Ye but waken my distress:
I am sick of loneliness
         Maria Gowan Brooks

This poem, written more than a century ago, reminds us how much we are all social beings. This is not to say that we must always and forever be in the company of others. Indeed, while viewing "Grizzly Adams" or absorbed in reading *Robinson Crusoe*, many of us have undoubtedly been tempted by the lure of living in splendid isolation—away from the need to study for an exam or to work on a schedule dictated by the clock and away from the responsibilities of being a son, daughter, father, mother, lover, or leader of the cookie sale for the benefit of the school band. A few moments reflection should dispel the notion that we can lead a fruitful, productive, fulfilling, and satisfying life in the absence of other human beings.

There have been numerous attempts to catalog social motives. Some lists are extremely long, and very few agree with one another in all respects. We shall be discussing three of the more widely accepted of these motives.

Affiliation

affiliation: the need to be with others and to form attachments to them.

The need to be with others—**affiliation**—is one of the most compelling of human motivations. This is as it should be. At birth, we were completely helpless and our survival hinged on the availability of others to meet our basic needs. Thus, dependence on others is woven in the fabric of our existence. Indeed, we were created by a social act—sexual intercourse—and we survive on the basis of social acts committed throughout our lives.

We gain much from affiliating with others. Most of our learning, formal and otherwise, takes place in a social context. People take interest in each other. Parents, guardians, or care givers may spend hours repeating words and phrases so that the child begins to acquire the rudiments of language. They also dispense rewards in both the physical (e.g., food) and the psychological (e.g., praise) realms of our existence. Moreover, they provide a gauge in terms of which we can judge our impact on the external world. Are you well liked by your peers? How do you know? We judge whether or not others like us by their reactions to us. If they find all manner of different reasons for not sharing our company, we may hazard a guess that we're not among their favorite people. If they come to us for help with an assignment, we judge that they respect at least some aspect of our abilities.

They also provide companionship in times of distress. In one study, female undergraduate students volunteered to participate in a study in which shock was to be administered. Some were warned that the shock would be severe and painful; others were told that the shock would be very mild. While waiting to participate, they were given the choice of waiting alone or in the company of another subject. The high-shock subjects preferred to have company, particularly if the companion was to receive severe shocks. Subjects in the mild-shock condition were largely indifferent, expressing no preference or preferring to wait alone (Schachter, 1959).

In another study, subjects anticipated participating in an embarrassing (sucking on a metal breast shield) or nonembarrassing (sucking on a lollipop) situation. They were more likely to choose waiting alone under the embarrassing condition (Teichman, 1973). If there is no choice about whether or not to have a companion, subjects in the embarrassing condition prefer to wait with someone who does not know about their upcoming humiliation. Anticipation of physical pain and anticipation of humiliation appear to have opposite effects. The expected reaction of the other person (understanding or ridicule) makes a difference.

Achievement

achievement motive:
the desire to do well and succeed.

underachievers:
people with low levels of achievement motivation whose performance does not live up to their ability.

Some people work hard and strive for success while others just sort of slide through life. The desire to do well and attain success characterizes the **achievement motive.** People with low achievement motives who do not perform up to their level of ability are called **underachievers.** Do you know any people like that?

In school, students with high achievement motives try harder, study more, and are usually more successful than those with a low achievement drive. At work, those with a high drive to achieve hustle more and seek more prestigious and responsible positions. Workers with low achievement motivation are usually content just to do their work and keep their jobs. How strong is your motive to achieve?

Look at the picture in Figure 4.3. Before reading further, write a brief story about it. Tell what is happening, what led to the situation shown, what the man is thinking, and what will happen.

Now read the following story written by a business executive in one of the early studies of achievement motivation (McClelland, 1962).

> The engineer is at work on Saturday when it is quiet and he has taken time to do a little daydreaming. He is the father of the two children in

FIGURE 4.3 MOTIVATION ASSESSMENT: Look at this picture and write a story about it. Tell what is happening, what led to the situation shown, what the man is thinking, and what will happen. You may get some idea of the strength of your achievement motivation by comparing your story to those presented in the text.

Courtesy *Harvard Business Review*

the picture—the husband of the woman shown. He has a happy home and is dreaming about some pleasant outing they have had. He is also looking forward to a repeat of the incident which is now giving him pleasure to think about. He plans on the following day, Sunday, to use the afternoon to take his family for a short trip. (McClelland, 1962, p. 101)[2]

Do you see any evidence of the achievement motive in the content of this story? Before you answer, read the following story written by another subject.

The man is an engineer at a drafting board. The picture is of his family. He has a problem, and is concentrating on it. It is merely an everyday occurrence—a problem which requires thought. How can he get that bridge to take the stress of possible high winds? He wants to arrive at a good solution of the problem by himself. He will discuss the problem with a few other engineers and make a decision which will be a correct one—he has the earmarks of competence. (McClelland, 1962, p. 101)[3]

[2] Reprinted by permission of *The Harvard Business Review*. Excerpt from "Business Drive and National Achievement" by David C. McClelland (July–August 1962). Copyright © 1962 by The President and Fellows of Harvard College; all rights reserved.
[3] Ibid.

The first subject was concerned only with the family picture on the man's desk. No statement was made of goals or ways of achieving them. In contrast, the second subject emphasized what the man in the picture was trying to do. He has a specific problem to solve and a successful solution is anticipated. If the content of subjects' stories reveals anything about underlying motivations, we would have to conclude that the first subject has a lower achievement motive than the second.

Studies have shown that achievement motivation in children is influenced by parental expectations. Our society puts great emphasis on achievement. Parents generally want and expect their children to achieve success. What did your parents expect of you? Do you feel you have lived up to their expectations? Most children accept their parents' expectations and make them their own. In one study, parents who expected independence at an early age tended to have sons with strong achievement motives (Winterbottom, 1953). Other studies have shown that parents with high achievement motivation have children who also have a strong desire to achieve (Singer & Singer, 1969).

Do you know people who hate to take chances because they are afraid of failing? If we consider the achievement motive as a need to do things that we can be proud of, *fear of failure* represents the need to avoid situations which lead to shame and embarrassment. When an individual feels the need to avoid failure, he or she may withdraw from the situation to escape feelings of anxiety or fear (Atkinson, 1964).

Imagine the following. There are two groups of people with strong achievement drives. However, one group has a high fear of failing, whereas those in the other group are confident and expect to succeed. Suppose we give each person a choice of three tasks. One is so easy that the chances of failing are small. The middle task has an equal probability of success or failure. The third task is so tough that everyone will fail. What level of task difficulty do you think the individuals in the two groups will select?

When such a study was actually conducted, the failure-oriented individuals were attracted to the easiest task where the probability of failure was low. It is interesting that many of those who feared failure also selected the most difficult task where they were almost sure to fail. Failure in an impossible situation doesn't reflect on an individual's ability. Most of those who feared failure shied away from the middle task. They would not expose themselves to possible failure in a situation where others would succeed. In contrast, those with a low fear of failure selected the middle task. There was no challenge in completing a task that *anyone* could do (the easy task). But there is a feeling of accomplishment when we succeed in a situation where other people may fail (Atkinson & Litwin, 1960). As the chances for success go down, one's pride in succeeding goes up. We all feel prouder when we do well on a difficult task than on an easy one. Indeed, there is evidence to show that male college students who expect to succeed select more difficult majors than those who fear failure (Isaacson, 1964).

People with a strong achievement drive tend to attribute success to factors within themselves—competence and effort. They find success extremely satisfying

Parents who have a strong motive to achieve often have children with high achievement motives.

The Museum of Modern Art/ Film Stills Archive

because it reflects on their ability. On the other hand, those with a high fear of failure tend to attribute success to factors outside themselves—good luck or an easy task. When those who expect failure *do* fail, they attribute it to a lack of ability and they try less in the future. In contrast, failure leads to increased effort in those who expect to succeed (Weiner, Frieze, Kukla, Reed, Rest, & Rosenbaum, 1971).

Why are women so grossly underrepresented in fields such as business, politics, and medicine? Much research has been done to answer this question. As a rule, society has not encouraged achievement in women. Very few women are executives, professionals, or hold high-ranking political office. When women do enter traditionally "masculine" fields, they tend to hold lower ranks and receive smaller paychecks (*U.S. News & World Report,* 1979). Women have to overcome many social and psychological barriers that men do not have to face.

Most studies on achievement motivation have focused on men. However, one classic study involving females produced some interesting results. In this study (Horner, 1972), intelligent and successful female undergraduates were asked to elaborate on the statement, "After first-term finals, Anne finds herself at the top of her medical school class." Sixty-five percent of the women gave responses that revealed an anxious *fear of success.* The following are some of their responses:

> Anne is an acne-faced bookworm. . . . She studies 12 hours a day and lives at home to save money.
> Anne doesn't want to be number one in her class. . . . She feels she shouldn't rank so high because of social reasons. She drops to ninth and then marries the boy who graduates number one.
> Although Anne is happy with her success, she fears what will happen to her social life.

When men were tested in this situation, the name Anne was replaced by John. Only 9 percent of the men told stories that contained a theme of avoiding success. What is even more striking is the fact that women rarely made negative comments when the name John was substituted.

Do women fear success in all fields or just in those traditionally defined as masculine? Much of the evidence suggests that women do not always fear success, particularly in conventionally female jobs. For example, when women reacted to a woman's success in nursing school, they didn't fear success—they wanted it (Feather, 1975). Thus, fear of success may be related to whether or not the job is considered "appropriate" for one's sex. One study confirmed this view (Janda, O'Grady, & Capps, 1978). College men feared success in the nursing field while college women showed fear at succeeding in the engineering profession—a field usually monopolized by men. One observer concludes,

> The catch for women is that "masculine" jobs and careers also tend to be the ones with the highest prestige and pay. Thus while men may be just as likely to fear success in "feminine" jobs as women are to fear success in "masculine" settings, women face the problem more often. Many college women want to break into "masculine" careers—like law, medicine, and

business. Not too many college men are dying to be nurses or secretaries. So, as a practical matter of fact, women are more likely to experience fear of success than men. (Middlebrook, 1980, p. 105)[4]

Self-Actualization

Mark just can't get out of bed this morning. For the past few days sleep has eluded him and it's a real struggle to keep his eyes open. His mind is a jumble of thoughts and desires. Tired or not he's hungry. He hasn't had a "solid" meal in days. He's out of money. If he doesn't show up at work he risks losing his job. He promised to do a favor for his closest friend. There's a term paper that must be completed. He has a job interview which represents the best opportunity for growth and development that he has ever been offered.

Can you identify the motives shown in this little scenario? There are physiological needs (Mark is tired and hungry), safety needs (threats to his economic well-being), social and recognition needs, and a need to realize his full potential. Some of these needs, like hunger, are clearly biological in nature. Others are highly influenced by our experiences and social interactions. How are all these motives related? Is it possible to organize them into some meaningful framework?

Abraham Maslow has proposed a way to organize the many and diverse motives operating in our lives (Maslow, 1962). He suggested that our needs can be arranged in a hierarchy based on their relative importance to our survival (see Figure 4.4). Maslow believed that we must satisfy our most basic needs before we can move on to the higher levels. According to this view, what needs do you think Mark will attend to first?

At the top of Maslow's hierarchy is the need to *self-actualize*—the need to realize one's full potential, to "be the best one can." Maslow had an exceptionally optimistic view of life. He believed that all our experiences can contribute to our personal growth and add meaning and richness to our lives. Even such mundane needs as hunger and safety can be satisfied in ways that improve the self. We can learn to appreciate the subtle differences in the taste and feel of foods so as to enhance our appreciation of the eating experience. Our homes should provide more than just shelter. They should be expressions of ourselves—unique, warm, and creative. Our lovemaking should be sensual, tender, and satisfying. We should express ourselves in creative and constructive ways to improve the quality of our existence. We should go beyond the ordinary and reach a little higher to achieve our own self-established goals and standards.

To characterize the self-actualizing person, Maslow studied self-actualizers. How did he identify them? Do you know a self-actualized person? Would others agree with you? Getting a group of people to agree on who's fully actualized is difficult. As a start, Maslow relied on general reputation. He studied the biogra-

---

[4] From *Social Psychology and Modern Life*, second edition, by Patricia Niles Middlebrook. Copyright © 1980, 1973 by Alfred A. Knopf, Inc. Reprinted by permission of the publisher.

FIGURE 4.4   MASLOW'S HIERARCHY OF MOTIVES: At the base of the hierarchy are the *physiological motives* that promote survival of the individual and of the species. These needs must be satisfied before the higher needs are activated.

The *safety needs* at the second level include the desire for shelter, security, and freedom from fear.

When the *belongingness* and *love needs* at the third level are not satisfied, we feel lonely. In today's society, these needs often go unfulfilled.

Needs concerned with *self-esteem* emerge when lower needs are satisfied. We need respect, both from ourselves and others, status, prestige, or other types of regard from other people.

When all the lower needs are satisfied, we reach the top of Malow's hierarchy—the need for *self-actualization.*

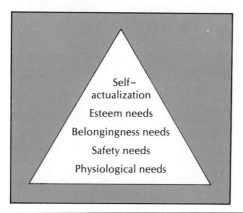

phies and autobiographies of such people as Albert Einstein, Helen Keller, and Albert Schweitzer. He also interviewed people who were judged by their friends and acquaintances to be "exceptionally healthy." He looked for individuals whose basic needs were satisfied and who had fulfilled their potential.

What are some of the qualities of the self-actualizing person? From his studies, Maslow compiled a list of their characteristics, as shown in Table 4.1.

Maslow found that many of the self-actualizing people he studied were devoted to some cause or life's work through which they found meaning and satisfaction. He identified self-actualizing people as ones who are better able to experience life vividly, fully, and without feeling self-conscious. They have the courage to be honest—to be themselves. They accept themselves and others and the realities of life. They take joy in the mere experience of being. They are spontaneous, creative, and have a keen sense of humor. They laugh at absurdities, not at other people's failings. They make the most of their abilities and seek higher goals for their fulfillment.

Maslow believed that the drive to self-actualize is universal. We all strive to develop our fullest potential. The popularity of such self-improvement techniques

TABLE 4.1   CHARACTERISTICS OF SELF-ACTUALIZERS

Astute and accurate perceptions of reality.

Can accept themselves as well as others.

Spontaneous in both thought and action, although
    not extremely unconventional.

Problem-centered rather than self-centered.

Look for periods of privacy and solitude.

Relatively independent of their immediate environment.

Capable of deep appreciation of life's experiences.

Capable of deep concern about social issues.

Able to achieve satisfying personal relationships.

Democratic in attitude, with a good sense of humor.

Able to clearly distinguish means from ends but enjoy
    the means toward their ends.

Source: A. Haber and R. P. Runyon, *Fundamentals of Psychology,* 3d
ed. (Reading, Mass.: Addison-Wesley Publishing, 1983).

as transcendental meditation (TM), Ehrhard Seminars Training (EST), biofeed-back, psychotherapy, zen, and yoga testifies to the strength of this drive.

Although Maslow's theory has captured the imagination of many, there are those who caution, "need hierarchy as a theory continues to receive little empirical support . . . the available research should certainly generate a reluctance to accept unconditionally the implications of Maslow's hierarchy" (Korman et al., 1977, pp. 178–9).

SUMMARY

In this chapter we discussed motivation—the forces that determine the arousal and direction of goal-seeking behavior.

- We cannot observe motivation. We must infer it from behavior and the circumstances surrounding that behavior.

- They may be concealed from others but known to ourselves. Or, they may be concealed from both ourselves and others. Finally, they may be open to anyone, ourselves and others.

- It is difficult to guess other people's motives. We can't always guess motivation from behavior. The same behavior may be prompted by a variety of different motives. Moreover, all people are not motivated by the same needs.

- Motivation directs our behavior. The amount of effort we are willing to expend is determined by the strength of the underlying motivation.

- Our motives and goals change over time.

- Biological drives are basic to our survival. As long as these drives are satisfied, they play relatively minor roles in our everyday lives.

- Centers for the arousal and inhibition of the hunger drive are found in the hypothalamus.

- The eating behavior of obese individuals appears to be more influenced by external factors than by internal bodily cues.

- Several techniques for weight control were discussed.

- The electroencephalograph (EEG), used to monitor electrical activity of the brain, has led to a description of different stages of sleep.

- Night terrors, occurring during stage 4 sleep, and nightmares, occurring during REM sleep, are two types of upsetting dreamlike experiences.

- Individuals clinically diagnosed as insomniacs differ in a number of ways from light and short sleepers.

- The sex drive is like other biological drives in that it builds up with deprivation; its arousal leads to activity and restlessness; orgasm results in the relief of sexual tension; following orgasm, the drive appears to be satiated.

- The male sex hormones, androgens, are involved in motivating and arousing sexual behavior in both males and females. Although the role of hormones is important, psychological factors also play an important part in human sexual behavior. The incentives involved in sexual behavior go beyond the reinforcing properties of orgasm itself.

- We appear to have an inborn need to seek certain kinds of stimulation. We call this class of motivations stimulus needs.

- Research findings suggest that there is an optimal level of stimulation required for normal functioning. We cannot tolerate an extreme absence of stimulation (sensory deprivation) or an extreme excess (sensory overload).

- We show a preference for change, novelty, and complexity in our environment.

- Affiliation, the need to be with others, is one of the most compelling of human motivations. We were created by a social act and continued survival depends on social acts throughout our lives. Affiliation brings many benefits: we learn from others, receive rewards from them, and we use their response toward us as a gauge of our own impact on others.

- The desire to do well and achieve success characterizes the achievement motive. Fear of failure and fear of success have important implications for our achievement-oriented behavior.

- Abraham Maslow suggested that human needs can be arranged in a hierarchy with self-actualization being the highest human motive.

TERMS TO REMEMBER

Motivation	Stimulus needs
Biological drives	Sensory deprivation
Excitatory nucleus	Sensory overload
Inhibitory nucleus	Sensory adaptation (Box 4.5)
Lipostat	Affiliation
Electroencephalograph (EEG)	Achievement motive
Rapid eye movement (REM)	Underachievers

CHAPTER 5

EMOTIONS

It looked as if it were going to be one of those days. Here is was only eight o'clock in the morning and Jimmy and Patti were already locked in mortal combat. What was it this time? A jurisdictional dispute about who gains control over the tube? Was Patti dipping into Jimmy's toys or vice versa? Whatever! Clearly Ellen's two children had already resumed their weekend warfare, and she would have to intervene. What crazy poet wrote of the joys of maternal bliss? A swinging single, no doubt.

A familiar scene greeted her as she rushed into the family room. The two combatants stood glowering at one another, poised to deliver the finishing stroke. If she weren't so emotionally involved, Ellen might have viewed the scene as laughable. Jimmy, seven years old, towered over his four-year-old sister. In spite of his clear physical superiority, she stood up to him and clung to her ground—perky, defiant, and ready to burst into tears.

"All right children, what's the problem?" Ellen demanded. Her question was answered by a veritable flood of accusations.

"Jimmy took my Raggedy Ann."

"Yech, I wouldn't touch that dirty old thing. Patti started it. She wouldn't give me back my Porsche."

"Well I was playing with it first. He only wanted it 'cause I was playing with it."

"Liar, liar, caught your face in a wire."

"I did not." Patti burst into tears.

"Jimmy, was she playing with your Porsche?" Ellen demanded crossly. Jimmy did not answer, but Patti cried out, "Yes he did, he did," between huge sobs and tears.

"Well it's mine. You and daddy gave it to me for my birthday. It's mine."

"I asked you if Patti was playing with it first."

"It's mine. It's mine."

"Give it back to Patti this instant!" Ellen felt a surge of anger course through her body. "Do you hear me? Give it back to her."

"Take the dirty old thing." He flung it at his sister. "I never liked it anyway." He rushed from the room, tears of rage streaming down his face.

"I hate my sister," he screamed out. "I hate Patti. I hate her, hate her."

Ellen ran after Jimmy, her anger suddenly stilled. She wanted to, needed to comfort him. She finally captured him, tried to envelope him in her body. He resisted. "Go way," he shouted, "Go way. I hate fatty Patti. You always give her my toys."

Ellen felt his resistance suddenly crumble. She hugged him tightly and he snuggled closer. "You don't really hate your sister, Jimmy. You love your sister."

"No, I hate her."

"Jimmy, don't say that. Tell me you love her. Brothers and sisters love one another. They don't say 'hate.' You really love Patti. You love her."

In this little slice of life, we are introduced to almost the entire spectrum of our emotional lives—anger, tenderness, love, hate, and rage. We are reminded of the extent to which the affective side of life is a constant companion to our every thought and action. Jimmy has a right to "hate" his sister temporarily. The feeling is OK even though the aggressive behavior is not.

Our emotions add spice to life, flavoring every experience with a full range of seasonings from the subtle flavors that can barely be perceived to those that overwhelm the senses. They stir up the body, causing different "happenings" in the internal organs and structures of the body—including the heart, the adrenal glands, the stomach, the intestines, the liver, the pancreas, and the genitals. Their expression in everyday life also serves to communicate with other people, imparting information about our changing moods and feelings about shared experiences.

Finally, emotion and motivation are two companion forces. On the one hand, emotions accompany motivated behavior. We feel good when our motives are satisfied, and sad or unhappy when our motives are frustrated. On the other

In the movie *Rocky III,* Sylvester Stallone displays nearly the whole spectrum of human emotions.

hand, emotions can serve to motivate and direct our behavior toward certain goals and away from others. Or they can provide the impetus to behave in a certain way to *avoid* an unpleasant emotion. For example, an individual may be motivated to spend much time and effort cleaning up to avoid the disagreeable feelings experienced whenever his roommate gets upset.

At times, it seems our emotions are like a conductor of a symphony orchestra, carefully coordinating the various parts of our body, directing when and how strongly to respond. At other times, our emotions are like the villain in a melodrama, an uncaring force dedicated to filling our lives with misery.

COMPONENTS OF EMOTION

Sam is overjoyed when he receives a birthday card. Joel appears indifferent as his father hands him the keys to a brand new 280Z. Marie cries as she watches a sad movie on TV. No tears from Flora at her closest friend's funeral. Jennie flares up at the slightest provocation and seems upset all day. Al always has a smile on his face no matter what happens. Bert is petrified at the sound of thunder. David wouldn't think twice about fighting off a would-be mugger.

We see these differences all the time in the people we know. But how do we explain them? What happens to Sam when he feels joy, to Jennie when she feels anger, or to Bert when he feels fear? These questions are easy to raise but not quite so easy to answer. Although we have learned much about emotions, in many ways they remain a puzzle. Like so many processes that psychologists study, emotions cannot be directly observed, but can be inferred from a variety of sources. We don't actually *see* joy, anger, or fear as such, but our judgment that somebody is experiencing one of these emotions is based on a number of different lines of evidence. For example, we may notice that when thunder sounds, Bert becomes agitated, his voice quivers, beads of perspiration form on his forehead, and he searches frantically for cover. Based on these observations, we suspect that Bert is experiencing fear. Our own experiences also play a vital role in judging emotions in others. If thunder makes us fearful, we are more likely to attribute the signs we observe in Bert as fear.

Emotions are complex states involving physiological reactions, situational factors, **cognitions,** feelings, and behavior. Let us look more closely at each of these components.

emotion: a complex state involving physiological reactions, situational factors, cognitions, feelings, and behavior.

cognitions: an individual's thoughts, ideas, and knowledge.

Physiological Reactions

The physiological response depends on the type of emotion and its intensity. Strong negative emotions, like anger and fear, lead to sweeping changes that involve virtually every system of the body. Even the mild emotional states go hand in hand with a variety of bodily changes. Think of the last time you were angry, joyful, afraid, or anxious. Can you recall the bodily states that accompanied these emotions?

Do you think you could differentiate the various emotions based solely on the bodily changes you are undergoing? For example, suppose your heart is beating a mile a minute, your palms are sweating, and your breathing is irregular. What emotion are you experiencing? Fear? Anger? Anxiety? Love?

There have been many attempts to differentiate the various emotional states based on unique physiological reactions. For the most part, these studies have not been successful. Generally, a strong emotional reaction is accompanied by a generalized state of excitement within the individual. But it has not been possible to obtain a one-to-one relationship between specific emotions and distinctive physiological changes. An exception to this is fear and anger. One investigator (Ax, 1953) demonstrated that fear and anger have different physiological patterns. Fear is accompanied by secretion of **epinephrine,** a hormone produced by the adrenal glands. Anger is more likely to produce the **neurotransmitter norepinephrine.**

In another study, the urine of hockey players was analyzed both before and right after a game. The norepinephrine levels of the players who actively participated in the game showed a striking increase. In contrast, those players who were benched because of injury and presumably were fearful showed marked increases in their epinephrine levels (Elmadjian, 1959).

There are a number of theories of emotion that have concentrated on the relationship between emotional feelings and physiological or bodily changes. One theory, called the James-Lange theory, proposed that emotions *follow* changes in bodily states. According to this theory, we see a bear, start running, and *then* we become conscious of fear. If we cry over bad news, we feel sad *because* we are crying. In other words, changes in bodily states precede the emotion that is experienced.

To support this view, James pointed out that there are many instances in which we do not experience an emotion until *after* we have reacted. For example, while driving your car have you ever had to instantaneously apply your brakes to avoid an oncoming vehicle? The chances are that you reacted immediately, without thought or fear. Only after you stopped did you notice that your heart was pounding, you were breathing rapidly, and your muscles were tense. You then recognized your fear. According to the James-Lange theory, changes in the *autonomic nervous system* are communicated to the **central nervous system** which, in turn, interprets these changes as specific emotions.

An American physiologist, Walter Cannon, showed that dogs continue to manifest emotional behavior even after the connections between the autonomic and central nervous systems are severed (Cannon, 1929). Indeed, people with spinal cord injuries are still able to experience emotion, even though they cannot feel the normal bodily sensations of arousal (Hohmann, 1966). Based on these types of findings, Cannon proposed that the emotional experience and bodily arousal occur simultaneously. According to the Cannon-Bard theory, when emotion-arousing stimulation is received, a signal is transmitted to the lower brain which activates a state of physiological arousal and, at the same time, signals the higher brain centers so that the emotional state can be interpreted.

epinephrine: a hormone produced by the adrenal glands that activates the body during times of emotion or stress.

neurotransmitter: chemical substance that transmits messages between nerve cells.

norepinephrine: a neurotransmitter produced by the adrenal glands that leads to the physiological changes associated with anger.

central nervous system: the brain and spinal cord.

Situational and Cognitive Factors

Whereas the previous theories were concerned mostly with emotion as physiological responses, other theorists have concentrated on situational and cognitive factors as determinants of the emotional experience. According to one theorist (Schacter, 1964), the emotional response is a combination of physiological arousal and the *label* that is applied to this arousal.

In a classic experiment (Schacter & Singer, 1962), subjects were injected either with adrenalin, a hormone causing arousal, or a **placebo** (an inactive substance). One group of subjects was informed about the effects of adrenalin (sweaty palms, heart pounding). Another group was either given no information or misinformed as to the effects. Subjects were then placed in a room with a confederate of the experimenters. The confederate was trained to act very happy or very angry. Subjects who knew what to expect about the effects of adrenalin were not affected by the behavior of the confederate. Neither were those who received the placebo. However, subjects who did not know that their physiological arousal was due to the drug appeared to experience emotions similar to that of the confederate.

placebo: an inactive substance given in place of a drug in an experiment.

Based on these results, Schacter and Singer proposed that a specific emotion is experienced when we are physiologically aroused *and* we have a specific label that we can apply to the emotional feelings. The label that is applied ("I feel angry," "I feel happy") is determined by previous experiences, reactions of others, and the situation in which we find ourselves (see Box 5.1). It should be noted that replications of the Schacter-Singer experiment have not always been successful (e.g., Maslach, 1979). Although more research is needed, it is clear that emotions are more than stirred-up bodily states. Knowing the situation that preceded the physiological reactions would certainly help to identify the emotion that is being experienced.

However, knowing the situational factors and the physiological responses may still not be sufficient to identify the emotional state. Often subjective reality—what is in our heads—is of greater importance in determining our responses than is objective reality itself.

Let us suppose that you pass a friend on the street whom you have not seen for several weeks. You call out, "Hi, Bill, long time no see." You are shocked when he passes you by without a sign of recognition—not a smile, a friendly gesture, or even the slightest cue that he acknowledges your passing. At first you are confused and disoriented. You ask yourself, "What have I done to merit that?" When you can find no answer, your confusion gradually gives way to annoyance and anger. Hostile thoughts begin to race through your mind. "Well, to hell with him it that's the way he feels. See if I'll help him out next time he needs a ride. I can get along very well without his friendship." By the end of the day, you have been stewing so much about Bill's unwarranted slight that your anger has been transformed into enmity. "I don't care if I never see him again," you tell yourself while tossing in bed, unable to sleep.

The next day you bump into a mutual friend. You mention casually,

BOX 5.1: THE THINK-DRINK EFFECT

We know him and try to avoid him at parties: the fellow who after a few drinks suddenly turns into a pawing letch or a would-be Sugar Ray. The belief that people become sexually aroused or aggressive after drinking is deeply entrenched, so much so that we suspect the lout at the party is just using alcohol as an excuse. He's not really that far gone.

Before reading on, ask yourself what your own beliefs are about how alcohol affects you. Does it make you feel more sociable and extroverted, or more withdrawn? Do you believe alcohol makes you feel more relaxed? More or less sexually aroused? More prone to angry outbursts?

We now have the first solid evidence that psychological processes have as much—or more—to do with some drinking behaviors than do the physical effects of alcohol. In a series of experiments with a unique "balanced placebo" design, psychologists have shown that people will act in certain stereotypical ways when they drink, even if they are drinking tonic water but have been told they are drinking vodka and tonic. In other words, the think-drink effect is as dramatic as a placebo's seemingly miraculous curative power.

We tried to choose a drink for our studies that most people would already be familiar with, but one that could not easily be distinguished from a placebo drink. Pilot testing revealed that drinkers could tell a mixture of one part vodka to five parts tonic water with no more than 50 percent accuracy, or chance odds. (The method works best when drinks are chilled and a squirt of lime juice is added, both of which make it harder to detect the vodka taste.) Most of the studies reviewed employed these beverages.

We also had an ethical dilemma to resolve. The balanced-placebo design requires that some subjects drink alcohol after being told they will be given a nonalcoholic drink. But informed consent dictates that they know they may be drinking alcohol since it may affect their physical and psychological functioning. Accordingly, we informed all subjects beforehand that they might be receiving alcohol as part of the procedure. Later on, an assistant of the researcher's tells each that he or she has been randomly assigned to either the group that will receive vodka or the group that will not; at this stage of the study, of course, some subjects are being deceived.

BALANCED-PLACEBO DESIGN: The four conditions in the experiments. The expect-no-alcohol/receive-alcohol condition is uniquely able to isolate purely physiological effects of alcohol on behavior.

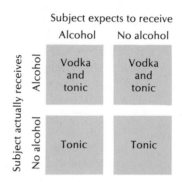

The studies strongly suggest that cognitive processes—our beliefs about how people are supposed to act when drinking—influence our reactions to alcohol in ways we have previously failed to acknowledge. For example:

- Men who believe they have been drinking alcohol become less anxious in social situations even when they have not been drinking the real thing. Women, strangely, become more anxious. But both types of response are determined by expectations (beliefs, hopes, and fears) about what happens when people drink.

- Many experts believe alcoholics develop a craving for liquor after just one or two drinks because a small amount of alcohol triggers a physiologically based addictive mechanism. However, studies show alcoholics experience the same craving after one or two placebo drinks. Even more surprising, alcoholics report little or no craving when they are given drinks containing alcohol that they believe are nonalcoholic.

- Men become more aggressive in laboratory situations when they are drinking only tonic but believe that it contains vodka. They also become relatively less aggressive when they think

BOX 5.1 *(concluded)*

they are drinking only tonic water, even though their drinks actually contain vodka.

- Men also tend to become more sexually aroused when they believe they are drinking the real thing—even when they're not. Women report feeling more aroused when they believe they have been drinking alcohol, but curiously, a measure of their vaginal blood flow shows that they are physically becoming less aroused.

MENTAL SET AND SETTING

Observers of various drug subcultures have frequently mentioned the role played by expectancy (mental set) and situational factors (setting) in a "high." Andrew Weil, in his pioneering book *The Natural Mind,* suggested that marijuana users did not need the substance to get high. "Pharmacologists do not understand," Weil wrote, "that all psychoactive drugs are really active placebos since the psychic effects arise from consciousness, elicited by set and setting, in response to physiological cues. Thus, for most marijuana users, the occasion of smoking a joint becomes an opportunity or excuse for experiencing a mode of consciousness that is available to everyone all the time, even though many people do not know how to get high without using a drug."

Because of our exposure to drinking models presented both in real life and in the media, we have come to expect that people will sometimes do things under the influence of alcohol that they would never do otherwise. Alcohol is frequently consumed in relaxed, convivial settings in which sexual advances, for example, are appropriate. In this sense, alcohol acts as a cue for sexual behavior. The cue effects are the same regardless of the pharmacological properties of alcohol, as long as the people involved believe they are really drinking liquor.

Early indications suggest that classical conditioning may play a role in this process: just as Pavlov's dogs learned to salivate at the sound of a bell that had been previously associated with a food reward, so the experienced drinker may achieve a conditioned high when presented with the signal or cue properties (sight, smell, taste, and so on) of a drink, regardless of whether the drink actually contains alcohol.

In addition, another important component would seem to be the attributions we make about alcohol as the "cause" of certain behaviors ("I wasn't myself"). The ingestion of alcohol itself seems to produce little more than an indefinite or ambiguous physiological reaction, an amorphous change in mood, at least at the dose levels most social drinkers are accustomed to. The interpretation or "framing" of this diffuse reaction appears to be more influenced by our prior beliefs, the drinking environment, and personal payoffs than by the physical effects of alcohol.

Source: G. Alan Marlatt and Damaris J. Rohsenow "The Think-Drink Effect," *Psychology Today.* 15 (December 1981), pp. 60–7.

---

so as not to betray your depth of feeling, "What's with Bill these days? I haven't seen him in quite a while."

"Oh, haven't you heard?" your friend replies.

"Heard? Heard what?" you ask.

"He was near that explosion in town a week, 10 days ago. He's suffering some sort of temporary hearing loss. In fact, I ran into him a couple days ago and he didn't even hear my greeting. At first I was offended. Then I realized what had happened."

In an instant, the anger and hostility you have nourished over the past 24 hours disappears like a thief in the night. It is replaced by vague and disquieting feelings—perhaps a bit of guilt or shame. In any event, you feel remorse and you are anxious to see Bill again so that you can reassert your friendship.

Transactions of this sort remind us of the fragility of human relationships. A misunderstanding here, an inappropriate emotional reaction there, and a relationship can be shattered just as surely and with the permanancy of a porcelain figurine that has fallen off the shelf. With this in mind, it is important to remind ourselves constantly that our perceptions and cognitions are not infallible. It is vital that we seek independent confirmation of the objective facts before taking precipitous and irreversible actions. By so doing, we may avoid the misperceptions and misunderstandings that can make shambles of the relationships we hold most dear.

Feelings

A constant companion to the thoughts and bodily reactions summoned forth by emotions is the ever-present affective side, the feeling of sadness, happiness, remorse, warmth, guilt, shame, tenderness, and anger. Sometimes several of these feeling tones occur simultaneously or in rapid succession in response to a given situation. This should not surprise us, since it is rare that any circumstance gives rise to a single unbridled emotional response. We may be overjoyed at the prospects of devouring the latest dairy delight at the corner ice-cream parlor, but we may also experience a tinge of guilt or sadness when we contemplate the calories involved in our "gluttony." We may look forward to the long-anticipated visit of a distant relative, but we harbor misgivings about the loss of freedom the visit will necessarily entail.

Indeed, we should not be surprised if on occasion we have some difficulty naming a particular emotion we are experiencing. We are often at a loss to explain our feelings to ourselves, since they are more often a stew rather than a single menu item. We may also have difficulty communicating our feelings to others as well. To illustrate, when I say "I feel sad," it may not be interpreted in the same way by others. We all have our own personal and unique scale by which we identify, measure, and evaluate our emotions.

Behavior

We also vary in the intensity with which we *display* emotions. We may throw a temper tantrum when angry or merely swear under our breath, cry out with elation or smile with pride when our team wins the game, or weep at the loss of a loved one. However, there is not always a correspondence between the feelings accompanying emotions and our behavior. We have all known moments when we have masked our true emotions behind a facial expression or gesture that did not mirror our real feelings. To illustrate, a visiting aunt is highly critical of the way you discipline your children. You deeply resent her intrusion into your life but decide to avoid a confrontation by taking the line of least resistance. Although you simmer inwardly, you nod your head, smile weakly, and try to change the topic of conversation. There are times when this type of behavior is adjustive since it avoids unpleasant and possibly damaging interactions. However, if bottling up our emotions becomes a way of life, we may suffer harmful consequences in the long run. In Chapter 6 we examine in greater detail the possible effects of concealing emotions.

In this section, we examined the complexity of our emotional lives. We have seen that our emotions include bodily reactions, situational factors, cognitions, feelings, and behavior. But how do our emotions develop? How do we learn to apply the appropriate labels to our different emotional states?

HOW DO WE LEARN TO LABEL EMOTIONS?

Maxine is a bright, bubbling three-year-old with an insatiable appetite for learning. She is constantly pointing to objects and asking, "What's that?" Her desire to find labels for anything and everything is almost an obsession. This is natural. Labels allow her to talk about things and events. For example, once she has learned the name of her favorite book, she can say, "I want Dr. Seuss." In this way, she can gain a certain measure of control over her environment.

Labeling is one of the most important aspects of language development. It is easy to learn and apply labels to observable and concrete things such as a book, a table, or a toy. But emotions are not public events. They are private. A parent cannot point to an emotion in a child and say, without fear of error, "You are happy," or "You are sad." Only the child is experiencing the emotion, not the parent. It is difficult for a child to learn the appropriate label for a particular internal state since the parents will often be wrong about the labels they apply.

How does a young child learn to use emotional words correctly? Let's look at a possible sequence of events. Suppose a situation arises which elicits an emotional reaction in Maxine (e.g., she is spanked by one of her parents). There are several aspects to her emotional reaction. One is a private event, an inner-directed feeling of some sort. This is the feeling that Maxine must learn to label. Other facets of her reaction include a set of behaviors such as crying, breaking furniture, and kicking the pet cat. Her parents may then respond in any number of different ways. For example, they may say, "You are angry," or "You are naughty." Each of these constitute a possible label for her feelings.

If her parents used the label naughty, Maxine might learn to identify her feelings as naughty. In other words, the label Maxine uses may mimic the label her parents use. The next time she experiences the same inner state, she may mislabel her anger as naughtiness. This is not even an emotional label, but Maxine has no way of knowing that. All she knows is that, whenever she feels this way, "naughty" is the name of the feeling. Moreover, she may also have learned that naughty is bad. Thus, the next time circumstances elicit the same inner feeling, she may conclude, "I feel naughty, therefore I am bad," even if anger is appropriate to the situation. It may be a long time before she learns to correctly label the feelings of anger. Indeed, she may even suppress these feelings because they are associated with being bad.

A factor further complicating the labeling of our emotions is our state of arousal at the time. If we are already in an aroused state (e.g., arousal from exercise,

How do you think Billy Martin would label the emotion he is experiencing?

United Press International

sex, or even humor) and then are made angry, we may interpret our arousal as anger. There is, therefore, a danger that our angry reaction may be completely inappropriate to the situation (Zillman, Johnson, & Day, 1974; Zillman, 1971; Mueller & Donnerstein, 1977).

This inherent difficulty in learning the appropriate labels for our inner states has important implications for adjustment. We may go throughout life with some degree of confusion about our own emotional feelings. Although we may successfully learn to distinguish the strong emotions from one another (e.g., anger, grief, and joy), subtle distinctions may always leave us somewhat perplexed. How can we tell if we are a little happy, very happy, or ecstatic? Can we always distinguish between sadness, depression, and grief?

One of the most important principles of effective adjustment is know thyself. Therefore, confusion concerning the identification of our ever-present emotional states can leave us in a quandry, to say the least. In more extreme instances, this confusion can lead to turmoil and chaos. Surely a person who cannot distinguish between love and sexual arousal is likely to have difficulty in establishing and maintaining a successful intimate relationship.

To make matters worse, it is rare that love is experienced as a pure emotion. At times, it is spun in the same web as its opposite emotion, hate. This should not surprise us. Psychoanalysts are quick to point out the fact that our early notions of and experiences with love are acquired during countless interactions with our parents. Parents are generally fickle love objects for children. At times, most parents lavish love and attention on the child. They are dependable providers of security and comfort. They are pillars of strength to whom the child can turn when troubled. At other times, many parents are like avenging demons, scolding their child for wrongdoing and threatening to withdraw their love, stated either directly ("I can't love a naughty child") or through implication. Thus, at almost the same moment or in rapid succession, the parents may evoke in their child feelings of both love and of hate. As we saw in Chapter 2, the pairing of these two emotional states provides the ideal circumstances for classically conditioning these emotional responses to one another. Thus, after many pairings of love and hate, the feeling of love acquires the capacity to elicit feelings of hate, and vice versa. The tragedy is that we may carry these *ambivalent* emotional feelings with us throughout life and later visit them upon our own marriage partners and children.

These ambivalent emotional reactions are illustrated in the following case example of a 10-year-old girl who was antagonistic at school and generally unhappy.

> From the mother's story, it was evident that the child was particularly upset whenever her younger brother received special attention. If the boy had a cold and was permitted to share the mother's bed, for example, or if he was included in a family outing, the little girl was likely to have what her mother called a "stormy spell." She hid in a closet and cried, or announced that she would not go to school, or she played with her friends so roughly and aggressively that the neighbors complained. Toward her brother, however, she was overtly affectionate and protective.

Is it possible for a child to both love and hate her mother?

Sue Markson

Sue Markson

It was only after prolonged behavior analysis that the little girl displayed her hostile reactions to her brother. She told stories about boys who played the most exciting games, who were allowed to be untidy and to skip their nightly baths, but who "couldn't possibly have nice personalities." With her dolls she constructed dramatic scenes in which little boys were so much trouble that they were left outside and forgotten by their parents. It was clear that this little girl maintained overt attitudes of love and affection, simultaneously with covert attitudes of rivalry and hostility, toward her brother. The consequence of this conflict was a failure of both competing responses to achieve consummation. (Cameron & Magaret, 1951, p. 255)[1]

Note the key thought in this case example—neither of the competing emotions was able to achieve satisfaction. One wonders to what extent the failures of many adults to find lasting and satisfying intimate relationships may involve confusion about these two ingredients—love and hate—in the emotional soup that feeds the affective aspects of our lives.

RECOGNIZING EMOTIONS IN OTHERS

The following is excerpted from a round table discussion involving four medical doctors. They were talking about the value of attending to nonverbal cues when communicating with patients.

[1] Excerpted by permission from Norman Cameron and Ann Magaret: *Behavior Pathology*, p. 255. Copyright © 1951 by Houghton Mifflin Company, renewed 1979 by David Hooke and Gretchen Ann Magaret.

RAKEL: A patient's posture and gestures during the history often provide better clues to sensitive issues than what he says. I'm going to demonstrate some common nonverbal responses, with Dr. Longmire acting as my patient.

Here's a familiar sign of resistance—crossed arms. Dr. Longmire is showing us that he's feeling very uncomfortable behind those crossed arms and crossed legs. His hands are nearly hidden. He may even be clenching his fists.

LONGMIRE [*as the patient*]:   You're right. I am.

WARD: Society says the patient can't hit you, the physician, for asking questions about uncomfortable issues in his life.

RAKEL: Instead, he's saying with his posture: "I'm trying to stay as far away from you as I can." [This means] that you need to spend more time than usual to get beyond the patient's resistance. But other nonverbal clues may signal the significant issues in the history. . . . A common clue is the respiratory avoidance response—throat clearing, if you prefer. If you hear that very often—and the patient doesn't have postnasal drainage—you know the patient doesn't like what is being said. A gesture that means the same thing is the nose rub, my favorite diagnostic clue. You can be reasonably sure the patient is rejecting what you or he has said when you see him flick his nose with his index finger.

MANAHAN: Maybe he's just scratching his nose.

RAKEL: No. Rubbing the nose to relieve an itch is more vigorous. It's a back-and-forth, sawing motion. The nose rub is no more than a quick flick of the nose. Johnny Carson gives a beautiful example in practically every "Tonight Show" program when he's about to discuss a sensitive or controversial subject. It must make him uncomfortable because, consistently, he first flicks his nose.

MANAHAN: Give me an example of how this can actually help me take the history.

RAKEL: In getting a sexual history from a 30-year-old man, I asked, "Have you ever had VD?" The answer was a quick and short: "No." But it was accompanied by the nose flick. If I hadn't been looking at the patient, I'd have missed it. Later, I asked, "How are things at home?" and got the same double-barreled answer: "Fine," and a flick of the nose.

HOLLISTER: Surely you don't make a diagnosis on the basis of the nonverbal clue.

RAKEL: No, but I do interpret the gesture as meaning, "I don't like what you're asking me," or "I'm uncomfortable with my answers; things really aren't going very well at home."

MANAHAN: So the nonverbal clue raises questions in your mind about the patient's verbal response. What do you do about it?

RAKEL: Ask another question, usually just a simple comment. In this case, I paused a moment and then asked, "You mean you don't have any arguments or anything?" At that, the patient poured out a tale of marital strife that included his acquiring a sexually transmitted disease from his wife. So the practical help is that the nose rub can point to areas in the history that need more exploration.[2]

The preceding round table discussion showed how certain nonverbal cues, or "body language," can be used to determine what a person is *really* feeling. But why is it necessary to look at indirect indicators of emotions? Why can't we just come right out and ask, "What emotion are you feeling?" There are at least two answers to this question. As we have already seen, there are times when we are unable to accurately describe our emotional states to ourselves. Under these circumstances, how can we be expected to describe our feelings to others? Secondly, from childhood on, we are taught not to "wear our feelings on our sleeves." Probably all of us can remember such parental admonitions as big boys don't cry, and good girls don't fight. Indeed, a certain degree of concealment of our true feelings is expected and encouraged in our society.

We all know people we say are "emotional" and those we call "unemotional." But are they *feeling* something distinctly different or merely *expressing* their feelings differently? Several possibilities exist. Many so-called emotional people may be playacting, exaggerating their display of feelings for dramatic effect. On the other hand, unemotional people may have rich and varied emotional experiences but, for various reasons, choose consciously or unconsciously to keep them in check. Thus, subjective reports of emotions cannot always be accepted at face value. No wonder we so often misjudge the emotions of others.

The language of emotions is obviously more than just words. We convey information about our feelings through nonverbal signs or cues, as well. The tone of our voice, our facial expression, body posture, and mannerisms all serve to communicate our emotional feelings to others. Think about it for a moment. What cues do we use to judge another person's emotions? Since the verbal reports of others are not always dependable, we must look elsewhere. How about looking at their facial expressions? A substantial body of research provides evidence that there are universal facial expressions for many of the emotional states. (see Figure 5.1). Various studies of different cultures suggest that anger, disgust, happiness, fear, sadness, and surprise can be identified from photographs of facial expressions (e.g., Ekman, Sorenson, & Friesen, 1969; Ekman, 1975). Even societies that are isolated from Western civilization, such as the Fore tribe in New Guinea, express sorrow by a down-turned mouth, anger by a red face, and happiness by laughing or smiling. Moreover, children in this country who were born blind and deaf display their feelings with the same facial expressions as normal seeing and hearing individuals (Goodenough, 1932). This is in spite of the fact that they never had the opportunity to observe the facial expressions associated with emotional states.

Suppose you walked into a room and saw Jerome with a broad smile on his face. You would probably conclude that he was feeling happy. You would probably

FIGURE 5.1   A young girl of the Himba tribe showing coyness in response to a compliment.
                    This emotional response is a universal cross-cultural one.

Irenaus Eibl-Eibesfeldt, "Strategies of Social Interaction"

be correct most of the time. However, as Box 5.2 shows, you might learn more
about what emotion he was experiencing by looking at his bodily gestures as
well as his facial expression.

Table 5.1 provides a summary of the "meaning" of various body signs. It
should be noted that, like facial expression, body language is not an infallible
guide to the inner life of the individual. Some studies have shown that humans
are not always able to accurately judge the emotions of others from facial expressions or other expressive behaviors (Plutchik, 1980). However, when used in
conjunction with other cues, movements and gestures may permit us to fine
tune our judgments.

What are these other cues? One of the most important is knowledge of the
context in which the emotion is evoked. When we saw Jerome smiling, we would
feel more secure in judging his emotion to be happiness if we knew that he
had just received good news. But what would we say if Irene's eyes were filled
with tears? Is she unhappy? Not necessarily. She may be overjoyed at receiving
a phone call from her runaway son. Clearly, knowing the situation may help to
clarify many circumstances in which the underlying emotion is ambiguous.

However, we don't always need to know the situational factors to correctly
label an emotion. For example, Dick's wife is usually sensitive to his changing
moods—his bouts of irritability as well as his moments of euphoria—without

---

BOX 5.2: SHEEPISH SMILES DON'T HIDE EMBARRASSMENT

People tend to laugh or smile when they are embarrassed. Do their smiles "save face" by concealing their discomfort? According to an experiment conducted by two psychologists at the University of London, Robert Edelmann and Sarah Hampson, face saving takes more than a face: in an embarrassing moment, body language gives people away almost every time.

The researchers showed 33 subjects silent videotapes of smiling people who had just learned that they had unwittingly criticized a painting in front of the artist who did it and who later said that the emotion they were feeling was embarrassment. For comparison, the subjects saw tapes of people in the same situation who later claimed they were genuinely amused by it. The viewers, aged 20 to 70, had been recruited from among students and people living near the university. A third of them saw faces only, a third saw bodies from the neck down, and a third saw the faces and bodies together. The viewers then had to select a phrase describing the emotion of the person from a list that included amusement and embarrassment.

From the faces-only tapes, most correctly identified the signals of amusement, but embarrassed expressions were mistaken for amused ones. Tapes of the body alone provided little help in identifying either emotion. With tapes of the face and body together, viewers were able to recognize both amused and embarrassed behavior most of the time.

In another experiment, different subjects saw the tapes showing the faces and bodies together and pinpointed the areas of the body that helped them decide what emotions they were seeing. All who got the amused behavior right said they noted the mouth; less than 4 percent mentioned behavior occurring in any area besides the face. In successfully detecting embarrassment, 68 percent mentioned using the eyes; 61 percent also said they used the hands; 50 percent, the mouth; and 44 percent, the lower legs.

Apparently, then, it is a too-quick hand movement or leg crossing that makes an ordinary smile look like a sheepish grin. The researchers propose that most people who smile when they are embarrassed do not really think they are fooling people. Rather, they realize that they bodies are giving away their embarrassment and use smiles to "qualify" their emotions, signaling others not to take them too seriously.

Source: Reprinted from *Psychology Today*, Magazine, Copyright © 1981. American Psychological Association.

---

knowing the underlying cause. Similarly, parents can usually tell when their children are sad even with no knowledge of the precipitating circumstances.

SOME SPECIFIC EMOTIONS

As you may have already gathered, emotions are exceptionally complex states that are difficult to classify. Indeed, no single classification system has gained general acceptance by psychologists. Part of the difficulty stems from the fact that the language of emotions is often confusing. There are thousands of different words used to describe our emotional states. Our everyday language simply does not provide clear distinctions among the various feelings and moods. To illustrate, the following words may all be used as synonyms for *depression:* dejection, sadness, melancholy, despair, hopelessness, pessimism, despondency, gloominess, discouragement, downheartedness, torpor, sluggishness, lassitude, ennui, and the blues.

Moreover, emotions rarely, if ever, exist in a pure state. They are commonly

TABLE 5.1   READING BODY LANGUAGE: They're not infallible signals, but body movement and gestures can give you clues to a person's emotional state during an interview. Here are some common body clues that may help you evaluate a person's mood.

Body Clue	What It Suggests
Rigid body posture, little movement	Tension, authoritarian values
Well-defined, localized movements, such as arm folding.	Resistance or protectiveness
Leg movement	Anxiety, fear, or aggression
Face picking	Fear of personal attack
Hand and shoulder shrugs	Confusion or uncertainty
Downward head tilt and lip contraction, poor eye contact, infrequent hand movements	Depression
Legs and feet together with legs extended	Meticulousness, sense of order, tendency toward anxiety
Arm and leg position asymmetry, sideways lean, open arm position, frequent gestures	Relaxation

Source: D. B. Adams and P. J. Michels, "History-Talking. The Subtleties of Body Language," *Diagnosis,* December 1981, p. 38.

a mixture of many different moods, feelings, bodily reactions, and cognitions. In fact, it is common to hear people say that they have mixed emotions about a particular situation or event in their lives. Think back for a moment to the last time you aced a test. Did you experience pure joy or was it mixed with many other sentiments? Did you perhaps feel a touch of compassion for a close friend who did not do as well? Even a tinge of guilt because the professor grades on the curve? Maybe even a hint of anger because the professor forced you to make a choice between doing well on the test and distressing some of your peers?

Finally, emotions exist in varying degrees of intensity. For example, fear versus panic, contentment versus ecstasy, annoyance versus rage, or sadness versus grief. The feelings associated with the different intensities can be extremely varied as are the resulting behaviors. It is not unusual for actors, teachers, politicians, and other "performers" to experience moderate degrees of anxiety just before facing their audience. Many of these people suspect that the anxiety they are experiencing is actually a positive force. Indeed, mild to moderate intensities are usually accompanied by increased alertness, slight changes in the tension level, and closer attention to relevant stimulation in our surroundings. The subjective experience is usually quite pleasant, even with the so-called negative emotions like anxiety or fear. We may even strive to obtain these mild negative emotional states by taking a roller coaster ride or going to see a horror movie. We will experience these emotions as pleasurable as long as we feel we are in control of the situation.

Higher intensity levels lead to a distinctly different state of affairs. In strong negative emotions such as fear and anger, our entire body is placed on an emergency basis. Our metabolism speeds up, sugar in the bloodstream and fats in body tissues are burned at a faster rate, and nonemergency functions like salivation and digestion are suspended. Other strong negative emotions such as grief lead to a slowdown in physiological functions such as lower blood pressure, pulse rate and respiration. High intensity levels of the negative emotions are usually experienced as unpleasant.

At the highest levels of intensity, emotions are usually quite disruptive of ongoing behavior. It is difficult to enjoy a well-prepared meal while in the throes of a violent rage reaction. A person in a state of panic can rarely be sexually aroused by the presence of a loved one. Indeed, even excessive positive emotions can be disruptive of ongoing behavior. Imagine trying to study for an exam after learning that you have just won first prize in the state lottery or that your lawyer has settled with the insurance company to the tune of $100,000.

In the next section we will look at a few selected emotional states, concentrating on the conditions that typically evoke them and examining ways of dealing with them in our everyday adjustments.

Anger

Imagine the following situation.

You have just received a notice that you have exceeded the limit on your credit card by $2,000. "Preposterous! Impossible!" you exclaim. "I'll call them this minute and get the whole thing straightened out."

Little did you realize that you were about to be snared in a web of bureaucracy. You call the number listed on the notice and ask the loan officer to please tell you what the charges are so that you can immediately clear up this misunderstanding. She tells you that her department does not get a record of the charges—only Customer Relations does.

"Fine," you say, "I'll call them."

"No, you can't *call* Customer Relations, you can only write to them," you are told in a cold and biting manner. "Unless you have the money in within three days, we'll be forced to cancel your card."

"OK," you say in a conciliatory manner, "tell me how I am going to write Customer Relations, get their reply, dispute an obvious error, and pay the bill all within three days?"

A moment of silence at the other end. "I am only citing company policy. Unless you pay the charges in three days, we must cancel."

"But wait, what are the charges?" you protest.

"That's not our department. I told you, you will have to write if you intend to dispute this bill."

"What bill? I haven't even received my bill yet, only this notice that I am overdrawn. How can I dispute charges when I don't even know what they are? You're setting up an impossible situation."   ·

No doubt you have been classified as a chronic spendthrift who recklessly

Do you think you would be likely to lose your temper after waiting many hours in long lines?

George W. Gardner

abuses credit card privileges. You deeply resent this implied accusation, especially in view of an unblemished track record extending over a period of 10 years. You are furious.

frustration: the blocking or thwarting of goal-directed activities.

In this scenario drawn from a real-life situation, we see a common circumstance that provokes anger—**frustration.** The blocking of paths to goals may take different forms. There may be physical barriers, such as a traffic jam on the road in front of you; social barriers, such as the action of a committee that denies you membership in an organization you are eager to join; personal and psychological barriers that drastically reduce the scope of your activities because of real or imagined inadequacies.

Here are numerous other situations that may arouse anger. Many victims of criminal acts report a variety of emotional reactions, among them anger. "I should have grabbed the gun and showered that mugger with bullets," we frequently hear the victim proclaim. Other conditions leading to anger include physical pain, insults, and threats.

aggression: physical or verbal attack intended to harm or injure. Whereas anger is an emotion, aggression is behavior. Anger does not always lead to aggressive behavior and aggression does not always stem from anger.

At one time or another, most of us have probably reacted to anger with a strong impulse to express **aggression** against the source of our anger. How often have you kicked a piece of equipment that refused to work properly or railed against the weather for canceling the long-anticipated family outing? Have you ever been tempted to retaliate in kind for an act of physical or psychological aggression against you? Clearly, aggression is a common reaction to anger. However, the link between anger and aggression is not forged in iron. Anger can lead to a variety of responses other than aggression. For example, anger may evoke sullen withdrawal, destructive, self-defeating, and nonproductive responses. Admittedly, this abundance of conflicting feelings and impulses may provide some positive gains. You may *feel* better after wallowing in self-pity, bawling out the loan officer at the credit card company, or kicking a flat tire. However, your situation is usually not improved by such behavior. Self-pity rarely leads to goal-directed behavior; insulting loan officers does not usually result in rulings in your favor, and flat tires remain flat even after the most forceful kick.

Because of its great potential for crippling human lives and relationships, it is vital that you learn how to recognize anger when it occurs and direct it along nondestructive avenues. Foremost, you must recognize it for what it is—an emotional response to frustration, threat, or social slight. You should not bury your anger in a mound of denials and hackneyed words. "I'm not really angry. I'm just annoyed," ignoring the seething caldron within you.

When we thrust anger or, for that matter, any emotion out of consciousness, we lose control over it. It may manifest itself in many different forms and disguises (blaming others, accusing others of being hostile or aggressive, blaming ourselves) while we remain unaware of its intrusion into our emotional and mental life. This is definitely not one of those situations where we can say, "What you don't know can't hurt you." Rather, we should say, "The greater our ignorance and self-deception, the greater the risk of damaging our lives and lives of others."

internal communications: thoughts that create stress. They may occur so quickly that we are often unaware of them. However, they may influence our behavior by interacting with the environment situation.

Sometimes our thoughts can intensify negative feelings and lead to aggressive behavior. These thoughts, or **internal communications,** may occur so quickly that we are unaware of them (Beck, 1976). But they may influence our behavior by interacting with the environmental situation. For example, Michael is concerned about his adequacy as a student. His roommate Todd always seems to do well with a minimum of effort, whereas Michael must struggle constantly to achieve passing grades. When his roommate asks, "How'd you do on that exam?" Michael snaps, "What's it to you?" His internal communication: "It's so unfair, he *always* does well," led him to behave aggressively. Because internal communications occur so fleetingly, Michael doesn't really understand why he felt angry at Todd or why he acted that way. Normally, we do not perceive our internal communications unless we work to tune them in. Some investigators have suggested that we should relive upsetting experiences to help us get in touch with our internal communications (Meichenbaum & Turk, 1976). In one study, subjects who were taught adjustive internal communications (e.g., "Take it easy"; "Don't get upset"; "I didn't do well but he's not to blame"; "Don't expect her to act the way you would") coped more effectively with their anger and showed lower arousal during confrontations than subjects who were taught relaxation skills (Novaco, 1974). The participants in this study learned to think about a provocation as a problem calling for a solution rather than as a threat calling for aggression.

We should pay particular attention to our fantasies and the silent conversations we constantly conduct within ourselves. The themes and content of these quiet dramas may be more self-revealing than our overt verbalizations and behaviors. If we find much or our mental life populated by themes of anger, hostility, and aggression, we can be quite certain that negative emotions constitute significant components of our emotional makeup. Knowing this, we should not respond with feelings of guilt and self-contempt. Anger turned inward is a dangerous force. Rather, we should attempt to identify circumstances that lead to anger with a view toward changing or modifying these circumstances. For example, if a person who is significant in your life plays a frequent role in your negative daydreams and inner conversations, it would be helpful to try to get at the cause of these feelings. At times, it may be found that relatively minor and easily corrected incidents serve to trigger anger and hostility. A calm and quiet conversation with that person will often result in shared insights that improve your relationship, e.g., "I can't stand it when you pop you bubble gum while we're watching TV." At other times, it may require considerable effort on the part of both parties to identify and correct sources of antagonism. If the relationship is valuable to you, the time and effort will be well spent.

How about "letting it all hang out"? Is it not harmful to bottle up anger? Isn't it best to get everything out in the open and lay it on the line? Although venting anger is often described in the popular literature as a healthy and normal means of gaining emotional relief, the bulk of research suggests that it will often damage rather than repair relationships. For example, if subjects are encouraged to respond aggressively toward a person who antagonizes them, they will later feel even more hostile and unfriendly toward that person (Kahn, 1966).

There are ways to deal with anger without hurting or humiliating another

assertive behavior: standing up for your rights without violating the rights of others.

person. You can use **assertive behavior** to stand up for your rights without violating the rights of others. Unlike aggressive behavior, with assertive behavior you do not demand that your needs be met at the expense of others. You do not hurt other people by attacking or belittling them. Rather, to be assertive is to look the other person straight in the eye and talk to them directly. You make or refuse requests without hurting or putting the other person down. You firmly request that someone modify their behavior without threatening or humiliating them. For example, suppose you ordered your roast beef rare and the waiter brings it well done. You could respond aggressively: you shout and insult the waiter, "You're really dumb! Does this meat look rare to you?" Or you could use an assertive alternative: you calmly inform the waiter of the error and request the correct order. We shall look at some assertiveness techniques in Chapter 9.

Anxiety

anxiety: vague unpleasant feeling; a premonition that something bad will happen.

Do you remember the last time you approached a strange or new life situation? A new challenge you were about to undertake? A decision in which the outcome was uncertain: Did you feel jumpy, nervous, or tense? If so, you were probably experiencing **anxiety**—a complex emotional state with far-reaching effects on behavior. Let us look at a couple of examples.

While driving across the eight-mile-long San Francisco Bay Bridge, John Masterson, a 48-year-old business executive, was suddenly seized by an acute anxiety attack. At first he felt a mild apprehension, then a tightening of the muscles around his head and shoulders. Soon his heart was pounding so rapidly and loudly that the sound seemed to echo in his ears. John was terrified and sure that death was imminent. He could not breathe, broke out in a profuse sweat, and felt on the verge of fainting.

Joanne Wilson was known by her college friends as a worrier. She worried about anything and everything: failing in school, making friends, eating the right foods, maintaining her health, and being liked. Joanne also had difficulty making decisions. Her insecurity was so great that even the most common decisions—what clothes to wear, what to order at a restaurant, which movies to see—became major problems. At night, Joanne reviewed and rereviewed every real and imaginary mistake she had made or might make. This added yet another concern—not being able to sleep.[3]

The examples presented above illustrate some of the ways anxiety is evidenced. Anxiety is manifested in four ways: in one's thoughts, behavior, physical or biological reactions, and feelings (see Box 5.3).

Anxiety is frequently described as a vague fear of something threatening. The feeling is similar to the emotion of fear. Indeed, fear and anxiety are often confused. The main difference is that fear is a reaction to a specific *real* danger, whereas anxiety usually does not have an obvious cause. it is this vagueness of anxiety that makes it so difficult to handle. Not being able to explain why we feel as we do creates an extremely uncomfortable state. However, anxiety may be realistic. It may be a normal and appropriate reaction to a specific situation. When anxiety results from an objective perception of real danger, it is similar to fear. Let us look at some examples.

You may feel anxious about taking an exam when you *know* you are not adequately prepared. You may feel anxious about traveling alone to a strange place if you know your car is likely to break down, particularly if there have been reports of high crime in the area. Or you might be anxious about attending a social function when you are aware that the last time you were in the company of these people you behaved in a rude or unacceptable manner.

What can you do about realistic anxiety? The first step is to try to identify the source of your fear. Once you have done so, you are then in a position to take steps to alleviate the anxiety. For instance, in the examples cited, you could prepare for the exam or try to work out a make up. You could fix your car or arrange to have somebody accompany you. You might try to engage in conversation with those people you previously insulted. You could apologize or try to explain your poor actions and go out of your way to behave in a charming, polite, and acceptable way.

Anxiety has been extensively studied by many different investigators. One distinction that has been made is between *general* and *specific* anxiety. Some

---

[3] Sue, Sue and Sue, *Understanding Abnormal Behavior*, p. 149. Copyright © 1981, Houghton Mifflin Company, used by permission.

BOX 5.3: ANXIETY

Anxiety is manifested in four ways: *cognitively* (in a person's thoughts), *motorically* (in a person's actions), *somatically* (in physical or biological reactions), and *affectively* (in a person's emotions).

Cognitive apprehensions may vary from mild worry to panic. Severe attacks can bring a conviction of impending doom—the end of the world or death; a preoccupation with unknown dangers; an inability to concentrate or come to decisions; and difficulty in sleeping.

Motor behaviors are often affected; anxious persons exhibit random movements, ranging from fine trembling to more pronounced skeletal shaking. A whole assortment of behaviors such as general restlessness, pacing, squirming, tics, lip biting, fingernail biting, knuckle cracking, and jumpiness may be exhibited. One can almost imagine that the body is prepared for flight from some threat that will suddenly appear. If the dreaded thing remains unknown to the person, what he or she experiences is considered a **free-floating anxiety.**

Somatically, changes in the autonomic nervous system are often reflected in shallow breathing, mouth dryness, cold hands and feet, diarrhea, frequent urination, fainting, heart palpitations, elevated blood pressure, increased perspiration, muscular tenseness (especially in the head, neck, shoulders, and chest), and indigestion.

However, the most pronounced manifestation is the affective domain; a feeling of tense excitement, bordering on terror, is characteristic of a state of chronic anxiety. In this state a person maintains a basic level of uneasiness and worry about imminent danger, no matter how well things are going. This may be punctuated by acute panic attacks, such as the one experienced by John Masterson in our first example. Psychologists use different tools to assess the different kinds of anxiety symptoms: self-reports, observations of motor behavior, and physiological measures.

---

free-floating anxiety: anxiety that is diffuse and without focus.

Source: Sue et al., *Understanding Abnormal Behavior,* p. 150. Copyright © 1981, Houghton Mifflin Company, used by permission.

---

people feel anxious in most situations, even those that do not ordinarily provoke anxiety. They feel uneasy about the future and worry about almost everything. These people are experiencing general anxiety. In contrast, some people display anxiety only in specific types of situations (Spielberger, 1972). Some examples of specific anxiety with which you are probably familiar include stage fright and test anxiety.

We have all experienced anxiety at some time in our lives and, life being what it is, we will continue to experience it to some degree. Therefore, to keep our reactions within normal bounds and ensure our well-being, we must learn the most effective ways to cope with anxiety when it does occur.

Alcohol and tranquilizers relieve anxiety, but they also reduce the ability to cope realistically with one's environment (Gray, 1978). In addition, the effects are only temporary, and the source of the anxiety remains after the effects of the drugs have worn off. Thus, although drugs can be a potent way of alleviating anxiety, they are, at best, a temporary solution.

For some people, professional psychotherapy is the answer to chronic and prolonged states of anxiety that interfere with effective functioning. Counseling and crisis centers are available for short-term assistance for those experiencing an acute life crisis. Anxiety is an unpleasant experience, and we avoid it whenever we can. Sometimes a change in lifestyle is the only way to avoid the various stresses in life. In Chapter 7 we examine the various defense mechanisms used to protect the self from anxiety.

progressive relaxation: a method of achieving deep relaxation by alternately tensing and relaxing different muscle groups.

There are a number of techniques that have been developed in which you alleviate anxiety and tension by learning to manage your body states. One experiment showed that anxiety can be lowered by consciously regulating one's breathing to half the usual rate (McCaul, Solomon, & Holmes, 1979). Another technique, called **progressive relaxation** (see Box 5.4), has been used successfully to reduce tension and anxiety (Paul, 1969).

BOX 5.4: PROGRESSIVE RELAXATION

Most people simply do not know how to relax. One investigator (Jacobson, 1938) noted that people tend to contract their muscles when they are tense. But many people are unaware of this tightness and, if told to relax their muscles, would not know how to let go. Jacobson developed a technique called progessive relaxation in which you alternately tighten and then relax different muscle groups throughout the body. Through progressive relaxation, the individual learns to distinguish the different sensations arising from tensing and relaxing muscles. After practicing tensing and relaxing for a while, you can go on to just relaxing muscles.

Using the instructions below, you can learn to relax. Make sure that you are absolutely comfortable and not likely to be disturbed. You can have a friend read you the instructions or put them on a tape recorder. Once you have practiced progressive relaxation a number of times and feel comfortable about your ability to relax, you can modify and shorten the instructions yourself. It is probably a good idea to go through the entire instructions once in a while to sharpen your relaxation skills.

RELAXATION INSTRUCTIONS

Relaxation of Arms (time: 4–5 minutes)

Settle back as comfortable as you can. Let yourself relax to the best of your ability. . . . Now, as you relax like that, clench your right fist, just clench your fist tighter and tighter, and study the tension as you do so. Keep it clenched and feel the tension in your right fist, hand, forearm . . . and now relax. Let the

fingers of your right hand become loose, and observe the contrast in your feelings. . . . Now, let yourself go and try to become more relaxed all over. . . . Once more, clench your right fist really tight . . . hold it, and notice the tension again. . . . Now let go, relax; your fingers straighten out, and you notice the difference once more. . . . Now repeat that with your left fist. Clench your left fist while the rest of your body relaxes; clench that fist tighter and feel the tension . . . and now relax. Again enjoy the contrast. . . . Repeat that once more, clench the left fist, tight and tense. . . . Now do the opposite of tension—relax and feel the difference. Continue relaxing like that for a while. . . . Clench both fists tighter and tighter, both fists tense, forearms tense, study the sensations . . . and relax; straighten out your fingers and feel that relaxation. Continue relaxing your hands and forearms more and more. . . . Now bend your elbows and tense your biceps, tense them harder and study the tension feelings . . . all right, straighten out your arms, let them relax, and feel that difference again. Let the relaxation develop. . . . Once more, tense your biceps; hold the tension and observe it carefully. . . . Straighten the arms and relax; relax to the best of your ability. . . . Each time, pay close attention to your feelings when you tense up and when you relax. Now straighten your arms, straighten them so that you feel most tension in the triceps muscles along the back of your arms; stretch your arms and feel that tension. . . . And now relax. Get your arms back into a comfortable position. Let the relaxation proceed on its own. The arms should feel comfortably heavy as you allow them to relax. . . . Straighten the arms once more so that you feel the

BOX 5.4 (continued)

tension in the triceps muscles; straighten them. Feel that tension . . . and relax. Now let's concentrate on pure relaxation in the arms without any tension. Get your arms comfortable and let them relax further and further. Continue relaxing your arms ever further. Even when your arms seem fully relaxed, try to go that extra bit further; try to achieve deeper and deeper levels of relaxation.

Relaxation of Facial Area with Neck, Shoulders and Upper Back (time: 4–5 minutes)

Let all your muscles go loose and heavy. Just settle back quietly and comfortably. Wrinkle up your forehead now; wrinkle it tighter. . . . And now stop wrinkling your forehead, relax and smooth it out. Picture the entire forehead and scalp becoming smoother as the relaxation increases. . . . Now frown and crease your brows and study the tension . . . Let go of the tension again. Smooth out the forehead once more. . . . Now, close your eyes tighter and tighter . . . feel the tension . . . and relax your eyes. Keep your eyes closed, gently, comfortably, and notice the relaxation. . . . Now clench your jaws, bite your teeth together; study the tension throughout the jaws. . . . Relax your jaws now. Let your lips part slightly. . . . Appreciate the relaxation. . . . Now press your tongue hard against the roof of your mouth. Look for the tension. . . . All right, let your tongue return to a comfortable and relaxed position. . . . Now purse your lips, press your lips together tighter and tighter. . . . Relax the lips. Note the contrast between tension and relaxation. Feel the relaxation all over your face, all over your forehead and scalp, eyes, jaws, lips, tongue and throat. The relaxation progresses further and further. . . . Now attend to your neck muscles. Press your head back as far as it can go and feel the tension in the neck; roll it to the right and feel the tension shift; now roll it to the left. Straighten your head and bring it forward, press your chin against your chest. Let your head return to a comfortable position, and study the relaxation. Let the relaxation develop. . . . Shrug your shoulders, right up. Hold the tension. . . . Drop your shoulders and feel the relaxation. Neck and shoulders relaxed. . . . Shrug your shoulders again and move them around. Bring your shoulders up and forward and

back. Feel the tension in your shoulders and in your upper back. . . . Drop your shoulders once more and relax. Let the relaxation spread deep into the shoulders, right into your back muscles; relax your neck and throat, and your jaws and other facial areas as the pure relaxation takes over and grows deeper . . . deeper . . . ever deeper.

Relaxation of Chest, Stomach and Lower Back (time: 4–5 minutes)

Relax your entire body to the best of your ability. Feel that comfortable heaviness that accompanies relaxation. Breathe easily and freely in and out. Notice how the relaxation increases as you exhale . . . as you breathe out just feel that relaxation. . . . Now breathe right in and fill your lungs; inhale deeply and hold your breath. Study the tension . . . Now exhale, let the walls of your chest grow loose and push the air out automatically. Continue relaxing and breathe freely and gently. Feel the relaxation and enjoy it. . . . With the rest of your body as relaxed as possible, fill your lungs again. Breathe in deeply and hold it again. . . . That's fine, breathe out and appreciate the relief. Just breathe normally. Continue relaxing your chest and let the relaxation spread to your back, shoulders, neck, and arms. Merely let go . . . and enjoy the relaxation. Now let's pay attention to your abdominal muscles, your stomach area. Tighten your stomach muscles, make your abdomen hard. Notice the tension. . . . And relax. Let the muscles loosen and notice the contrast. . . . Once more, press and tighten your stomach muscles. Hold the tension and study it. . . . And relax. Notice the general well-being that comes with relaxing your stomach. . . . Now draw your stomach in, pull the muscles right in and feel the tension this way. . . . Now relax again. Let your stomach out. Continue breathing normally and easily and feel the gentle massaging action all over your chest and stomach. . . . Now pull your stomach in again and hold the tension. . . . Now push out and tense like that; hold the tension . . . once more pull in and feel the tension . . . now relax your stomach fully. Let the tension dissolve as the relaxation grows deeper. Each time you breathe out, notice the rhythmic relaxation both in your lungs and in your stomach. Notice thereby how your chest and your

BOX 5.4 *(concluded)*

stomach relax more and more. . . . Try and let go of all contractions anywhere in your body . . . Now direct your attention to your lower back. Arch up your back, make your lower back quite hollow, and feel the tension along your spine . . . and settle down comfortably again relaxing the lower back. . . . Just arch your back up and feel the tensions as you do so. Try to keep the rest of your body as relaxed as possible. Try to localize the tension throughout your lower back area. . . . Relax once more, relaxing further and further. Relax your lower back, relax your upper back, spread the relaxation to your stomach, chest, shoulders, arms and facial area. These parts relaxing further and further and further and ever deeper.

Relaxation of Hips, Thighs and Calves Followed by Complete Body Relaxation

Let go of all tensions and relax. . . . Now flex your buttocks and thighs. Flex your thighs by pressing down your heels as hard as you can. . . . Relax and note the difference. . . . Straighten your knees and flex your thigh muscles again. Hold the tension. . . . Relax your hips and thighs. Allow the relaxation to proceed on its own. . . . Press your feet and toes downwards, away from your face, so that your calf muscles become tense. Study that tension. . . . Relax your feet and calves. . . . This time, bend your feet towards your face so that you feel tension along your shins. Bring your toes right up. . . . Relax again. Keep relaxing for a while. . . . Now let yourself relax further all over. Relax your feet, ankles, calves, and shins, knees, thighs, buttocks, and hips. Feel the heaviness of your lower body as you relax still further. . . .

Now spread the relaxation to your stomach, waist, lower back. Let go more and more. Feel that relaxation all over. Let it proceed to your upper back, chest, shoulders, and arms, and right to the tips of your fingers. Keep relaxing more and more deeply. Make sure that no tension has crept into your throat; relax your neck and your jaws and all your facial muscles. Keep relaxing your whole body like that for a while. Let yourself relax.

Now you can become twice as relaxed as you are merely by taking in a really deep breath and slowly exhaling. With your eyes closed so that you become less aware of objects and movements around you and thus prevent any surface tensions from developing, breathe in deeply and feel yourself becoming heavier. Take in a long, deep breath and let it out very slowly. . . . Feel how heavy and relaxed you have become.

In a state of perfect relaxation you should feel unwilling to move a single muscle in your body. Think about the effort that would be required to raise your right arm. As you *think* about raising your right arm, see if you can notice any tensions that might have crept into your shoulder and your arm. . . . Now you decide not to lift the arm but to continue relaxing. Observe the relief and the disappearance of the tension. . . .

Just carry on relaxing like that. When you wish to get up, count backwards from four to one. You should then feel fine and refreshed, wide awake and calm.

Source: Relaxation instructions reprinted from Wolpe and Lazarus *Behavior Therapy Techniques* (1966), pp. 177–180. By permission of Pergamon Press Ltd.

desensitization: a technique for reducing anxiety by systematically pairing relaxation with the anxiety-arousing situation.

Desensitization is a method for reducing anxiety which involves training the individual to relax in the presence of a situation that previously aroused anxiety. The individual first learns to relax in a rather benign situation and is then gradually led through a series of anxiety-arousing stimuli that are increasingly intense for that individual. Finally, the person is able to relax in the situation that previously was the most anxiety arousing.

Investigators have found that anxiety associated with taking tests can be diminished through relaxation training and concentrating on the test rather than on

BOX 5.5: MATHEMATICS ANXIETY

For many students, courses involving mathematics and numerical concepts evoke high levels of anxiety. One investigator selected those students who scored high on a mathematics anxiety questionnarie and gave them a "treatment" consisting of a short-term course in which they learned to relax in the imagined presence of situations that aroused progressively greater degrees of anxiety (Suinn, 1970). For example, a tape recording described a situation that presumably elicited a relatively low level of anxiety ("consider two different summer job offers"). This was followed by a description of a neutral situation, one that should have aroused no anxiety. The students were then trained in relaxation techniques. The first scene was presented again, and the students were told to relax. This general sequence was repeated for scenes that became increasingly anxiety producing. By the time the subjects arrived at the most anxiety-arousing scene ("imagine you are taking a final examination in mathematics"), they are expected to show considerable skill at relaxing in the presence of anxiety-producing stimuli.

The basic assumption underlying the use of "relaxation" techniques is that relaxation is incompatible with anxiety. If people can learn to relax in anxiety-arousing situations, they can gain a measure of control over their anxiety. In doing so, they can reduce the debilitating effects of anxiety on learning and performance. The results of this study support both expectations. The subjects who received relaxation therapy obtained sharply reduced scores when retested on the mathematics anxiety questionnarie, and their performance on a test of mathematical ability improved markedly. Indeed, their performance on the mathematics test was superior to that of nonanxious control subjects. Some of the tape-recorded materials used in the first therapy session are described below.

SESSION 1

Scene 1

Now as you are relaxing like that, I want you to picture a scene. I want you to picture a scene in which you have two different offers for summer jobs. One will pay you a pretty good salary, while the other one pays a lower salary but includes a room and board and travel expenses. Just picture yourself sitting down in a comfortable, relaxed manner. You are beginning to figure out which of the jobs is the most lucrative. As you work out the problem, you remain relaxed and at ease. Just picture that scene.

Neutral Scene

Now let that scene go. Just let it dissolve away and picture another scene this time. Picture a peaceful scene. Just imagine that on a calm summer's day you lie on your back on a soft lawn and watch the clouds move slowly overhead. Just picture yourself on a lawn or meadow looking up at a blue sky and watching the clouds move slowly overhead. Notice especially the brilliant edges of the clouds as they slowly pass.

Relaxation

Now let that scene dissolve away. Just let it completely dissolve away and go back to relaxing. Just concentrate on letting your whole body relax more and more and deeper and deeper. Relax your forehead and your jaws. Relax your neck, shoulders, your chest and back, relax your stomach. Relax your hips and thighs, your knees, calves. Relax your ankles and feet. Relax your arms, your forearms. Relax your hands and fingers. Just let your whole body relax more and more. Get rid of any tension you might have in your body. Just let the relaxation take over.

Scene 1

Now once again as you are relaxing, I want you to picture a scene in which you have two different offers for summer jobs and one of them will pay you a pretty high salary while the other one pays room and board, travel expenses, but a lower salary. Now just picture yourself sitting down in a comfortable, relaxed manner and beginning to figure out which of the jobs is the most lucrative, and as you work on the problem, you remain relaxed and at ease.

Source: Haber/Runyon. *Fundamentals of Psychology,* © 1983. Addison-Wesley, Reading, MA. p. 352. Reprinted with permission.

one's feelings. Box 5.5 describes a technique that has been successfully used with students for whom the study of mathematics is fraught with anxiety. In general, when anxiety is associated with a specific identifiable stimulus situation, we can usually control these negative feelings through the use of desensitization techniques. When attempting to control specific anxiety, it is best to avoid thinking about your inner feelings. Rather, force yourself to concentrate on the specific event that precipitated the feelings of anxiety. By so doing, you may find yourself better able to function and will, perhaps, reduce the underlying anxiety. One of the major causes of anxiety is uncertainty. By ignoring the interfering negative feelings and concentrating only on the situation at hand, you may be able to reduce the uncertainty inherent in the situation and, thus, reduce the resulting anxiety.

Depression

Most of us have experienced feelings of depression, at least in a moderate form (see Box 5.6). Do you recall times when you felt discouraged and downhearted? Perhaps you felt nothing is going right and there was little hope for the future. You may have had thoughts like "I'll never make it" or "It's hopeless." Depressed feelings such as these are fairly common, particularly following a specific event such as a disappointment or a loss. Usually, these depressions do not persist for very long. However, sometimes depressions can last for years and involve more serious symptoms. It has been estimated that approximately 15 percent of American adults will suffer a major depression at some time in their lives, and that serious depression is about twice as common in women as men (American Psychiatric Association, 1980).

BOX 5.6 DEPRESSION

Feeling blue or depressed is a fairly common experience, especially among college students. It is estimated that, at any given time, approximately one fourth of the American college population is suffering some of the symptoms of depression. Moreover, roughly three quarters of all college students feel depressed at some time during the school year (Beck & Young, 1978). Some of the most common factors that trigger depressive feelings are:

1. Separation from family or friends if the student is away from home. A student may feel isolated or alone if cut off from his or her support group.
2. Academic pressures may be more than anticipated. Many students lack the basic skills that are necessary for academic success.
3. Internal or external pressures to make a career choice. Many students feel depressed as the college years pass and they still can't decide what they will do when they graduate.
4. Some students feel that they are not living up to expectations either academically or socially. They may feel like failures or that they are wasting both time and money. Often these students are performing satisfactorily but feel depressed because they set higher standards than they are able to meet.
5. Sometimes a breakup of an intimate relationship will precipitate a depression.

BOX 5.6 *(concluded)*

SYMPTOMS OF DEPRESSION

You usually know when you are feeling blue. However, if the following conditions exist, you can assume more than a minor mood change is involved.

1. You feel overwhelmed by demands and responsibilities.
2. You have a low opinion of yourself.
3. You blame and criticize yourself frequently.
4. Your future looks dismal and hopeless.
5. You find yourself upset over events that normally wouldn't bother you.

COPING WITH DEPRESSION

Once you start to have thoughts such as those listed above, you begin to feel even more worthless and helpless. A vicious cycle can begin making you even more depressed. One recommendation is to write down negative or self-critical thoughts as you have them, especially if they are followed by feelings of sadness (Beck & Greenberg, 1974). Once you have compiled these thoughts, try to write a rational response to each one. For instance, if you think, "I am no good at anything," list all the things you do well.

The following table lists a number of self-defeating thoughts or attitudes with a corresponding adjustive alternative.

Self-Defeating Thought	*Adjustive Outlook*
I can't do anything about it.	Maybe I can't think of something now, but if I try I may be able to come up with something.
I don't have the ability to do the job.	Maybe I need more training
This is the worst thing that ever happened.	That was certainly a bad experience. But life must go on.
I don't know anything about computers. I can't even try for the job.	There are books I can read and courses I can take.
It was all my fault.	I was to blame, but so were the other people.
I'm really a terrible person.	Nobody's perfect. I have strengths as well as weaknesses. Everybody does.
I never do anything right.	I may have messed this up, but there are other things I do well. I'll try harder next time.
It's hopeless.	If I ask someone, I may be able to find another way. Maybe if I tackle it a little bit at a time.

Make a daily schedule for yourself, making sure to occupy yourself every hour during the day (Beck & Greenberg, 1974). Start with relatively easy tasks and work your way up to more difficult ones. As you complete each activity, check or cross it off. A number of small successes can go a long way toward breaking the cycle of hopelessness and falling even further behind. Students who are depressed generally spend much time avoiding their assignments, often by sleeping. They fall behind in their work, which only makes them more depressed.

If you are lacking some of the skills necessary for success, don't hesitate to ask for help.

Try to get feedback from other people. When you are depressed it is usually difficult to have an objective perspective about yourself or your problems. Sometimes a friend or a counselor can help you view your situation more realistically and help you break the self-defeating cycle of feeling helpless and depressed.

Often people in nursing homes feel depressed because they believe they have lost control over their lives. Programs that provide opportunities for these people to make their own decisions give a great lift to their morale. At the Toms River Convalescent Center, a representative group of residents meet to plan their monthly recreational activities—shopping trips, concerts, museum visits, or just sightseeing tours via the center's privately owned, specially designed Winnebago recreational vehicle.

Phyllis Luber

The milder forms of depression are usually triggered by a specific environmental event. In the case of severe depression, a number of studies have found an extremely high incidence of stressful life events (e.g., failure to meet perceived male or female role demands; changes in marital relationship; a move, often involving changes in work) that may have precipitated the depressive episode (Leff, Roatch, & Bunney, 1970).

Most people experience losses, failures, or disappointments at some time in their lives. But only some people become severely depressed. How can we explain this difference? There is a growing body of evidence that suggests that various life experiences may interact with biological factors to produce the depressive reaction.

Some researchers have proposed that depression is associated with low levels of certain neurotransmitters, e.g., norepinephrine. Indeed, certain drugs that combat depression appear to act by increasing the norepinephrine levels in the brain. Based on experiments with rats, one investigator suggests that prolonged stress where the individual has no control may lead to deficiencies in norepinephrine

(Ellison, 1977). Rats subjected to prolonged shock who were unable to do anything about it developed low levels of norepinephrine, whereas rats who could control the shock did not (Weiss, Glazer, & Pohorecky, 1974). In an extensive review of the evidence relating biochemical factors to major depression, the reviewers suggest that life stressors may cause long-term biochemical changes in the brain, and these changes may be implicated in the onset and maintenance of depression (Barchas, Akil, Elliott, Holman, & Watson, 1978).

Social-learning theorists focus on the importance of prior learning experiences and stress the relationship between reinforcement and depression. We all depend on other people for reinforcement. Depression results when we lose people close to us, resulting in a loss of an important source of reinforcement (Ferster, 1973). According to social-learning theorists, we lose interest and slow down when someone close to us dies or leaves. This may start a vicious cycle—when we lose interest, we are less likely to do things that would lead to social reinforcement or approval from others. Not having the proper skills can also lead to depression because the unskilled person will usually not be reinforced as often as the skilled individual (Lewinsohn, 1975). Moreover, depressive behavior is sometimes maintained because it is reinforced by sympathetic friends and relatives. Indeed, for the depressed person to become motivated to cope with depressive feelings, the sympathy must sometimes stop.

Depression is often associated with feelings of low self-esteem. When people feel negative about themselves and the world, they often feel guilty and blame themselves when confronted with failure or disappointment. They may feel worthless and helpless and be unable to act effectively. One theorist (Seligman, 1975) has suggested that people become depressed when they feel that their actions are ineffective and have little to do with the outcome of a situation. He calls this phenomenon **learned helplessness**—the belief that one's actions bear no relation to rewards and punishments received.

learned helplessness: the belief that one's actions are ineffective and have little to do with the outcome.

Seligman feels that early childhood experiences are critical. When children are rewarded or punished indiscriminately and inconsistently, they begin to feel that there is no relationship between their actions and the final outcome. Children must learn that they have control over their environment and that positive and negative reinforcements *are* contingent upon their actions. Seligman believes that when individuals feel they lack control over their lives, they give up trying. This feeling of ineffectiveness leads to passivity and then depression. The depressed individuals are caught in a vicious cycle. They experience a few failures which lead to the belief that they can't do anything about their situation—they expect to fail. Expecting the worst, they stop trying because they believe that continued effort is futile. Since they don't try, they do in fact, fail, which only serves to confirm their expectations.

Some investigators believe that the phenomenon of learned helplessness can be used to explain the high incidence of depression in women. Since women have traditionally been trained from early childhood to be helpless and dependent on others, they are more likely to feel ineffective and, thus, depressed. Consider the following example.

Ms. T is a 39-year-old homemaker with three children, ages 9, 11, and 14. Her husband is the sales manager for an auto agency. Although the family does well financially and has a comfortable lifestyle, Mr. T began to notice that his wife was becoming more and more depressed. She reiterated constantly that she lacked any goals in life. Mr. T would try to reassure her, pointing out that they had a nice home and that she had no reason to be unhappy. He suggested that she find some hobbies or socialize more with neighbors. But Ms. T became progressively more absorbed in brooding over her belief that she had no goals in life.

After a while, she no longer bothered to keep the house clean, cook, or take care of the children. At first, Mr. T had thought she was merely in a "bad mood" and that it would pass, but now he was worried. Mr. T was quite puzzled about her behavior and could not imagine why she felt this way. He decided to have a long talk with her. Ms. T told him she no longer had any motivation; simple household chores took too much energy. While believing that she loved him and the children, Ms. T indicated that she had lost strong feelings for anything. She did display some guilt about her inability to take care of the children and to be a wife, but everything was simply too depressing. Life was no longer important, and she just wanted to be left alone. She began to cry, uncontrollably. Nothing Mr. T said could bring her out of the depression or stop her from crying. He felt it was imperative that she see a physician and made an appointment forthwith.

The next day, Mr. T decided to work only till noon, so that he could spend the rest of the day with his wife. On arriving home, Mr. T found his wife nearly unconscious; she had taken sleeping pills in an apparent suicide attempt. She was taken to the hospital. Ms. T is currently receiving medication and psychotherapy to treat her depression.[4]

Ms. T's life is an example of the close connection between depression and suicide. Depression is the major predisposing factor for suicide throughout the industrialized world (Guze, 1981). As two investigators observed, "a depressed person is emotionally incapable of perceiving realistic alternative solutions to a difficult problem. His thinking process is often limited to the point where he can see no other way out of a bad situation other than that of suicide" (Farberow & Litman, 1970, p. 85).

Who commits suicide? Sometimes it's difficult to know for sure. Statistics on suicide are often unreliable because it is difficult to know for sure how many officially recorded accidental deaths were actually completed suicides. The peak age for suicide attempts is between 24 and 44, but the majority of people who kill themselves are between 55 and 65 years of age. More men than women commit suicide, but women make more attempts than men. About 10,000 college students attempt suicide each year, and about 1,000 of them succeed (see Box. 5.7).

Although there is no doubt that depression plays a major role in suicide, not

---

[4] Sue, Sue and Sue, *Understanding Abnormal Behavior*, pp. 238–240. Copyright © 1981, Houghton Mifflin Company, used by permission.

BOX 5.7: WARNING SIGNS FOR STUDENT SUICIDE

A change in a student's mood and behavior is a significant warning of possible suicide. Characteristically, the student becomes depressed and withdrawn, undergoes a marked decline in self-esteem, and shows deterioration in habits of personal hygiene. This is accompanied by a profound loss of interest in studies. Often he or she stops attending classes and stays at home most of the day. Usually the student's distress is communicated to at least one other person, often in the form of a veiled suicide warning. A significant number of students who attempt suicide leave suicide notes.

When college students attempt suicide, one of the first explanations to occur to those around them is that they may have been doing poorly in school. As a group, however, they are superior students, and while they tend to expect a great deal of themselves in terms of academic achievement and to exhibit scholastic anxieties, grades, academic competition, and pressure over examinations are not regarded as significant precipitating stresses. Also, while many lose interest in their studies prior to the onset of suicidal behavior and their grades get lower, the loss of interest appears to be associated with depression and withdrawal caused by other problems. Moreover, when academic failure does appear to trigger suicidal behavior—in a minority of cases—the actual cause of the behavior is generally considered to be loss of self-esteem and failure to live up to parental expectations, rather than the academic failure itself.

For most suicidal students, both male and female, the major precipitating stressor appears to be either the failure to establish, or the the loss of, a close interpersonal relationship. Often the breakup of a romance is the key precipitating factor. It has also been noted that there are significantly more suicide attempts and suicides by students from families where there has been separation, divorce, or the death of a parent. A particularly important precipitating factor among college males appears to be the existence of a close emotional involvement with a parent that is threatened when the student becomes involved with another person in college and tries to break this "parental knot."

Although most colleges and universities have mental health facilities to assist distressed students, few suicidal students seek professional help. Thus, it is of vital importance for those around a suicidal student to notice the warning signs and try to obtain assistance.

Source: From *Abnormal Psychology and Modern Life,* 6th edition by James C. Coleman, James N. Butcher, and Robert C. Carson. Copyright © 1980 Scott, Foresman and Company. Reprinted by permission.

---

everyone who commits suicide is depressed. In fact, severely depressed patients rarely commit suicide (Mendels, 1970). They are usually so listless that they simply do not have the energy to commit a suicide act. Severely depressed individuals are more likely to commit suicide right after they come out of depression—when their spirits begin to rise. Although not all suicides are preventable, greater awareness of this problem could make a difference.

What is the best way to treat depression? Mild forms of depression, which most people experience, require no treatment. Even though the depressed individual feels desperate about his or her current circumstances, depressive episodes are generally self-limiting, and the condition will probably taper off in time. However, there are certain strategies that can be employed to help lift a person out of his or her depressive state.

Try this simple experiment. Look in a mirror and set your face into an expression of sadness. Do you feel a little bit sad? Now change your expression into one of joy. Did your mood change? It has been suggested that we can change our feelings by purposely changing our behavior (James, 1884). In James' own words, "If we wish to conquer undesirable emotional tendencies in ourselves, we must assiduously, and in the first instance cold bloodedly, go through the *outward motions* of those contrary dispositions we prefer to cultivate."

James' advice does not always work. Sometimes, restraining or disguising our true feelings can have harmful effects. For example, the individual who suppresses grief after the death of a loved one may suffer a lot internally. However, studies have shown that consciously maintaining a false front can often lead to the desired effect (e.g., Lanzetta, Cartwright-Smith, & Kleck, 1976). Thus, consciously changing our behavior *can* result in a change in our feelings.

Severe or prolonged depression is usually amenable to psychotherapy or behavior therapy. In some cases, chemotherapy or electroshock treatments have proved effective in dealing with severe depression. Moreover, as the following example demonstrates, the social environment can have a powerful impact on depressed behavior.

> The patient, a 37-year-old housewife, was severely depressed and had been since the death of her mother. She complained about somatic symptoms, paced, withdrew, and frequently cried. Members of her family responded to these depressed behaviors with helpfulness, sympathy, and concern.
>
> The therapist began rating two classes of behavior for the patient, *coping behavior*, such as cooking, cleaning the house, and tending to her children's needs, and *depressive behavior*, which included crying and complaining. The therapist then joined the patient's entire family and instructed the husband and children to pay instant and frequent attention to her coping behavior and to ignore her depressed behavior. The therapist taught family members to acknowledge her positive actions with approval, interest, and encouragement and to shift their attention from the "sick woman" to the homemaker and mother.
>
> Figure 5.2 shows the effect of the treatment. The first seven days of treatment were used to obtain pretreatment baselines for both depressive and coping behavior. You can see that the daily rates of coping behavior in the first week are very low and the rates of depressive behavior are very high. At the end of the first week, the family was instructed to change their response to the mother's behavior. Dramatic increases in coping behavior occurred for the next week.
>
> Recall for a moment that we have said that depressed episodes are frequently self-limiting. How then are we to know whether the change in the behavior of the family is producing the behavior change in the mother or not? The answer is that the researcher conducted a *clinical experiment* to demonstrate the causal link between her behavior and the responses generated in her family. On the 14th day, the therapist instructed the family to return to their previous behavior. That is, they were again to provide attention and concern for her complaints. Within three days, the investigators note, she was once again showing high levels of depression. The effect can be seen in the "reversal days" of Figure 5.2. After the 18th day, the treatment was reinstituted and dramatic improvement again occurred in the behavior of the patient. (Liberman & Raskin, 1971)

FIGURE 5.2 MODIFICATION OF DEPRESSIVE BEHAVIOR USING REINFORCEMENT AND EXTINCTION TECHNIQUES TAUGHT TO FAMILY MEMBERS

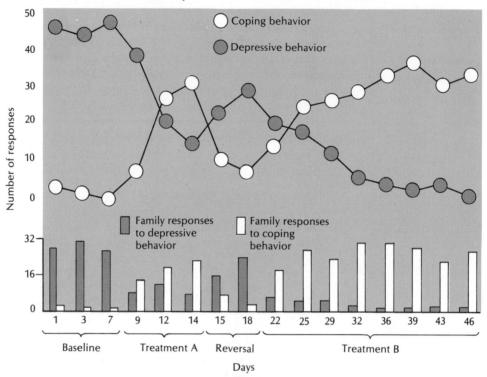

Source: R. P. Liberman and D. E. Raskin, "Depression: A Behavioral Formulation," *Archives of General Psychiatry* 24 (1971), pp. 515–23. Copyright 1971, American Medical Association.

Love

What is love? Although one of the most powerful of human emotions, psychology has had relatively little to say about it until recent years. There were, of course, many words about sexuality by Freud and efforts by some of the neo-Freudians to define the elusive emotional and motivational state called love. But by and large, we have left it to the poets to weave their words about love into the fabric of our everyday lives. Who has not heard such expressions as, "Love makes the world go round" or "Love is a many splendored thing"? However, if we turn to the poets, we find that love is a confusing array of flowers, vegetables, humors, illnesses, and what have you. As a sample, love is: a perpetual anaesthesia, a wild plant, a devotion that never dies, a flame, a kiss, a mood, a proud and gentle thing, a sickness. Moreover, it is: like a flower, full of showers, like a dizziness, like a landscape, like a red red rose, like the measles, and it is the lord and slave of all.

It is clear that, in the eyes of the poets, love is many different things. However, when a sociologist by the name of John Lee asked Americans, Canadians, and Britons the meaning of the words "I love you," he also uncovered a variety of different notions (Lee, 1974). After classifying and categorizing the answers, he arrived at six different definitions:

Eros: A strong and immediate attraction to beautiful people. Erotic lovers are attracted to their beloved by their hair, skin, muscles, body proportions, fragrance, and so forth. Such love does not usually survive the fading of the initial bloom.

Mania: An obsessive type of love in which the lover alternates between peaks of rapture, when his or her love seems to be present. This is the love most often portrayed in literature—an anguishing, tormenting, jealous type of love that rarely provides lasting satisfaction and often ends in tragedy.

Ludus: A love characterized by playfulness. It is a game to be played, involving both challenges and strategies. However, we must not become too attached to our partners or make any long-range plans.

Storge (pronounced *stor-gay*): A quiet type of love, without fever or tumult. An affection for the other person as a friend. This type of love is often referred to as companionate love.

Agape (pronounced *ah-ga-pay*): A patient, kind, unselfish, and undemanding type of love, shared by all the great religions. Of this type of love, Lee notes:

> I found no saints in my sample. I have yet to interview an unqualified example of agape, although a few respondents had brief agapic episodes in relationships that were otherwise tinged with selfishness. For instance, one of my subjects, seeing that his lover was torn between choosing him or another man, resolved to save her the pain of deciding; he bowed out gracefully. His action fell short of pure agape, however, because he continued to be interested in how well his beloved was doing, and was purely and selfishly delighted when she dropped the other man and returned to him.[5]

Pragma: This is a practical type of love in which the individual tries to find the right match in terms of personality, background, education, religious views, and interests. Emphasis is placed on making a sensible choice. Having made the choice, deeper feelings frequently develop.

Lee also describes three other types of love which are various combinations of the six basic types shown above. He states that, to find a mutually satisfying partner, we should search out one who shares the same definition of love. The further apart they are, the less likely are they to share a common language of and about love. Box 5.8 provides a test developed by Lee as a means of diagnosing your style of love.

A psychologist by the name of Zick Rubin has spent considerable time and

---

[5] Reprinted from *Psychology Today* magazine. Copyright © 1974 American Psychological Association.

BOX 5.8: GRAPH YOUR OWN STYLE OF LOVING

Consider each characteristic as it applies to a current relationship that you define as love, or to a previous one if that is more applicable. For each, note whether the trait is *almost always true* (AA), *usually true* (U), *rarely true*, (R), or *almost never true* (AN).

		Eros	Ludus	Storge	Mania	Pragma
1	You consider your childhood less happy than the average of peers.	R		AN	U	
2	You were discontent with life (work, etc.) at time your encounter began.	R		AN	U	
3	You have never been in love before this relationship.					R
4	You want to be in love or have love as security.	R	AN		AA	U
5	You have a clearly defined ideal image of your desired partner.	AA	AN	AN	AN	AA
6	You felt a strong gut attraction to your beloved on the first encounter.	AA	R	AN	R	
7	You are preoccupied with thoughts about the beloved.	AA	AN	AN	AA	
8	You believe your partner's interest is at least as great as yours.	U	U	R	AN	U
9	You are eager to see your beloved almost every day; this was true from the beginning.	AA	AN	R	AA	R

		Eros	Ludus	Storge	Mania	Pragma
19	You try to force beloved to show more feeling, commitment.	AN	AN		AA	
20	You analyze the relationship, weight it in your mind.			AN	U	AA
21	You believe in the sincerity of your partner.	AA			U	
22	You blame partner for difficulties of your relationship.	R	U	R	U	
23	You are jealous and possessive to the point of angry conflict.	U	AN	R		
24	You are jealous to the point of conflict, scenes, threats, etc.	AN	AN	AN	AA	AN
25	Tactile, sensual contact is very important to you.	AA		AN		R
26	Sexual intimacy was achieved early, rapidly in the relationship.	AA		AN	AN	
27	You take the quality of sexual rapport as a test of love.	AA	U	AN		R
28	You are willing to work out sex problems, improve technique.	U	R		R	U

#						
10	You soon believed this could become a permanent relationship.	AA	AN	R	U	U
11	You see "warning signs" of trouble but ignore them.	R	R	AA	R	
12	You deliberately restrain frequency of contact with partner.	AN	AA	R	AA	
13	You restrict discussion of your feelings with beloved.	R	AA	U	U	
14	You restrict display of your feelings with beloved.	R	AA	R	U	
15	You discuss future plans with beloved.	AA	R	R	AA	
16	You discuss wide range of topics, experiences with partner.	AA	R	AA		
17	You try to control relationship, but feel you've lost control.	AN	AN	AN	AA	
18	You lose ability to be first to terminate relationship.	AN	AN	AA	R	
29	You have a continued high rate of sex tactile contact throughout the relationship.	U			R	R
30	You declare your love first, well ahead of partner.	AN	AN	R	AA	
31	You consider life your most important activity, even essential.	AA	AN	R	AA	R
32	You are prepared to "give all" for love once under way.	U	U	AN	U	AA	R
33	You are willing to suffer abuse, even ridicule from partner.	AN	R	AA	AN	
34	Your relationship is marked by frequent differences of opinion, anxiety.	R	AA	R	AA	R
35	The relationship ends with lasting bitterness, trauma for you.	AN	R	R	AA	R

To diagnose your style of love, look for patterns across characteristics. If you consider your childhood less happy than that of your friends, were discontent with life when you fell in love, and very much want to be in love, you have "symptoms" that are rarely typical of eros and almost never true of storge, but which do suggest mania. Where a trait did not especially apply to a type of love, the space in that column is blank. Storge, for instance, is not the *presence* of many symptoms of love, but precisely their absence. It is cool, abiding affection rather than *Sturm und Drang.*

Source: Reprinted from *Psychology Today* magazine. Copyright © 1974, American Psychological Association.

effort distinguishing between romantic love and liking. He developed two scales of 13 items each to help differentiate these two different feelings about a partner, date, spouse, relative, or friend. Figure 5.3 shows three items from each scale. Complete this scale, if you wish, choosing a number from 1 (disagree completely) through 9 (agree completely) that represents your feelings about the person you are rating. Your score on each scale is the sum of the values you assigned to the items on the scale. Keep in mind, however, that this is only a small part of the total scale. For this reason, the results must be regarded as incomplete and inconclusive. Nevertheless, it should give you some idea about how the distinction between romantic love and liking is made.

For all its simplicity, the full scales have been found to be useful in distinguishing romantic love from liking. To illustrate, without their knowing it, Rubin observed the amount of eye contact between couples while they sat in the room waiting for the study to begin. He found that couples scoring high on the love scale spend more time looking deeply into one another's eyes than those scoring lower on the scale.

But how does a person go about finding someone to love? In their excellent book *A New Look at Love,* Elaine and G. William Walster (1978) list the following practical suggestions:

1. Make sure you're surrounded by people. Invite acquaintances to dinner, a movie, or a party. Assume you must ask first.

FIGURE 5.3

Romantic Love Scale

1. I feel that I can confide in _____ about virtually everything.

```
/       /       /       /       /       /       /       /       /
1       2       3       4       5       6       7       8       9
```

2. I would do almost anything for _____.

```
/       /       /       /       /       /       /       /       /
1       2       3       4       5       6       7       8       9
```

3. If I could never be with _____, I would be miserable.

```
/       /       /       /       /       /       /       /       /
1       2       3       4       5       6       7       8       9
```

Liking Scale

1. I think that _____ is unusually well adjusted.

```
/       /       /       /       /       /       /       /       /
1       2       3       4       5       6       7       8       9
```

2. I have great confidence in _____'s good judgment.

```
/       /       /       /       /       /       /       /       /
1       2       3       4       5       6       7       8       9
```

3. _____ is one of the most likable people I know.

```
/       /       /       /       /       /       /       /       /
1       2       3       4       5       6       7       8       9
```

2. Be extra friendly to people in your neighborhood, school, and at work. They are most likely to become—or introduce you to—compatible mates.
3. Get deeply involved in something, an activity you genuinely like. If you feel you are not deeply interested in anything, you have identified a problem. People without strong interests are not themselves very interesting.
4. Sheer exposure can frequently work to your advantage. Repeated exposure to anything or anyone tends to produce positive feelings toward that thing or person (p. 29).

SUMMARY

In this chapter we looked at emotions, a constant companion to our every thought and action.

- The emotions add spice to life; they stir up the body; their expression serves to communicate with other people; and they motivate and direct our behavior toward certain goals and away from others.

- Emotions are not directly observed but inferred on the basis of a number of different lines of evidence.

- Factors associated with emotion include bodily reactions, situational factors, cognitions, feelings, and behavior. What's in our head is often an important determinant of how we respond emotionally to situations. If we believe something is true, we will respond accordingly, even if the objective facts indicate otherwise. Moreover, changing our perceptions and/or interpretations of events may alter the nature and intensity of our emotional responses.

- The theories of emotion differ in terms of the causes and the sequence of events. The James-Lange theory maintains that emotions follow changes in bodily states. According to the Cannon-Bard theory, the physiological state and the emotional experience are triggered simultaneously. Schacter and Singer propose that emotion is explained by the combination of physiological arousal and the cognitive interpretation of the emotion-arousing situation.

- Learning to label emotions is not as simple as it might seem at first blush. It is relatively easy to learn the labels for publicly observable things. However, emotions are private. Children are dependent on others to provide labels for their emotions. Incorrect labeling by an adult may lead to confused labeling by the child.

- Confusion concerning the identification of our emotional states violates an important principle of effective adjustment, i.e., know thyself. Many relationships hinge on our ability to distinguish one emotion from another and to express whichever is appropriate to the situation.

- Emotions are rarely expressed in pure form. Sometimes conflicting emotions become conditioned to one another. The result is feelings of ambivalence.

- Nonverbal cues or body language are often important in judging the emotions of others, particularly when people are unwilling or unable to reveal their emotions directly.

- Facial expressions provide universal clues to certain underlying emotional states—anger, disgust, happiness, fear, sadness, and surprise.

- Emotions vary in kind and intensity. The feelings and behavior associated with different intensities can be extremely variable. Mild negative emotional states may even be desired by many people. However, strong negative emotions cause "emergency reactions" in our bodies and are usually experienced as unpleasant.

- Anger may arise from a variety of circumstances—frustration, physical pain, insults, and threats. We should not bury our anger in denial and hackneyed words. When anger is thrust into unconsciousness, we eventually lose control over it. Anger is an emotion, aggression is behavior. Our internal communications can sometimes intensify negative feelings and lead to aggressive behavior. We can use assertive behavior instead of aggression to stand up for our rights.

- Whereas fear is a reaction to a specific real danger, anxiety usually does not have a specific or identifiable cause. However, anxiety may be a realistic and normal reaction to a specific situation. Anxiety may be general, in which case its victim tends to worry about many things indiscriminately. Anxiety may also be specific, in which case it is elicited by a narrow range of circumstances, e.g., test anxiety. Relaxation and desentsitization techniques may frequently succeed as a means of reducing specific anxiety. Drugs may, at best, provide only temporary relief.

- Depression is accompanied by feelings of discouragement, hopelessness, and low self-esteem. When people have little control over the outcome of a situation, they often develop attitudes of learned helplessness in which they believe their actions bear no relation to rewards and punishment. Depression is a major predisposing factor in suicide. Mild depression, however, is common and usually self-limiting.

- Efforts to give coherent meaning to love have resulted in the observation that many different definitions are used by people when they say "I am in love." When the definitions are classified, they yield six basic definitions: eros, mania, ludus, storge, agape, and pragma. It has been suggested that we should seek out as partners, individuals whose definition of love is similar to our own. The following practical suggestions have been made in relation to finding someone to love: surround yourself with people; be extra friendly to people in your neighborhood, school, and at work; get deeply involved in some activity you enjoy; and increase the amount of exposure to those who interest you.

TERMS TO REMEMBER

Emotion

Cognitions

Epinephrine

Neurotransmitter

Norepinephrine

Central nervous system

Placebo

Frustration

Aggression

Internal communications

Assertive behavior

Anxiety

Free-floating anxiety

Progressive relaxation

Desensitization

Learned helplessness

C H A P T E R 6

STRESS AND STRAIN

I Shoulduv Stayed in Bed

"This is one of those days I shoulduv stayed in bed," moaned Al as he kicked off his shoes, stretched his legs out on the hassock, and drained the last of his Oly Gold. "I tell you Mildred, any more days like today and we're flat broke." He mused for a moment on the implications of being unemployed and completely out of funds. Finding this train of thought disturbing, he flicked it off as easily as he then flicked the TV set on. "What's this?" he shouted angrily, "Only April and already everything is reruns."

He got up and paced the floor nervously, turning his back on the flickering television set. As little as he liked the prospects of playing a rerun of his day's activities, they still beat the usual TV fare by a mile. "Some day I'm gonna write a book about my life," he thought. "Probably make a million. Leastways, I can't make less than I am as a builder."

The word "builder" triggered a short burst of annoyance. "Builder, hell, I'm a messenger boy for the Department of Building Inspections. You put in a few wires and you call for an electrical inspection. No more wiring until it's been inspected. No matter that I got five people on payroll doin' nothing but collecting pay. I called in two inspections yesterday. Two! And in plenty of time. Who shows up? My workers. That's who. Sittin' on their butts half the day while I keep calling the Building Department." He felt his annoyance being transformed into a seething anger. "And what do they do when they come? They redline me for a violation that coulduv been corrected in a minute or two. But no. I gotta fix it and then call in another inspection. A whole day, maybe two, lost because of bureaucratic red tape. They're tryin' to strangle me, that's what they doin'. Strangle me in red tape."

He was now pacing furiously about the living room. When Mildred suggested that he put his excessive energy to use by taking out the garbage, he blew his stack. "All day long I'm taking orders, and I'm the boss." He let out a string of choice four letter words. "And now I gotta take out the garbage. Well, Mildred, you can take the garbage and stuff it. In fact, they can take the whole building industry and stuff it." He threw open the rear door and paced onto the patio.

"I gotta stop thinking about the job," he told himself. "When I started in business for myself, I promised that I would never take my work home with me. So calm down, Al. Think of something pleasant that happened to you today."

"Well, damn it, nothing good happened except that I'm still alive. I'm not even sure that's good." He recalled the appointment he had had with a local businesswoman. She wanted to put up an office complex way out in the boondocks.

But she never showed up. Left him standing there for two, maybe three hours. "Of course, I got nothing better to do with my time." He swore again, and then entered the fantasy world for a few moments. He had a vision of this woman putting up the office complex, using another builder.

149

And then, two or three months later, the building collapses. In the follow-up investigation, he is called as an expert witness. "As I see it," he reports, "shoddy construction techniques were used. There were shortcuts—dangerous violations of the building code to save a few bucks. They should never have been passed by the building inspectors. If you ask my opinion, somebody was on the take." In his mind's eye, he observed the businesswoman quake and the building inspectors blanch under the force of his testimony. He found the fantasy incredibly satisfying. He sat down quietly on the lawn furniture and began elaborating on it.

In this brief slice from Al's life, we see that smooth sailing on uneventful seas is not an enduring characteristic of everyday existence. Stress is so much a part of our daily life that, rather than rail against it, we often pay it little attention. But then one stressful event begins to pile up on another and, before we know it, we are overwhelmed by the mental pain known as anxiety. Anxiety, when out of control, has a way of producing unexpected reversals in implementing our plans or continuing our goal-directed activities. All of us have unquestionably experienced days like Al's, days we should have stayed in bed. Perhaps we missed an important class or an examination which could not be made up, or maybe we put the foot to the pedal a bit too forcefully and wound up in traffic court. We may even have been forced to change vocational objectives because a single course, like chemistry, refused to capitulate to hours of intensive and largely unproductive study. And so it goes. Big and small frustrations, conflicts, and other stressful circumstances are mixed in with other ingredients in that stew we call life and are served up to us on an almost continuous basis. But few people complain about getting fat on these ingredients. And there are times when all of us wish we could go, at least temporarily, on a stress-free diet. In this chapter and the next, we examine the various sources of stress, bodily reactions to stress, and psychological means of coping with the circumstances that induce stress reactions.

STRESS AND STRAIN

stress: conflicts, pressures, and other external situations or circumstances that impinge upon the organism.

Al is experiencing difficulties in meeting his financial obligations; he is on a constant hustle to land new contracts; he is regularly faced with bureaucratic delays and consequent financial losses on jobs that are presently underway; people fail to show up for appointments, further aggravating his financial crisis. Most of us would agree that Al has been confronted with many stressful events.

But what is **stress?** Stress is conflict, internal and external pressure and other troublesome conditions in life. When stress is experienced, the person generally feels tense and jumpy. We use the term **strain** to refer to these bodily reactions to stress (Maddi, 1983). The heart seems to be pounding a mile a minute, there

strain: intense and sometimes harmful physical reactions to stress.

Which is more stressful for this bridal couple—hanging high above the street on the window washer's scaffolding where they met, or getting married?

United Press International Photo

is shortness of breath, a funny feeling in the stomach, and, occasionally, painful symptoms as in a headache.

Is strain always caused by some sort of calamity or disaster that engulfs the individual? In other words, is strain always caused by bad or undesirable things that happen to us? Surprisingly, it is not. Based on thousands of interviews of people from all walks of life, two psychiatrists devised a Social Readjustment Rating Scale (Holmes & Rahe, 1967). This scale deals with 43 different life events and shows the relative degree of stress associated with each. Examination of Table 6.1 shows that the five most stressful events are, indeed, personal disasters—death of a spouse, divorce, marital separation, jail term, and death of a close family member. However, marriage, retirement, and pregnancy are usually considered favorable and desirable events. Nevertheless, all rank fairly high as causes of personal strain.

Thus, it appears that *any* change in important aspects of our daily routines can be a source of strain. Recognizing this fact, many large corporations keep mental-health professionals on call to provide counseling for personnel who have recently received promotions. Quite often a depression, varying between mild and severe, sets in shortly after receiving such "good news."

Later in this chapter, we will look at various bodily reactions to stress and physical disorders that are, at least in part, stress related. Interestingly, several studies have found that people who experience numerous stressful events within a relatively short span of time run an increased risk of developing a physical illness (see, for example, Dohrenwend & Dohrenwend, 1974).

The adverse effects of strain also appear to be cumulative—the greater the number of life changes taking place within a given period of time, the greater are the adverse effects on a person's health and well-being. You can run a little test on yourself. Using Table 6.1, check your life changes that have occurred over the past year. Add up the total value of all the items you have checked. If your total score is between 0 and 150, your stress score is within the normal

TABLE 6.1	SOCIAL READJUSTMENT RATING SCALE	
Rank	Life Event	Mean Value
1	Death of spouse	100
2	Divorce	73
3	Marital separation	65
4	Jail term	63
5	Death of close family member	63
6	Personal injury or illness	53
7	Marriage	50
8	Fired at work	47
9	Marital reconciliation	45
10	Retirement	45
11	Change in health of family member	44
12	Pregnancy	40

TABLE 6.1 *(concluded)*	Rank	Life Event	Mean Value
	13	Sex difficulties	39
	14	Gain of new family member	39
	15	Business readjustment	39
	16	Change in financial state	38
	17	Death of close friend	37
	18	Change to different line of work	36
	19	Change in number of arguments with spouse	35
	20	Mortgage or loan over $10,000	31
	21	Foreclosure of mortgage or loan	30
	22	Change in responsibilities at work	29
	23	Son or daughter leaving home	29
	24	Trouble with in-laws	29
	25	Outstanding personal achievement	28
	26	Wife begins or stops work	26
	27	Begin or end school	26
	28	Change in living conditions	25
	29	Revision of personal habits	24
	30	Trouble with boss	23
	31	Change in work hours or conditions	20
	32	Change in residence	20
	33	Change in schools	20
	34	Change in recreation	19
	35	Change in church activities	19
	36	Change in social activities	18
	37	Mortgage or loan less than $10,000	17
	38	Change in sleeping habits	16
	39	Change in number of family get-togethers	15
	40	Change in eating habits	15
	41	Vacation	13
	42	Christmas	12
	43	Minor violations of the law	11

You can measure the amount of stress during a year by the total number of life change units. These units are obtained by adding the mean value associated with the events you have experienced during the year. For example, suppose the following events occurred during the past year: personal injury (53), change in health of family member (44), sex difficulties (39), change in financial state (38), and change in living conditions (25). Thus, your score is 199.

To interpret your score, compare the total to the following:

0 to 150:	No significant problems.
150 to 199:	Mild life crisis.
200 to 299:	Moderate life crisis.
300 and above:	Major life crisis.

This scale is a research rather than a diagnostic instrument. If you obtain a high score, you should not feel unduly alarmed. However, it might be beneficial to consider making some adjustments in your lifestyle.

Source: Reprinted with permission from *Journal of Psychosomatic Research*. T. H. Holmes and R. H. Rahe. The social readjustment rating scale. Copyright © 1967, Pergamon Press, Ltd.

range. Scores between 150 and 199 show mild stress; 200 to 299 suggests moderate stress; a score over 300 suggests a major life crisis. Too many significant changes are taking place within too short a period of time. Holmes and Rahe (1967) found that about 80 percent of individuals scoring over 300 within a one-year period also developed serious medical problems. In contrast, only about 30 percent of people scoring 150 and under presented similar physical complaints. Thus, stress does more than increase our psychological discomfort in the form of anxiety. As the TV commercial says, "It can also be dangerous to your health" (see Box 6.1).

BOX 6.1: "JOB BURNOUT": GROWING WORRY FOR WORKERS, BOSSES

AN INTERVIEW WITH PROFESSOR CARY CHERNISS

Q: Professor Cherniss, some people say they dread getting up in the morning and going to work because they're unhappy and frustrated in their jobs. Is that a widespread complaint?

A: Everyone has that feeling occasionally. When people experience it regularly, day in and day out, we call it "job burnout."

Q: What does that mean?

A: It refers to a situation where a person has been experiencing high levels of stress and hasn't been able to cope with it.

Such a person gets more and more discouraged, and finally just gives up and withdraws from things. So burnout is really a reaction to a stressful job.

Q: Can you describe the symptoms and give us an example of burnout?

A: Probably the most common one is exhaustion—emotional as well as physical. It's the feeling that one just can't go any further.

There are more subtle symptoms, too, such as cutting corners at work or losing one's idealism. The latter reaction shows up particularly among young professionals who are new to their jobs. I recall a young woman lawyer in her first year of practice, dealing with people at the poverty level.

She had been a student activist, was very idealistic, and felt that poverty law would be her life's work—an opportunity to do something constructive for the needy.

Within a few months, she had become ex-

tremely frustrated. She found that her clients would lie to her and were ungrateful for her efforts on their behalf. They considered her a part of the "system."

She was robbed at gunpoint a couple of times by clients. Her car was stolen. She got little support from her colleagues, all of whom were young and overworked.

She started using drugs heavily and put on a lot of weight. Her attitude changed dramatically. She considered going to work for the prosecutor's office, she said, so she could "put these people behind bars." Hers was a classic case of burnout.

Q: What kind of impact can burnout have on one's personal life—on family relationships and on health?

A: People who experience burnout tend to have a lot of health problems. The physical symptoms include headaches, problems with sleeping, gastrointestinal disturbances. Those are all reactions to stressful and frustrating work situations. People who are bored or frustrated at work show differences in blood chemistry. They tend to have more ulcers also.

We're just becoming aware, though, of the kind of spillover effect that burnout and dissatisfaction in work can have within the family. People who are burned out are more likely to have marital problems. And there is much more tension within the family from the stresses that they bring home from the job. . . .

BOX 6.1 *(concluded)*

Q: Do you believe there are specific on-the-job conditions that can lead to this type of problem?

A: One of the biggest factors is simply lack of control over one's work environment. Often we think of the assembly-line worker as epitomizing that situation. But it applies to people at higher levels, too.

   Administrators in public agencies, for instance, frequently feel that they must deal with so many constituencies, so many pressure groups, so many regulations that they have little control over their own organizations.

   And it's that lack of control—the sort of thing a teacher might feel in an inner-city classroom with 30 active kids—that is a major factor that can contribute to burnout. . . .

Q: How do you advise people who are experiencing job burnout? What is the solution?

A: While there are clearly things that individuals can do, I would emphasize the importance of personal control and effectiveness within the workplace. When a job is structured in a way that really limits the worker's self-control and his chances for experiencing a sense of success and competence, then that person is going to experience frustration and burnout.

   The emphasis really has to be on what employers can do to structure jobs and work settings to make them more meaningful to workers.

Q: Aren't there some lines of work where it would be almost impossible for an employer to make those kinds of changes?

A: Obviously there are limits on what can be done within the workplace. Needs for productivity and efficiency will limit what can be done. But in most work situations, some changes can be made to increase the extent to which workers can exercise control over their own jobs.

   Something as minor as having workers periodically fill out a survey in which they rate their supervisor's performance is an example.

   Not only does that sort of thing give workers a feeling that they are being consulted, but it also has been found that many supervisors respond positively to the feedback and do, in fact, change in ways that the workers find desirable. And when that happens, then the workers feel they have been given some control over their own work lives.

Source: Reprinted from *U.S. News & World Report,* February 18, 1980, pp. 71–72. Copyright © 1980, U.S. News & World Report, Inc.

A number of researchers have criticized the Social Readjustment Rating Scale as being too simplistic. They argue that prediction is too complex to be based solely upon 43 major life events. Lazarus, one critic, has developed a "hassle quotient" which he uses to demonstrate the effect of minor everyday irritations on physical and mental health (see Box 6.2).

One investigator (Selye, 1978) has challenged the notion that stress is always harmful. He believes that some stress—he calls it **eustress**—can actually be good. According to Selye, stress can facilitate functioning in certain areas. Whereas some people thrive on calmness and serenity, others require adventure and excitement in their lives. What is stressful to certain individuals may be exhilarating to others. If eustress is to be beneficial, we must recognize our own reactions to stress and modify our lifestyles accordingly.

eustress: according to Selye, "good" stress that is beneficial to the individual.

Recent research has turned to identifying resistance resources whereby persons can remain healthy despite encountering stressful circumstances. Investigators have identified a number of variables that appear to moderate the debilitating effects of stress on the individual. These variables include personality characteris-

BOX 6.2:   LITTLE HASSLES CAN BE DANGEROUS TO YOUR HEALTH

The impact of hassles on our physical and mental health depends to a great extent on their frequency, duration, and intensity. A person's response to a given hassle depends on a variety of other factors: personality, coping style, other resources, and how the rest of the day has gone. When someone is under pressure, petty problems that otherwise might be ignored—a broken shoelace, for example—can have a much greater effect than if they had occurred at less anxious times.

For that reason, the particular hassles cited by the people we surveyed are less important than their overall intensity and the individual reactions to them. And though our data do not yet allow us to say this, we suspect that some of the impact of hassles stems from their personal meaning and significance or from our ineptness in coping with certain interpersonal difficulties. As I pointed out in an interview with *Psychology Today* ("Positive Denial: The Case for Not Facing Reality," November 1979), "Psychological stress resides neither in the situation nor the person; it depends on a transaction between the two. It arises from how the person appraises an event and adapts to it."

The kind of hassles that affect a person's overall psychological economy have several possible sources. Major life events, in addition to their obvious or immediate impact, can create continuing hassles— a kind of "ripple effect." Divorce, for example, might force a man inexperienced at such tasks to make his own meals, do the laundry, or clean the house; it might force a woman to handle household finances or repair a leaky faucet for the first time.

Some hassles may recur because of a permanent but not always harmonious relationship in marriage or at work, such as sexual incompatibility with a spouse or personality conflict with a co-worker. Other hassles may occur not as a result of any major life change or permanent relationship, but from a momentary situation—an unexpected phone call, an uninvited guest, a flat tire.

While our data show a stronger correlation between hassles and health than between life events and health, we do not mean to deny the very real impact of major setbacks. Clearly, the death of a loved one or a divorce can cause great emotional pain, and when such events are compounded, they can increase a person's susceptibility to illness.

Indeed, our results reaffirm a relationship between such major events and illness a year or two later for some people. But as other researchers have found, the link between life events and illness is not invariable; most people who score in the highest ranks of life change do not suffer from a major illness in the following year or two.

Our results also suggest that the effects major life events do have may occur through the daily hassles they provoke. Under statistical analysis, life events do not seem to have any independent effect on health beyond that produced by hassles. In sum, it is not the large, dramatic events that make the difference, but what happens day in and day out, whether provoked by major events or not. Take the case of the middle-aged man who learns that his brother, who lived in a distant city, has died. He may grieve at the loss, but his daily life will be disturbed little, if at all. Should his business partner die, in contrast, he would not only feel the emotional loss but might also have to cope with myriad hassles in adjusting to his partner's absence. In the latter case, he would presumably be a more likely candidate for physical or psychological illness.

When we added the information from the mood scales and daily logs of emotions to the data on hassles, we found that particularly for men, the more hassles and the more negative emotions, the worse a person's subsequent health. Our results strongly suggest that hassles trigger unpleasant emotions, which, in turn or in combination, have an adverse effect on health.

Source: Reprinted from *Psychology Today* Magazine. Copyright © 1981. American Psychological Association.

tics, social supports, health practices, constitutional predisposition, and coping techniques (e.g., Kobasa, Maddi, & Courington, 1981; Antonovsky, 1979; Kobasa, Maddi, & Puccetti, 1982). For example, it has been demonstrated that certain personality characteristics increase resistance to the disabling effects of stressful life events on health. One investigator (Kobasa, 1979) has proposed the *hardy personality style* as that which encourages constructive coping.

> Hardy persons have considerable curiosity and tend to find their experiences interesting and meaningful. Further, they believe they can be influential through what they imagine, say, and do. At the same time, they expect change to be the norm, and regard it as an important stimulus to development. These various beliefs and tendencies are very useful in coping with stressful events. Optimistic cognitive appraisals will be made, such that changes will be perceived as natural enough, meaningful, and even interesting despite their stressfulness, and in that sense held in perspective. Decisive actions will also be taken to find out more about the changes, to incorporate them into an ongoing life plan, and to learn from their occurrences whatever may be of value for the future. In these ways, hardy persons will transform stressful events into less stressful forms.

> In contrast, persons low in hardiness tend to find themselves and the environment boring, meaningless, and threatening. They feel powerless in the face of overwhelming forces, believing that life is best when it involves no changes. As such, they have no real conviction that development is either possible or important, and are passive in their interactions with the environment. When stressful events occur, such persons will have little basis for optimistic cognitive appraisal or decisive actions that could transform the events. As their personalities provide little or no buffer, the stressful events are left free to have a debilitating effect on health. (Kobasa et al., 1982)

What kinds of learning experiences build hardiness? It has been suggested (e.g., Kobasa & Maddi, 1977) that certain kinds of experiences in childhood tend to build the three crucial personality characteristics that constitute a hardy personality—commitment, control, and challenge.

> The major factor in learning a sense of commitment or involvement (rather than alienation) is for a majority of the child's daily experiences to be positive rather than negative. Through this, the belief develops that it is interesting and worthwhile to involve oneself in whatever is going on. Most important in learning a sense of control or influence (rather than powerlessness) is for the child to have had regular experiences of stretching to accomplish something and succeeding. If parents can engineer things to be slightly (neither overwhelmingly nor easily) within children's grasp, [the children] will come to think of themselves as influential persons. Finally, a sense of challenge (rather than threat) is learned by having a wide range of experiences in childhood and receiving encouragement to construe their meaning in a variety of ways through exercise of symbolization, imagination, and judgment. Through this, the child will learn to expect change rather than the status quo, and be prepared to reflect on changes as a stimulus to development. (Kobasa et al., 1982)

In the next three sections we shall be looking at three sets of circumstances that commonly produce stress: frustration, conflict, and pressure.

FRUSTRATION

Frustration is defined as blocking or a thwarting of goal-directed activity. In other words, whenever we are on some path toward a goal and something intervenes to impede or block our progress, we are undergoing frustration. As you might imagine, this definition implies that frustration is a common event in everyday life. After all, there is hardly a moment when we are not in pursuit of some goal or goals. Moreover, there is hardly a moment when we are completely free of any obstacle that may stand in the way of this pursuit. When we are driving somewhere, there are always stop signs, other vehicles competing for their share of the road, and traffic signals. When we wish to pursue an occupation, we must establish credentials in the form of educational background, work-related experience, proof of capabilities, or what have you. When we wish to go on a date, we must convince the other party that our company is desirable and worth that person's investment in time. When we wish to establish credit so that we are eligible for our first loan, we are told that we must prove that we have previously satisfied a loan. Such "Catch 22s" abound in everyday life.

Try the following exercise. Compile a list of goal-directed activities in which you can be reasonably certain that there are no obstacles, physical or otherwise, that might impede your progress. A rather short list, isn't it? Let us look at why this is so.

Frustrating or goal-blocking circumstances may take an almost unlimited number of different forms. However, we may place them in one of three broad categories: physical, social, or personal barriers.

Physical barriers are, as their name implies, actual physical impediments on the path to a goal. Many physical barriers are encountered in everyday life. Fences, walls, locked buildings, and impenetrable hedges are all obvious physical obstacles that may prevent us from going from one place to another. Not so obvious but just as real are barriers that relate to our state of well-being. People mired in poverty, for example, may suffer deprivation of nutrients that are essential for normal growth and development. The effects of these dietary deficiencies are most devastating during infancy and childhood when a growing body makes insistent dietary demands. The stunted growth, physical and perhaps mental, may foreclose future possible opportunities for a person so afflicted.

There are also social sources of frustration. Humans are eminently social organisms. Virtually everything we do involves others and has some impact on them and their relationships with us. Inevitably and inescapably, constraints are placed on our behavior. These restrictions may come in the form of religious commandments; laws passed at the federal, state, county, city, or community level; contracts made between interested parties; rules defining acceptable and unacceptable behavior in a social group or organization; and so on. Each of these constraints is a possible source of frustration since it may block ongoing goal-directed activities.

This student may be frustrated because she has left too little time to complete too much work.

Sue Markson

Many builders, like Al, are constantly frustrated by the requirement that building inspectors must pass on whether or not each stage in construction is up to code before work can progress further. Similarly, many students must have silently revolted at the notion that they must pass a test to be certified as having satisfactorily completed a course.

We may all be equal under the law but we are not, in fact, equal in terms of our physical, mental, emotional, and social competencies. When we attempt to achieve goals far beyond our reach, we are destined to experience frustration. Students with limited abilities in math are likely to encounter many frustrations if they decide to pursue a major in engineering. Similarly, those who have difficulty constructing a coherent sentence might encounter numerous obstacles in the pursuit of a career in journalism.

This is not to say that our grasp must never exceed our reach. At times, it is necessary to put forth more than 100 percent if a particular goal is to be attained. Witness the total absorption and dedication necessary to become an Olympic competitor. However, frustration is likely to be a constant companion to individu-

---

BOX 6.3: COPING WITH FRUSTRATION

Consider how much effort a young child expends when learning a new motor skill such as walking. An adult would probably be overwhelmed by an equivalent amount of frustration. Typically, adults can tolerate just so much failure before they give up. If an adult, learning a new and difficult task, were willing to stumble and fall as often as a child learning to walk, he or she would almost always be successful. Persistence can be rewarding. However, our persistence should be expressed in the effort to achieve desired goals rather than in specific repetitive behaviors. In other words, we must be flexible in the means by which we attempt to reach goals, or else behavior may become rigid, repetitive, and nonproductive. We must know when to change our response and try a new approach.

How do you know if persistence will be productive? Some things cannot be changed, and it is just as valuable to know when to quit as to know when to keep trying. The following suggestions can help determine whether or not perseverance will be fruitful.

1. Identify the source of the frustation and determine whether it is internal or external.
2. Is the barrier real or imagined? You may need to talk to others about this to gain a more objective perspective.
3. Can you do anything about the source of frustration? Is it worth the effort?
4. If you have reasonably persisted in one direction without success, are there alternative courses of action?

---

als who make it a habit to pursue goals where their interests and/or competencies are low (see Box 6.3). Habitual frustration is the breeding grounds for personal dissatisfaction, low self-esteem, anger, aggression, and other maladaptive attitudes and behaviors.

CONFLICT

conflict: the simultaneous arousal of two or more incompatible motives.

One of the most common sources of stress is **conflict.** A person in a true conflict experiences anxiety, uncertainty, and is generally uncomfortable. That's why conflict is a potential threat to adjustment.

Life is full of conflicts. Should I stay home and study for that big exam or go out on the town with my friends?

Should I lie to the insurance company about how the car got smashed up? Should I major in psychology, law, or business? Should I stay locked in a marriage with a person I don't love—what will happen to the children?

Conflicts are subjective experiences and may not always reflect the realities of life. For example, Carol may feel that she lacks the skills for a particularly desirable and well-paying position. An objective appraisal of the situation reveals that she is extremely well qualified. Plagued by self doubts, she may hesitate to even apply. It doesn't matter to Carol what the external reality is. She is experiencing what is, to her, a genuine conflict.

Our conflicts are rarely simple. Usually they are so complex that we have difficulty understanding them, much less resolving them. Generally, conflicts arise from clashing motives, such as wanting to continue school, yet at the same time wanting to earn enough money to support one's family. Or they may be the product of a clash between behavior and one's inner standards or values, e.g., lying to get something we want yet feeling that it is wrong to lie. Many conflicts are little more than an annoyance, like a cockroach swimming in one's soup. However, when they involve major life decisions, such as the choice of a career, a mate, or whether or not to have children, they add significantly to the amount of stress we experience.

To help simplify our understanding of conflicts, it is helpful to note that some of our motives move us toward a desirable goal *(approach tendency)*, while others make us want to avoid something unpleasant *(avoidance tendency)*. Many years ago, psychologists (Lewin, 1935; Miller, 1944) classified conflicts into the following four types: approach-approach; avoidance-avoidance; approach-avoidance; and multiple approach-avoidance.

Approach-Approach Conflict

There is a sign in our office which says, "When confronted by two good things, choose both." Wouldn't it be wonderful if life were that simple?

Approach-approach conflict. He can buy only one. Which will he choose?

© Joel Gorden 1983

The least stressful type of conflict is the approach-approach conflict. In this type of situation, we find ourselves simultaneously attracted to two desirable but incompatible goals. Have you ever wanted to do two things at the same time or be in two places at once? Perhaps you had to choose between two jobs, two majors in college, or two restaurants to have dinner at last night. If so, you were experiencing an approach-approach conflict.

You may vacillate or waver back and forth for a short time before making a decision in an approach-approach conflict. But generally, these types of conflicts are relatively easy to resolve. All you need is to find reasons why one job, one major, or one restaurant is better or more desirable than the other. Maybe one job is closer to home, one major requires less lab time, or one restaurant offers faster service. Once you decide between the goals, you have resolved the conflict.

Avoidance-Avoidance Conflict

When we must choose between two unpleasant or negative goals, we are placed in an avoidance-avoidance conflict. A variety of sayings express this dilemma, "Caught between the devil and the deep blue sea," "From the frying pan into the fire," or "Damned if you do, damned if you don't."

In an avoidance-avoidance conflict, you don't like either choice, but you must choose anyway. Do you study or flunk the course? Do you have an unwanted child or an abortion that is against your principles? Do you take a required course you don't like or not graduate? When you try to avoid one of these undesirable alternatives, you find yourself faced with the other. That is the essence of the avoidance-avoidance conflict—you cannot escape both. Thus, you are in a dilemma and experience anxiety when trying to resolve this conflict.

Avoidance-avoidance conflicts usually result in indecision and vacillation. The individual may freeze—be unable to make a decision and thus take no action. Sometimes this can be disastrous. Suppose, for example, you are caught in a fire. The building is about to collapse. You either have to jump many stories or run through the flames. Freezing in this situation will result in certain death.

In other situations, lack of action may result in a decision being made for you. For example, if the woman pregnant with an unwanted child delays too long in making an abortion decision, she loses her chance to make that choice. Likewise, waiting too long to study for an upcoming exam may result in a decision by default. Before you know it, the exam is here, you are unprepared, and you fail.

These dilemmas are viewed as conflicts only on the basis of the individual's own values or needs. If, for example, a woman doesn't see anything wrong with abortion and she really doesn't want the baby, she experiences no conflict.

If the conflict is intense, adjustment problems may result. No matter what the choice is, there will inevitably be stress and pain rather than relief. The individual may try to escape, if this is possible. For example, faced with an undesirable course, the student may decide to change majors or even drop out of school.

Approach-Avoidance Conflict

In most cases, goals do not produce *either* an approach *or* an avoidance tendency. More frequently, there are conflicting tendencies to both approach and avoid. We want something but we don't want it. We'd like that second helping of dessert but, oh, those calories. There's an apartment we would really like to live in but the rent is too high. An example of an approach-avoidance conflict

Avoidance-avoidance conflict. Sometimes a person has to choose between unemployment and an unpleasant job.

Sue Markson

is the student who sat outside the school auditorium for hours. She wanted to audition for a part in the school play, but the prospect of facing an audience made her anxious. Fearing that she would be laughed at, she finally left without trying. The conflict was resolved in favor of avoidance of the situation.

Many people have difficulty making a commitment to a lasting relationship with another person. There are many positive aspects they find attractive—the sense of security, their feelings for the other person. But at the same time, they hesitate to take on the responsibility and lose their freedom. Approach-avoidance conflict. This child is caught in an approach-avoidance conflict: to move closer or to retreat?

In today's society we still have to deal with sexual conflicts. Homosexuality, premarital relations, and infidelity are often at the core of many approach-avoidance conflicts. These conflicts may set the stage for emotional problems that last throughout an individual's life. For example, a man may find himself plagued with homosexual desires. At the same time he may feel guilty and ashamed of these feelings. If he is approached by another man, he may feel both attracted and repulsed at the thought of a sexual encounter.

Approach-avoidance conflict. This child is caught in an approach-avoidance conflict: to move closer or to retreat?

© Chicago Sun-Times, 1983. Photograph by Don Bierman, reprinted with permission.

The tendency to approach an attractive goal increases as we get nearer to the goal. However, the strength of the tendency to avoid also increases as we approach the undesired goal. Of critical importance in an approach-avoidance conflict is the fact that the negative emotions (e.g., anxiety) increase at a faster rate than the positive emotions (e.g., liking) as we get closer to the goal. Thus, as we approach closer and closer to the goal, the stronger is our tendency to avoid it (Miller, 1944). That's why approach-avoidance conflicts are usually characterized by much vacillation and indecision. The conflict is usually more intense the closer we are to the goal object. For example, suppose you have a job interview scheduled for Wednesday at 9:00. On Tuesday you are very excited and eagerly looking forward to this opportunity. However, you are also a little nervous and apprehensive. By 8:00 Wednesday morning, you find your anxiety is increasing. By 8:30 you start to have second thoughts about going to the interview. The closer you get, the more anxiety you feel and the more you hesitate.

How do we resolve approach-avoidance conflicts? Do you remember the last time you had a conflict about attending a class or, perhaps, an examination? Either you went or you didn't. Thus, you somehow resolved your conflict. Anything which affects the relative strength of either the approach tendency or the avoidance tendency will lead to a resolution of the conflict. For instance, in the example above, suppose you learned that very few people were applying for this particular job. Moreover, you heard that the interview was fun. This information would probably increase your tendency to approach the situation. When either the approach becomes stronger or the avoidance tendency weakens, the conflict will be resolved by approach. However, if the approach tendency weakens or the avoidance tendency strengthens, the individual will either remain in conflict or escape the situation altogether.

Multiple Approach-Avoidance Conflict

Ten-year-old Laurie has a problem. Karen and Missy are fighting with each other. They have each made it clear to Laurie that she cannot be friends with both—she must choose one.

At first glance, this appears to be an approach-approach conflict. However, upon further reflection, we see that there is more to this situation than meets the eye. Laurie's feelings toward both Karen and Missy include negative elements along with the positive. This is not at all unusual. There is probably no one in our lives who elicits approach tendencies uncomplicated by negative elements. Children may love their parents but still harbor resentment for the many times they have blocked goal-directed activities.

The reverse is also true. Love of children for parents and playmates is almost inevitably tinged with negative feelings. So it is with Laurie. At times, she finds Karen demanding, uncompromising, and irritable. Missy, on the other hand, is given to stubborn streaks. No matter what Laurie suggests as a playtime activity, Missy balks. During such times, neither girl enjoys herself. But then there are occasions during which pleasure abounds when either friend is a playmate.

Multiple approach-avoidance conflict. In this painting the young man puzzles over choices—and their conflicts.

Jack Lavine, "Judgement of Paris—Greenwich Dreamer," 1965. Private collection of Mr. and Mrs. Charles Benton

These mixed and contradictory feelings bring us to the crux of multiple approach-avoidance conflicts. They are exceedingly difficult to resolve. The closer Laurie gets to resolving the conflict in favor of one playmate, the more anxiety she feels about making this particular choice. She then moves toward the other friend. As she approaches nearer to selecting that friend, the avoidance tendency with its associated anxiety goes up.

Many of our most important decisions involve multiple approach-avoidance conflicts. We usually have several goal objects from which to choose, all fraught with positive and negative aspects. Whom should Cyndi marry? Dependable, rich, but very boring Norman? Or exciting ne'er-do-well Steven? Should we take that course that offers no outside assignments and no credit or the more demanding one that satisfies a needed requirement? If you think for a moment about your own goals and desires, you will find many pluses and minuses. Are you striving for a career that offers many exciting rewards and challenges? Is the road to that goal filled with long hours of diligent study and hard work? Should you buy that inexpensive, gas-saving used car from your friend, or bury yourself in debt for that flashy sports car you've always wanted?

Multiple approach-avoidance conflicts are an inescapable part of everyday life. Almost any course of action has both positive and negative aspects. Choosing one alternative means giving up another. Moreover, many motives operate simultaneously within an individual. These motives may be incompatible with each other. Each motive presses for its own goal. The goals may have both positive and negative aspects and may be at variance with each other. Box 6.4 offers some suggestions on how to cope with conflicts more effectively.

BOX 6.4: COPING WITH CONFLICT

Many of the suggestions in Box 6.3 can also be utilized to handle conflicts more effectively. In addition, the following may be helpful in a conflict situation or in making a tough decision.

1. Give yourself some time to consider the various alternatives. Don't rush a decision that you may later regret. If you know you did everything you could to avoid a bad decision, you will be better able to live with the outcome.
2. Try to find compromises that are feasible. You must get as much information as possible. You may think there are only two or three choices, but you may be missing other viable alternatives.

3. If you can, try out an important decision partly before making a total commitment. If you are considering moving in with someone, spend a few days or a week together first. Look over the textbooks for courses you are undecided about. Try renting ski equipment for a while before making an investment in a new venture.
4. When you have exhausted all possibilities, make a decision and stick to it. Vacillation and indecision produce anxiety. Unless you have made a really bad decision, it is best to choose a direction and learn to live with it.

PRESSURE

So far, we have looked at one side of the coin—the frustrations and conflicts that impede our progress toward goals. On the other side of the coin are the pressures that cause us to speed up and intensify our efforts to carry our activities to their conclusion. Probably all of us have experienced extreme pressure at one time or another—before athletic competition, prior to an important engagement, or while trying to juggle a busy schedule to accommodate the many activities to which we are committed. The pressure is often felt as extreme muscular tension and is commonly accompanied by self-invoked goads. "I've just got to complete this assignment within the next 15 minutes or . . . ." Such pressures often seem the rule rather than the exception. They are everywhere, arising from many sources, both within and external to ourselves.

Internal Sources of Pressure

Some of the internal sources of pressure include our value system, our self-esteem, and our personal commitments. A person with high standards of moral and ethical behavior must constantly be on the alert to see that these standards are not compromised. This is not an easy task in the complex society of today where the standards of conduct are not regulated by a uniform and universally accepted set of norms. What might be perfectly acceptable behavior for one person may be the apex of immorality for another.

While there is pressure to conform to the inner voices of conscience, there may also be pressure to relax our standards. It is generally much easier to blend with the noises of the crowd than to maintain our voice as a separate and distinct entity. Thoughts like "Why not cheat on that term paper? Most everyone else does" come easily to the mind. While there is danger that some people will establish such strict personal standards of morality that they can be maintained only at great cost to the individual, there is also the danger of slipping into an "all's fair in love and war" mentality that may bring us into conflict with our peers and other elements of society.

Additional pressure may come from our own self-concept, our self-esteem. If we regard ourselves as perfect and consider everything short of perfection as failure, we place an enormous additional burden on ourselves. In spite of our capabilities and competencies, we are almost certain to taste, on occasion, the bitter fruits of defeat. In this extremely complex technological society, the harvest of our efforts is not always under our direct control. Thus, in spite of giving it our best, we may not always achieve the goal we so devoutly pursued.

expectancy: anticipating or predicting an outcome based on past experiences.

Some people create their own internal pressures by the **expectancies** they have about the results of their behavior. This is particularly true if the expectations are negative—if they anticipate that something bad is going to happen. Most people are usually not aware of the things they tell themselves that make a bad situation worse. In the last chapter (Box 5.6) we saw that self-defeating thoughts can intensify feelings of depression. This is also true of stress. Indeed, what people tell themselves may well compound the pressure or frustration they are already experiencing and can become a major source of stress. For example, suppose you are taking an exam and find that you cannot answer the first two items. If you then tell yourself, "I'll never finish," or "I'll probably fail," the chances are your behavior will be influenced by your expectation of the outcome. One investigator (Meichenbaum, 1976) suggests that we carefully observe and monitor

catastrophizing: exaggerating the importance or significance of a situation; blowing up a problem into a major disaster.

catastrophizing thoughts and develop adjustive alternatives. For instance, instead of saying, "I'll never pass this test," say, "Wait a minute. I studied for this test. I'm sure there are questions I can answer if I just stop these distracting thoughts and concentrate on the exam." Each time you catch a disruptive thought and effectively change it, reward yourself.

We may also place additional pressure on ourselves by overcommitting our time and talents. It is often easier to say yes than no when a parent, spouse, lover, boss, friend, or associate asks us for a favor, particularly if it is not "due" before a considerable period of time has elapsed. But time is a ruthless traveler and, before we know it, the remote future is the present and we are expected to make good on our promise. If we have made too many such promises, we may find ourselves overwhelmed with prior commitments.

One final word. It is likely that each of us has our own optimal level of pressure. Some people thrive on levels of pressure that might send others scurrying for the psychoanalytic couch. Moreover, if there are sudden changes in the pressure level demanded, either increases or decreases, the individual may suffer adverse physical and/or psychological consequences. It has often been noted that people who live in a pressure cooker most of their lives frequently collapse after they retire, many dying at an early age.

External Sources of Pressure

Recall the tribulations of Al, the builder with whom we began this chapter. He was frustrated by red tape that caused costly delays in ongoing projects. He also made appointments in which the other party failed to show. However, his work-related problems were only the tip of the iceberg. As the owner of his business, he had responsibilities toward his employees, his clients, the profession he practiced, and the broader community he served. Moreover, he had commitments to the savings and loan that held a mortgage on his home, the bank that provided the funds for his construction equipment and even the family car, the raising and education of his children, and so forth.

Most of these responsibilities are regulated by time pressures. Payments must be made on schedule or he suffers financial penalties. If payments are delayed too long, he runs the risk of having the loan called in. In a phrase often used by attorneys, "Time is of the essence." If you reflect for a moment, you will realize how many of our daily activities are regulated by the clock.

In school, classes and labs are scheduled for an entire semester, term papers are scheduled for submission by certain dates; exams are designated to take place at a specific time and location; varsity sports follow a time schedule.

At work, the clock often rules supreme. You must be at your place of employment at a specific time, eat your lunch at the noon hour, and end the day's work at a specific time. Why, even the time and duration of coffee breaks are regulated by many employers. One of the authors witnessed an amusing example of the extent to which we often live by the clock. While visiting an agency of a major state government, he noticed a person sleeping soundly on a couch in a lounge area. This was early in the morning. Later that day, when returning for a cup of coffee, the same gentleman was still putting in sack time. Suddenly he awoke, glanced at his watch, jumped into full alertness and mumbled disconsolnately, "My God! I'm missing my coffee break."

Time pressures can overwhelm us if we don't plan ahead. Before we know it, the term paper is due, three exams are scheduled for the week, homecoming weekend is upon us, guests are arriving for a lengthy visit, the long-awaited concert is coming up, and the car is scheduled for an emissions checkup.

There are also pressures to meet the conflicting and sometimes contradictory demands of others. We fill many different roles at any given time during the course of a lifetime. Each of these roles carries with it different expectations of us. We may be a student in one context, a teacher in another; parent and child; employer and employee; friend and lover, etc. Often these expectations are in conflict. As a son or daughter, we are expected to reflect the values our parents taught us; as members of a peer group, an entirely different set of values may prevail.

All of these pressures, internal and external, can intensify the effects of frustration and conflict. To illustrate, if you are running late for an important appointment, a red traffic light may provoke an emotional outburst where ordinarily the reaction is one of mild annoyance.

GENERAL ADAPTATION SYNDROME

What happens when an individual is subjected to severe and prolonged stress? Canadian psychiatrist Hans Selye (1956) noted that the body responds in the same way to any stress, be it inner conflict, infection, a perceived danger, or a significant life change. He called this series of responses the *general adaptation syndrome*. It consists of a three-stage physiological reaction: the alarm stage, the resistance stage, and the exhaustion stage.

1. The Alarm Stage. Imagine this situation. You are driving home from class at a leisurely pace. Suddenly a small child darts directly in front of your car. You can actually feel the bodily changes that occur in such a situation. All your resources are mobilized and you are ready to cope with threat or danger. Many people who have had this experience feel the need to rest for a while afterward until their bodies resume normal functioning. Sometimes the shock of the situation may overwhelm effective or adaptive behavior. We have seen instances of this in mass panic reactions which can occur in a fire or uncontrolled mob situation.

2. The Resistance Stage. With continued stress, the most effective behavior is energized to meet the threat. However, the level of arousal is not as high as in the alarm reaction. The body now attempts to restore its lost energy and to repair whatever damage has been done. The body appears to return to normal and all bodily resources turn to adapting to the stress situation. However, we pay dearly for this outward appearance of normality. Although the body is better able to cope with the original source of stress, it experiences a diminished capacity to deal with other sources of stress. All our resources have been used up in adapting to the original source of stress. It is during this resistance stage that the first signs of bodily illness begin to appear.

3. The Exhaustion Stage. If the stressor is still not adequately resisted, we pass the point of no return. Our resources are depleted and we function less effectively. Although our capacity for resisting stress varies, we all ultimately become exhausted with persistent and prolonged stress. Eventually we stop functioning until the threat or danger is removed. In this stage, it is difficult not to break down. Our resistance goes and the result is tissue damage in one of the organ systems. Continued stress leads to deterioration, collapse, and finally death.

**PSYCHOSOMATIC
DISORDERS**

> Most standard medical textbooks attribute anywhere from 50 to 80 percent of all disease to . . . stress-related origins. . . . Among your friends, how many can you count who have suffered or are suffering from migraine, hypertension, asthma, hay fever, arthritis, peptic ulcer, nervous tension, or alcoholism? If you can answer "None," you have a rare group of friends indeed. (Pelletier, 1977, p. 7.)

You're making me sick! A bit melodramatic perhaps, but this statement may not be far from the truth. There is much evidence to suggest that many physical symptoms may indeed be brought on or aggravated by emotional factors. Prolonged or severe stress can lead to physiological disorganization of the body, one aspect of which is an increasing susceptibility to infections and other physical disorders. In other words, environmental conditions can radically alter our physical well-being. In fact, the most recent classification of mental illnesses (*Diagnostic and Statistical Manual of Mental Disorders,* 1980) includes a category called "psychological factors affecting physical disorders."

> We now recognize that the human organism must be viewed as a totality in which physical and emotional factors constantly interact. Every so-called physical disorder may have a strong emotional component. Thus, people seem less resistant to the common cold when they are under stress or suffering unusual emotional duress. Moreover, many doctors have observed that their patients' emotional health significantly affects their ability to recover from a physical illness. For example, there have been many reports of people "hanging on" long after a serious physical disorder should have terminated their lives. On the other hand, some people with relatively minor disorders have succumbed as if welcoming death. As one pioneering investigator of the relationship between emotional and physical factors has observed, it is often "more important to know what kind of patient has the disease than what kind of disease the patient has" (Dunbar, 1943, p. 23). Clearly, then, the physician of today must treat more than merely the physical aspects of disease. Emotional factors should receive at least equal consideration.[1]

The pressures and responsibilities of today as well as uncertainties about tomorrow keep many of us in a chronic state of anxiety. How many physical ailments are a direct result of this unrelieved stress that is so much a part of our everyday

---

[1] Haber/Runyon. *Fundamentals of Psychology* © 1983. Addison-Wesley, Reading, MA. Pp. 345–346. Reprinted with permission.

lives? There are certain physical disorders in which stress plays a key role. These are known as **psychosomatic disorders** and they include such conditions as ulcers, asthma, headaches, hypertension, and heart disease.

The autonomic nervous system, which controls such processes as heart rate, blood pressure, and skin temperature, was originally thought to be beyond voluntary control and not responsive to change through learning. However, studies using **biofeedback** have shown that such involuntary processes as irregular heart beats (Bleeker & Engel, 1973), blood pressure (Miller, 1972), tension headaches, and asthma (Fuller, 1978) can indeed be modified through conditioning. The results of these and other studies suggest that certain autonomic processes can be controlled voluntarily. Thus, it is possible that many physical disorders are learned and can, therefore, be treated using the principles of conditioning.

Certainly learning plays an important role in the development of physical disorders. If autonomic responses are influenced by environmental circumstances, it is indeed possible that psychosomatic disorders are learned in the same way as any other behavior pattern. For example, attention and concern can reinforce and maintain a physical problem. As one observer has noted,

> When sickness behavior is more strongly reinforced than is wellness behavior, it will persist after the organic cause has disappeared. Some of the considerable variety of sickness behaviors are extreme dependence, asking for medication, fatigue, weakness, various complaints, wincing, limiting physical activity, and other signs of pain. For such patients, the treatment is to discover how sickness behavior is being reinforced, remove those reinforcements, and find ways of adding additional reinforcements for wellness behavior. The attention and sympathy of care-facility staff and of family members can be a powerful reinforcement. All too often "it is the squeaking wheel that gets the grease"; complaints, difficulties, and symptoms of suffering elicit the attention and sympathy. Other common reinforcements are relief from arduous duties and responsibilities, disability payments, and pain-killing or sleep-inducing medications. After organic causes have been ruled out, *and one must not make the mistake of neglecting those that can be corrected by purely medical treatment*, a sophisticated behavioral analysis must be made of the reinforcements that are effective for the individual patient. Then behavior therapy is indicated if reinforcement for the symptoms is evident, and it is practicable to withhold reinforcements for sickness behavior and provide adequate reinforcement for wellness behavior first in the health-care situation and then in the patient's normal environment. (Miller, 1983, pp. 24–5)[2]

The following is an example of how attention and concern can help to maintain a specific problem, i.e., asthmatic attacks:

A child may get little or no attention from crying, but the gasping or wheez-

---

[2] Reproduced, with permission, from the Annual Review of Psychology, Volume 35, © 1983 by Annual Reviews, Inc.

ing reactions that often follow crying spells may obtain immediate attention and concern for him. If this pattern is repeated, the infant might learn an asthmalike response as a means of obtaining parental attention and alleviating distress. In addition, an asthmatic reaction—as a means of reducing anxiety—might generalize to other types of stressful situations. By virtue of its anxiety-reducing quality, it would continually be reinforced, and hence tend to persist. Even when more adaptive ways of coping with anxiety were later acquired, the individual might still resort to asthmatic attacks under severe stress. (Coleman, 1976, p. 510)[3]

The organ system that suffers first under the strains of chronic stress differs across individuals. Why some people develop ulcers, others heart disease, and still others no observable body symptoms is a question that has intrigued many scientists. Some investigators have suggested that we inherit a predisposition to certain psychosomatic disorders. Indeed, certain ailments, such as asthma and hypertension, tend to run in families (Price & Lynn, 1981). However, many of our emotional responses are learned through imitation. Thus, learned factors cannot be ruled out.

Another explanation that has captured the imagination of many is the *somatic weakness hypothesis*. According to this view, certain organ systems possess an inherited or acquired vulnerability and, with sufficient stress, break down. Thus, the particular physiological disorder that develops would be determined by whichever system was the "weakest link" in the body. For example, one study of asthmatic patients reported that 80 percent had had prior respiratory infections as compared to only 30 percent of the nonasthmatic controls (Rees, 1964).

Let us now turn our attention to two disorders—ulcers and heart attacks—in which stress has been strongly implicated.

Ulcers

Ulcers represent the most well-documented case for the role of stress in physical disorders. Normally, when food enters, or is about to enter, the stomach, acid is secreted. When digestion of the food is completed, this secretion stops. Emotional stress or worry can stimulate the flow of stomach acid. If this acid is not absorbed by food, it attacks the stomach tissue leading to inflammation and crater-like sores called ulcers.

Why do some people secrete stomach acid where there is no food in the stomach? Various studies have implicated stress as a factor in the high rate of stomach acid secretion (Wolf & Wolff, 1947; Phillip & Cay, 1972).

One of the most demanding and stressful jobs is that of an air traffic controller. Fear and uncertainty are constant companions of these people. They must remain alert and vigilant at all times. A momentary lapse can spell disaster. No matter

---

[3] From *Abnormal Psychology and Modern Life* by James C. Coleman. Copyright © 1976. Scott, Foresman and Company. Reprinted by permission.

how careful they are, the possibility of an accident always exists. Air traffic controllers suffer from an alarmingly high rate of ulcers.

Heart Attacks

Approximately 700,000 Americans die every year of heart disease (*World Almanac*, 1980). Although the causes of coronary disease are still not well understood, stress appears to be a major contributing factor.

Research by two cardiologists (Friedman & Rosenman, 1974) has identified the personality characteristics of people who are especially prone to heart attacks. They classified people into two personality types: Type As run a high risk of heart disease while Type Bs are unlikely to have a heart attack.

Type A people are aggressive, extremely ambitious, and highly competitive. They feel a chronic sense of time urgency as they hurry from one activity to another in a continual race against the clock. They drive themselves unmercifully to achieve self-imposed goals. They push themselves to the limit and then deny they are tired (Glass, 1976). In contrast, Type B personalities deal with problems in a more relaxed way and set more realistic goals. An eight-year follow-up study found twice as many heart attacks among Type As than Type Bs (Rosenman, Brand, Jenkins, Friedman, Straus, & Wurm, 1975).

Do you know any Type A people? Table 6.2 presents a checklist to help you recognize Type A personality characteristics. One way to avoid the destructive stress associated with Type A personalities is to avoid the types of behavior identified in this list.

Which of these executives is a Type A person? Who do you think is more likely to experience a medical problem?

Sue Markson

Wide World Photos

TABLE 6.2   ARE YOU A TYPE A? Check the items that apply to you. Do you:

_____ Always move, eat, and walk quickly?

_____ Become very impatient when you are stuck in slow traffic or get caught in a slow-moving line?

_____ Continue to think about your own concerns while someone is talking to you?

_____ Frequently try to do several things at one time?

_____ Almost always try to catch up on work instead of relaxing on a vacation?

_____ Feel a tinge of guilt when you *do* relax or just do nothing for a period of time?

_____ Tend not to notice your general surroundings because you are so involved in your work?

_____ Find yourself taking on more and more responsibilities in less and less time?

_____ Tend to rate yourself in terms of the *number* of things you have accomplished?

_____ Have a habit of accenting key words in everyday conversation?

_____ Feel an urgency about doing things quickly and immediately?

_____ Find yourself interrupting other people to finish their sentences for them?

Although this short test is not meant to be a diagnostic tool, a pattern of ''yes'' responses probably suggests Type A behavior.

Source: Developed from descriptions in M. Friedman and Rosenman, *Type A* (New York: Alfred A. Knopf, 1974), pp. 82–85.

SUMMARY

In this chapter we saw that stress and its associated anxiety is a common element of everyday living. Most of us have learned to adapt to the many stresses we encounter in daily living. However, occasionally a single event can be so stressful or the cumulative effects of many stressful events can be so great that we find our coping abilities strained to the limit.

- The physiological state of strain does not always result from a calamity or even from an undesirable event. In fact, any change in an important aspect of our daily routines can serve as a source of strain.

- In this chapter we reviewed three common sources of strain: frustration, conflict, and pressure.

- Frustration is a blocking or thwarting of goal-directed activity. It may result from physical, social, or psychological barriers on the path to a goal.

- Conflict is a consequence of two or more competing motives. Four types of motivational conflict have been described: approach-approach, avoidance-avoidance, approach-avoidance, and multiple approach-avoidance.

- In approach-approach conflicts, there are two desirable goals. However, accepting one means relinquishing the other.

- In avoidance-avoidance conflict, both goals are aversive. Selection of either one will entail some degree of discomfort to the individual.

- In approach-avoidance conflicts, a single goal contains both positive and negative elements. The closer we approach the goal, the more pronounced are the effects of the negative or aversive elements. These conflicts are very stressful to resolve: we have difficulty getting to the goal because of the aversive components, and we do not want to flee from the situation since we are attracted to the positive elements.

- Multiple approach-avoidance conflicts are similar to the approach-avoidance conflicts. However, more than one goal object is involved, each with both positive and negative elements. Like approach-avoidance conflicts, these are also extremely difficult to resolve and for the same reasons.

- Pressure speeds up and intensifies our efforts to reach goals. Pressure may arise from within the individual (e.g., value system and self-esteem) or from external sources (e.g., time pressures and demands of others).

- Pressure can intensify the effects of frustration and motivational conflict.

- When people are exposed to severe and prolonged stress, a three-stage reaction, called the general adaptation syndrome, has been described.

- During the alarm stage, all of our physical forces are mobilized to meet the threat.

- The resistance stage is characterized by a continual struggle against the long-term source of strain. Outwardly, the body appears to return to normal. However, if another source of strain is suddenly introduced, we may find that the body is unable to withstand the onslaught.

- With persistent and prolonged strain, bodily defenses become exhausted (the exhaustion stage). The individual is susceptible to a physical and/or emotional breakdown.

- Many physical disorders have strong emotional components.

TERMS TO REMEMBER

Stress	Expectancy
Strain	Catastrophizing
Eustress	Psychosomatic disorders
Conflict	Biofeedback

CHAPTER 7

COPING

Sounds of Silence   During the ensuing months, things did not get any better for Al. Indeed, they continued to deteriorate. After completing the last project, no more contracts had come through. In fact, there wasn't even one good lead. Oh, plenty of people were calling, proposing possible building projects, and wanting to discuss his involvment. But that was as far as things went. A call or two, several meetings, rising hopes, and then the deafening "sounds of silence." Perhaps it was the pendulumlike swings of emotions and moods that hurt the most—more even than the prolonged inactivity. Joy at one moment, profound depression at the next. Anger, anxiety, and guilt were constantly vying for center stage in the arena of his mind. Through it all, hope seemed forever to be tugging at his line, but no one would take the bait. "Sorry, Al, but times are bad for everybody. I just can't raise the financing for the project. Tight money, expensive money. What's a person to do?"

During these times, he thought often of the extent to which failure is a very personal and private thing. The fact that he was not alone in his misery provided little consolation. If the truth were known, he would welcome the news that some of his many friends and competitors in the building trade were making it. He had sufficient confidence in his own reputation and ability that, given some activity in the building industry, he would grab off his fair share.

To make matters worse, he had begun to take his problems home with him. When he felt frustrated and angry, he would take it out on Mildred or the kids. "Nothing physical," he would tell himself, "I just yell at them. That's all. But why do I yell at them? For nothing at all. I even find myself inventing excuses for getting angry at them." Then sharp stabs of guilt would cut his spirit to the quick.

This brief view of Al reminds us of the linkage between stress and the emotions. Frustration commonly leads to anger, and occasionally aggression. However, aggression is unlikely to occur when the cost to the individual (e.g., the possibility of retaliation or subsequent punishment) is too high (Bandura, 1977; Montagu, 1976). Expression of anger and/or aggression as well as forbidden desires and impulses often trigger guilt reactions. Further, threats to the individual's well-being or self-esteem are likely to lead to anxiety. In the case of Al, the long layoff threatened both his financial security and his favorable image of himself, (e.g., he had thought of himself as his own boss, a successful builder, and a good provider). Often our efforts to cope with stress are directed as much to alleviating the emotional component as they are to correcting the underlying cause of the threat. This is an important point to keep in mind. Successfully stilling the emotional turmoil often has little impact on the conditions that produced the strain. In contrast, when our efforts are directed either at removing the causes of strain or finding satisfactory alternative routes to pursue, we usually receive, as a bonus, relief from emotion-induced tension.

FIGHT, FLIGHT, OR FREEZE

In the animal world, there are three built-in coping mechanisms that are waiting to be activated when the organism confronts a dangerous situation. If the threat is another animal with no overwhelming physical advantage, *fight* might well be the most adaptive response. The attacking animal might pause if there is risk of either injury or a prolonged and exhausting battle. However, if the danger is a rapidly spreading grass fire, remaining to put up a fight is likely to be the last foolish act in the animal's life.

At times, the better part of valor is to flee. This will be particularly true when the defending animal is overmatched. A gazelle that stands up to an attacking lion will not receive a reward for finishing second. Moreover, in the case of the rapidly spreading grass fire, the only adaptive response may involve *flight.*

Finally, when neither fight or flight are viable options, such as when the potential victim is sealed in a box canyon, *freezing* may spell the difference between living and providing a tasty snack for a predator. Freezing might be effective since the potential victim provides fewer and less distinctive visual cues (i.e., there is no motion) and olfactory cues (less of the animal's scent is dispersed in the surrounding terrain).

At the human level, the same broad categories of adjustive behavior are available. However, because of our astonishing adaptibility, flexibility, and resourcefulness, the behaviors are not limited to fighting, fleeing, and freezing in the literal sense of these words. Rather, we may stand up and oppose the source of stress, withdraw, or take no action whatsoever. Depending on the circumstances, any of these behaviors may be either adaptive or maladaptive.

Let's look at some of the options open to Al. He can simply bide his time, hoping that something will happen to bail him out; he can withdraw from the building trade and actively pursue a career in another field; or he can stick it out while pursuing a more aggressive and creative approach to obtaining contracts whenever new projects are open to bidding. Each of these possible courses is analogous to the built-in coping mechanisms we discussed earlier: freezing (biding his time), withdrawal (entering a new career), or attack (trying to remove or overcome the source of strain).

If Al decides to take the direct approach—to strike out against the source of strain—he is committed to trying to obtain a livelihood from a field with opportunities that are dwindling at present. Like the tennis player who is losing the match, he must develop new strategies or new procedures to take him out of the rut. To illustrate, he might decide that extraordinary circumstances demand extraordinary solutions. "I can't just wait for them to come to me. I've got to get out into the field and start to beat the bushes."

The question must be asked, "Is this solution realistic?" It is possible that he is up against one of those situations in life where increased effort yields no further dividends. If this is the case, Al is subjecting himself to further strain and greater pressure. Indeed, there is the danger that his arousal level will become so great that his competencies will be diminished. For example, he may begin to pursue leads in which the chances of success are minimal and the payoff so small that further efforts simply are not justified. In short, he is in danger of spreading himself too thin.

The truth of the matter is that we do not exercise complete control over our own destinies. At times, factors external to us play a predominant role—accidents, natural disasters, war, and so on. In the case of Al, a severe and prolonged slump in the building industry rendered his knowledge and skills useless as a means of earning a livelihood at this juncture in his life. On such occasions, withdrawal from the situation and pursuit of other goals may be the most viable options.

Like the general on the battlefield, it is not easy for most of us to make a strategic withdrawal. Self-esteem, feelings of security, self-confidence, and public image are all at stake. Many of us are known by what we do and how well we do it. To abandon one line of endeavor in favor of a second is to admit defeat in the eyes of many. Nevertheless, to persist in nonproductive and self-defeating behavior when alternative actions are available is likely to court disaster. Students who are hopelessly lost in a course to which they have given their best effort may be acting wisely when they elect to withdraw.

Biding one's time may also be appropriate on occasion. Many setbacks and their associated strain are temporary in nature. This is often the case when external forces and pressures, over which we have no control, are at work. Loss of employment, a chance outbreak of personal misfortune, or grief associated with the loss of a loved one may overwhelm us at the time they occur. We cannot attack and defeat these circumstances other than to give vent to our rage, dismay, or grief. This venting of emotions may be adjustive in the sense that it often relieves the immediate tension and, in doing so, provides more favorable conditions for seeking solutions. But to withdraw may simply not be warranted by the permanency of the impact of these events on our lives. Employment opportunities come and go, chance occurrences include desirable as well as undesirable consequences, and the acute grief following the loss of a loved one will diminish with time. In short, there are times when just waiting to see what will happen is the wisest course of action.

Given that three broad classes of responses are available to us in times of stress, how do we decide among them? This question takes us right to the heart of coping mechanisms.

COPING MECHANISMS

Coping mechanisms are the means by which we adapt to the stresses of daily living. They include the entire arsenal of human capabilities—behavioral changes, thoughts, feelings, information processing, learning, remembering, and so forth.

Earlier in the chapter we distinguished between behavior that results in some resolution of the source of strain as opposed to responses that alleviate the emotional components of strain. We shall use the term **coping mechanisms** to refer to those behaviors and thoughts that come to grips with the causes of strain. Later in the chapter, we shall examine various **defense mechanisms.** Typically, the defense mechanisms leave untouched the underlying causes of strain and their accompanying emotional reactions; rather, their primary function is to ease the acute discomfort of the emotions associated with frustration and unresolved motivational conflict.

coping mechanisms: those behaviors and thoughts that deal directly with the causes of strain.

defense mechanisms: devices used to alleviate or avoid anxiety associated with strain.

Humans are capable of such highly complex cognitive activities as shown here.

Use of Cognitive Abilities for Coping

A major advantage we humans have over lower animals derives from our cognitive abilities. Our options are not restricted to the here and the now. Through the use of language and other symbolic processes, we can represent the past, the present, and the future. The very fact that you are reading this book and attending lectures on human adjustment testifies to your confidence that words and thoughts can have an impact on your life. In fact, they can even move mountains, symbolically, that is.

Use of Reasoning.   We are capable of setting up various "what if . . .?" situations in which we are free to invent symbols representing events and processes in the real world, manipulate them mentally, and arrive at hypotheses or hunches concerning possible future outcomes. To illustrate, we can set up some of the following what if propositions:

> Contemplating the bleak outlook of his present circumstances, Al asks, "What if I purposely underbid the next contract, assuming that there will be no lost days due to inclement weather, that by diligent searching I can find the least expensive suppliers, and that I can improve the efficiency of my entire operation by greater attention to detail?"
> Having identified these factors, he can then investigate, again symbolically, the chances that these conditions can be met. "During the next three months, the weather is usually ideal. Over the past five years I have lost less than 5 percent of work hours due to bad weather. However, during the rest of the year, that figure is closer to 15 percent. And, because of the recession in the building industry, the suppliers are also hurting. By shopping around, I can surely find someone willing to trim the profit margin. But increasing efficiency, that's a horse of a different color. I don't think much can be done to improve efficiency. Every time I have tried to institute campaigns to cut the waste, our labor costs have mounted. People spend too much time trying to save a piece of wood here, recycle a nail there. . . ."

Let's look at another example.

> LuAnn had been informed by the obstetrician that her newborn child was certain to be retarded. Only the degree of retardation was at issue. After initially rejecting the physician's prognosis, she gave way to grief.

Courtesy National College of
Education

Later, she began to contemplate various options open to her. "If we keep little Joey, there will be hardships for all of us. His older brother and sister would have to understand that Joey is someone special, and he would have to be treated differently. He could never engage in the usual horseplay that takes place among siblings. Also, they may be too embarrassed to bring their friends home, too embarrassed to admit that Joey is their brother. We'll have to deal with that problem if we decide to keep Joey. And there's the problem of our own shame.

"Joey will also require a great deal of attention and care, much more than Mark and Frances. He may or may not learn to take care of himself, learn to speak or read. That will be hard for us to take emotionally. Clearly, we cannot apply the same standards of growth and development to Joey that we use to judge the progress of Mark and Frances.

"But, on the other hand, I have spoken to people with Down's syndrome children. They tell me they're perfectly lovable, well-behaved, and sociable children. A few of these parents say they wouldn't part with their child under any circumstances—the benefits so outweigh the disadvantages.

"Now we must decide what is best for Joey. . . ."

As you might imagine, these explorations of various alternative routes through the use of language can take us down many strange and unfamiliar paths. Indeed, they should. Unlike behavior in the real world, there is little cost to such activity and an enormous potential payoff. Moreover, at the cognitive level, there is no commitment to a course of action. Commitment should come only after considered weighing of the risks, costs, and benefits.

objectivity: giving facts as they are without a bias toward either side.

Objectivity. The use of our logical reasoning ability, as powerful as it is, still entails some risk. When the stakes are high, it is easy for our thoughts and reasoning processes to be influenced by our feelings, emotions, wants, and desires. We may readily overlook the negative elements in a plan and embrace the positive elements with an excess of fervor. One of the most important mechanisms for preventing the intrusion of irrelevent issues is **objectivity.** When we maintain an objective attitude, we are able to disentangle the emotional from the logical components in thought, reasoning, and action. We are also able to distinguish between thoughts that relate to the problem from those that do not. Let's look at an example.

For as long as he can remember, Frank has wanted to pursue a career in forestry. He intensely dislikes "desk jobs" but loves the great outdoors. His greatest pleasures come from backpacking expeditions in wilderness areas, living much of the time off the land. He envisions the life of a forest ranger as ideally suited to his emotional and intellectual needs. However, a number of people warned him that there are few job openings in the field of forestry relative to the number of qualified applicants. Resisting the temptation to push aside these warnings, he began an extensive review of career opportunities in this field. He soon discovered that the warnings were accurate. When he spoke to recent graduates from the program, he found that many had been forced to accept positions outside forestry, often in areas for which they were poorly equipped. Of those who had been successful in finding a position, many wound up in desk jobs. Frank is now looking into related fields, like field biology and soil biology, where he could still find the lifestyle he wanted and the opportunities for employment appeared to be better.

Concentration.   Another cognitive feature that provides a mechanism for coping is our ability to focus our complete attention on the problem at hand. This capability, known as **concentration,** permits us to put aside disturbing thoughts and ideas while we narrow the scope of our efforts to the stressful situation in which we find ourselves.

concentration: focusing complete attention on the situation at hand.

> Fanny is a star of stage and screen. This is the night she is going to open with the lead role in a widely anticipated Broadway play. An hour before curtain time, she learns that her mother has just died. In spite of her grief, she is able to put aside thoughts of her personal loss and concentrate her efforts on the demands of the evening. In the "show must go on" tradition, she goes through with her performance and wins critical rave reviews. Only after she returns to the dressing room does she permit her grief to find expression.

Humor.   Humor is another means by which we can often defuse potentially stressful situations, especially those involving abrasive interpersonal relationships. Making yourself the butt of a joke can get people laughing together. This makes for better conditions for establishing accord instead of a shouting match. To illustrate:

> Following a particularly bad year, the annual meeting of the board of directors of a public corporation promised to produce many sparks. Aware of this fact, the president of the company preceded his opening remarks with this announcement, "Before stepping into the room, I was offered $100 to resign my position. But my good friend Charlie talked me out of it. He told me I could get a much better offer than that." The laughter that followed relieved many tensions and permitted the board to take up urgent matters of business without an underlying hostility that often defeats rational discourse.

Two authors of a book about Judaism argue that, among Jews, verbal jousting often takes the place of physical violence (see Box 7.1).

Suppression.   We also have the capacity to suppress our immediate reactions to situations, giving us time for a more considered and constructive response. The old expression, "When someone makes you angry, count 10 before answering," carries the wisdom of **suppression.** This inhibition may take the form of complete immersion in other activities that successfully compete with the disturbing thoughts. Many distressful events involve interpersonal relations. Consider the following:

suppression: consciously inhibiting thoughts and reactions to events that cause strain.

> Jim and Ellen have been close and valued friends for many years. You and your partner have shared many good times and a few moments of

BOX 7.1 :   JEWISH JOUSTING

A Jewish woman is told by her son's psychiatrist that the boy has an Oedipus complex.

"Oedipus, Schmoedipus," she replies. "As long as he loves his mother."

That was one example of Jewish humor provided by Rabbi Joseph Telushkin, co-author of the book *The Nine Questions People Ask About Judaism.*

The "Oedipus, Schmoedipus" joke played upon the supposed ignorance of the traditional first-generation Jewish mother. Telushkin used another story to illustrate the other side of the coin, the Jewish psychiatrist.

Goldberg, the psychiatrist, tells his patient that after 10 years, he is finally cured. The man doesn't believe him and says he's not ready to cope on his own. Goldberg tells him that he doesn't ordinarily do this, but he's going to give the man his home phone number.

"Call me any time you have a crisis you don't think you can deal with," Goldberg tells the man.

Two weeks go by and Goldberg is awakened by a call from the man at 6 in the morning.

"Dr. Goldberg, I had such a horrible nightmare," the man says. "I dreamed you were my mother."

"What happened then?" Goldberg asked.

"Well, I decided I'd better have some breakfast. So I had a cup of coffee and then called you."

"A cup of coffee?" the doctor said. "You call that a breakfast?"

Telushkin told his audience that Jews traditionally have not engaged in physical violence. So they make up for it in verbal violence. No one is safe from it. Not even the leaders of Israel.

"When President Eisenhower met Israel's David Ben-Gurion, Eisenhower said, 'I greet you as the president of a nation of 160 million people.' Ben-Gurion replied, 'I greet you as the prime minister of a nation of a million-and-a-half prime ministers.' "

Telushkin said humor is a factor in mother-son relationships, the method of prayer, psychology, even anti-Semitism.

"When Groucho Marx was denied membership in a country club because he was Jewish, he sent a letter to the membership committee asking if his daughter could wade into the pool up to her waist, because she was only half-Jewish."

"A Jew sat on the subway reading the *Jewish Daily Forward* (a Yiddish newspaper) and noticed a Jewish friend sitting opposite him reading an American Nazi propaganda newspaper. After most of the other passengers got off the subway, the first man went over and sat next to the man reading the Nazi paper.

" 'Why are you reading such hateful trash?' he asked.

" 'Look,' his friend replied, 'If you read the *Forward,* you find out how the Arabs are bombing children in Israel, how the economy there is so bad, how many problems Jews have with assimilation, people who don't have enough to eat, and whatnot.

" 'But look, in this Nazi paper, you read how we own all the banks, how we're so influential in governments all around the world and how powerful we are. If you ask me, we're doing better in this paper.' "

Yet humor can be a potent weapon against prejudice, even if the prejudiced person believes Jews are smarter than other people, therefore, a more dangerous enemy.

An anti-Semite was sitting on a train in Europe watching a Jew eat a piece of herring.

"What it is about you Jews that makes you so smart?" he demanded.

The Jewish fellow was perplexed for a moment, then told the man it was because of all the herring his people ate.

The anti-Semite asked how much herring the man had with him and how much it would cost him to buy it.

The Jewish man said he had 10 pounds and he would sell him all the herring for 20 drachmas, an outrageously high price.

The anti-Semite paid the price and started to furiously wolf down the herring. But after a while, he realized he had been had.

"I don't feel any smarter!" he shouted. "This is ordinary herring that I could have bought in any store for only three drachmas."

The Jewish man smiled.

"See," he said, "it's working already."

Source: S. Pollak, "Jewish Jousting," *Arizona Daily Star,* 9 March 1982, p. 13.

Suppression.

"I'm beginning to think you were better off when your hostility was suppressed..."

From *The Wall Street Journal,* with permission of Cartoon Features Syndicate

adversity together. You always look forward to getting together with them. You were stunned earlier in the day when you bumped into a mutual friend who asked if you were going to attend the big bash at their home tomorrow night. Of all people, you had not been invited. You are hurt, angry, and depressed, all at once. A few moments after learning of the social slight, you notice Jim and Ellen walking ahead of you. You are tempted to catch up to them and give them a piece of your mind. But you suppress the urge, realizing that many relationships may be fractured in a moment of thoughlessness. "Count to 10," you tell yourself, and then take a different path so that you don't accidently meet up with Jim and Ellen. You don't trust yourself to maintain a calm exterior.

The next day you receive a battered letter in the mail, with a note from the post office attached. The note explains that the letter had been caught in automatic processing equipment. Thus, its poor condition and the delay in receiving it. You open it and find an invitation to attend a party at Jim and Ellen's that night. You breathe a sigh of relief that you had suppressed your initial urge.

Tolerance for Ambiguity.   Ambiguity is one of the basic facts of human life. It is rare that we can enter a situation and feel perfectly assured we understand all that is going on. In the above example of Jim and Ellen, the entire future of your relationship had become clouded by what had appeared to be an unforgiveable social slight. As a student, you have unquestionably experienced ambiguity concerning the expectations of one or more of your instructors on forthcoming examinations. When dating another person of whom you are very fond, you have probably wondered to what extent that person returns your feelings. You have detected ambiguous cues—professions of love and evidence of concern mingled in with moments of irritability and disregard.

Generally, we don't like ambiguity. It generates negative feelings ranging from mild discomfort to agonizing anxiety. Thus, our motivation is high to clear up the uncertainty accompanying ambiguity, even if we must force things at times. Unfortunately, in the absence of clear clues, any action we take is in ignorance. Had you confronted Jim and Ellen in anger, you may indeed have resolved the ambiguity, but the price you paid in terms of shattered human relationships may have been greater than you wished to bear. It is wise to develop a tolerance toward ambiguity, recognizing it as a normal aspect of everyday living. Ambiguity is, in fact, another of life's problems. Like any problem, it is best solved when our information base is large and we do not respond with haste. It is more likely to yield to objective and reasoned analysis than to emotional outbursts.

Sublimation.   There are times when the goals we seek cannot be reached for one reason or another. **Sublimation** involves substitution. To illustrate:

sublimation: the substitution of alternative or secondary goals for those that are denied.

> Michael B has overpowering sexual urges that fill him with anxiety and shame. Virtually every time he sees a beautiful woman, he is almost overcome by a desire to fondle her. Knowing that direct expression of this urge is likely to bring him much grief, he expends a large amount of energy fighting it. But life is hell for him because he is never confident that he will be able to resist the urge. He is counseled to take up sculpturing as a hobby. There he is free to place his hands on the female form—in wax—without fear of social disapproval. He takes to the hobby as a duck takes to water. The forbidden urge remains, but at a level of intensity that he is able to handle.

When Freud introduced the concept of sublimation, he singled out the sexual drive. This drive is insistent, demanding satisfaction. However, society has formulated numerous prohibitions relating to the satisfaction of sexual urges. Thus, our most significant frustrations revolve about the thwarting of this powerful force. Sublimation provides a socially acceptable way of redirecting sexual energy into socially approved outlets.

Historically, sublimation has been considered a defense mechanism rather than a coping mechanism. However, since the use of sublimation does not appear to incur any long-term undesirable consequences, its use is often made by choice, and it alters potentially destructive tendencies, many contemporary theorists regard it as coping (Kroeber, 1973). Its use has also been expanded to encompass antisocial impulses other than prohibited sexual activity. For example, fear, rage, and sorrow are often expressed in antisocial ways, such as withdrawal into isolation or aggression.

A Frenchman weeps unashamedly as the French regiments leave the Nazi occupied country during World War II.

Wide World Photos

Draining Off the Tension

As we have noted, strong negative emotions can seriously interfere with our ability to cope successfully with stress. They tend to produce levels of arousal that are not conducive to objective consideration of the facts, focusing our thoughts on the relevant issues, and rational weighing of alternative courses of action. It is also difficult to be funny when your emotional life is in turmoil.

In our culture there are often attitudes that oppose the use of natural outlets for the draining of tension associated with stressful events. Little boys are told big boys don't cry. Although a greater degree of permissiveness exists with respect to little girls, the prevailing attitude is that we should learn to keep the expression of our emotions in check. Many adults tend to frown upon and children make fun of people who cry when distressed. Yet crying is a perfectly natural response to pain, grief, and despair. It seems to relieve the tension and permits a person to get back on track faster following a catastrophic event in his or her life. It should be encouraged rather than discouraged.

Talking things out is another way of reducing the tension associated with frustration and motivational conflict. Perhaps one of the most important functions served by friends is that they provide accepting environments in which we can talk about our life-threatening adventures, our doubts, our grievances, and our fears. In doing so, we often become less sensitive to the impact of these events on our lives and are able to regard them and deal with them more objectively.

Moreover, friends often provide feedback that allows us to view our reactions in a different light. "You are so upset that Donna wants a separation," observes Fred's closest friend and confidant. "Are you aware of how often you put her down when you're together? You do it in thousands of little ways. You belittle her achievements, her intelligence, her emotional responses to situations. . . ."

Donna's decision to call it quits reminds us of the fact that the need to affiliate is among the strongest of human motivations (see Chapter 4). Indeed, many of the stresses we experience in life result from the souring of interpersonal relationships—voluntary separation from someone who has shared significant moments in our lives, divorce, drifting away from friends. Often the culprit is our inability to put ourselves in the other person's shoes. **Empathy** is the term we use to describe our capacity to see things from the perspective of the other person. Fred regarded many of the things he said to Donna as a form of playful teasing. He was sure she delighted in hearing such witticisms as: "When the Lord doled out Donna's brains, He must have used a teaspoon."

empathy: the ability to see things from another person's perspective.

Had Fred asked himself, "How would I like it if someone said something like that to me?" he might have thought twice before inflicting it upon Donna. Of course, Donna is not without blame of her own. Early in her relationship with Fred, she smiled or laughed whenever he inserted the verbal dagger. She had been taught that it was undignified and improper for young ladies to express their true feelings, especially when they were negative. Perhaps the relationship would have been quite different, with a better prognosis for success, had she said right up front, "No, that's not true, Fred. I've got a good head on my shoulders, and you know it. You make me angry when you put me down. I'm sure you wouldn't jump for joy if I called you stupid. If I am expected to put up with more of this nonsense, we had better call it quits right now." Sometimes an honest expression of feelings will provide the feedback necessary to put a relationship on an even keel. If it doesn't, the relationship may not have had much going for it at the very outset.

DEFENSE MECHANISMS

Freud was more than the founder of psychoanalytic theory. He was also an astute observer of the human scene. He noticed that people are extremely sensitive to threats to their ego or to their self-esteem. They will do almost anything to avoid, escape, or shield themselves from the anxiety elicited by these threats. They erect barriers to protect themselves from both external threats, such as failures and disappointments, and internal threats, such as guilt-arousing desires or behavior, personal limitations, and real or imagined feelings of inferiority. Freud called these barriers *defense mechanisms.* As we noted earlier, defense mechanisms do not come to grips with the causes of strain, but rather they help us live with the emotional pain that strain often leaves in its wake. They may be considered maladaptive if they become the primary means of coping with stressors, because they usually involve a degree of self-deception and distortion of reality. Thus, they may actually interfere with effective resolution of an underlying problem.

It should be emphasized that the use of defense mechanisms is not in and of itself a sign of abnormality. We all use defense mechanisms at different times and to varying degrees. Some of the following may already be familiar to you: "I missed the shot because the sun got in my eyes." "Good thing I was passed over for the promotion. The extra pressure would probably give me ulcers." Or "I would have done better in the course but the instructor didn't know how to teach." These all appear to be examples of rationalization which we shall soon discuss.

But are they? That is, do people make these statements to protect themselves from acknowledging their own failings or inadequacies? Or do they represent a true and undistorted view of reality? For example, did Dick *really* miss that shot because the sun got in his eyes, or did he just say that to protect himself from acknowledging his own lack of skill? All defense mechanisms involve some degree of self-deception and are often accompanied by some degree of reality distortion. To ascertain whether Dick was rationalizing, we would need to know more about Dick, his feelings about himself, and his motivations.

The behavior of the individual often provides valuable cues. When the behavior is inappropriate to the situation, the possibility should not be overlooked that defense mechanisms are being used. For example, suppose we see Amy smile when we know she is disgusted, or Paul laugh when we know he is sad, or David smiling and whistling when we know he's scared to death. It probably would be a good guess that they are hiding their true feelings—from themselves as well as others—under the blanket of defense mechanisms.

It is also helpful to look at the intensity of the behavior. Defense mechanisms characteristically represent exaggerated forms of behavior. Amy's smile is a bit too broad; Paul laughs too loud and too long; and David's whistle seems forced. This exaggeration of behavior is exemplified by the well-known line from Shakespear, "The lady doth protest too much, methinks."

Let's turn our attention to a variety of different defense mechanisms. While doing so, we should keep the following in mind: Each defense mechanism does not necessarily operate independently of or in isolation from other defense mechanisms. We shall frequently find that several mechanisms operate in concert to achieve a blending of the many diverse behaviors, attitudes, motives, and emotions that characterize ongoing activity.

Repression

Many people have experienced moments when they have thoughts, feelings, and urges that they would rather forget. Jane is furious at her mother for interfering in her relationship with Charlie and she thinks, "I wish she would drop dead." Natalie finds herself uncomfortable and anxious whenever her sister Margaret is around. Erotic fantasies float through her mind as if they have a will of their own. Bill is plagued with memories of stealing from his best friend.

repression: a defense mechanism in which anxiety-arousing thoughts or desires are automatically ejected from consciousness.

Like Jane, Natalie, and Bill, many of us have experienced conflicts that are unsolvable at the time or we have done something we deeply regret and wish we could "take it back." How do we deal with the anxiety that is bound to persist as long as these events occupy center stage in our thoughts and feelings? Wouldn't it be wonderful if we could banish all objectionable thoughts and desires from consciousness? This is precisely what **repression** does.

Repression does not wait for us to summon it forward. It operates automatically to force unacceptable content from consciousness. It is also selective—not all anxiety-arousing material is a candidate for repression. These thoughts and impulses must have great personal significance and they must elicit high levels of anxiety, usually centering on forbidden urges.

When material is forced into the unconscious, it does not die, neither is it rendered harmless. In a sense, it is buried alive. It still festers at the unconscious level and occasionally shows up in behavior, usually in a disguised form. For example, it may intrude in our dreams and our fantasies. It may reveal itself in the inadvertent slip of the tongue such as the following one reported to Freud by Dr. Brill, "While writing a prescription for a woman who was especially weighted down by the financial burden of the treatment, I was interested in her saying, 'Please do not give me any *big bills,* because I cannot swallow them.' Of course she meant to say pills" (Freud, 1915, p. 103).

Repression can also produce distortions and aberrations in ongoing behavior. Consider the following example:

Many soldiers coped with their battle experiences by repression, unconsciously blocking memories from awareness.

> A young man who had recently become engaged was walking along the street with his fiancee. Another man greeted him and began to chat in a friendly fashion. The young man realized that he must know this apparent stranger, and that both courtesy and pride required that he introduce the visitor to his fiancee. The name of the other man, however, eluded him completely; indeed, he had not even a fleeting recognition of his identity. When in his confusion he attempted at least to present his fiancee, he found that he had also forgotten her name.
>
> Only a brief behavior analysis was necessary to make this incident comprehensible as an example of normal generalized repression. The apparent stranger was in fact a former friend of the young man; but the friendship had eventually brought frustration and disappointment in a situation identical with the one described. Some years before, our subject had become engaged to another young woman, and in his pride and happiness he had at once sought out his friend and introduced the two. Unfortunately, the girl had become strongly attached to the friend and he to her; at length she broke her engagement and married the friend. The two men had not seen each other until this meeting, which repeated exactly the earlier frustrating situation. It is hardly surprising that the newly engaged man repressed all recognition of his former friend, all hints as to his identity, and even the name of the fiancee. (Cameron & Magaret, 1951, pp. 367, 368)[1]

----
[1] Excerpted by permission from Norman Cameron and Ann Magaret: *Behavior Pathology,* pp 367–368. Copyright © 1951 by Houghton Mifflin Company, renewed 1979 by David Hooke and Gretchen Ann Magaret.

United Press International Photo

In many ways repression is the master defense mechanism. It underlies other defense mechanisms and must be activated before they can be called into play.

Rationalization

rationalization: a defense mechanism in which the individual represses underlying motives and invents plausible and acceptable reasons to justify behavior.

Of all the defense mechanisms, you are probably most familiar with **rationalization.** Indeed, the moral in one of the most beloved of Aesop's Fables involves this mechanism. When the fox was unable to reach the grapes after exerting itself to the limit, it justified giving up the effort by rationalizing that the grapes were probably sour anyway. Benjamin Franklin summarized the spirit of rationalization as follows, "So convenient a thing it is to be a reasonable creature, since it enables one to find or to make a reason for everything one has a mind to do."

There are times when we are unable to face up to the real reasons behind certain experiences, e.g., poor performance in spite of intense effort, disappointment in love, or taking credit for something a friend has done. We need to invent plausible and acceptable reasons to justify our behavior and feelings. To illustrate, Ginny and Phil were childhood sweethearts. Everyone expected that they would someday marry. But Phil has other ideas. In the heat of an argument, he lists all the reasons "You aren't my type of girl," and terminates the relationship. Ginny is overwrought. He has deeply wounded her self-esteem. She finds it impossible to face up to all the accusations Phil has made. The mechanism of repression automatically rejects much of what Phil has said. By the next day, she has invented a rationale for the breakup which is acceptable to both herself and to her friends. "We have been together so long that we were unable to develop our own potentials." "I want to pursue a career and marriage would only interfere." "Phil has a long way to go before he's ready for marriage. I can understand why he wants his freedom at this time."

Rationalization is not the same as lying. The essence of lying is the desire to deceive someone else when you are fully aware of your own motives. Both involve the use of reason to protect the person's self-esteem. However, when you rationalize, you have repressed awareness of the underlying motivation so that, in actuality, you are deceiving both yourself and others. If Ginny really accepts her reasons for the breakup with Phil, she is rationalizing; otherwise, she is lying. If you call in sick when you are not ill but would rather be doing something else, you are not rationalizing even though you are using reason to achieve a goal other than the one you are publicly espousing.

Projection

Almost every day many us have thoughts, feelings, and urges that we keep very private. Perhaps we have fantasies involving some illicit sexual activity, a negative feeling toward someone we love, or an urge that fills us with guilt. Perhaps we have some personality trait we do not wish to acknowledge. If these characteristics are sufficiently threatening to our self-esteem, we may repress them.

projection: a defense mechanism in which individuals attribute their own unacceptable impulses or feelings to others.

However, in **projection** we go one step further. We attribute these undesirable characteristics to other people, events, or things. This mechanism allows you to remain blind to certain intolerable aspects of yourself while their influence distorts the picture of the outside world.

There are some people who severely criticize in other persons the very same faults which are the weak points of their own character. They completely fail to recognize the fact that they themselves possess the objectionable traits or motives. To illustrate, Sheila can't seem to get Ted out of her mind. There is no question that she is sexually attracted to him. However, the thought of having an extramarital affair is repugnant to her. She now projects these same feelings and tendencies on her husband Leonard. She becomes very suspicious of his every move. "Where were you last night? Who were you with?" Nothing he says can convince her of his innocence. His denials serve only to add more fuel to the fire. Sheila has successfully repressed her sexual urges toward Ted.

But repressed impulses continually strive to break through at the conscious level. Consciously acknowledging her attraction to Ted evokes too much anxiety for Sheila. However, feelings of guilt which led to anxiety may be alleviated if you are able to cast the blame for shameful tendencies or wishes onto others, leaving yourself guiltless, or even victimized. In other words, you may feel less guilty if someone else can be made to feel guilty.

Projection of blame is commonly found in such everyday situations as the following. Matt clears the plates off after dinner. He piles several plates on top of each other. Before he makes it into the kitchen there is a loud resounding crash. He turns defiantly to his mother and exclaims, "It's all your fault, you told me to hurry."

Reaction Formation

reaction formation: a defense mechanism in which anxiety-arousing impulses are controlled by acting in the opposite way.

In **reaction formation** a person represses the unacceptable aspects of him or herself and then develops behavior and/or attitudes that are the exact opposite of the repressed urges. For example, as a child Adam loved wallowing in dirt and mud. There is nothing unusual about this behavior. It is a normal part of the child's exploration of the world. However, Adam's father saw things differently. He punished Adam severely both physically and verbally. He yelled, "You're filthy. You disgust me." Adam repressed this urge for dirt and disorder. To prevent the forbidden impulse from emerging, he adopted attitudes and behaviors that were the direct opposite. He became excessively clean and orderly, a behavioral characteristic he carried into adulthood.

In this example as in others involving reaction formation, the individual adopts a socially acceptable mode of behaving and thinking. By doing so, many secondary benefits are realized. Adam was able to gain the approval of his father as well as other adults. "What a nice boy he is. So clean and neat." This behavior is not hypocritical. It is a sincere expression of an individual's *conscious* beliefs.

Ironically, even though the behavior is in direct opposition to the repressed urge, the underlying impulse may still achieve some partial satisfaction. Consider the following: When her daughter Evelyn was born, Marion's first impulse was to reject the child. She had three children already and did not want to have a fourth. Besides, the little infant brought into her hospital room was crinkled and ugly. Her initial reaction was accompanied by overwhelming feelings of guilt. Repressing her negative reaction, she manifested an opposite reaction to the child. "She is beautiful. Just what I always wanted." However, like any repressed impulse, her underlying hostility toward Evelyn struggled to gain expression. She imagined all sorts of harm that could befall her daughter. She became overzealous in her efforts to shield Evelyn from danger. As a result, Marion became overly protective. In effect, she was smothering instead of mothering. She restricted Evelyn's interactions with other children saying, "You'll catch your death of pneumonia if you go out today." She told herself that she loved her child and pointed to her concern as evidence of her love. In actuality, she was hurting Evelyn through her behavior by stifling and interfering with her normal development. Thus, Marion's original hostile impulse was being satisfied to some degree even though her behavior might be regarded by herself and others as genuine love. Beneath this apparent devotion there lurked an unrecognized feeling of hostility or even wishes for her daughter's death. Her devotion served to appease a sense of guilt.

How can you tell if behavior is hiding behind the mask of reaction formation or is a sincere expression of a person's underlying beliefs? In truth, it is not always possible. However, the defensive character may be betrayed by exaggerated and rigid behavior accompanied by severe attitudes. Both Adam's excessive need for cleanliness and Marion's extravagant professions of love and concern were distortions of normal hygienic practices and love for one's child.

In more extreme forms, reaction formation is found in the "pacifist" who shouts, "Kill those who make war"; the self-appointed censor of public morals who voraciously devours pornographic literature to accumulate "evidence"; and the person struggling with repressed sexual urges who proclaims, "Castrate all sex offenders."

Regression

Growth is a continuous process of change. Behaviors that "worked" at an earlier time may be perfectly appropriate and relevant at that stage of development. However, we change, our motivations change, and our abilities to adjust to new situations undergo a continuous process of modification. Through the mechanism of *regression*, the individual returns to earlier modes of behaving as he or she tries to regain the gratifications of an earlier period in life. The arrival of a new sibling may precipitate a return to earlier, previously rewarding forms of behavior. For example, the child who is toilet trained may start wetting the bed again. Adults who throw tantrums or pout when frustrated or disappointed may be concealing their anxieties by retreating to immature patterns of emotions and/ or behavior. When the responsibilities of maturity become too much, you might

When this 17-year-old psychiatric patient found the old photograph of herself (B) at 5, she cut her hair and tried to make herself look as she had at 5 (C).

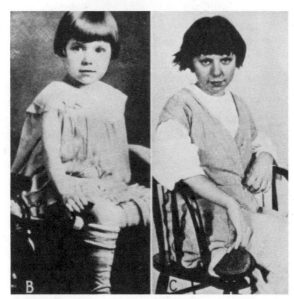

Dr. Jules Wasserman

regress to the dependency of childhood to allay the fears and insecurities of adult life.

It is likely that all of us, at one time or another, have displayed some form of regression. Do you remember the last time you were sick? Did you behave as a mature adult or did some childish characteristics creep into your behavior? Did you complain a lot? Were you perhaps a bit more demanding than usual, looking for and expecting a little extra attention? Illness is one type of stress situation that tends to bring out the baby in many of us.

Isolation

In many of life's situations the cognitive and emotional components are at war. Beverly is a loan officer at The First Bank. A warm and friendly person, she readily established trusting personal relationships with many of her customers. For the most part, she enjoys her work. Occasionally, however, she learns that one of her friends, with an outstanding loan at the bank, is in deep financial trouble. She finds it extremely difficult to put pressure on them to cure a delinquent account and simultaneously maintain her emotional composure. In the beginning, she had many sleepless nights knowing that she was, in a sense, contributing to the distress of her friends. The incessant conflict between her feelings and her actions threatened to shatter her ability to function.

After a while she developed what some call a hard shell. She managed to split off and isolate her emotional life from her business activities. This is the essence of **isolation.** Thoughts, actions, and feelings are placed in separate compartments where they do not interact. She tells herself and others, "You know, I love Kate and Howard like a brother and sister. I would do anything in my power to help them. But this is a business matter. Either they pay or the loan falls due. My own feelings have nothing to do with the decision."

isolation: a defense mechanism in which one separates conflicting thoughts or impulses by putting them into separate "compartments."

This situation is not unique to Beverly. Many of us compartmentalize to keep conflicting tendencies isolated from one another. Business people often say, "Business and friendship are like oil and water. They simply do not mix." Some surgeons make it a point to keep an emotional distance from their patients. Indeed, many will not operate on members of their own family. Instructors are often reluctant to establish close personal ties with their students, fearing a conflict between their feelings for their students and the necessity that they make judgments about the adequacy of their academic performance.

Denial

Janet's parents have just been informed that she has a disease that is usually terminal. At first they are utterly devastated by this tragic news. Their entire lives are suddenly thrown out of focus and they begin to doubt the very meaning of life. Amidst the emotional turmoil, Carl grasps at a straw of hope, "He didn't say it is necessarily fatal. He said 'usually.'" Edna grasps at the straw along with her husband of 20 years. "Maybe she doesn't have it after all. I have heard of diagnostic errors. We have all heard of such mistakes. We must get a second opinion."

Up to this point, most physicians would agree with this decision. Second opinions, made independently of the first, will occasionally raise doubts about the initial diagnosis. Under these circumstances, even a third opinion may be sought. But this is not the way the scenario enfolded for Edna and Carl. The second opinion confirmed the first, the third confirmed the two, the fourth confirmed the three . . .

In fact, the three distraught people embarked on a pilgrimage of all the prestigious medical centers of the nation. When yet another physician uttered the fateful words, they screened out the unfavorable words and clung to such phrases as, "Of course, I may be wrong. . . ." Both Carl and Edna are using the mechanism of **denial.** Denial is like closing one's eyes to the true state of affairs and pretending it does not exist. Like other defense mechanisms, it operates without conscious guidance. Carl and Edna are not purposely denying the accuracy of the diagnosis, but they are unconsciously filtering the information so that only part of it gets through—the words of hope rather than those of despair.

denial: a defense mechanism in which one simply denies an unpleasant reality.

Denial is not always passive. Look at the plight of Kate and Howard. In the face of impending financial disaster, they acted as if their finances were as sound as the Rock of Gibraltar. Indeed, they went one step further. They engaged in a wild spree of compulsive buying, thereby actively denying the reality of their situation.

We have noted several times in this book that effective adjustment requires that one face reality. Generally speaking, avoiding the true state of affairs is a sign of poor adjustment. However, one observer (Lazarus, 1979) has argued convincingly that there are times when denial can contribute positively to adjustment. Lazarus studied surgical patients. He found that those patients who used denial had a better postoperative recovery than those who insisted on knowing all the details about their operation. Based on his research, Lazarus concluded that denial can be useful in situations where the individual has little control over the outcome (see Box 7.2).

Displacement

Stress often makes us angry. We rage against the source of our frustration. Indeed, on occasion we may find ourselves overcome by the urge to strike out against the instigator of our anger and to inflict punishment on it. Nevertheless, in spite of these intense impulses to express our aggression, most of us do not often obtain direct gratification. Why?

The causes of our frustrations are numerous and varied. As we previously noted, they may be physical barriers, events, or other people. How do you vent anger against a computer that keeps mailing your book club selections long after you have cancelled your membership? Do you dare to challenge an authority figure whose ability to retaliate is greater than your ability to inflict harm? What

BOX 7.2: A CASE FOR DENIAL

For many years, the traditional wisdom in psychology has been that people should "face facts." People should be able to recognize their own shortcomings, threatening situations, and other unpleasantries. Most mental-health professionals believe that efficient perception of reality is an important characteristic of well-adjusted individuals.

Over the past few years psychologist Richard Lazarus at the University of California at Berkeley has been conducting extensive research on the topic of stress that has prompted him to arrive at some surprising conclusions. Lazarus believes that both denial (refusing to "face facts") and illusions (false beliefs about reality) can be important to psychological health—for some people on some occasions. When Skylab was about to fall to earth in 1979, Dr. Lazarus' advice, when asked how to deal with the threat, was to ignore it—advice that was consistent with his research findings.

Much of his research has been conducted with surgical patients. What he has found was that patients who did use denial and who insisted on maintaining their illusions had a better postsurgical recovery than those patients who insisted on knowing all the facts about their surgery and having a detailed account of their prognosis. To illustrate, a patient who uses denial wanted to know very little about his upcoming operation. When asked about the operation the patient might say "I leave that to my doctor. He's the best in the world." After the operation, such patients have relatively few complaints. They may perceive any discomfort as something to be expected and not even report it to their physician. Furthermore, illusions can speed the recovery process. By believing they can make a speedy recovery, such patients may actually try harder. And physicians have long been aware that the patient's attitude plays an important role in the recovery process.

On the other hand, patients who "face the facts" are likely to be much more anxious about their operations—which can in turn lower the chances for success. Following surgery, these patients are acutely aware of every ache and pain. Their inability to have illusions may cause them to be more pessimistic about their chances of recovery. Again, this attitude may interfere with the recovery process.

Lazarus is quick to point out that denial and illusions are not appropriate for every situation. He cited cases of women who denied the potential risk of a lump on the breast until it was too late for treatment. Men who were having heart attacks have begun to exercise to prove to themselves that nothing serious was wrong with them.

It is in situations where one has little control that denial and illusions can be most useful. Certainly Skylab's falling was beyond our control, and ignoring its threat was the best solution. So too, denial and illusions concerning a major operation could lessen anxiety and lead to a quick recovery.

Source: From "Positive Denial: A Case for Not Facing Reality" by Richard S. Lazarus interviewed by Daniel Goleman. Reprinted from *Psychology Today* magazine. Copyright © 1979 American Psychological Association.

about your moral and ethical values? Most people have been taught that aggression is wrong except under special circumstances.

Why do some people pound the desk, kick the wastebasket, or throw the pliers? Are they really angry at these inanimate objects? The fact of the matter is that feelings of anger and hostility may be so intense that they cannot be consciously tolerated. Through the mechanism of **displacement,** we transfer the emotional feeling from the original source to a substitute. By shifting to another person or object, the individual is protected from consciously acknowledging these feelings.

An amusing example of displacement is provided by a four-year old girl who was locked in the closet by her mother for being bad:

displacement: a defense mechanism in which unacceptable impulses are redirected to something or someone other than the original source.

After a rather long silence, the mother inquired from her side of the door, "What are you doing?" The child said, "I've spat on your coat, I've spat on your shoes. Now I'm waiting for more spit." (Landreth, 1967, p. 327)

PUTTING IT ALL TOGETHER

In this chapter, we have looked at both coping and defense mechanisms. We have seen that coping mechanisms get to the heart of the matter. They serve to surmount, remove, or alter the underlying causes of strain. They represent effective means of adjusting to the stresses of daily life. Defense mechanisms, on the other hand, attempt to reduce or alleviate the extreme discomfort of such emotions as fear, anxiety, and guilt.

In this section we shall look at several stressful situations and see how a defense mechanism and then coping behavior might be brought into play.

Repression and Suppression

Repression. In a moment of overriding temptation, Bill stole a sum of money from his best friend, Barry. He felt remorseful and guilty. Gradually, details of the crime began to fade. Within days, he could not even recall the incident. But other things began to happen. For reasons he couldn't understand, he began to avoid Barry or even thinking of him. Moreover, he turned down invitations to parties where he might run into Barry. He spent so much time worrying about his incomprehensible split with Barry that other areas of functioning were adversely affected—study, work, and even recreation.

Suppression. Shortly after transgressing toward Barry, Bill found that feelings of guilt and remorse were interfering with his ability to function. He said to himself, "I must have a talk with Barry at the very first opportunity. I am sure he will understand that I took the money in a time of great personal stress and weakness. In the meantime, life must go on. I'll just have to stop thinking about Barry until I can do something about it. I'll immerse myself in work. That's a surefire way to take my mind off what I did to Barry."

Rationalization and Use of Reasoning

Rationalization. Alice was having a ball at college—going to parties every night, attending athletic events, and generally doing anything that would take her away from her studies. Then the crash came. Her midterm grades were in. Catastrophe. "You know," she told a friend, "I'm in the wrong major. Those advisors we had back in high school were the pits. I'm saddled with a whole bunch of courses that are as interesting as watching grass grow. It's too late now to do anything about it."

Use of Reasoning. After receiving her midterm grades, Alice sits down to take stock of the situation. She admits to herself that she has been trying to burn the candle at both ends. She decides that it is time to take college more seriously. "Is it too late?" she asks herself. "Not really. I know my own capabilities. What if I cut down on the partying? That will certainly give me time to study and make up some of the lost work. What about dropping that math course where I am hopelessly lost? Then I can get a tutor for the other courses. Yeah, I think I can work this out."

Projection and Empathy

Projection. Diane has just been in a fender bender. She rushes out of the car and begins to scream at the other motorist, "Why don't you watch where you're going? Look what you did to my car!"

Empathy. Diane takes a deep breath before she gets out of her car. The face of the other motorist mirrors her own distress. She sees the damage that has been done to the other person's car and realizes that it is more extensive than her own. Her heart goes out to him. She says, "I don't know who's at fault but I'm sure neither of us did this intentionally. Let's see what we can work out."

Regression and Humor

Regression. Neal was already feeling the pangs of regret for accepting the invitation to give a speech before a local service organization. He always felt anxious whenever he was the focus of attention of a large number of people. He was afraid they would not like him, not accept him. He remembered similar uncomfortable situations when he was younger. For example, when a child, he would play the part of a clown to break the ice. He would make faces and generally act silly. As the moment of truth drew near, Neal started clowining around with the other participants. In spite of the fact that his behavior drew stern looks of disapproval, he continued acting in a silly manner.

Humor. Neal was aware of the fact that the forthcoming speech would elicit much anxiety in him. Knowing that humor is one means of alleviating tension, he prepared a humorous story to introduce his speech. He told the story well and was rewarded by looks of approval.

Isolation and Objectivity

Isolation. Jeanette was a biology instructor. She was faced with a perplexing problem. Cathy was one of the most brilliant students she had ever had in class.

Her fund of knowledge and zest for learning seemed to be unlimited. However, there was a problem. In exam situations, Cathy froze. In fact, so high was her anxiety level that beads of perspiration dropped from her forehead. She was in danger of failing the course. Jeanette felt sympathy for Cathy but concluded that sympathy has no place in the classroom. Either Cathy must overcome her anxiety attacks or she would fail the course.

Objectivity. Instead of retreating into a hard shell, Jeannette reasoned as follows: "The purpose of an exam is to assess the learning of my students. Obviously, the anxiety attacks interfere with Cathy's ability to demonstrate the knowledge she has acquired in the course. What I really want to know is how much Cathy has learned. Suppose I put her in a nonthreatening test situation." She decided to give Cathy an oral examination in which great pains were taken to see that Cathy was both relaxed and comfortable.

Denial and Concentration

Denial. Kate and Howard are in serious financial trouble. Every day the mail brings more bills. They remain unopened. Their banker, Beverly, has telephoned and left messages. They have not returned the calls. Life appears to continue as usual.

Concentration. Kate and Howard sit down and spread all the bills in front of them. Then they list their assets. They spend the entire evening trying to work out a method of payment that will satisfy their creditors. They each work out a means to supplement their income until they resolve this crisis. In addition, they figure out ways to cut back on some of their expenses.

Displacement and Sublimation

Displacement. Luis has had it with his boss. For the second time in a row, he has been overlooked for a raise. He is furious. However, he needs a job and so far there are no other offers on the horizon. Thus, he avoids a confrontation with the boss. Seething with anger, he turns his wrath on his subordinates.

Sublimation. Luis has a hobby. He loves to write poetry. Instead of venting his anger on his co-workers, he spends his lunch hour writing poems about war, crime in the streets, and violence in the cities.

SUMMARY

- Efforts to cope with stress may be directed at alleviating the emotional component and/or dealing directly with the causes of strain.

- In the animal world, there are three built-in coping mechanisms: fight, flight, or freeze. At the human level, the same broad categories of adjustive behavior are available.

- Coping mechanisms are those behaviors and thoughts that deal directly with the causes of strain. They may involve the use of cognitive abilities or draining off the tension associated with stress.

- Through the use of reasoning, we weigh the risks, costs, and benefits of various alternative courses of action.

- Maintaining an objective attitude means considering an issue without being influenced by personal feelings or beliefs.

- Another cognitive mechanism for coping is the ability to concentrate or focus complete attention on the problem.

- Through the use of humor, potentially stressful situations are often defused.

- Immediate reactions to stressful situations can be consciously held back or suppressed.

- Ambiguity and uncertainty should be recognized and accepted as a part of everyday life.

- Sublimation involves the substitution of alternative, usually socially desirable, goals for those that are denied.

- We may release some of the tension associated with strain through crying or talking things out with a confidant.

- Empathy is the ability to see things from another person's point of view.

- Defense mechanisms are devices used to protect the individual from the anxiety associated with strain. The defense mechanisms discussed include repression, rationalization, projection, reaction formation, regression, isolation, denial, and displacement.

- Finally, we looked at a variety of situations and showed how the individual might use a defense mechanism or a coping mechanism to deal with strain.

TERMS TO REMEMBER

Coping mechanisms	Repression
Defense mechanisms	Rationalization
Objectivity	Projection
Concentration	Reaction formation
Suppression	Isolation
Sublimation	Denial
Empathy	Displacement

C H A P T E R 8

LIFE SPAN DEVELOPMENT

Judy's obstetrician was careful. Of this she heartily approved. But wasn't he carrying things a bit too far? After confirming that she was pregnant (a fact that she had suspected because of changes in her body which she could already sense), he told her he wanted to remove some tissue from the inside of her cheek to do a chromosomal analysis. A chromosomal analysis indeed! Why only that morning her grandmother, with characteristic candor, had warned her, "Don't let him suggest any high fallutin' ideas, honey. When my generation had a baby, we didn't make such a fuss over it. We had our babies any which way you could imagine. Some were delivered by old Doc Kroak and others by a midwife. Didn't much matter. Somehow we got along OK. Now they got so much fancy equipment in the delivery room, it's a wonder they can find the mother."

"I don't understand, doctor. Why do you want a chromosomal analysis?"

"Just a precautionary measure, that's all."

"Precaution against what?" she asked, feeling a slight edge come to her voice.

He must have noticed too. He reassured her, "Nothing to concern yourself with. Every once in a great while, we find a prospective mother with chromosome abnormalities. Since they can lead to birth defects, we think it is important to check these things out early in the pregnancy. But don't worry. It's rare and I'm sure everything will be fine."

He was wrong. He called Judy several days later and asked her to stop by his office. He cut off her question, "Why?" before it could be asked. "It won't take long," he assured her, "Just something I want to check out with you."

Judy entered the obstetrician's office with an uneasy feeling, almost a sense of foreboding. She felt better when he seemed to be relaxed and at ease. "Judy, I'm going to give it to you straight." She felt a sudden rush of panic at these words. He continued, "We found some evidence of chromosomal breakup. It may not mean a thing, but I think we should check it out just the same." He paused, smiling reassuringly. "Tell me, are you aware of any history of birth defects in your family?"

She searched her memory for a few moments and recalled that Aunt Grace, on her mother's side, and Cousin Charlene had had some problems. Aunt Grace had aborted a couple of times in her fifth month and Charlene had a child who was placed in a children's hospital at a very early age. She informed her physician of these facts and promised to inquire further if it would be of any use.

"Yes, it would be most helpful if you would. The more we know about you and your family the more intelligently we can proceed."

He then began to explain what he had in mind. First, he delivered a brief course on genetics, explaining that there are 46 chromosomes in each body cell of a normal human being. They form 23 pairs. In the female, one of these pairs consists of two X chromosomes. In the male, there is one X and one smaller Y chromosome. These two chromosomes are often called the sex chromosomes, since together they determine the sex of the child. The fertilized egg always receives an X chromosome from the mother. It may receive either an X or a Y from the father. If an X, the child has two X chromosomes and will be female. If a Y, the combination of and X and a Y yields a male child.

Each chromosome in the human body carries over 1,000 genes. These determine the characteristics that distinguish us from all other species on earth—our physical form and appearance, eye and hair color, etc. They are truly our genetic links to the past. As you might imagine, if anything is wrong with only a single chromosome that makes up the fertilized egg, there is a potential for widespread physical and mental abnormalities in the developing individual.

amniocentesis: the surgical procedure used to obtain fluid from a pregnant woman. This fluid is then analyzed to determine whether there are genetic abnormalities in the fetus.

After obtaining more information on birth defects in Jane's family background and weighing the possibility of damage to her chromosomes, her obstetrician advised **amniocentesis.** This is the technique of obtaining cells from an unborn infant for intensive analysis.

This is how it works. First, echo-location is used to find the precise position of the fetus in the mother's womb; high-frequency tones are bounced off the fetus and the record of the echos provides a "picture" of its size and location. This procedure avoids the necessity of X rays, which are potentially dangerous to the unborn child. The fetus is surrounded by the amnion, which is filled with fluid in which loose cells float about. All of these cells are genetically identical to the original fertilized egg.

A hypodermic syringe is injected into the prospective mother's abdomen and about six tenths of an ounce of amniotic fluid is withdrawn. The cells found in the fluid may be studied directly or grown as tissue cultures for more exhaustive study. Although the culture method can provide more information, a delay of at least one month is involved. In some cases, this delay cannot be tolerated.

The study of the cells will reveal whether or not there are chromosome abnormalities. To illustrate, occasionally an extra chromosome will appear in the cells under analysis. If it occurs among the middle-sized groups of chromosomes and the fetus is permitted to go to term, the child will almost certainly die during infancy. Other anomalies may lead to retardation. For example, chromosomes are occasionally found with a condition referred to as a "dangling tip." If this is found in the X chromosome or chromosomes identified as number 16, 6, 7, or 8, retardation is a distinct possiblity ("Retardation," 1982).

In addition to the chromosomal analysis, biochemical methods can be applied to the amniotic fluid itself and detect congenital conditions, such as defects in the neural tube. In fact, more than 40 metabolic disorders can be detected by amniocentesis (Crain, 1982).

A procedure called amniocentesis is used to detect various genetic defects in the fetus. A needle is inserted through the abdominal wall of a pregnant woman in order to obtain amniotic fluid for analysis.

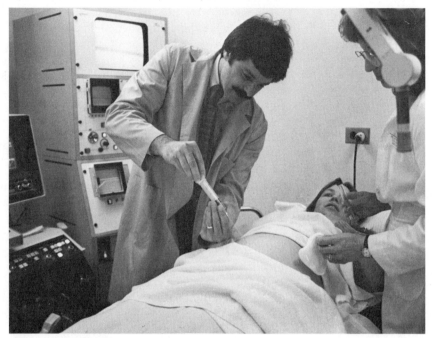

Sue Markson

Amniocentesis may provide the information that allows parents to decide whether or not to permit the pregnancy to go to full term. Not all parents decide to terminate a pregnancy when an abnormality is found. Many of these people have found support groups or professional help beneficial in helping them to make and live with their decisions.

Amniocentesis may provide favorable as well as unfavorable news. For example, in situations where past family history casts a shadow of doubt over the pregnancy, amniocentesis may remove some of the doubts concerning the prospects of the unborn child. This is what happened in the case of Jane. Since the analysis of the amnion cells was favorable, she carried her child to term. She now has an infant daughter her obstetrician proclaimed "normal and beautiful."

ENVIRONMENTAL FACTORS IN PRENATAL DEVELOPMENT

zygote: product of the union of an ovum and a sperm; the fertilized egg.

embryonic period: human development from the time of implantation to about the eighth week after conception.

fetus: the unborn infant from about the end of the second month after conception until birth.

Life begins as a single microscopic cell, a product of the union of an ovum (egg) and a sperm. This fertilized egg, called the **zygote,** contains the genetic information that directs the growth of the individual throughout life.

Within one day after fertilization, the zygote divides into two joined cells, each containing the same genetic information found in the original cell. After about two weeks of this type of division, the cluster of cells forms a hollow ball containing three distinct layers of cells. The outer layer will give rise to the skin, the nervous system, and the sense organs. Bones, blood, and muscles will develop from the middle layer. Finally, the organs of the digestive system will develop out of the inner layer.

During the **embryonic period** (2 to 8 weeks), some of the basic features of the anatomy are formed. Although the embryo is only about an inch long at the end of the eighth week, the limbs and distinguishable facial features may be discerned.

Beyond the eighth week until birth, the developing child is referred to as the **fetus.** The structures that were formed during the embryonic period are now refined and finished. By the fifth month, the mother may let out a startled cry, "I can feel it moving." Its heart is also beating by this time. If the child is born during the 28th week, it is capable of surviving if given proper medical attention since all body systems can function by this time.

During the approximately nine-month period from conception to birth, is it safe to say that the developing individual is free of any environmental influences? In other words, can we attribute any and all characteristics of the child at birth to the enfolding of the genetic plan for that child?

It may surprise you to learn that only a few generations ago it was widely believed that the mother could positively influence the later development of the child by selectively exposing herself to desirable environments. Expectant mothers advocating this view went out of their way to attend art exhibits, museums, concerts, and plays so that their children would grow up with an appreciation of the arts. When this view was discredited, very little scientific interest was directed to the possible effects of the prenatal environment on the developing individual. However, by ignoring the fact that the mother's body provides a very complex chemical environment for the embryo and fetus, researchers were, in effect, discarding the baby with the bath water.

We now know that alterations in the chemical environment can produce tragic consequences for the child. The following are a few of the variables that may be related to problems at birth and thereafter: age of mother, her nutritional habits, her use of drugs, alcohol, and/or cigarettes, illnesses contracted during pregnancy, and the number of previous pregnancies (see references in Parmelee & Haber, 1973). To illustrate, rubella (German measles) contracted by the mother during the first few weeks of pregnancy increases the risk that her child will be born with an affliction such as deafness.

Let's first take a look at the effects of the nutritional habits of the mother on the developing fetus. Have you ever heard a folk wisdom to the effect, "For every baby the mother loses a tooth"? The implication is that the fetus has first call on the nutritional resources of the mother. Thus, if the mother has an unbalanced and nutritionally inadequate diet, the fetus will get what it needs first, leaving the mother seconds and leftovers. According to this view, the mother will suffer greater nutritional deficiencies than the child. However, this does *not* appear to be the case. Rather, it looks as if the mother's body takes care of itself first and then attends to the needs of the child within her.

Let us suppose for a moment that an expectant mother is suffering from malnutrition. Who is likely to suffer more, the mother or the child? To answer this we should know that the time of maximum environmental risk to an organ or a body structure is when it is developing. Once it is completely formed and functioning, it is less susceptible to environmental stress. It is no accident that rubella can be so damaging to a fetus but usually leaves the mother symptom-free. So it is with dietary deficiencies in the mother.

Malnutrition, particularly during the fetal period and the first few months after birth, leads to a loss of brain cells in the unborn child that can never be recaptured (see Birren, Kinney, Schaie, & Woodruff, 1981, for example). Thus, malnutrition in the pregnant mother may lead to permanent physical or intellectual impairment of her offspring. This is particularly worrisome because of the rapidly growing number of teenage pregnancies. Younger girls may be more likely to follow a "coke and chips" diet. Pregnancy is not the time to go on a crash diet or to ingest the latest miracle drug that promises to shave off pounds a week with no effort on the dieter's part.

Although there is no direct mingling of the mother's blood with that of the fetus, various substances that the mother is taking can reach the child via the umbilical cord. This makes the fetus a potential victim of its mother's life-style. Thus, if the mother is addicted to morphine, heroin, or methadone, the child may be born with a drug addiction and must undergo drug withdrawal. Not only does this ordeal involve difficult psychological aspects, it is also life threatening.

Even anaesthetics are not free from suspicion. They are frequently used during delivery to ease the pain of childbirth and to simplify the delivery by the physician. One of the consequences of this practice is that the child often emerges in a semidrugged state. When children delivered with the assistance of anaesthetics are compared to those for whom no medication was used, it has been found that the drugs may interfere with the coping behaviors of the newborn (Aleksandrowicz, 1974; Scanlon & Alper, 1974). The effect may last as long as 28 days. However, not all experts regard these effects as serious (Yang, Zweig, Douthitt, & Federman, 1976). Nevertheless, many mothers choose delivery procedures that do not involve the use of medication.

A wise approach to pregnancy is to avoid taking any compound that is not essential for the mother's health and to avoid excessive amounts of those that are. A partial listing of potentially harmful drugs reminds us of the need for caution in this area. Besides compounds we have previously examined, we may include some barbiturates and tranquilizers, synthetic sex hormones, and excessive amounts of vitamins A, D, B6, and K (Cox, 1979). Even smoking cigarettes appears to reduce the weight of the newborn child and increase the likelihood of the Sudden Infant Death Syndrome in infancy.

MATURATIONAL READINESS AND SENSITIVE PERIODS

maturation: developmental changes that follow a genetically proprogrammed growth process.

The birth of the baby increases the child's vulnerability to environmental influences. During the prenatal period, the basic structures of the body are being formed and maturing. A given structure appears to be most "at risk" when it is in its formative stages. However, this process of **maturation** does not end at birth. The brain is still an incomplete structure in which many billions of neural connections must be made before the child is ready to skip, talk, socialize, reason, and do the many other things that are uniquely human. Early development follows a maturational timetable fairly closely, but interaction with the environment occurs through the life span.

critical period: a time of maximum readiness for the development of a particular skill or behavior.

It has been proposed that, just as there are periods in prenatal development when environmental irregularities can cause widespread structural and functional harm, so also there are similar periods after the child is born. These time intervals during which we appear to best be able to benefit from experience have been called **critical periods.** To illustrate, when children are placed in institutional settings at an early age, they sometimes receive sharply reduced environmental stimulation and very little personal attention from care givers. They may lie in cribs for long periods of time during which their only human contact is when their diapers are changed and when they are fed. This minimal human attention is often dispensed in a cold mechanical fashion. These children evidence retarded motor development, emotionless reactions to others, slowed development of language skills, and intellectual impairment (Spitz, 1945; Dennis, 1960; Skeels, 1966).

sensitive period: the period of time during which a particular skill or behavior is likely to develop.

The initial observations suggested that the effects of deprivation during the critical period are permanent and irreversible. More recent evidence indicates that the effects are reversible to some extent and some ability to benefit from experience extends beyond the critical period. For these reasons, the term **sensitive period** is coming more into general use. As one reviewer expressed it, "[In humans] the effects of experience become less irreversible and more plastic, so the term 'sensitive' may be more appropriate than is 'critical'" (Hunt, 1979, p. 136).

There are three major lines of evidence supporting the concept of sensitive periods in humans: the social smile, social attachment, and intellectual development.

The Social Smile

Many different stimuli elicit the smiling response in infants during their first month, including a high-pitched voice, gas in the digestive system, the human face and facsimiles thereof, and tactual stimulation of the face. It is generally

Which environment is more likely to lead to normal development? Why?

Suzanne Arms/Jeroboam, Inc.

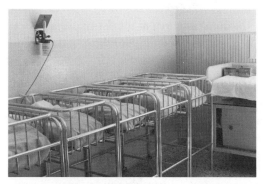

Suzanne Arms/Jeroboam, Inc.

believed that the smiling response does not acquire social significance until about the fifth week (Ambrose, 1963). For about the next 9 to 10 weeks, the infant will smile in response to objects, strangers, and care givers. At about the 20th week, however, the stimuli eliciting the smile become discriminated. Thus, familiar objects and faces will evoke smiling behavior but strange objects and unfamiliar faces will not. It is believed that the maximum sensitive period occurs between the time the social response first appears until the child reacts with fear to unfamiliar faces and objects.

Studies of blind children provide strong support for the notion of sensitive periods for the acquisition of the smiling response (Fraiberg, 1976). These children evidence the social smile about the same age as sighted children. However, unless the smiling response is specifically reinforced by providing some sort of nonvisual stimulation (e.g., touching, cooing) whenever they smile, the social smile diminishes and disappears altogether. It is extremely difficult to regain the response through direct instruction.

Social Attachment

When discussing motivation, we noted that humans are preeminently a social species. Virtually everything we do throughout life is in a social context—eat, play, learn, and so forth. Studies of lower animals demonstrate that the initiation of social attachments in many species is almost regulated by the clock. Failure to establish social ties within a relatively narrow time frame can have long-lasting effects on adult social attachments.

Is there an analogous period during which the human infant develops a strong, clearly differentiated tie to a care giver? The other side of the relationship—the parents to the child—is quite clear. When the pregnancy is wanted, the bonding of the mother to her child begins even before the child is born. She typically begins anticipating the pleasures she expects to experience once delivery takes place. If the pregnancy is not wanted, however, this anticipation of joy is missing. Thus, the initial strength of the parental bonding may be weak or even negative.

Even if the pregnancy is wanted, however, the child must pass muster. The child may fall short of parental expectations in appearance, frequency of crying, or responsiveness to the parents (Blehar, Lieberman, & Ainsworth, 1977). In one long-term study of infant development (Chess, Thomas, & Birch, 1965), the researchers found that about 7 to 10 percent of the children were "difficult." Their eating, sleeping, and toilet habits were irregular. They tended to cry a lot, were inclined to be irritable, and had difficulty adjusting to change. The investigators concluded that, because the mother did not experience pleasure in her interactions with the child, the temperamental difficulty mushroomed into a totally unsatisfactory mother-child relationship. Alone or in combination, these immediate reactions can impair the early transactions between parent and child. However, human adaptability is enormous. Care givers can be taught to engage in activities that will bring smiles and laughter into the interactions of the participants (Hunt, Mohandessi, Ghodssi, & Akiyama, 1976; Levenstein, 1976).

But what about the bond between the infant and the care giver? Does there appear to be a sensitive period? Some of the most convincing evidence comes from studies in which infants are shifted from foster mothers to adoptive parents (Yarrow, 1967). If the separations occurs at six months or less, there is little evidence of distress in the child—prolonged anger or depression—as long as their physical needs continue to be satisfied. However, if separation occurs at eight months or older, the infants respond with strong negative emotions, including protest and withdrawal. What about the other side of the sensitive period? According to one researcher, "The most sensitive time may be the period during which the infant is in the process of establishing stable affectional relationships, approximately between six months and two years. A break in relationship with a mother-figure during this period would presumably be most traumatic" (Yarrow, 1964, p. 122).

However, the child is capable of flexible and varied forms of attachment. Once the infant becomes attached to the mother, it can expand its trust to include the father, grandparents, and siblings (Ainsworth, 1973). Moreover, infants in kibbutz nurseries in Israel identify and respond affectionately to their parents in spite of frequent separations (Newman & Newman, 1979).

What are the critical factors in establishing a warm, trusting attachment to a care giver? The evidence suggests that it is the quality rather than the quantity of the care and transactions between infant and care giver. As expressed by one observer, "Evidence from longitudinal studies is suggesting that what may be most important for the infant's relationship with its mother is the mutual delight that each takes in their transactions with each other" (Hunt, 1979, p. 126).

Intellectual Development

Earlier in the chapter we took brief note of studies of institutionalized children who experienced minimal sensory, perceptual, social, and intellectual stimulation. In one of these studies, children from comparable backgrounds were raised in two quite dissimilar institutions in Iran. The following passage describes the child-care practices in Institution A:

> On the average there were eight children per attendant. . . . The attendants have no special training for their work and are poorly paid. The emphasis on the part of the supervisors seems to be on neatness in the appearance of the rooms, with little attention to behavioral development. In his crib the child is not propped up, and is given no toys. . . . Except when being bathed, the younger children spend practically their entire time in their cribs. (Dennis, 1960)

Contrast the above with the care provided in Institution B:

> The number of children per attendant is three to four. Children are held in arms while being fed, are regularly placed prone during part of the time they are in their cribs, are propped up in a sitting position in their cribs at times, and are placed in playpens on the floor daily when above four months of age. Numerous toys are provided. Attendants are coached in methods of child care, and supervisors emphasize behavioral development as well as nutrition and health. (Dennis, 1960)

Do you imagine that the differences in care giving might influence the intellectual development of the children in the two institutions? In a word, the answer is yes. The children in institution A were found to be seriously retarded in physical, intellectual, and motor development. Indeed, only 8 percent of the children in Institution A could walk by the age of three contrasted with 94 percent in institution B. A critical factor in their intellectual retardation may have been the lack of visual stimulation. When confined to cribs in the prone position, the children in institution A had little opportunity to follow people and objects with their eyes. Children raised in a normal setting spend a considerable amount of time watching things that move or have contrasting edges (Hunt, 1979).

Further evidence for a sensitive period in intellectual development is described in the work done by researchers from Harvard University. The investigators had observed that, by the age of six, two types of children can be observed: Type A children who are outstanding in their ability to cope with problems in and out of the classroom; and Type C children, who manage both their academic and social lives rather poorly (White & Watts, 1973; White, 1975).

The investigators next turned their attention to the mothers of these children. They found that mothers of Type A children provided a rich and intellectually stimulating environment for their children. They provided freedom to roam and a variety of toys. They encouraged their children to explore their environment. If a child ran into a problem, the mother would speak to the child and offer new ideas for the child to consider. The small child began to identify him- or herself as a "doer," as he or she moved around to actively explore the environment. This exploration and learning about cause and effect adds greatly to the intellectual performance of the Type A children. In contrast, mothers of Type C children ruled by the words, "Don't do that." They placed many restrictions on their children's freedom to explore and made no attempt to stimulate their curiousity.

At the age of 10 months, the two types of children did not appear to differ from one another in their overall coping abilities. However, by the age of 18 months, the differences were clear-cut. Thus, it appears that the sensitive period for intellectual development starts at about one year of age and extends to at least one and a half years and possibly longer. Since the brain grows rapidly between birth and the age of three, achieving 80 percent of its adult size by that time (Scrimshaw, 1969), it has been suggested that the sensitive period for intellectual development comes between one and three years of age.

What are the adjustment implications of research on sensitive periods of development? Since most of you are or someday will become parents, it is important to be aware of how profoundly your behavior can affect the development of your children. A few good rules to follow are:

1. If you are female, maintain a well-balanced diet throughout pregnancy and avoid the use of alcohol, drugs, and cigarettes.
2. After the child is born, do not hesitate to handle and hug the infant.
3. Engage in activities that produce reciprocal laughter—smiling, cooing, making faces, etc.
4. Provide a stimulating environment for the child—mobiles hung above the crib, safe toys for the baby to touch and manipulate, and walks in a carriage. Above all, talk to your child. The child is learning much about language long before he or she is able to speak a first word.

**COGNITIVE
DEVELOPMENT**

Children are amazing little creatures. From the moment they are born, they examine, manipulate, and search for ways to understand their environment. Even the little ones who have not yet acquired language have "ideas" about how to interact with the world around them. How do children come to *think* the way they do?

Jean Piaget, one of the foremost leaders of cognitive psychology, found that watching the intellectual development of children blossom and grow was not only fascinating but provided valuable clues to understanding and interacting with children at different stages of development. Although it was clear that children act smarter as they get older, Piaget was the first to spell out the special differences in thought processes. He believed that mental growth takes place in a series of stages. In each stage, the child thinks and behaves quite differently. The speed at which the child climbs the intellectual ladder may vary quite a bit from one child to another, but the sequence is the same for all children. Can you speed up the process? One study found that you cannot rush a child's intellectual development by trying to teach reasoning skills appropriate to more advanced levels (Brown, 1965). However, if a child is maturationally ready, the transition to the next cognitive level can be accelerated through increasing the complexity of interactions with the environment. Let's look at Piaget's developmental stages.

sensory-motor stage: according to Piaget, the first stage of cognitive development during which the child comes to know the world through sensory and motor experiences.

Sensory-Motor Stage (Birth to 2 Years). In the first, or **sensory-motor stage** of development, children form their ideas of the world largely on the basis of the outcomes of their actions. They examine, handle, and manipulate objects and then observe what happens. If they see a mobile hanging above their crib, they may reach out and try to pull it down. They shake objects and listen to the sounds, jump up and down on a toy to see what happens, and suck almost any object they can grasp. Through these sensory and motor activities, they are learning to know their world in terms of their own actions and the consequences of these actions.

object permanence: the recognition that an object continues to exist even though it is out of sight.

During the first few months of life, infants seem to have no sense of **object permanence.** If you take an object and move it across a six-month-old's field of vision, he or she will typically follow the object with the eyes. But what happens when the object disappears? The child will show no disappointment and will not appear to anticipate that the object will come back. Did you ever try playing "peek-a-boo" with a young infant? It's usually not too much fun because the infant doesn't seem to understand what the game is all about. By the time the infant reaches about nine months of age, he or she will reach for an object that is hidden out of view, but only if the child has seen the object being hidden. Now "peek-a-boo" is fun to play. By the time the child reaches about 18 months of age, he or she will begin to search for something even if the child has not seen it hidden. Because such behavior is "natural" for adults, we rarely pause to reflect on what a remarkable intellectual achievement this is for the child. For the first time, the child realizes that an object can exist separately and independently from his or her involvement with it.

By the end of the sensory-motor period, children are able to symbolically represent problems and invent solutions. Piaget observed the following example of sensory-motor invention in one of his children:

Jacqueline, at 1 year 8 months, arrives at a closed door—with a blade of grass in each hand. She stretches out her right hand toward the knob but sees that she cannot turn it without letting go of the grass. She puts the grass on the floor, opens the door, picks up the grass again and enters. But when she wants to leave the room things become complicated. She puts the grass on the floor and grasps the doorknob. But then she perceives that in pulling the door toward her she will simultaneously chase away the grass which she placed between the door and the threshold. She therefore picks it up in order to put it outside the door's zone of movement. (Piaget, 1952, p. 339)

Preoperational Stage (2 to 7 Years).   The appearance of language signals a major break in cognitive development. In the **preoperational stage,** children acquire the ability to imagine doing things and to imagine the possible consequences of their actions. They can now think and talk about objects in terms of symbols, instead of having to actually manipulate them. It is during this period that imaginative play begins to take shape. The world of make-believe opens to the child. He or she can take a truck and pretend it's a spaceship, play house in a most realistic and elaborate manner with nothing but building blocks as props. But children at this stage cannot manipulate symbols the way an adult does.

preoperational stage: in Piaget's theory of development, the stage in which language begins to dominate cognitive development.

One of the most difficult things for many adults to accept is that children don't think the same way adults do. Piaget believed that the nature of the thinking process is very much different in younger children (see Box 8.1). For example,

A whole new world opens to children at the preoperational stage as they learn to use symbols.

Monika Franzen

BOX 8.1: STAGE THEORY AND THE COGNITIVE GAP

One of the fascinating implications of a stage theory of cognitive development is the inevitability of communications gaps between individuals perched at different cognitive levels. Consider the following account of an encounter among a 2-year-old boy, his 5-year-old sister, and their 45-year-old father.

David is seated on the floor, completely absorbed in play with two hand puppets. Without warning or preamble, Laurie suddenly grabs one of the puppets. David's response is instantaneous and vigorous. He screams, stamps his feet, and displays all of the signs of acute emotional distress. Between sobs and tears, he manages to voice a protest, "Mine! Mine!" Laurie becomes very annoyed with David. "Don't you know you can't have two toys by yourself? You must share." Unimpressed with the force of Laurie's logic, David remains restive. "Mine! Mine!" he continues to shout. Finally, in the role of ombudsman, Daddy decides to intervene. "Laurie, you should not have taken the puppet away from David. He was playing with it."

"But he wasn't sharing," Laurie replies, a tear beginning to form at the edge of her voice. "You always tell me I must share. So I *was* sharing. David wasn't sharing."

"But David's only a baby," Daddy replies placatingly. "He doesn't understand sharing."

"Well, he's supposed to share," Laurie affirms, confident of the basic righteousness of her stand. As she leaves the room, she defiantly displays the trophy she had wrested from David by her obedience to the rule of sharing.

Looking at the above transaction from the point of view of a stage developmental theorist, several interesting observations may be made that bear directly on personal-social interaction at many stages of life. David is just beginning to emerge from the sensory-motor period in which the outstanding feature is egocentrism. Egocentrism in the young child shows that he or she has not yet developed a sense of self as a separate being in the world. The baby sees the world revolving round him- or herself and is unable to take another person's point of view. In fact, the baby is unable to distinguish clearly between self and nonself. To David, the puppets are not only *his* but they are *him*. At least, they are as much him as an arm or a leg.

Laurie's admonition to share is beyond David's comprehension. The gap between Laurie and David is not one of quantity (how much they differ in the *same* point of view) but of quality. The concept of sharing is different in *kind* from the concept "all the world is part of me." But just as Laurie and David are destined to undergo many similar confrontations until both have achieved the blessed state of the same level of cognitive development, so also are Laurie and her father. At Laurie's cognitive stage, rules are treated as God given. Rules are rules and must not be violated. She has not yet reached the level of cognitive development in which such rules are recognized as the "inventions" of people, constructed to achieve a degree of social harmony.

In this single real-life situation, we see how stage theory may shed light on several gaps that have captured the imagination of many observers of the contemporary scene—the generation gap, the credibility gap, and the communications gap. We may add the "cognition gap."

Source: Haber/Runyon, *Fundamentals of Psychology,* © 1983. Addison-Wesley, Reading, Ma. pp 396–7. Reprinted with permission.

children at this stage are still *egocentric*—they see everything only from their own point of view. If a three-year-old closes his or her eyes, the child cannot see you. Since he or she cannot see you, the child also believes you cannot see him or her. What are the adjustive implications of egocentric thinking? If a child believes he or she is at the center of the universe, that the world revolves around him or her, the child is also likely to believe that he or she can make things "happen." Thus, children at this age are particularly susceptible to believing that something happened because they thought about or wished it to happen.

Imagine the four-year-old who angrily wishes her father gone. How do you suppose she will deal with death or divorce?

To Piaget, one of the main characteristics of the preoperational stage is the child's inability to visualize that a given quantity, weight, or volume of a substance doesn't change regardless of its shape or the way it is arranged. The concept of **conservation** begins to appear in the preoperational stage but is not fully mastered until the next stage of development. Ask children under four years of age to choose between four candies spaced close together or four candies spread out. Most of the children will choose the latter, presumably because they think there are more candies. Now try the following experiment: Show the child two identical glasses. Pour water from one glass into the other. By the time children reach the age of four, they can usually recognize that the quantities are the same. Now, take another glass that is taller and thinner and pour water into it from one of the other glasses. Even though the young child sees you pour from one glass to the other, he or she will say that the taller glass has more water. The ability to distinguish between appearance and reality is beyond the intellectual capabilities of the preoperational child. By the age of six or seven, most children recognize that, regardless of the way things are packaged, divided, or shaped, quantity remains the same.

conservation: the concept that certain properties (e.g., quantity, volume) of objects remain the same in spite of alterations in their appearance.

Concrete Operational Stage (7 to 11 Years). Children at the *concrete operational stage* can now handle the concept of conservation. They are able to classify things and reason logically. They have a set of rules that help them adapt to their environment. They can apply these rules, especially to objects they can see and feel. Instead of manipulating things, they now can manipulate symbols, but they cannot yet deal with completely abstract concepts. They can reason logically, but only if relationships are stated in concrete terms. For example, if they know that Barbara is smaller than Arnie, and Arnie is the same size as Mindy, they will understand that Barbara is also smaller than Mindy. However, they would probably have difficulty if you confronted them with this problem: A is smaller than B and B is the same size as C. Which is smaller, A or C?

concrete operational stage: in Piaget's theory, the third stage of cognitive development during which the child develops the ability to think logically.

Formal Operational Stage (12 Years and Beyond). The ability to deal with abstract relationships develops during the **formal operational stage.** Children can now reason about the possible and the abstract. They are no longer tied to what is real and concrete. They can deal with hypothetical situations and can imagine rather than experience the consequences of their actions. This is also a time for thinking about one's thoughts—how thoughts are organized and where they are leading. Some of the cognitive focus is shifted from the present, and the past and future become part of one's world. What happened before is considered, discussed, and evaluated. What is done now is seen as affecting the future and long-term planning begins. Perceiving time as continuous, and recognizing the impact of the past and the future on current activities, is one of the basic qualities of human thought. It is at this highest

formal operational stage: in Piaget's theory, the final stage of cognitive development during which the child develops the ability to deal with abstract relationships.

In the formal operational stage adolescents can conceptualize thoughts, think about thinking, and arrive at conclusions.

Bruce Forrester/Jeroboam, Inc.

level of cognitive development that this appreciation of the time perspective emerges.

Piaget originally believed that formal operations was the final and inevitable stage in cognitive development. The child is no longer "different" from adults. Of course, experience and knowledge will add to one's cognitive abilities, but the final stage of intellectual growth was reached by around 12 years of age. This view has since been revised by Piaget (1972) and others. It is now believed that, unlike the other stages, formal operations may not be universal. Aptitude, education, and the experiences of life may well determine whether or not an individual ever reaches this stage and, if so, to what degree. We usually associate abstract ability with training in such areas as mathematics, science, and logic. But people who cannot handle the abstract relationships in mathematics and science may still reach the formal operational stage in their own area of interest. A mechanic may be able to formulate and test hypotheses when trying to fix an automobile engine; a plumber may form abstract concepts of plumbing lines when trying to locate a leak; and a retail shopkeeper may display exceptional logic when dealing with a merchandise supplier.

One final thought. Piaget may have believed that the final stage of cognitive development was reached by the age of 12, but several studies have taken issue with this conclusion. These studies suggest that certain aspects of cognitive growth continue well into adulthood (Rubin, Attewell, Tierney, & Tumolo, 1973; Papalia, 1972). Certain cognitive abilities stay intact in old age, and little or no impairment in any cognitive area is found in some people well along in years (Baltes & Schaie, 1976).

MORAL DEVELOPMENT

Suppose your friend pleaded with you to help him cheat on a test. Would you? Is it ever right to lie? Should you obey a law you sincerely believe to be unjust? Is it wrong to tell on someone to get yourself out of trouble? Throughout our lives, we are continually faced with moral dilemmas. How do we develop moral principles?

Jean Piaget (1948) saw moral development as an aspect of cognitive growth. He believed that, like the development of thinking and reasoning, there are universal and fixed stages in the development of moral judgments. How morality is judged at a later stage may be incomprehensible to a child at an earlier stage of development. Perhaps that's why it is so difficult to teach moral judgments.

Piaget posed moral dilemmas to children at varying ages. For example, he asked children to judge "which child is naughtier": the one who accidentally breaks 15 cups or the one who deliberately breaks 1 cup? The way children react to such dilemmas appears to change with age and stage of moral development. Very young (preoperational) children focused on the extent of the damage—they judged breaking 15 cups naughtier than breaking just 1 cup. Older children said that purposely breaking one cup was worse—in other words, they considered the child's intentions. Piaget believed that preoperational children can only understand results and outcomes and base their moral judgments on this information alone. To make moral judgments on the basis of what another person is thinking, the child must pass beyond the stage of egocentric thought.

Another cognitive psychologist, Lawrence Kohlberg, went beyond Piaget's theorizing and proposed more complex stages of morality. Kohlberg devised a series of moral dilemmas such as the following:

> In Europe, a woman was near death from a special kind of cancer. There was one drug that the doctors thought might save her. It was a form of radium that a druggist in the same town had recently discovered. The drug was expensive to make, but the druggist was charging 10 times what the drug cost him to make. He paid $200 for the radium and charged $2,000 for a small dose of the drug. The sick woman's husband, Heinz, went to everyone he knew to borrow the money, but he could only get together about $1,000, which is half of what it cost. He told the druggist that his wife was dying and asked him to sell it cheaper or let him pay later. But the druggist said: "No, I discovered the drug and I'm going to make money from it." So Heinz got desperate and broke into the man's store to steal the drug for his wife. Should the husband have done that?[1]

---

[1] Source: Kohlberg, L.: The Development of Children's Orientation toward a Moral Order. I. Sequence in the Development of Moral Thought." *Vita Humana*, Vol. 6, pp 18–19 (Karger, Basel 1963).

According to Kohlberg, a child at the preconventional level of moral development might reason that snitching is OK as long as you don't get caught.

Ilka Hartmann/Jeroboam, Inc.

There are no right or wrong answers to these dilemmas. Kohlberg was not as much interested in the positions subjects took as he was in the *reasons* they gave to justify their answers. Through the use of this technique, Kohlberg has described seven stages of moral development organized into three levels.

Between the ages of about 4 and 10, children are at the *preconventional* level of development where they are mostly concerned with the consequences of their actions. In the first stage, they act to avoid punishment. Even though their actions correspond to what is usually considered right or wrong, there is no sense of underlying reasoning. They merely obey rules to avoid trouble and escape punishment. An individual at this stage might respond, "Heinz shouldn't steal the drug because he'll get caught and sent to jail" (Liebert, Poulos, & Strauss, 1974).

At the second stage of the preconventional level, moral judgments are based on self-interest. The primary motivation is to gain rewards and the return of favors. The biggest advance at this stage is that other people are sometimes considered but only in terms of "If you scratch my back, I'll scratch yours." Here a person might respond to the Heinz dilemma, "Heinz isn't really doing any harm to the druggist, and he can always pay him back. If he doesn't want to lose his wife, he should take the drug because it's the only thing that will work" (Rest, 1974).

Stages three and four are at the *conventional* level of moral development, a level many people never pass. In stage three, the child tries to be "good" to gain approval or avoid disapproval. At this stage, the *intentions* of the person become important. Thus, a person at this stage might justify stealing the drug on the grounds that Heinz had intended to pay the druggist and that people would think he was inhuman if he didn't do everything he could to save his wife's life.

By stage four, the individual recognizes the need for law and order. The social order must be maintained and rules obeyed, even if the individual doesn't agree with those rules. Thus, a person at this stage might reason, "You can't let somebody die like that, so it's Heinz's duty to save her. But Heinz can't just go around breaking laws and let it go at that—he must pay the druggist back and he must take his punishment for stealing" (Rest, 1974).

The final stages of moral development are at the *postconventional* level of morality. All involve reasoning rather than emotions. In stage five, the individual is concerned with gaining the respect of others, and feels duty bound to conform to the laws and standards of the majority. If the laws are wrong or unjust, then they should be changed. Thus, a person might reason, "Heinz will lose the respect of others if he lets his wife die. He will have to go to jail since that is the law. Perhaps the law should be changed to provide for such an emergency."

By stage six, the individual listens to the dictates of his or her own conscience. Morality is defined in terms of abstract values which are objectively defined. Individuals at this stage might reason that the higher principle of saving a life justifies stealing the drug. Kohlberg believes that very few people reach this stage or the next.

The seventh stage of moral development has been reached by such great leaders as Spinoza, Martin Luther King, Jr., and Gandhi (Kohlberg, 1980). At this highest stage, individuals transcend the limitations of human frailty and judge morality in an infinite perspective.

SEX ROLES

sex roles. social expectations about how men and women are supposed to behave simply because of their sex.

The social forces that define what men and women "should" be like are set in motion from the moment we are born. These **sex role** expectations influence how we view ourselves, how we interact with others, and even what we do with our lives.

At a very early age, children learn to label themselves as female or male. They actively teach themselves and each other what behaviors are appropriate for each sex. When parents tell their sons "boys don't cry" or encourage their daughters to help in the kitchen, they are sending clear messages about how boys are supposed to behave (because they are boys) and how girls are supposed to behave (because they are girls). Sex role expectations are so pervasive that even feminists may be affected by them. One study found that feminist mothers had no difficulty treating their daughters in a nonsexist way, but were upset if their sons played with dolls or showed any "feminine" tendencies (Van Gelder & Carmichael, 1975).

Children also learn sex roles through observing and imitating their parents or other adult models. In households where the father works and the mother stays home to take care of the family, the parents are providing the traditional sex role models for the child.

Girls can go across sex barriers with less impunity than boys can.

George W. Gardner

But what happens when the mother works outside the house? Generally, the father helps with the household chores and shares in the care of the children (Hoffman & Nyé, 1974). Since sex role models in these households are less traditional, you might expect the children to hold less traditional views of women and men. Indeed, children of working mothers see men and women doing many different things both inside and outside the house (Miller, 1975). They also see women as less tied to the house, more active outside, and generally more competent and effective. There is evidence to suggest that these feelings carry over to the daughters' own views of themselves. Career-oriented college women are more likely to be the daughters of working women than of nonworking women (Hoffman & Nye, 1974).

The educational system also tends to perpetuate the traditional sex-role stereotypes. Girls and boys soon learn that their teachers have different expectations about their behavior and which subjects they will do well in. The contents of textbooks generally portray girls as passive, dependent, and helpless, while boys are seen as resourceful, creative, and independent. Adults are similarly submerged in conventional sex-role stereotypes. Men work outside the house at interesting, exciting jobs. Women, when they do work, are portrayed in typical "women's" occupations—teacher, nurse, secretary (Wirtenberg & Nakamura, 1976). It should be noted that there has been a concerted effort by both authors and publishers in recent years to remove sexist references from the literature. For example, the American Psychological Association suggests that authors "be aware of the current move to avoid generic use of male nouns and pronouns when content refers to both sexes. . . . [and] avoid overuse of the pronoun *he* when *she* or *they* is equally appropriate" (*Publication Manual*, 1974).

In the final analysis, what it means to be a male or female is not so much dictated by biological factors as by expectations about behavior. In virtually every aspect of life, men and women are "assigned" different roles and expected to behave in different ways. There is much evidence to document the existence of sex-role stereotypes. People generally believe that women are not aggressive, not independent, not very competitive, and have no business sense. But they are tender, gentle, and compassionate (Broverman, Vogel, Broverman, Clarkson, & Rosenkrantz, 1972). Not all women accept the traditional sex-role stereotypes, and those that don't have higher career and educational aspirations, cope more effectively with stress, and perform better in competitive situations (Peplau, 1976; Stewart, 1978). Thus, women who reject the conventional stereotypes are better able to cope and compete—the very qualities necessary for success in the business world.

How have men been affected by the traditional sex-role stereotypes? According to the stereotypes, men are aggressive, highly competitive, ambitious, and unable to express tenderness (Broverman et al., 1972). There is evidence to suggest that men pay dearly when they adhere to the traditional male role. Men have a greater vulnerability to heart disease related partly to aggressive and competitive behavior (Harrison, 1978). Living up to the traditional male standard means hiding true feelings and emotions, since it is not manly to be anxious or afraid. This means keeping problems and feelings bottled up.

Fathers are becoming more actively involved in the responsibilities of child care. As they do so, they are learning that they can be tender, warm, and gentle without sacrificing their "masculinity."

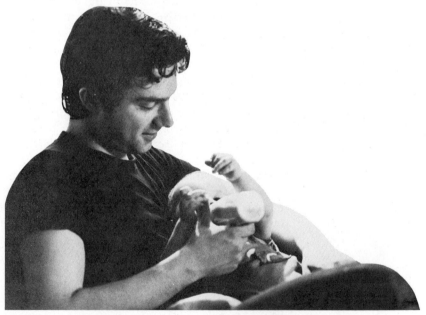

© Joel Gordon 1978

Sex-role stereotyping carries the implication that masculinity and femininity are at two opposite ends of a pole. If a man is manly, he cannot also be feminine. Results from a number of studies support the view that there really are two separate dimensions (Broverman et al., 1972). The masculine dimension includes such traits as aggressiveness, independence, and competitiveness. Ability to express emotions and feel warmth and concern for others are some of the traits in the other, feminine dimension. According to the stereotypes, man is high on the masculine dimension and low on the feminine dimension. The stereotypic woman is just the opposite.

In recent years, psychologists have raised questions such as, "Is a man any less of a man if he cleans the house, cares for the children, is warm, tender, and affectionate? Or a woman any less of a woman if she is highly motivated, aggressive, and has a keen business sense?" In contrast to the traditional stereotypes, a number of studies have found that aggressive, masculine men may also be warm and gentle and that a compassionate, tender woman can also be highly competitive and aggressive (Bem, 1974).

androgyny. the ability to integrate both "masculine" and "feminine" characteristics as the situation requires.

Combining qualities of both the masculine and feminine sex roles is **androgyny** (Bem, 1974). People who combine the best of each score high in both dimensions and are viewed by some as the most effective functioning adults. Indeed, androgynous people do better at school, have higher self-esteem, and earn more awards than those mired in traditional and rigid sex roles (Spence, Helmreich, & Stapp, 1975). Androgynous women and men are more flexible and better able to adapt to the demands of the situation. They can be assertive when required, or they can be warm and expressive when the situation calls for it (Bem & Lenney, 1976).

Although some say the distinctions between the sexes are blurring, there is still a lot of ambivalence and confusion about sex roles. The traditional stereotypes linger on and place restrictions on both men and women. Is androgyny the answer? Only time will tell.

ADULT DEVELOPMENT

Until relatively recently, it was widely assumed that development was a process that started at conception and ended at adolescence. As we saw in Chapter 2, however, Erikson and others have argued convincingly that development is a lifelong process that continues until death. In other words, we do not reach a certain age and then stop growing emotionally, socially, and intellectually.

Although the major classes of problems that confront us during our adult years tend to correlate with age, it is important to note that age does not lock us into specific roles and behaviors. As one psychologist has observed: "It no longer surprises us to hear of a 22-year-old mayor or a 25-year-old university president or a 35-year-old grandmother or a retiree at 50. No one blinks at a 70-year-old college student or at the 55-year-old man who becomes a father for the first time" (Neugarten, 1980, p. 66).

There is no universal agreement about how to divide the adult years into various age groups. Any classification is arbitrary. When we speak of the young adult, we refer to someone between 17 years of age and about 40; middle adult extends from 40 to about 60; and later adulthood starts at about age 60.

As we grow older we face different challenges. One of the first struggles confronted by the emerging adult is the push and pull away from parental domination toward the responsibilities of adulthood. By the time most young people step into their 20s, they leave home and develop new relationships with other adults. The future seems scary and there is much anxiety about which paths to follow.

Although there are broad individual differences, a number of generalizations have been made by the various investigators studying adult development. In her book *Passages*, Gail Sheehy (1976) described the 20s as a time during which people start to build their lives. They search for areas of competence and concerns are directed toward occupational and educational decisions, and establishing intimate relationships. During this time, many people start to build a family (see Box 8.2).

The early 30s are seen by many as a time of soul-searching and reevaluation (Sheehy, 1976; Gould, 1975). Many people start to question and doubt their choices and their values. Those who have married may feel discontent. Extramarital affairs and divorces are often symptoms of this rocky period. This is the first major time of reassessment when the individual starts to question, "Where am I going? What is life all about?"

By the second half of the 30s, there is a settling down (Levinson, Darrow, & Klein, 1978). Pressures to succeed at a chosen career or achieve desired goals intensify as the individual becomes aware that the clock is ticking and time is passing (Gould, 1975). However, it is at about this time that many people experience what has been called a *midlife crisis*. Somewhere around the age of 40, the individual becomes aware that life may be more than half over and that many dreams will never be realized. For those who feel trapped in a life with no meaning, the future may look bleak and feelings of depression may be overwhelming.

Daniel Levinson and his colleagues (1978) found that about 80 percent of the men they studied experienced a painful and disruptive midlife crisis. About half the men saw the midlife period as their last chance to achieve desired goals. Often the goal was something specific such as a certain position in their career or a specified level of income. Some of the men experienced a serious decline during this period. This decline was sometimes associated with their failure to achieve certain goals or the realization that their lifestyle or job was leading nowhere. During this time, these men felt that life had no meaning and that what they were doing was meaningless. Other men attempted to break out of the routines of their lives by changing jobs, marriages, or lifestyles. Certain aspects of life that were once accepted were now seen as intolerable, causing the individual to make dramatic changes. In many cases, these changes entailed much risk and sacrifice and may literally have meant starting all over. Although these men took many years to rebuild their lives, many of them ultimately achieved a new rewarding stability.

BOX 8.2: PARENTING

Sally Forth by Greg Howard, Field Newspaper Syndicate

As the above cartoon suggests, one of the most challenging tasks of early adulthood is learning what it takes to be a good parent. Generally, the only training we have for the job comes from our own experiences as children and, usually, the only thing people learn from that is what they are *not* going to do. So—what can you do as a parent to ensure that your child will develop in a healthy, happy, and productive way? Although there are no easy prescriptions to follow and no guarantees of success, certain areas have been identified in which parental influence plays a key part in the shaping of the child's personality.

Most investigators agree that healthy development requires an atmosphere of love and acceptance. But love is not enough. Of equal importance is *discipline* and the setting of limits. One of the most difficult problems for parents is learning to strike a balance between harsh authoritarian discipline and total permissiveness. Because many parents waver between these two extremes, the child may receive conflicting messages at different times. *Consistency* is crucial to the child's sense of insecurity, and the child views the world as unpredictable and unreliable. As long as parental standards are consistent, discipline provides the

> Needed structure and guidance for promoting healthy growth on the part of the child. Where coercion or punishment is deemed necessary, it is considered important that the parent make it clear exactly what behavior is considered inappropriate; it is also considered important that the child know what behavior is expected, and

that positive and consistent methods of discipline be worked out for dealing with infractions. In general, it would appear that freedom should be commensurate with the child's level of maturity and ability to use it constructively. (Coleman, 1980, p. 149)

Another key area in parent-child relationships is communication. Faulty communication patterns are more prevalent in the background of emotionally disturbed young people than in those who show adequate adjustment (Alexander, 1973). For example, some parents are so preoccupied with their own interests and concerns that they fail to listen to their children. Thus, they have no real understanding of the stresses and conflicts the child is experiencing. Consequently, they don't provide the support needed during times of crisis. Another faulty communication pattern is what has been called the *double bind* (Bateson, 1960). In this type of communication, the parent conveys one message verbally and another through his or her behavior. An example of this might be a mother who tells her daughter that she is gaining too much weight and must watch her diet. Yet she continues to urge the daughter to clean her plate and continually provides high-calorie treats at the dinner table.

Some parents find it difficult to allow their children to grow up. They watch over them constantly, protect them from even the slightest risks, and make all decisions for them. The overprotective parent stifles normal growth and development by failing to provide the child with opportunities to test competence and reality. As a consequence, the child often feels inade-

BOX 8.2 *(continued)*

quate and threatened by the real world. The following example illustrates some of the problems of overprotection.

> I was a girl who had almost everything: a beautiful home; money for personal pleasure whenever I asked; nice clothes; and parents who coddled me, picked up after me, and chauffeured me wherever I wanted to go. What didn't I have? Well, I didn't have any knowledge of how to sort out laundry or run a washing machine. I didn't know how to discipline myself to use time properly, to make sure I got enough sleep, to feed myself the right food. I didn't have the basics for coping with life on my own.
>
> My parents—undoubtedly out of love, but with a mixture of guilt added—had, for some reason,

> overcompensated during my childhood. They had done too much for me. And when the time came for me to be on my own, I struggled for independence from this overprotective nest, stumbled over my newfound physical, moral, and social freedoms, and suffered a crushing fall. But by the time I hit bottom, I had learned one principle that I hope will guide me throughout the rest of my life: I can make it on my own. I learned this the hard way. I only hope that, by sharing my experience, I can help others become independent young adults without the physical and emotional trauma I endured.

In addition to those discussed, other parent-child relationships have been associated with faulty development in children. These are summarized in the accompanying table.

SUMMARY CHART OF FAULTY PARENT-CHILD RELATIONSHIPS

Undesirable Condition	Typical effect on Child's Personality Development
Rejection	Feelings of anxiety, insecurity, low self-esteem, negativism, hostility, attention-seeking, loneliness, jealousy, and slowness in conscience development
Overprotection–domination	Submissiveness, lack of self-reliance, dependence in relations with others, low self-evaluation, some dulling of intellectual striving
Overpermissiveness–overindulgence	Selfishness, demanding attitude, inability to tolerate frustration, rebelliousness toward authority, excessive need for attention, lack of responsibility, inconsiderateness, exploitativeness in interpersonal relationships
Perfectionism with unrealistic demands	Lack of spontaneity, rigid conscience development, severe conflicts, tendency toward guilt and self-condemnation if there is failure to live up to parental demands
Faulty discipline:	
Lack of discipline	Inconsiderateness, aggressiveness, and antisocial tendencies
Harsh, overly severe discipline	Fear, hatred of parent, little initiative or spontaneity, lack of friendly feelings toward others
Inconsistent discipline	Difficulty in establishing stable values for guid-

BOX 8.2 *(concluded)*

Undesirable Condition	Typical effect on Child's Personality Development
	ing behavior; tendency toward highly aggressive behavior
Inadequate and irrational communications	As in case of "double bind" communications, the tendency toward confusion, lack of an integrated frame of reference, unclear self-identity, lack of initiative, self-devaluation
Undesirable parental models	The learning of faulty values, formulation of unrealistic goals, development of maladaptive coping patterns

The exact effects of faulty parent-child relationships on later behavior depends on many factors, including the age of the child, the constitutional and personality makeup of the child at the time, the duration and degree of the unhealthy relationship, his or her perception of the relationship, and the total family setting and life context, including the presence or absence of alleviating conditions and whether or not subsequent experiences tend to reinforce or correct early damage. There is no uniform pattern of pathogenic family relationship underlying the development of later psychopathology, but the conditions we have discussed often act as predisposing factors.

Source: From *Abnormal Psychology and Modern Life,* 6th edition by James C. Coleman, Robert N. Butcher and Robert C. Carson. Copyright © 1980 Scott, Foresman and Company. Reprinted by permission.

The midlife crisis, if it occurs, can be exciting. It can provide opportunities for achieving old but not forgotten goals, for working out new identities, and for preparing the individual for later maturity and aging.

Some investigators have challenged the view that the midlife period is a time of upheaval and turmoil (Vaillant, 1977; Costa & McCrae, 1980). Instead they feel that there is a smooth and gradual transition from a younger self-concept to an older one. Moreover, the relevance of these findings to women has been questioned (Barnett & Baruch, 1978).

By the late 40s, much of the previous anxiety and urgency gives way to an acceptance of one's life and a feeling that one can live with previous decisions and choices. Many individuals with children become more willing to let their children develop in their own directions instead of pushing them toward parental goals. For example, a parent may finally give up on the idea that the child will take over the family business and accept and even encourage the child's pursuit of his or her own interests.

For many, this is the time that the last of the children leave the home. One investigator (Neugarten, 1970) found that the average age of the mother is about 47 and the father about 50 when the youngest child breaks the family ties and begins a new and independent life. The house is empty and life is very different for the parents. After mother and father spend about 20 years adjusting to the role of parents, new adjustments are now required, particularly if life has centered on the children. For some people, the least satisfying time of life is when the children leave home. In contrast, there are those who are actually relieved and look forward to the time when the last child takes off (Lowenthal & Chiriboga, 1972). Moreover, relationships between parents and their children actually tend to get better *after* the children have left home (Sullivan & Sullivan, 1980).

Most people in their 40s and 50s find their strength, physical vigor, and attractiveness diminishing, making them aware that they have used up half their lives. As they settle into their 50s, they begin to mellow out, become more interested in daily happenings and less concerned with accomplishments and abstract goals. They are more likely to be satisfied with the direction their lives have taken and accept the fact that certain goals will never be achieved.

menopause: the period in a woman's life when menstruation ceases.

For women, **menopause** (in the mid to late 40s or early 50s) represents the reality of aging. Menstruation stops, the woman is no longer able to bear children, and certain physical changes sometimes cause dramatic alterations in mood and appearance. Some women find menopause difficult to adjust to and they become anxious, depressed, or irritable. Many women find menopause is not as bad as they thought it would be and that much of their anxiety stemmed from *not* knowing what to expect. Although some women fear menopause signals the end of their sex life, in actuality many women find sexual relations more enjoyable once the fear of pregnancy is removed.

climacteric: the time of life associated with various glandular and bodily changes in men.

Although men do not experience a sudden physical change comparable to menopause, many go through a **climacteric** (Zaludek, 1976). There is decreased hormonal output, but they still remain fertile. Many of the psychological symptoms experienced at this time—anxiety, depression, irritability—often stem from the realization that their strength and vigor are declining and their appearance is changing.

As we saw in Chapter 2, Erik Erikson believes that the major challenge of

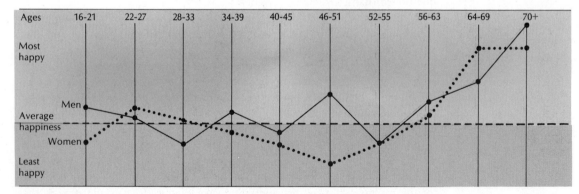

FIGURE 8.1   THE HAPPIEST YEARS: A comparison between men (—) and women (....)

| Ages | 16-21 | 22-27 | 28-33 | 34-39 | 40-45 | 46-51 | 52-55 | 56-63 | 64-69 | 70+ |

Most happy

Men

Average happiness

Women

Least happy

Source: Gail, Sheehy, *Pathfinders* (New York: William Morrow and Company, 1981), p. 253.

the middle years is achieving generativity—feeling that one is making significant contributions to the next generation. Many middle-aged people strive to achieve generativity through their work. More and more women and men are changing jobs or careers during the middle years as they search for more rewarding or satisfying work. During this time, many women start a new career or pick up an old one now that their children are in school or have left home.

Many young people tend to view the later years as "downhill all the way." But, based on four years of research, Gail Sheehy (1981) found that the happiest people are in their mid-50s and older. She found that older people were less bored, less lonely, and more in control of their inner needs and outer environment (see Figure 8.1).

At 85, George Burns still continues to live a productive life.

Courtesy G. P. Puttman's Sons

Aging is inevitable. But as the saying goes, "You are only as old as you think you are." One investigator (Neugarten, 1971) distinguishes between the "young-old" and the "old-old." The young-old accept that they are aging but don't think of themselves as old and refuse to accept the role of "old person." In contrast, the old-old accept the inevitability of being old, see themselves as old, and accept the role of "old person."

As with every other period of life, there are tremendous variations in aging. At the extremes are the older people who are healthy, alert, and still active in society and those who are confused, childlike, dependent, and senile. It is certainly a misconception to believe that all old people are sickly or senile. Only about 5 percent of the elderly are in nursing homes or institutions. And many of those

FIGURE 8.2

Carrie VanVliet, 95-year-old nursing home resident, spends much of her daily time in the activities room firing and painting ceramics. Her creations are eventually sold to the community during the facility's annual holiday bazaar. (This is excellent therapy for hands and fingers as well as being mind-stimulating.)

Phyllis Luber

Mae Corrigan, 89-year-old nursing home resident, still begins her day by applying her face makeup as the finishing touch to dressing. (She won't leave her room unless "totally dressed.")

Phyllis Luber

who are in nursing homes are still creative, productive, and vain enough to care about their appearance (see Figure 8.2).

As people grow older, there are certain inevitable and predictable social changes they will experience that will affect whom they spend their time with and what they do. Some of the most important changes associated with late adulthood include retirement and the death of one's spouse, friends, and relatives.

In the next three chapters, we deal with various aspects of adult development: Interpersonal Relationships; Marriage and Other Intimate Relationships; and Sexuality.

SUMMARY

In this chapter we looked at life span development and some of the adjustive requirements that typify various ages of development.

- Conception occurs when a sperm unites with an ovum to form a zygote. Twenty-three chromosomes are contributed by each parent. Each chromosome, in turn, carries in excess of 1,000 genes.

- When there is good cause to suspect the possibility of birth defects or inherited disorders, amniocentesis provides a means of identifying some potential problem areas or, alternatively, providing a clean bill of health for the fetus.

- Environmental factors are also at work even during the prenatal period. Alterations in the chemical environment can produce tragic consequences for the child. Contrary to popular belief, the mother will satisfy her nutritional needs before meeting those of the fetus. Consequently, maternal malnutrition can inflict irreparable harm on the fetus. Other factors that may produce adverse prenatal development include: use of drugs, alcohol, and cigarettes by the mother; illnesses contracted by the mother during pregnancy; and number of prior pregnancies.

- We examined sensitive periods in the maturation of the individual, focusing on evidence provided by the social smile, social attachment, and intellectual development. We proposed four rules to follow when you are a parent of a newborn child. These involved diet, handling and hugging the child, engaging in reciprocally satisfying activities, and providing environmental stimulation for the child.

- During the course of intensively studying the development of children, Piaget concluded that cognitive development proceeds by stages. Although the stages are not fixed by the calendar, they do follow a predictable sequence. The various stages he observed were: sensory-motor, approximately 0 to 2 years; preoperational, 2 to 7 years; concrete operational, 7 to 11 years; and formal operational, 12 years and beyond.

- Both Piaget and Kohlberg concerned themselves with moral development. Piaget noted that moral concepts are tied to cognitive development. At early stages of development, children assessed blame in terms of the amount of damage inflicted. At later stages, however, they took into account the intentions underlying the acts.

- Kohlberg has proposed a seven-stage theory of moral development in which more abstract principles of assessing blame characterize higher levels of morality. Kohlberg believes that very few people reach stage 6 (morality defined in terms of abstract values) and stage 7 (in which morality is judged from an infinite perspective).

- Sex role expectations influence how we view ourselves, how we interact with others, and what we do with our lives. They are set in motion at the moment of birth. Sex roles are learned by children through observing and imitating their parents and other adult models.

- The meaning of being male or female is not dictated by biological factors but rather by expectations about behavior.

- Women who do not accept the traditional sex role stereotypes have higher career and educational aspirations, cope more effectively with stress, and perform better in competitive situations.

- Androgynous individuals—who combine the "best" qualities of both masculine and feminine sex roles—are more flexible and appear better able to adapt to the demands of the situation.

- Development continues throughout life. Although certain developmental problems are correlated with age, we are not locked into specific roles and behaviors by the clock. The next three chapters are concerned with three major areas of development in the adult.

TERMS TO REMEMBER

Amniocentesis	Preoperational stage
Zygote	Conservation
Embryonic period	Concrete operational stage
Fetus	Formal operational stage
Maturation	Sex roles
Critical period	Androgyny
Sensitive period	Menopause
Sensory-motor stage	Climacteric
Object permanence	

C H A P T E R 9

INTERPERSONAL RELATIONS

It was a soft summer day, one that Lena liked to refer to as a lazy day. Bill and she sprawled on the park lawn, eyes closed and welcoming the warm touch of the sun on their faces after so many days of rain and cloudiness. When a puffy white cloud crossed the sun and cast a brief shadow on their faces, Bill opened his eyes and followed the cloud impassively.

"There's a swan up there, a big white swan," he murmured.

Lena was suddenly wide awake and alert. She had never seen a swan out of water, "Where is it?" she demanded, her eyes rapidly scanning the terrain but coming up empty.

"Up there in the sky. Oops, it's turning into a dragon."

"You're crazy," Lena said, laughing quietly. "If anything, it's my Aunt Tildy."

They both enjoyed this moment of supreme tranquillity and relaxation. Wishing to prolong the moment, Bill observed a young man walking across the lawn about 25-feet away. "What do you suppose he does for a living?" he asked.

Rapidly picking up the game, Lena observed, "Well, he wears a black leather jacket, his hair is long and scraggly, and he's got a spare tire bigger'n yours. He's a biker, no doubt about it. Probably got a chain concealed under his jacket. I wouldn't turn my back on him if I were you."

"Me, a spare tire?" Bill acted offended. "You know perfectly well that I'm in my sixth month and it's beginning to show." They both laughed together. "But I agree with you. A biker he is. Now what about that young lady over there?"

"Unh, unh. No fair. It's your turn to go first."

"OK if you insist. Well, first thing I see is that she is well-dressed and meticulously groomed. That means she's very careful about herself and about her appearance. On the other hand, she wears her hair in a rather severe style, her clothing is kind of mannish, and she wears glasses. Everything points in one direction. She's another biker, no doubt about it. Probably got a chain hidden underneath her skirt."

Lena was only slightly amused. "Seriously, Bill. What do you think about her?"

"I think she's some sort of business executive. Those glasses give her away. She's definitely the intellectual type. But don't be misled by external appearances. Beneath that harsh and stern exterior beats a heart of ice."

In this good-natured exchange between Lena and Bill, we see the importance of appearance in forming first impressions about people. This is due to the fact that we all carry stereotypes in our heads concerning the relationship of appearance

What would you say about each of these groups of people, strictly on the basis of your first impression?

Ellis Herwig/Stock, Boston

Jim Whitmer/Nawrocki Stock Photo

Ken Yee

with the occupation, status, political leanings, and personality characteristics of the individual. Moreover, our descriptions of the *appearance* of people are so interwoven with *inferences* concerning the underlying significance of their surface features that we are frequently unaware of where description ends and inference begins. Thus, we might describe a person as "lean, hard muscled, cold, and calculating," forgetting that "cold and calculating" are inferences.

First impressions lead to wide-ranging and immediate inferences about the friendliness of people (Argyle, 1975), the emotions they are experiencing, their personality traits, and whether we find them attractive or unattractive (Hochberg, 1978). Surprisingly, these first impressions appear to have a lasting impact. We tend to apply labels to people based on the first impressions. If we are introduced to a person who is abrupt and aloof, we might label this person as cold and unfriendly. We have, in effect, made a judgment about an enduring aspect of that person's personality. Future interactions with that individual will be strongly influenced by this initial assessment. If you later encounter this "cold and unfriendly" person, you may respond in kind by remaining aloof and uncommitted. This could well set in motion a vicious cycle in which each of you continues to behave in ways that perpetuate and confirm your first impression.

One study illustrates several important aspects of first impressions (Luchins, 1957). In this study, the subjects read either one or two paragraphs about a hypothetical person named Jim. One of the paragraphs portrayed him as friendly and the other as unfriendly. Those who read the "friendly" description overwhelmingly rated Jim favorably (95 percent) while only 3 percent did so after reading the "unfriendly" paragraph.

Even more striking is what this experiment showed about the impact of first impressions. When given two paragraphs to read, the subjects were more strongly influenced by the first passage they read (first impressions) than by the second. Thus, if the first paragraph described Jim as unfriendly, the subjects rated him as unfriendly even though the second paragraph was favorable. Conversely, when a "friendly" description preceded an "unfriendly" one, 78 percent saw him in a favorable light. Thus, first impressions tend to be lasting impressions.

Let us suppose that you have just had a brutal day. Absolutely nothing has gone right. You are suffering from a severe headache and are feeling irritable and generally out of sorts. In the midst of all of this, you are introduced to your employer's spouse. You're not in the mood for small talk and are really quite anxious to get home. Consequently, you excuse yourself immediately after the introduction, mumbling some excuse about having to go somewhere right away. Later you realize what a bad first impression you had made. How do you go about combating unfavorable first impressions?

The experimenter in the Luchins study described above found two techniques that were effective. Subjects appeared to be less ruled by first impressions when they were cautioned not to make snap judgments and to wait until more evidence was in. Also time was found to be a great healer. When a long interval elapsed between reading the two paragraphs, subjects were more likely to judge on the basis of what they read last rather than first. Thus, if you have made a bad first impression, it would be wise to allow a period of time to pass before seeing that person again. Memories of your prior impression will have faded to some extent. It is important, however, that you make every effort to behave in ways that will counter the first impression.

COMMUNICATION

Hi, how are you?''

How do you answer a question like that? Is the person asking the question really interested in your state of health? Or is the question merely a social amenity that doesn't require anything more than, "Fine, how are you?" Suppose the person who asked the question is a close friend. Would you be more likely to interpret the question as a genuine inquiry about your well-being? Clearly, the same set of words can communicate a number of different meanings, depending on the circumstances. In fact, sometimes we can talk without communicating anything. To illustrate, consider the following conversation between two friends:

FERNANDO: I saw Karen the other day. You wouldn't believe what has happened to her.

SHIRLEY: Oh, I bumped into Chuck this morning. He's had quite a week.

FERNANDO: Karen has been accepted into graduate school and won a beautiful fellowship.

SHIRLEY: His girlfriend, Evie—you remember her—got into a car accident.

FERNANDO: Free room, board, and pretty good pin money.

SHIRLEY: She wasn't too badly hurt but it's going to be Chuck's first law case.

parallaction: a form of noncommunication in which the conversations parallel one another without interacting.

On the surface, Fernando and Shirley appear to be communicating but are they? They are alternating their turns at speaking but neither is listening to the other. Such conversations are known as **parallaction** (Luft, 1969). We encounter this sort of parallel talk when engaging in ritual types of greetings, e.g., "Nice day, isn't it?" "Not bad, think it'll rain?" Through rituals such as these we exchange words but no real information or feelings.

mystification: a form of miscommunication in which either one or both parties are hiding true feelings or intentions.

Sometimes we don't want to communicate our true feelings and/or intentions to another person. This is called mystification. **Mystification** occurs when a person talks, but intentionally miscommunicates what he or she is really feeling or thinking. We sometimes use mystification when we think we will hurt or disappoint someone if we reveal our true feelings or intentions. Or mystification may be used to deliberately deceive or conceal true intentions or motivations:

JENNIE: Wow, am I glad to see you. I was just thinking about you.

WAYNE: That's funny, I was just thinking about you, too.

JENNIE: If I remember correctly, don't you own a summer place up in the mountains?

WAYNE: Uh, yes, but it's occupied a lot of the time. Why do you ask?

JENNIE: Oh, no special reason. It's just that I was going to be up in that area next weekend and I thought maybe I could use your place.

"Has it ever occured to you, Leland, that maybe you're too candid?"

From *The Wall Street Journal,* with permission of Cartoon Features Syndicate

WAYNE: Gee that's too bad, but it's being used next weekend.

JENNIE: Well, how about the following weekend?

WAYNE: Sorry, but it's busy then too.

In both parallaction and mystification, there is no authentic communication between parties—no give and take, no revelation of innermost feelings, no disclosure of personal problems, a little chance of developing a deep and rewarding relationship. In *real* communication, individuals take a chance—they allow other people to know who and what they are, what they are feeling and thinking. In short, there is trust.

But real communication is a two-way street. Effective communication requires active listening as well as talking. Although there are no set rules for increasing awareness of what the other person is really trying to say, there are ways to improve sensitivity to another person's feelings and needs.

1. Tune in to all the verbal and nonverbal cues. Often the tone of voice, facial expression, or gestures can help you discover the person's true feelings.

2. Be responsive to the other person's *feelings* as well as thoughts. Ask direct questions, "How do you *feel* about this situation?" rather than, "What do you *think* about this situation?"

3. Try to repeat or reflect the feelings that the other person appears to be commu-

nicating. You may be able to help him or her openly express feelings so that together you can examine and discuss them.

Often people do not say what they are truly feeling. This may lead to fraudulent interpersonal transactions and deception in the relationship. An example of this is the double-bind communication pattern mentioned in Box 9.1, which presents three poems that illustrate the double bind situation.

On the other side of the street is the ability to openly and honestly reveal yourself to another person.

> There is much evidence that indicates that healthy relationships are based on self-disclosure. If you hide how you are reacting to the other person, your concealment can sicken the relationship. . . . Being silent is not being strong; strength is the willingness to take risks in the relationship, to disclose yourself with the intention of building a better relationship. (Johnson 1972)

self-disclosure: the act of openly and honestly revealing certain aspects of oneself to others.

In most cases, **self-disclosure** tends to invite self-disclosure. When you trust someone enough to share your most intimate thoughts and feelings, they will usually return this trust and reveal themselves to you. A number of studies have demonstrated that the overall level of intimacy is usually reciprocated. It has been suggested that when someone discloses something personal, the other

---

BOX 9.1: THE DOUBLE BIND

A great deal of frustration can result from the double-bind situation. The following three poems illustrate the emotional tangles that can result from this pattern of communication.

> They are playing a game. They are playing at not playing a game. If I show them I see they are, I shall break the rules and they will punish me. I must play their game, of not seeing I see the game.

Jill   You think I am stupid
Jack   I don't think you're stupid
Jill   I must be stupid to think you think I'm stupid if you don't: or you must be lying.
          I am stupid every way:
          to think I'm stupid, if I am stupid
          to think I'm stupid, if I'm not stupid
          to think you think I'm stupid, if you don't.
Jill   I'm ridiculous
Jack   No you are not

Jill   I'm ridiculous to feel ridiculous when I'm not.
          You must be laughing at me
          or feeling you are laughing at me
              if you are not laughing at me.

How clever has one to be to be stupid?
The others told her she was stupid. So she made herself stupid in order not to see how stupid they were to think she was stupid,
because it was bad to think they were stupid.
She preferred to be stupid and good,
rather than bad and clever.
It is bad to be stupid: she needs to be clever to be so good and stupid.
It is bad to be clever, because this shows how stupid they were
to tell her how stupid she was.

Source: From *Knots,* by R. D. Laing. Copyright © 1970 by the R. D. Laing Trust. Reprinted by permission of Pantheon Books, A Division of Random House, Inc.

person is then *expected* to respond with an equally intimate revelation (Ehrlich & Graeven, 1971). This reciprocal exchange does not necessarily occur at each and every encounter. One party may simply have nothing to disclose at the time or may decide to listen rather than to talk. Of such stuff are friends made.

If you think about your own relationships, you probably place them in some order that reflects the degree of mutual self-disclosure. Marginal friends and acquaintances may exchange information that is factual and devoid of emotional intensity. However, you and your closest friends may share intimate information concerning your experiences and innermost feelings. There is an unspoken pact between very close and intimate friends: "I do not have to prove my trustworthiness at every encounter. I will not violate your confidence, neither will I stand in judgment of you because of what you say." Any violations may signal the end of the relationship.

Self-disclosure is not easy. But certain things are more difficult than others to talk about. In general, the past is easier to talk about than the present. Moreover, we tend to avoid any disclosures that might cause others to judge us, be used against us, embarrass or humiliate us. This is one of the reasons that parallaction and mystification are found in so many conversations. One observer (Johnson, 1972) has suggested the following order of disclosures from easiest to most difficult:

You tell me how Sue felt about Virginia (neither person present).

You tell me how Sue now feels about Virginia (neither person present).

You tell me the way you felt about Virginia (not present).

You tell me the way you now feel about Virginia (not present).

You tell me the way you used to feel about me.

You tell me the way you now feel about me.

There is more to communication than just words (see Box 9.2). As we saw in Chapter 5, facial expressions, gestures, and other mannerisms often convey a wealth of information above and beyond the spoken word. In fact, one observer has estimated that only 35 percent of the total meaning is communicated via the spoken word in two-way conversations (McCroskey, Larson, & Knapp, 1971). What happens if you are unable to use these nonverbal cues and have to rely solely on words to communicate? When we talk on the telephone, we cannot see the other person's facial expressions, body movements, or any other nonverbal cues. In view of these apparent limitations, is it possible for telephone communication to be effective?

Surprisingly, in many situations it is on a par with face-to-face communications and, in some, it is even more effective. Part of the reason for the telephone's unexpected advantage derives from the fact that there is better speech meshing in telephone communications, that is, there are shorter statements by each party, fewer long pauses, more evenhanded sharing of time, and fewer mix-ups that lead to both people speaking at the same time (Muson, 1982).

BOX 9.2: PERSONAL SPACE

Imagine the following situation. You have a number of things on your mind and you would like to be alone for a while. You decide to have a cup of coffee by yourself. The cafeteria is almost empty. No sooner are you settled than a stranger sits down at your table. Do you think you would be annoyed? Would you feel as if that person was invading your privacy—that he or she was violating your *personal space?* Personal space is an invisible boundary that surrounds us and allows us to maintain a certain distance from other people. We permit only certain types of interpersonal communication and behaviors to occur within our space and feel anxious or even angry when we feel our personal space has been invaded.

Personal space serves very definite functions. We define our own borders, but there are mutually accepted conventions. For example, did you ever walk into a movie theater that was only sparsely filled? Where did you sit? If you are like most people, you probably chose a seat one or two places removed from some other person. Suppose the next person who came in decided to sit down in the seat next to you in spite of the fact that the theater was almost completely empty. Would you think the behavior was not appropriate? Now imagine it is a few minutes later. The theater has pretty well filled up and there are only a few seats left. You wouldn't blink an eye if a stranger sat next to you now. This is because personal space both protects us and communicates to others something about our relationships with them. If a stranger sits down next to you when there are so many other seats available, you feel uncomfortably aroused because the experience is stressful. You feel as if your freedom has been restricted when your personal space is invaded. You usually keep your distance from other people unless you want to start or maintain a relationship with them. This is particularly true in smaller rooms (M. White, 1975) and indoors as contrasted with outdoors (Pempus, Sawaya, & Cooper, 1975).

Four personal zones have been identified (Hall, 1968) in terms of the amount of distance between people. Only certain types of interpersonal interactions are allowed to occur within each zone, and only certain people are allowed to enter a given zone.

The most intimate zone ranges in distance from body contact to about a foot apart. Relationships between lovers, very close friends, and family are considered appropriate within this zone. We are likely to repel anyone who tries to enter this zone without permission. Think of the people you allow within your intimate zone. How about your physician?

We maintain a personal distance of about one to four feet with close friends and daily acquaintances. At this distance we play cards, sit around in small groups, or eat in a restaurant with two or three other people.

Impersonal contacts are maintained at a distance of about 4 to 12 feet. Certain topics of discussion such as business, the weather, or politics are considered appropriate within this zone, whereas intimate conversations are usually not "acceptable" and may make others uncomfortable.

Finally, more formal contacts such as between a speaker addressing an audience or a spectator at a sports event, tend to occur beyond a distance of 12 feet.

There are some interesting differences between men and women with regard to personal space. In general, men prefer sitting *across* from a person they like and are uncomfortable when a stranger sits across from them. The reverse is true of women—they are only comfortable sitting *next* to a person they like. If they don't know or like someone, they would rather sit across from them (Byrne, Baskett, & Hodges, 1971; Fisher & Byrne, 1975). One may speculate on the implications of these findings. Suppose a man, wanting to make a woman feel comfortable, sits *next* to her rather than across from her. If she doesn't know him, she might regard his behavior as aggressive and offensive.

Under what circumstances would she be better off with a face-to-face confrontation?

© Joel Gordon 1976

Imagine that you are having a dispute with someone over some important issue. You know that you have the stronger case. Do you feel you would have a better chance of persuading the other person to your point of view via the telephone or in a face-to-face confrontation? A number of studies have produced rather intriguing results: strong arguments are even more powerful over the phone. Why is this so? One observer suggests, "Since [the telephone] offers little in the way of personal intimacy, negotiators can keep their minds on the case, argue their institutional positions without developing too much empathy for the other guy, and prevail on the basis of stronger bargaining points" (Muson, 1982, p. 47).

Equally striking is the evidence that people are not as readily manipulated and mislead on the telephone as in person-to-person conversations. If people are specifically trained to produce a favorable impression, they will be more successful in person than on the telephone. The telephone does not permit them to take advantage of nonverbal communications (eye contact, body language, etc.) as manipulative techniques. Someone who is trained to read the language of the body can monitor the other person's nonverbal reactions and then adjust their own responses accordingly.

These results are nicely summarized by Muson:

> If we stretch the findings of these various studies to emphasize the point, we can reach a few conclusions: If a person wants to leave a certain impression with a potential employer, but has something to hide, he may be better off arranging a face-to-face meeting than talking on the phone. On the other hand, if he wants to coldly assess another's intentions, he might have a better chance on the phone. Getting together enables people to schmooze, to become more intimate, and also to be taken in.
>
> Likewise, the businessman with a weak case in some deal being negotiated would be well advised to talk it over with his opponents in person; he may win some ground. But the businessman with a strong case should insist on telephone negotiations, especially if he has a generous nature; he is less likely to give away the store.
>
> All this ignores the complexity of human beings. Whether one person can influence another's attitudes, for example, may depend less on the medium of communication than on the personalities of the two people, their knowledge and experience, how they regard each other, and so on. (Muson, 1982 p. 49)[1]

JUDGING OTHERS

altruism: the act of helping others without expectation of personal gain.

Both Liz and Juan are deep into a discussion of ethical and moral responsibilities of living in a modern society. They both agree that most people are more concerned with themselves than they are with humanity in general. They both advocate greater **altruism** as one of the requirements of effective citizenship.

[1] Reprinted from *Psychology Today* Magazine Copyright © 1982, American Psychological Association.

During their discussion, an appeal is made by a radio announcer calling for blood donors to help supply plasma for victims of a recent disaster. Juan says, "There's a case in point. How many people do you think will answer the call? A handful at best."

"You're absolutely right. Most people are too selfish to give of themselves without receiving anything in return."

"No good to just sit here and talk about it. I'm going right down to the blood bank to give a pint."

"Great idea. I'm going to do the same thing."

Afterwards, Juan goes to the nearest Red Cross Blood Bank and donates his blood. He receives a card acknowledging his contribution. Liz goes to a private blood bank where she receives $75. She immediately goes to her favorite boutique, where she purchases a dress that she has been admiring for some time.

Having read about the actions of these two friends, answer the following questions. Whose action was more altruistic? Was Liz or Juan more sincere in their views about civic responsibility? If you are like most people, you chose Juan as more sincere and altruistic. Why?

attribution theory: a theory concerned with the rules we use to make judgment about the causes of behavior.

This question takes us to the heart of **attribution theory.** According to this view, we do not take the actions of others at face value. Instead, before judging the actions of others, we ask *why* they acted as they did. It is this attribution of cause that gives attribution theory its name. Generally, the underlying cause of behavior may be attributed to individual personality traits (dispositional factors) or to external (situational) factors. Thus, the way we judge a person depends on the attributions we make. Let's look at another example.

Julie and Marty have set a wedding date. Marty is extremely wealthy but his appearance leaves much to be desired. In fact, many people call him ugly. Is Julie marrying Marty because she loves him (an internal disposition) or because he is wealthy (a situational factor)? What if Marty is poor and struggling to make a living? Would you change your opinion about Julie's motivation for marriage?

When Marty is physically unattractive but wealthy, we would probably attribute Julie's intentions to a situational factor—his great wealth. But why are we inclined to dismiss true love as her underlying motivation? In our society, physical attractiveness is highly valued. We may pursue the following line of reasoning, "If he's not attractive, what other reason could she have for marrying him?" On the other hand, when Marty is both poor and unattractive, we are more likely to attribute Julie's decision to dispositional factors, her love for him.

Clearly, attributing underlying causes to behavior is not as straightforward or unequivocal as we would like. Why are people attracted to beautiful, wealthy, or successful people? Is it because of their physical appearance, their wealth, or because they are witty and have an intriguing personality? Since the causes of behavior are so ambiguous, how do we check whether or not our attributions are correct? In a word, we test our attributions in the everyday world. To illustrate, imagine that Marty suffers severe financial reverses prior to the wedding date. In spite of his poverty, Julie marries Marty and even picks up the tab for the wedding. Certainly, Julie's action would force us to reexamine our prior attribution. "Why she really does love him," we might exclaim.

In everyday life, we use several different criteria to test the accuracy of our attributions. These are: consistency, consensus, and freedom from external pressure.

Consistency

The first time we saw Brenda, we were charmed by her winsome manner. She was sprightly, spirited, buoyant, warm, and friendly. However, that sort of behavior is expected of a flight attendant. Even though our first impression was very favorable, we couldn't help wondering if her charm was more a function of the situation or an enduring aspect of her personality. The next time we see her, she has just received notice that her job has been terminated. Although she was obviously distraught at this unexpected news, she still took the time to respond calmly and warmly to a stranger's request for directions. Because of the consistency we have observed in two different situations, we are more likely to attribute her actions to dispositional factors (she really *is* a charming and friendly person). We see her on another occasion when she has two young children in tow. They are screaming, scrapping with one another, and making one big nuisance of themselves. Nonetheless, she remains unflappable, attempting to mediate between the two disputants in a cheerful and congenial manner. We are now convinced that our first impression was basically sound. However, had she responded with anger, irritability, or aggression in either of the two non-job-related situations, we might then attribute her behavior to situational factors—when the job requires her to be friendly, she can don the mask of charm.

Consensus

Whether we realize it or not, we often seek consensus for our opinions, attitudes, and beliefs. This is particularly the case when there is ambiguity and doubt. "From my observations of her, Brenda is one-in-a-million," says a friend in response to our query. "Absolutely nothing rattles her. She's 24 carat." Hearing this fortifies our prior judgment of Brenda.

There is much evidence to support the following view: Learning that others share our views increases our conviction that we are right. In contrast, our confidence diminishes when others disagree with us (Wells & Harvey, 1977; Middlebrook, 1980). However, if we suspect that others were not free to express an honest opinion or that they were responding out of ulterior motives, we would be less influenced by their opinions.

Freedom from External Pressure

Recall the great patience and cheerfulness Brenda displayed when interacting with airline passengers. If we had only that sample of her behavior, we might be reluctant to make inferences about her underlying personality traits. Why? Generally, when we perceive that external pressures are at work on an individual, we are more likely to attribute behavior to situational rather than dispositional factors. In other words, whenever we observe behavior that conforms to situational demands or expectations, we tend to discount the importance of an individual's underlying characteristics. Since our initial observations of Brenda were in a work-related situation, we might conclude, "Of course, she's friendly and effervescent. That's what airline personnel are supposed to be."

With these considerations in mind, indicate whether you would attribute the following statements to dispositional or situational factors:

"This previously owned car is a 'cream puff.' In my opinion, it's the best buy on the lot." Imagine this statement is made by *(a)* a used car dealer; *(b)* your closest friend with whom you are going to share the car.

"We can look forward to a sharp rise in the GNP and a decline in unemployment rates over the next six-month period," says *(a)* an incumbent senator one week before the election; *(b)* a professor of economics with no political affiliations.

An act committed under pressure, regardless of the form of pressure, is generally not very informative. We do not always know whether a person is playing a role or acting out of genuine feelings.

INTERPERSONAL ATTRACTION

Jennifer has the biggest, bluest eyes you've ever seen. Her long silky hair hangs loosely on her shoulders, framing her clear, near-perfect features.

Mabel is short and fat. Her mouse-colored hair hangs limply on her head, accentuating a complexion marred by pimples.

Who do you think will be more successful in life? Who do you think is more exciting, poised, and interesting? Who would you like to spend time with?

As much as most people don't like to admit it, we often judge a book by its cover. Indeed, there is a growing body of evidence that good-looking people appeal more to the opposite sex and are rated as more popular and persuasive than their unattractive peers (Berscheid & Walster, 1974). Moreover, people tend to see physically attractive men and women as more capable of achieving success in social and personal relations, happier, and more fulfilled (Dion, Berscheid, & Walster, 1972). Perhaps we expect more of attractive people and treat them accordingly. To illustrate, in one study, even when two children had identical report cards, fifth-grade teachers expected the more attractive children to be more intelligent and to achieve higher levels of education (Clifford & Walster, 1973).

An extreme case of judging a book by its cover is judging people by their names. Shakespeare said it first, "What's in a name?" Quite a bit if we can believe the results of research on the topic. When asked to select a beauty queen from an assortment of equally attractive photographs, college students overwhelmingly voted for those with a desirable first name (Garwood et al., 1980).

The following letter to "Dear Abby" provides an amusing example of a name that is well liked in spite of an unpleasant association.

How important is physical attractiveness?

Frank Schultz

Dear Abby:

We named our son "John" after his father. His grandfather, great-grandfather, and great-great-grandfather were also Johns. Abby, our son is named after a person—not a toilet!

Will you please tell me when, where, and how the toilet came to be known as a john? Thank you.

Wife and mother of a John
not a toilet

In researching the subject, I learned more about toilets than I cared to know. I found several conflicting theories on how the toilet came to be known as "the john," the most reasonable explanation being that the first toilet was called "john" after its English inventor back in the early 1800s.

I bought it, after checking it out with a plumber in Flushing.*

Box 9.3 illustrates the potential impact of various names. Perhaps we should exercise care in selecting a name.

The results of studies on interpersonal attraction should be viewed with a degree of caution. In most of these studies, subjects judge from photographs or from situations in which the amount of physical contact is minimal. It may well be that physical attractiveness is important only in the initial stages of a relationship. With increased contact and additional knowledge of the other person, the role of physical attractiveness may diminish in importance (Berscheid & Walster, 1974). You have probably known many people who initially turned you off because of their physical appearance. However, as you got to know them better, you discovered many desirable and appealing traits. They may have even begun to look better to you.

How often have you heard the expression opposites attract as a way of explaining the mutual attraction between people who differ in social, ethnic, or religious backgrounds? How much truth is there to this generalization? Think about some of the people you know. Why are you attracted to certain people, indifferent to some, and repelled by others? Are your closest friends really that much different from you?

In the typical study of the role of similarity in interpersonal attraction, subjects are shown questionnaires which are supposedly filled out by another person. In reality, however, the experimenter manipulates the "other" person's answers so as to vary the degree of similarity with the subject's answers to the same questionnaire. The subject is then asked, "How much do you think you would like this person?" The research results in this area tend to contradict the view that opposites are attracted to one another. We are more likely to be attracted to and like people who are similar to us in attitudes, education, status, interests, and personality (Laumann, 1969; Byrne, 1971). This relationship has been demonstrated across many populations—from young children to senior citizens.

---

* Taken from the Dear Abby column. © 1981, Universal Press Syndicate. Reprinted with permission. All rights reserved.

BOX 9.3:   WHAT'S IN A NAME?

Perhaps you find that you react unfavorably to certain names. Ask yourself how you would feel about a comedy writer and actor whose last name was Konigsberg, or a dramatic actor named Schwartz. If you think you might be less than favorably disposed, the owners of those names—Woody Allen and Tony Curtis—must have anticipated your reaction. In the performing arts, more than anywhere else, people seem to be aware of the power of a name. Consider these current and past stars, and the original names they chose to give up:

Alan Alda—Alphonso D'Abruzzo
Martin Sheen—Ramon Estevez
Eve Arden—Eunice Quedens
Danny Kaye—Daniel Kominski
Elliot Gould—Elliot Goldstein
Hal Linden—Harold Lipshitz
Nancy Walker—Anna Myrtle Swoyer

The stars may have a good reason for changing their names. On occasion, you may have found yourself envisioning what a person might be like merely on the basis of that person's first name. You may even like or dislike your own name on the basis of stereotypes you have about that name. Some recent evidence suggests that there are some widely shared stereotypes in our culture about certain names. Here are some examples:

Harvey—weak and bumbling.
John—trustworthy and kind.
Michael and James—masculine, active.
Tony—sociable.
Robin—young.
Agnes—old.
Matilda—unattractive.
Ann—nonaggressive.
Wendy—feminine, active.

Some of these stereotypes are particularly strong. In fact, in 1965 a New Yorker named Harvey Edwards became so tired of unfavorable portrayals of Harveys in the media that he organized a group of 150 men who shared his first name. They besieged advertising agencies and eventually won their fight to have the offending commercials removed.

But does a name really have any impact on person perception, or do we merely think it has an impact? Several studies have shown that, in general, we respond more favorably to people with usual names than to people with unusual names. In addition, we tend to like people with favorably stereotyped names, even if those names are somewhat less common. Here is some of the evidence.

- One study showed that male and female students had the same attitudes toward 20 male names. They saw the relatively familiar names (David, Gary, James, John, Joseph, Michael, Paul, Richard, Robert, and Thomas) as better, stronger, and more active than the less familiar names (Andrew, Bernard, Dale, Edmond, Gerd, Ivan, Lawrence, Raymond, Stanley, and Matthew).

- In the 1940s, students with unusual names were more likely to flunk out of Harvard than were their classmates.

- There seems to be more neurosis and psychosis among men with unusual names than among men with usual names. This difference does not show up among women, however, in general, there seems to be less of a stigma for a female to have an unusual name than for a male.

- A study of fourth- and fifth-grade children revealed that the children with the best-liked names were also the most popular.

- Teachers' evaluations of students may be biased by the "desirability" of the students' names. Teachers who read essays by fifth-grade children gave higher grades if the supposed author had a desirable name (Karen, Lisa, David, or Michael) than if the author had an undesirable name (Elmer, Bertha, or Hubert).

- Another study showed that children with well-liked names (Jonathan, James, John, Patrick, Craig, Thomas, Gregory, Richard, Jeffrey) were better adjusted, had higher expectations for academic success, and scored higher on achievement tests than children with disliked names (Bernard, Curtis, Darrell, Donald, Gerald, Horace, Maurice, Jerome, Roderick, and Samuel).

BOX 9.3 *(concluded)*

(In each of the last three studies, the desirability of names was obtained in previous ratings made by relevant groups of subjects.)

Source: From *Social Psychology and Modern Life,* second edition, by Patricia Niles Middlebrook. Copyright © 1980, 1973 by Alfred A. Knopf, Inc. Reprinted by permission of the publisher.

There are exceptions. When the relationship between similarity and liking is carried to the extreme, all of our friends might be expected to be clones of ourselves. Such friends would simply not provide the variety of new stimulation that we generally find desirable. They would not challenge our ideas, expand our horizons, or balance out our deficiencies. How unique and different would you feel if surrounded by carbon copies of yourself?

What happens if someone is perceived as similar to you on a characteristic you consider undesirable? When this happens, you will probably express a dislike for that person. Under these circumstances, the more similar that person is to you, the greater is your dislike of him or her (Novack & Lerner, 1968; Taylor & Mettee, 1972). Perhaps this is because that person reminds you of perceived

It has been found that people are more likely to be attracted to those who seem attractive, share similar beliefs, and provide opportunities for rewarding interactions.

Jean-Claude Lejeune

weaknesses in yourself. Moreover, no matter how great the similarity between you and another person, you will not like that person if you think their personality is unappealing (Ajzen, 1974).

SHYNESS

Carl glanced cautiously at his watch, as if fearing it would explode in his face. "Damn," he swore silently, "Time to go to that @#$%&, class again. How I hate it." He paused for a few moments, quickly ticking off in his mind reasons for skipping class one more time. But all reasons, either legitimate or otherwise, had been exhausted by the sixth week of the semester. He would just have to go and face the music. He smiled bitterly at the expression "face the music," wondering how it got into the language. "More like facing the firing squad," he thought, "What with all the questions what's-his-name fires at us."

The class wouldn't be so bad if the professor didn't ask all those questions: "Janine, on what date did the . . . ?" "Harvey, I would like you to outline for the class the eight reasons . . ." "Carl, how sharp do you feel today? Try answering this one. . . ." With only 15 students in the class, he was sure to be called on two or three times, maybe even more. Everytime he heard, "Carl . . . ," his heart would skip a beat, a lump would form in his throat, his mouth would go dry, his palms would drip like a leaky faucet, and his stomach would be tied up in knots. To make matters worse, he knew the answers most of the time. But somehow the connection between his mind and voice would be severed. In fact, more often than not, his mind would go blank and he would fumble for some response, any response. These experiences were absolutely humiliating. How he dreaded that class!

What was Carl's problem? In a word, he was shy. Although perhaps of little consolation to Carl, he is not alone. Here are some of the facts about shyness uncovered by Philip Zimbardo, one of the leading researchers in this area: More than 80 percent of those surveyed indicated that they experienced shyness at some point in their lives; 40 percent of these people considered themselves *presently* shy; and an astonishing 25 percent considered themselves *always* shy (1977). Based on the finding that only 7 percent of Americans surveyed never experienced shyness, Zimbardo regards shyness as a universal experience.

If shyness is so common, why be concerned about it? According to Zimbardo:

> Shyness may be a mental handicap as crippling as the most severe of physical handicaps, and its consequences can be devastating:
>
> > Shyness makes it difficult to meet new people, make friends, or enjoy potentially good experiences.
> >
> > It prevents you from speaking up for your rights and expressing your own opinions and values.
> >
> > Shyness limits positive evaluations by others of your personal strengths.
> >
> > It encourages self-consciousness and an excessive preoccupation with your own reactions.
> >
> > Shyness makes it hard to think clearly and communicate effectively.

A shy person often misses out.

United Press International Photo

Negative feelings like depression, anxiety, and loneliness typically accompany shyness. (Zimbardo, 1977, p. 12)[2]

Assuming that shyness is a dominant aspect of your personality that you would like to change, is there anything you can do about it? Or is shyness fixed and unchanging, like a physical trait such as eye color? Let's see what Zimbardo has to say in answer to this question:

A substantial body of evidence exists (including much of my own research) to support the opposite conclusion, namely, that human personality and behavior are quite changeable when the situation changes. Human nature is remarkably pliable, readily adapting itself to the challenges of whatever environment it finds itself in. Adaptability to environmental change is, in fact, the key to survival; humans and animals that fail to do so soon become extinct. Thus, to change behavior, we must look to factors in the current situation that maintain the undesirable behavior, as well as focus on alterations in the situation that will call forth and support desirable behaviors. (Zimbardo, 1977, p. 119)[3]

More specifically, Zimbardo recommends the following:

1. *Understand yourself better*—This includes understanding the image you project to others and the image you would like to project. Do you feel that your life is under your personal control or do you believe that events external to yourself are in command? Taking charge of your own life is one aspect of shedding the shell of shyness.

2. *Understand your shyness better*—Find answers to such questions as: What circumstances prompt feelings of shyness? How often do they occur? Are there any social situations in which you feel completely at ease? If so, what are they? Perhaps they may provide cues for decreasing feelings of shyness in other places.

3. *Build self-esteem*—Shyness and low self-esteem go together. Find something you do well, take pride in it, and share it with others. If you would like to model your behavior after someone else, pick your models carefully. Behind their masks of contentment, many people in the limelight are little more than hollow shells. Do not feel that you must be on center stage at all times to conquer shyness.

4. *Develop specific and successful social skills*—Recognize that all people are, at times, actors. The better your acting skills, the greater the acknowledgment you receive. When entering situations that make you uncomfortable, prepare your scripts in advance. Then act them out to the best of your ability.

5. *Help others who are shy*—It is said that the best way to learn is to teach. By helping others who are shy, you may gain insight into your own shyness. As stated by Zimbardo, *"Be something to other people that will enable them to be more to themselves"* (1977, p. 189).

---

[2] Philip G. Zimbardo, *Shyness*, © 1977 Philip G. Zimbardo. Published by Addison-Wesley, Reading, Massachusetts. Reprinted with permission.
[3] Ibid.

One final point. Shyness is not all quinine and vinegar. It has its positive elements. Approximately 10 to 20 percent of shy people prefer to remain shy, presumably because they have found its positive side (Zimbardo, 1977). Shyness can make us appear serious, introspective, and sophisticated. It also affords us greater privacy and some of the pleasures of solitude.

GROUP INFLUENCES

Have you ever noticed that you often behave differently when you are in a group than when you are alone? Have you gone to a recent performance of one of your favorite muscial groups and found yourself caught up in the excitement

It is easier to vent feelings such as anger when you are in a crowd.

Jean-Claude Lejeune

In much of our everyday behavior we use perceptual defenses to screen out potentially troublesome information. These smokers are ignoring a sign that would force them to stop smoking or to move to another location.

Sue Markson

generated by the crowd reaction? Did you find yourself singing, clapping, shouting, and joining the others in the heat of the moment? Do you think you would have acted this way if you were alone?

Have you ever had this experience? There is someone whom you intensely dislike, but you have refrained from saying or doing anything about it. You then see others arguing with this person and you jump right in and aggressively tell that person off.

When did you last attend a rally or a meeting only to find that your views were in the minority? Did you feel any pressure to go along with the majority point of view?

All of these situations testify to the pervasive influence of other people on all aspects of our lives—our beliefs, attitudes, likes, and dislikes. When we are in the company of others, we are somehow different than when we are alone. We may be fearful of others; we may be stimulated by them to achieve goals we believe are beyond our grasp; we may adapt our behavior or beliefs to go along with our perception of group values; we may even, at times, blindly follow the leader.

Every group has its own set of rules or social norms. Enormous pressures are exerted on us to mold our beliefs, attitudes, and behaviors according to these group standards. Groups often bestow handsome rewards on members in good standing and punish those who deviate from the norms of the group. This dual action of reward and threat of punishment (e.g., expulsion or social rejection) serves to keep the behavior of group members in line. As a result of these pressures, you may sometimes do or say something with which you are in disagreement to maintain your standing within the group. When you adapt your beliefs or behavior so that they are consistent with the expectations of others, you are *conforming.*

The concept of conforming always involves some disparity between the way that the group expects us to act and the way we want to behave. Thus, if we behave according to group standards because we accept these standards as valid guides to our own behavior, we do not speak of this behavior as conformity (Worchel & Cooper, 1979). The group does not explicitly command us to behave in a specific fashion. Rather, group pressures to conform are often unspoken but understood as part of the unwritten rules of the group.

Obedience is a "horse of a different color." Here the expectations are direct, explicit, and leave little to the imagination. If the drill sergeant says "When I call 'eyes right,' I want to hear your eyeballs click!" you had better find some way of obeying the command. Obedience may be either constructive or destructive. We all benefit from obeying rules that protect the rights of the individual, preserve the order of society (e.g., traffic, civil, and criminal laws), and promote the common good. But sometimes obedience demands unthinking and often mechanical responses to authority figures.

Every once in a while, we hear of the most outrageous and shocking atrocities committed by people who were just following orders. Recalling the Nazis' attempt at genocide before and during World War II, many Americans are tempted to say, "It cannot happen here." We found our faith shaken by the revelations of the massacre at My Lai during the Vietnam war. Are there circumstances under which the average person will obey an authority figure even though the demands conflict with that individual's personal values and beliefs? In other words, can any responsible and respected person be persuaded to inflict punishment upon another human being?

Suppose you are a subject in a psychological experiment on the effect of punishment on learning. In the role of "teacher," you are expected to administer an increasing amount of shock each time the "learner" makes a mistake. The intensity of shock can range from mild to very severe. You are instructed to move one level higher on the shock generator each time the learner flashes a wrong answer. When the shock level reaches a certain intensity, you hear the learner pounding on the wall. From this point on, the learner's answers no longer appear. What do you do now? If you turn to the experimenter for guidance, you are told to treat the absence of a response as a wrong answer and to shock the subject according to the usual schedule. Again you hear a pounding on the wall and then silence. Do you continue to administer shocks? If you balk, there are a series of prods, e.g., "Please continue"; "The experiment requires that you continue"; "You have no other choice, you *must* go on."

What do you imagine you would do in this situation? Refuse to go on? Surprisingly, if you are like the subjects who actually participated in such a study (Milgram, 1963), you would probably continue up through the highest shock levels (see Figure 9.1). These results were obtained in several repetitions using, as subjects, respected businesspeople, homemakers, and Yale University students. It should be noted that none of the subjects realized the experiment was rigged and shocks were never administered to the learners. In fact, the learners were confederates of the experimenter; i.e., they were aware of what was happening in the experiment and were acting their parts.

The surprising thing about this experiment is that the subjects were not bound and in chains. They were free to discontinue their participation whenever they wished. They had nothing to gain by remaining and nothing to lose by stopping. So why did they continue? Apparently they did not wish to subject themselves to the disapproval of the authority figure. However, it was not always easy to comply with the experimenter's demands. In fact, many subjects found themselves extremely tense and uncomfortable. The following is the way an observer described one subject's behavior:

> I observed a mature and initially poised businessman enter the laboratory smiling and confident. Within 20 minutes he was reduced to a twitching, stuttering wreck, who was rapidly approaching a point of nervous collapse. He constantly pulled on his earlobe, and twisted his hands. At one point he pushed his fist into his forehead and muttered: "Oh God, let's stop." And yet he continued to respond to every word of the experimenter, and obeyed to the end. (Milgram, 1963, p. 377)

FIGURE 9.1

OBEDIENCE: Subjects were told to administer increasing amounts of shock to a "learner." All 40 subjects administered shocks scaled "intense" or higher. Only 35 percent of the subjects broke off before the end.

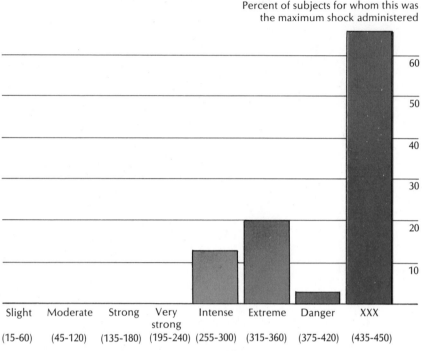

Percent of subjects for whom this was the maximum shock administered

Source: "Behavioral Study of Obedience" by Stanley Milgram, *Journal of Abnormal and Social Psychology* 67, 1963, pp. 371–78. Copyright © 1963 by the American Psychological Association and used by permission.

This study as well as similar studies have stimulated much controversy over the ethics of such research. In the face of severe criticism, Milgram has replied,

> I must say that I was totally astonished by the criticism that my experiment engendered. I thought what I was doing was posing a very legitimate question. How far would people proceed if they were asked to give increasingly severe shocks to another person? . . . I'm convinced that much of the criticism, whether people know it or not, stems from the results of the experiment. If everyone had broken off at slight shock or moderate shock, this would be a very reassuring finding and who would protest? (Milgram, 1977, p. 98)

If nothing else, this experiment reminds us of our own vulnerability and susceptibility to social pressures. Given the right circumstances, almost anyone might be capable of committing a heinous act when ordered to do so by someone per-

A   The "shock generator."

B   The experimenter asks the subject to help attach the shock electrodes to the "learner" (seated).

C   The experimenter explains the use of the shock generator.

D   A subject gives up and refuses to deliver any more shocks.

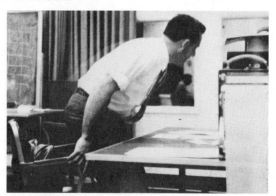

© 1965 by Stanley Milgram. From the film *Obedience*, distributed by The New York University Film Library

ceived as a legitimate authority figure. None of us can state with absolute certainty, "I would never do such a thing." Forewarned is forearmed. If you anticipate being placed in a situation where you may be pressured to do something you find objectionable, there are a number of courses of action open to you. You may avoid the situation altogether or you can take positive steps to resist the social coercion. For example, research has indicated that people are more likely to successfully resist authority when there is social support for their position (Milgram, 1965). In other words, when you enter such a situation, it is advisable to bring someone along who will buttress your position. In international confrontations, have you ever heard of a diplomat entering negotiations with the "enemy" without a massive contingent of supporting personnel?

ATTITUDES

Karen looked in the lobster tank at the local seafood establishment, grimaced, and pursed her lips in disgust. "How can anybody eat such things? They are so ugly."

Hank looked in the same tank, smiled broadly, licked his lips, and said, "Wow, they look delicious. Can't wait to bite into one."

"I think marriage is hazardous to your health," observed Peter following his third divorce.

What do these three statements have in common? They all represent attitudes—learned predispositions to respond in a certain way, negatively or positively, toward people, objects, or ideas. Our likes and dislikes, our reactions to various situations, and the choices we make in life are, to a large extent, reflections of our underlying attitudes.

Attitudes are comprised of three components—thoughts, feelings, and behavior. For example, we may infer from Karen's statement that she thinks lobsters are ugly, feels disgusted by them, and would not eat one. Peter's inability to maintain three marriages (behavior) may reflect his underlying negative thoughts and feelings about marriage.

Are these three components always in agreement? Not necessarily. Our behavior is not always consistent with our thoughts and feelings. Why? For one thing, we are not always aware of our own attitudes. For another, the situation may call for behavior which is inconsistent with our underlying attitudes. To illustrate, Paula thinks of herself as open-minded, impartial, and unprejudiced. Yet, she feels vaguely uncomfortable at the thought of minorities moving into her neighborhood. This disparity between the way she feels and the way she thinks about herself causes her many uneasy moments, even feelings of guilt. She doesn't want to admit how she really feels, so she has openly spoken out at meetings in favor of equal rights and desegregation. Thus, her public statements and actions are not consistent with her private feelings.

As we see in Paula's case, inconsistency leads to feelings of tension. Since tension is usually experienced as undesirable, the individual is motivated to reduce the inconsistency and thus reduce the tension. What means are available to lessen the inconsistency? One way is to change or modify our attitudes. This is easier said than done. Attitudes are relatively enduring dispositions to think, feel, and behave in certain ways and are usually resistant to change. A person who is prejudiced cannot suddenly decide to become unprejudiced by a simple assertion of the will. More is involved than mere verbal statements. If Paula wishes to reduce the inconsistency by lessening her prejudicial attitudes, she should permit and encourage a greater amount of interaction with minority group members. A number of studies have shown that increased contact decreases prejudice (Star, Williams, & Stouffer, 1965; Hamilton & Bishop, 1976).

Do scare tactics work?

Courtesy American Cancer Society

Attempts to change attitudes have generally focused on changing single compo-nents—thoughts, feelings, or behaviors. It is believed that the change in one component will generate pressures to change the others. This is, in fact, the rationale behind many desegregation laws and judicial rulings. It is assumed that increased contact (changing behavior) will lead to subsequent changes in feelings and thoughts about minority groups.

Some of the most effective techniques for changing attitudes have been devel-oped by advertising agencies and utilized by the mass media to advertise and sell products. The goal is to produce favorable attitudes toward certain products since a favorable attitude is more likely to lead to the desired behavior—buying that product. Some advertisers attempt to persuade the audience to buy their product by appealing to the thoughts or cognitive component of attitudes. Tooth-paste manufacturers and drug companies often cite the results of research to support their claims that their product will produce beneficial results for the consumer. The rationale behind this appeal to reason is that the consumer's feel-ings about the product might change along with thoughts about it. "So Decayless reduces cavities. That's exactly what I want. Anything that keeps me out of the dentist's chair and reduces my bills can't be all that bad." With both positive thoughts and feelings about a product, who can resist engaging in the desired behavior (buying the product)?

Famous celebrities are often used in advertising campaigns because of the desira-ble emotions they elicit in an audience. We tend to place our public figures on pedestals. We may admire certain actors and actresses for their acting ability, but we also respond emotionally to them. We regard them warmly and we trust them not to mislead us.

Negative emotions are also used effectively in persuading people to change their behavior. Pictures of mutilated bodies of people in automobile accidents are used to scare people into "sitting down and buckling up." We are encouraged to heed the warning to stop smoking as a "matter of life and breath." However, the research on scare tactics to change attitudes and behavior have yielded conflict-ing results. For example, one study (Janis & Feshback, 1953) found that high-fear provoking messages produce *less* behavior change than low-fear messages. Yet other studies have found the opposite (Leventhal & Singer, 1966). These conflicting findings may possibly be reconciled by the view that *moderate* fear arousal may be more successful in changing attitudes than either very low or very high levels of fear (Krisher , Darley, & Darley, 1973; Worchel & Cooper, 1979).

Finally, we can direct our efforts to modify attitudes by focusing on the behavior component. When a person's actions are at variance with their attitudes, they may change their attitudes to reduce the inconsistency. For example, suppose you are a debater and are assigned a position that is incompatible with your own views. As you defend this position, you may be surprised to find yourself tugged in the direction of this initially antagonistic attitude (Janis & King, 1954). In this connection, it has been observed that, if you repeat a lie often enough, you will wind up accepting it as the truth. It is almost as if you talk yourself into it.

THE GENTLE ACT OF PERSUASION

Maynard stood absolutely motionless in an attitude of stunned disbelief. One half-hour ago, he would have said it couldn't happen, but somehow it did. He had just signed a contract to purchase the latest edition of *Encyclopedia Ignoramus*, complete with a certificate of ownership which "the proud owner can display over the mantlepiece," one year's free subscription to a magazine of his choice, a Cosmic Atlas (including maps of the planetary orbits and major constellations), a genuine simulated hardwood book case, and the right to purchase, at cost, the valuable annual supplement to the encyclopedia.

How did it happen? Is the saleswoman, Erika, a practitioner of witchcraft? Did she cast some sort of magic spell over him? He began to go over his recollections of their encounter.

He was hard at work in his garden, a hobby he practiced at every opportunity. He took great satisfaction watching things grow and burst into their annual displays of color. He noted absent mindedly a woman leaving the house of his next-door neighbors, the Dunns. She looked up and down the street, spied him, and then sauntered (or did she slither?) over to where he was working.

"Oh what beautiful flowers," she exclaimed with obvious delight. "How do you get them all to bloom at one time?"

"Well, I must admit it takes some doing," he replied modestly. Inwardly, he was about to burst with pride.

"Your *Verbena Peruvianus* are so perfectly formed and so brilliantly red. Tell me, would you mind my bringing my husband over some time? We're both absolutely devoted to gardening."

"Why, of course not. Any time."

And so the conversation continued. Before long they were discussing the children, their education, and their educational needs. Erika would say such things as, "Don't you agree that education is so very important in this day and age?" and he would agree enthusiastically.

"Don't you think the parents have the responsibility to expose their children to all available educational resources?" She looked him straight in the eye and touched him lightly on the arm.

"Absolutely. As soon as my kids could walk, I got them library cards."

"Marvelous," she replied, nodding her head in approval. "Reading is such an important skill."

Before he know what hit him, he had signed the contract. Although he now regretted the decision and he knew he could legally cancel within three days, he had no intention of doing so. It would be embarrassing to reverse himself after having agreed with Erika on so many different issues.

In this scenario, we see several techniques for obtaining agreement. Had Erika approached Maynard and said, "I'm selling an encyclopedia and wonder if you are interested?" he would have answered in no uncertain terms, "No! I have all the references I need." By approaching him on an unrelated issue (his garden), she established a rapport with him and created the feeling that they had something in common. When Erika complimented him on his beautiful garden, Maynard developed a trust and liking for her. Erika's use of verbal reinforcers (e.g., Marvelous!) tended to strengthen this feeling. It is difficult not to like someone who says nice things about you. It is also difficult to refuse a request from someone you like or from someone who likes you. She reinforced this feeling of mutual regard by establishing eye contact and touching him. People are more likely to respond positively when you look them directly in the eye and emit favorable signals through the use of body language. For example, sitting or standing in an open, relaxed manner is more persuasive than a "closed" body posture, i.e., arms crossed, elbows clamped next to the body, and feet pressed together (McGinley, Le Fevre, & McGinley, 1975).

One of the most effective persuasive techniques is to obtain agreement on many small issues before the larger issue comes up. By getting Maynard to agree that education is important, that reading is an essential skill, and that parents have a responsibility to involve themselves in the educational process, she increased the likelihood that he would agree to a logical extension of this responsibility.

Other techniques that have been found to be successful include the following:

1. Asking questions that do not demand an answer because agreement can be assumed. Such questions tend to minimize the persuasive intentions of the communicator.
2. Spelling out the conclusion, particularly when the issue is complex or you think the audience may fail to draw the desired conclusion. However, if

We are more reluctant to change our minds once we have "signed on the dotted line."

Candee Productions/Nawrocki Stock Photos

Candee Productions/Nawrocki Stock Photos

the subject matter is relatively simple or if the audience is hostile, you may be better off letting them draw their own conclusions.

3.   Presenting both sides of the issue if the audience is either initially opposed or aware of conflicting arguments. Sometimes just telling your audience that there is another side without actually presenting the counterarguments may make your argument more effective. However, if the audience initially supports your position or doesn't know there is another side (and isn't likely to find out), you may be better off presenting just the one side. It can weaken your argument by confusing the audience with too many disparate facts.

4.   Repeating your points can be effective—to a point. Too much repetition can be boring and can antagonize the other person.

5.   Getting the individual to make a public commitment can be both powerful and binding, as we saw in the case of Maynard. The fact that he had placed his signature on the document made him more reluctant to back out.

ASSERTIVENESS

As you can see from the previous section there are many ways to sharpen your techniques of persuasion. What do you do when the tables are turned? Suppose you are confronted with a very persuasive individual who is pressuring you to do something you don't want. Do you have a hard time saying "no"? Can you stand up for your rights, refuse an unreasonable request, and express your true feelings without offending, abusing, or putting the other person down? Do you feel tense and uncomfortable whenever you make a personal request? You may need some **assertiveness training.** In Chapter 5, (the section on anger) we saw that it is possible to be assertive without being aggressive.

assertiveness training: training in the social skills required to be able to refuse requests; to express both positive and negative feelings; to initiate, engage in, and terminate conversation; and to make personal requests without suffering from excessive stress. (American Psychological Association, 1982)

Most of us have received requests from friends, acquaintances, or employers with which we did not wish to comply. However, out of fear of losing their friendship or favorable regard, we have honored the request, hating ourselves afterwards for our failure to speak up. It is often difficult to say no, particularly if our self-image is one of a friendly, helpful person. When learning how to say no, it is important to realize that people who withdraw their friendship or respect because we exercise our right to refuse a request were not terrific friends to begin with.

If you're a person who just can't say no, there are a few techniques you might find useful in resisting social pressures.

1.   Don't hedge or hem and haw. Words like, "Well, gee, maybe, but I don't know for sure," are a come-on and encourage the other person to pursue the issue further. Indeed, the other person might interpret your words as a tentative acceptance. If this is the case, it may be even more difficult to say no once you have thought it through. A simple "no" leaves less of an opening for badgering you.

2.   Repeat the word "no" each time the person pressures you to change your

mind. Unless you have previously committed yourself to honor this person's request, you owe nobody an explanation for your refusal. To illustrate:

HANK: You've never smoked marijane? You don't know what you're missing. Here, take a puff.

YOU: No.

HANK: Why?

YOU: I don't want to. See ya.

This technique is sometimes called the *broken record:* you repeat a statement of your position every time the issue comes up. Let's look at another example:

"I'm just looking, thank you," repeated Gail to the third salesperson who approached her as she passed their counters on her way to the Atari display. She *was* just looking. She wasn't going to buy anything this time and she didn't want to be bothered by someone trying to sell her something. So she kept repeating, "I'm just *looking,* thank you," a little more firmly each time until they all finally gave up.

3.   When you answer, do not leave an opening for a rebuttal. For example, if your reply to Hank is, "I think it's dangerous and hazardous to your health," you are inviting a deluge of counterarguments. He will almost certainly have constructed elaborate defenses in support of his habit. He may point out the fact that there is no absolutely conclusive evidence that marijuana is dangerous to humans. "Even if it is dangerous," he may concede, "Is it any worse than cigarettes, liquor, tranquilizers, and the thousands of additives that are crammed into our food?" On the other hand, suppose your response had been something like, "I really don't appreciate being forced to do something I don't want to do. So please don't try to convince me." This type of response will usually close the door to a rebuttal.

4.   Use *fogging.* Reword the person's request. Then nod your head in agreement or say something nice about the person. Finally, turn the person down anyway.

ERIKA: You should buy a set of encyclopedias.

MAYNARD: Yes, I should own a set. But I'm not going to buy one now."

SUMMARY

In this chapter we looked at various aspects of interpersonal relationships, including the formation of first impressions, communicating with others, judging others, shyness, group influences on behavior, attitudes, changing attitudes, and assertiveness.

- Based on another person's appearance at the time of our first contact, we often make inferences concerning their occupation, status, political leanings, and personality characteristics.

- First impressions appear to have a lasting impact. The inferences made on the basis of first impressions will often resist conflicting information arising from later encounters. If you have made a poor first impression, it is advisable to permit a period of time to elapse before seeing that person again.

- Much of what passes for communication fails, in actuality, to communicate meaning. Some conversations consist of parallaction, which is ritualistic talking with little communication of feelings or information. Another problem in communication is mystification. This occurs when the individual intentionally miscommunicates information. In real communication, the person takes a chance. There is mutual self-disclosure in which each individual is expected to achieve an equally deep degree of intimacy.

- Communication is not limited to spoken and written language. Facial expressions, gestures, body position, and other mannerisms often convey information above and beyond the spoken word.

- In many situations, telephone communication may be as effective as face-to-face discussions. When there is a dispute between two parties and one has the stronger case, telephone communications may be even more effective in persuading the person with the weaker case to change.

- When judging others, we do not take their behavior at face value. Before judging the actions of others, we wish to know why they behaved as they did. Attributing underlying causes to behavior may involve individual personality factors (internal dispositions) or situational factors. Three criteria used in checking on the accuracy of our attributions are: consistency, consensus, and freedom from external pressure.

- Factors influencing interpersonal attraction include physical appearance and perceived similarity of personality characteristics. However, if you dislike a person who is similar to you, the dislike will be greater than for a person seen as dissimilar.

- Shyness is a common difficulty, with about 80 percent of those surveyed in one study indicating that they experienced shyness at some point in their lives.

- The consequences of shyness can be devastating, interfering with the establishment of relationships, limiting the individual's defense of personal rights and points of view, and producing unfavorable impressions in others. Negative feelings like loneliness, depression, and anxiety often accompany shyness.

- Shyness is not a fixed and unchangeable aspect of personality. Various techniques for overcoming shyness were presented.

- We often behave differently when we are members of a group than when we are alone. Others influence all aspects of our lives, including our likes, dislikes, beliefs, and attitudes.

- When you adapt your expressed beliefs or behaviors to reflect group values, you are conforming. Group pressures to conform are typically unspoken but understood.

- In obedience, the expectations are direct and explicit. Obedience may be either destructive (e.g., following orders to commit a crime) or constructive (e.g., following rules that protect the safety of everyone).

- Attitudes are learned predispositions to respond in certain ways, either negatively or positively, toward people, objects, or ideas. They include thought (cognitive), feeling, and behavioral components. At times, these components are inconsistent with one another, causing tension.

- Attempts to change attitudes often focus on a single component of attitudes. However, changing one component will often alter the remaining components. Techniques of persuasion include appeals to thought (e.g., evidence of proof of a claim), feelings (trust of a celebrity), or changing behavior (debaters often change positions when forced to defend one they initially opposed).

- Techniques of changing the attitudes of others include: establishing a friendly and trusting relationship, obtaining agreement on minor points, using reinforcement, spelling out the conclusion when the issue is complex, repeating the main points, and getting the individual to make a public commitment on the issue.

- A number of assertiveness techniques were discussed. They include: no hedging; the broken record: taking a position and repeating it; leaving no opening for a rebuttal; and fogging, rewording the request and saying something nice before turning the request down.

TERMS TO REMEMBER

Parallaction	Altruism
Mystification	Attribution theory
Self-disclosure	Assertiveness training

MARRIAGE AND OTHER INTIMATE RELATIONSHIPS

A Day Alone

Diane could not quite believe her good luck. Here she was totally free for the day and absolutely alone. In times past, she would have dreaded the prospects of spending an entire day with no other companionship than her own thoughts. "But times change and, fortunately, me with them," she mused contentedly.

Her thoughts drifted back a year, almost to the day. How could she ever forget? That's when she saw Fred for the first time. "Funny," she thought, "I didn't hear a clanging of bells or a flashing of lights on our first meeting. In fact, he appeared rather unappealing in his sweat-stained tennis garb. It was what happened to our relationship afterward that fixed the date in my mind."

She continued to ruminate on their first meeting. She had been called in at the last moment to fill in at mixed doubles when his regular partner couldn't make it. It didn't take her more than a few moments warming up to see that Fred was a superb player, far outclassing her in strength and shot-making ability. Her first reaction was one of distress. She would make a fool of herself and there would be a scene, made all the worse by her unwillingness to submit meekly to criticism. She was sick and tired of macho males who equated physical strength with general superiority.

But Fred was a delightful surprise. Not a word of criticism did he speak. Rather, if anything, he was a bit too lavish in his praise. "Nice shot, partner," he would say after a rather routine crosscourt half volley. They lost the match but he maintained his good cheer. "How long you been playing?" he asked afterwards. To her reply of five years, he continued, "That figures. You've got all the shots. Pity the competition after we've played together a few more times." He was not just being nice. They played again two days later and have been inseparable ever since.

Her thoughts wandered over a broad landscape of friends and acquaintances. "It's funny. I have known some people almost all my life and we have never gone beyond exchanging observations about the weather." She had an amusing visual image of a montage of disembodied faces—the druggist, the manager of the local supermarket, the plumber, the school crossing guard—all saying in unison, "Good morning, Diane, nice day, isn't it?"

She began to wonder why some acquaintanceships remain essentially static while others flower into vibrant friendships. She wondered what made her relationships with people like Myrna, Sam, Betty, and Pedro so very special and central to her life whereas individuals like Eric and Lisa remained on the fringes, on speaking terms but with no shared intimacy. And why did Fred occupy a place at the very core of her existence? Why could she not imagine a life that did not include him?

CLOSE
RELATIONSHIPS

It has been reported that the great comedian Groucho Marx was offered membership in a posh Hollywood Country Club. He is said to have declined, giving the following as his reason, "Any club that would have me as a member cannot be all that particular about who it takes in."

Although undoubtedly meant to be humorous, Groucho's refusal embodies within it a profound insight into human relationships. The key to establishing close human relationships is found within ourselves. Unless we have a positive self-esteem and see ourselves as desirable and valuable, how can we possibly imagine that others will value us and wish to establish close personal ties? Remember that, from the point of view of attribution theory, the way you perceive reality is the most important determinant of your behavior. If you perceive yourself as unworthy, you are likely to attribute the same perceptions to others. You will assume that others will find you dull, boring, and without redeeming virtues. Unfortunately, such self-defeating attitudes can easily become self-fulfilling prophesies. When you hold a low opinion of yourself, you often *act* in ways that confirm your self-evaluation. You may compensate by behaving in a superior fashion or you may withdraw into a shell as if to say, "Don't look at me or pay me any attention. I am not worthy of your regard." Neither of these stances is likely to endear you to others. People you encounter in the course of daily living are more likely to see you as a person to be avoided rather than as one to be approached. Who can take genuine pleasure in the company of either a boor or a wet blanket? You are then able to look at this cumulation of "evidence" as proof of your unworthiness. "See, it's just as I said. There *is* something wrong with me" (See Box 10.1).

Ironically, just as well-balanced and healthy personality characteristics are essential for establishing effective interpersonal relationships, genuine personal growth depends in large part on the quality of the individual's interactions with others. Through good and honest relationships, we learn much about ourselves and we are provided the opportunities to express some of our finest characteristics, such as trust, love, and commitment. Thus, maladjusted individuals are doubly penalized—they are unable to accept and respect themselves and they are deprived of the types of social experiences that would allow them to grow and develop in positive directions.

Effective interpersonal relationships are not static; they are characterized by continued growth and development in honesty, supportiveness, meaningfulness, and selflessness. Let's take a further look at each of these characteristics.

1. Honesty. To varying degrees, all of us display a public self that differs from the private self that we know in our innermost thoughts and impulses. The public self is on display and consists of the parts we act out on the stage of everyday living. In contrast, the private self is usually under wraps, revealed only to our most intimate friends. When Jimmy Carter was running for President, he shocked many people by admitting that he had, on occasion, lusted after a woman "in his mind." The startled reaction of the public was probably more

BOX 10.1: THEIR OWN WORST ENEMIES

In my practice I have come to know a great many inveterate self-critics, given to asserting their failings in as much detail as the listener seems willing to endure. The species is not all that rare and includes a variety of breeds. Self-critics may be boorish whiners or charmingly droll, but these are only surface characteristics. The common denominator is the habit of putting themselves down.

While most people criticize themselves occasionally, the habitual self-critic does so with unusual frequency and severity. So heavy is his investment in always talking about his own inadequacies that if he is contradicted—if he is assured that his self-assessment is mistaken in whole or in part—he may only become angry and more entrenched in his beliefs about himself.

What most significantly distinguishes one self-critic from another is motive, and the possible motives of the self-critic are many and can combine like molecules. Usually we think of such people as lacking in confidence, or feeling inferior, or believing themselves wrong about something. While there is truth in these explanations, they overlook the personal and social functions of self-criticism. People make their "I'm no good" statements not just because they sincerely believe them to be so, but also in order to accomplish something. People can criticize themselves as a way of sending a message to others, as a means of, say, expressing hostility or anger, or of establishing social status or position. The adolescent who announces that he can't do anything right, that he is always messing up, may be seeking to avoid responsibility. The woman who keeps insisting to her husband that she is dull and stupid and a poor mother may be trying to frustrate and annoy him because he is insensitive to her real concerns. The motive for putting oneself down can be as self-sacrificing as a misguided effort to keep a family together or as self-serving as an attempt to be seen as someone who lives up to extraordinarily high standards.

Whatever the motive, the self-critical person causes himself discomfort and even pain, and may have little awareness that he is the perpetrator of his own distress. He also does not see that his excessive self-criticism is an understandable response to the circumstances of his life. But failing to grasp the reason behind his self-criticism, he is in a poor position to do much about it.

In analyzing the types of self-criticism, we must look at what the person is actually doing: what he intends, what he achieves, and what satisfaction he may gain.

MOBILIZING PRESSURE TO IMPROVE

Some people criticize themselves in an effort to get a better understanding of their actions or to force themselves to do better next time.

The line between sensible and unreasonable self-criticism is sometimes thin. A person who is critical of his own math ability may reasonably decide, for example, that he is poor at algebra and ought to avoid the course. And a young girl may question whether she is experienced enough or popular enough to date an older boy in her school. Is she right? Or merely afraid? Or both?

Self-criticism also mobilizes discomfort and brings pressure on people to do better. To get a job done, they "put the screws" to themselves. Especially when they have little interest in the job, they castigate themselves for lack of enthusiasm or energy and exhort themselves to try harder. Being really tough on themselves does increase motivation, at least temporarily, and often long enough to do the job. But if they fail, as occasionally happens, the result may be a cycle of disappointment and anger that leads to even harsher self-criticism.

People who criticize themselves as a way to self-improvement should ask themselves, "Is it working? Is more pressure going to work any better?" These questions should help them to realize that their self-criticism is a form of victimization, not a technique by which they continuously do better. For if their excessive self-criticism were indeed effective, they would be near perfect!

A CHECK ON AMBITION

Self-criticism may be a way of restraining oneself from trying to do something that may be dangerous

BOX 10.1 *(continued)*

or unethical. When a person criticizes his own abilities or status, he reminds—or convinces—himself that overly ambitious attempts to change that position may be doomed to failure.

Just such reasoning helps to explain why many teenagers are almost compulsively concerned about their appearance. According to the social expectations of their own group, teenagers should not only meet and date members of the opposite sex, they must also enjoy and be adept at such relationships. For some teenagers, these expectations are frightening threats to their self-esteem. They would rather criticize their own looks and limit their social activity than be publicly embarrassed.

PLAYING IT SAFE

People who have modest expectations, who play it safe, may be surprised by good news, but they will not be startled by failure or disappointment. They expect that. Issues of control are important in this case of self-criticism. People who put themselves down do not allow circumstances—or other people—to do it for them.

Obviously, self-criticism can also be a strategy to ward off attacks by others. People who present themselves as being insecure, frightened, or barely able to manage, tend to prevent other people from criticizing them. After all, one would have to be a hardhearted person to attack anyone who is such a mess!

HUMILITY AND SUPERIORITY

When a person acknowledges wrongdoing by saying "I was wrong" or "I was mean and selfish," he may be doing penance in the traditional sense. He is also showing good faith to others by saying, in effect, that the transgressed standards do count; in the process he affirms himself as a defender of what is right.

Let us see what else may be involved. By acknowledging guilt, people often set a precedent that invites others to acknowledge their own parts in a conflict. In many situations, admitting one's guilt becomes a way of getting others to admit theirs. As a result, the guilt is diffused, and one gains in moral stature by having been the first to say, "Yes, it was my fault."

Self-criticism can also be a device for asserting one's general superiority. . . . people establish the superiority of their standards by constantly renouncing their less than perfect performances. Their self-criticism, harsh and continual, announces that they are above making mistakes and that their imperfect behavior is not a reflection of their true selves.

Consider the graduate who cannot decide on any dissertation topic and stick to it. One topic is not interesting enough, another not important enough, and so on. The student wants to write something exceptional, but he has no guarantees that anything he starts will be outstanding. He renounces his attempts not because he feels inferior but to uphold his self-image as a person who expects great accomplishments from himself.

STATEMENTS TO OTHERS

Self-criticism can also be a statement to other people not to make any demands. The adolescent who insists on his lack of responsibility is an example. By declaring that he is irresponsible, he tells people that they should not expect anything of him. He is saying, [in effect] "Don't expect too much from me because, you see, I've got this wooden leg."

Yet another form of self-criticism aims at evoking sympathy. By being overly tough on themselves, people who feel lonely and unloved invite their friends and acquaintances to reassure them of their worth. These friends often will share in the misery, saddened by what they hear, and frustrated by an inability to do anything about it other than offer words of comfort. To the extent that misery loves company, self-critics of this type often get what they love. To the extent that they do, they gain an added advantage—avoiding an unfavorable comparison between their own unhappiness and the happier situation of their friends.

Sympathy-seeking self-critics tend to be hard on their friends. In the first place, these self-critics don't want the sympathy to stop. As long as friends keep attending to them, they need not do anything to change their situation. But after a time, friends tend to be weary of a constant stream of self-deprecation. Often they will drift away, leaving the lonely, sympathy-seeking self-critic even more lonely, more in need of sympathy, more self-critical, searching for new

BOX 10.1 *(concluded)*

sympathetic listeners. It is a cycle that can be broken only when the self-critic moves beyond egocentric unhappiness and learns to talk with people about something other than his or her problem.

HIDDEN MOTIVES

Some forms of self-criticism are not so much requests for a response as they are vehicles for expressing feelings that are difficult to express more directly.

Consider an incident in which a wife has spent hours making a special meal. The husband comes home late, eats mostly in silence, but comments that the duck is dry, perhaps overcooked. The wife states angrily that she is an awful cook, that absolutely nothing that she does is ever right. Dumping the dry duck in the garbage, platter and all, she runs from the room. The wife is ostensibly putting herself down, but by indirection, she lets her husband know that he has hurt her, and she tries to make him squirm.

Hostile self-critics do not always know that they are being hostile. If one of the wife's friends said that she would have been angry too, the woman might respond, "But I wasn't angry. I was just terribly hurt and upset." But if the friend said, "Your husband's comment was unfair and was enough to make you angry," such a remark would legitimize the anger and allow the woman to accept it.

Hostile self-critics have reservations about speaking up for themselves. They feel that it is selfish and wrong to put their own interests ahead of others'. They choose instead to camouflage their hostility by apparently turning it against themselves, and they strike out through self-criticism.

Self-critical people experience condemnation, degradation, and humiliation as if they had originated in someone else. Given the distress generated by extreme self-criticism—for no one enjoys believing that he or she is incompetent, unloved, ugly, or irresponsible—it is no surprise that self-critics are often unable to attribute their pain to their own choices and actions. But this leaves them in a poor position to think through these choices and actions.

People need to see that they do not condemn themselves merely because they believe that they are stupid or incompetent, but always to accomplish something: to pressure themselves to improve, to gain sympathy, to avoid responsibility, or any of the other reasons that we have discussed. Understanding the reasons for being self-critical is the first step in altering those reasons and breaking the pattern. . . . People who use self-criticism to evoke sympathy must be treated differently from those who use it to express anger. Both may need different advice than those who denounce themselves to stonewall further attacks. Finally, some people may be unduly self-critical for any combination of the reasons we have discussed, and thus pose more complex problems.

In every instance, however, self-critics need to understand that *they* are doing the criticizing. Once it dawns on them that they are acting on intelligible reasons and are in charge, that they are perpetuating their own unhappiness, they may find a way to silence the harsh critics inside themselves.

Source: Driscoll, R., Their Own Worst Enemies. *Psychology Today,* July 1982, 45–49. Reprinted from *Psychology Today* magazine. Copyright © 1982, American Psychological Association

in response to the admission than to the impulse. In other words, people in or seeking public office do not usually share their inner world with the general public. This world is carefully guarded from outside intruders since public revelations of private thoughts and impulses might be used against them. However, one of the great values of sharing close and intimate relationships is that each individual should feel free to peel off the surface layers that conceal the private self (Altman & Taylor, 1973). If you are unable to do so and you feel you must protect your public image at all times, you might well question the integrity of the relationship. Close friends should have access to deeper layers of your personality. Otherwise, many of the values of the relationship are lost—opportunities to test your ideas, express your doubts and fears, and share your personal goals and aspirations in a nonhostile environment.

2. Supportiveness. Marcia had just been divorced from her husband of 12 years and her entire life was in disarray. The visiting arrangements for the children were still in dispute; she had to find employment in spite of the fact that she had been out of circulation in the job market for 10 or more years; many of the valued friendships she and Ted had established were suddenly excised from the core of her life. Her few remaining friends described her as a nervous wreck. She was suddenly impatient, short-tempered, and unreasonable in her expectations of others. Throughout all the tempest and turmoil, her closest friend, Millicent, remained steadfast in her patience and loyalty to Marcia. Mutual acquaintances were perplexed. They demanded to know, "How can you put up with her? She goes around with a constant chip on her shoulder." Her reply was simple and direct, "She has always been my closest friend. Now of all times, she deserves all the support I can give her."

In her private world, Millicent admitted that Marcia's difficulties had put a strain on their relationship. But she had a well-formulated concept of friendship. In her conversations with herself, she reviewed her role as close and intimate friend to Marcia. "A fair weather friend is no friend at all," she would say to herself. "It is times like this that really put the fabric of a friendship to the test. If I abandon her now, I am admitting that our relationship was a sham. But it wasn't. I gained much from her companionship during the good times and expect to benefit from them in the future."

Being supportive does not mean humbling yourself at the other person's feet. It means suspending negative judgments, accepting the person for what he or she is, and not demanding conformity to your system of values.

3. Meaningfulness. Meaningful relationships change us, making us different from what we would otherwise have been. One test of the meaningfulness of a relationship is to answer the following questions, "Suppose I had never met this other person. Would I be any different now? In what ways? If the relationship were suddenly terminated, how would it affect me? Would something significant be missing from my life?" If the answers to these questions are in the negative—"No, I would still be the same person," and "I would just continue to go on as if nothing had happened"—the relationship lacked any real meaningfulness for the individual.

4. Selflessness. Two types of interpersonal relationships have been described by Martin Buber—I–thou and I–it relationships (1970). In the I–it relationship, the other person is treated as an object rather than as a unique individual, someone to be manipulated for the benefit of the "I." Examples of I–it relationships abound in the entertainment field where actors, actresses, and other performers are treated as commodities to be marketed and merchandised for personal gain. Even members of the medical profession have expressed concern about the use

Friends provide the support we need, particularly in times of crisis.

United Press International Photo

of patients as objects—they are sometimes referred to as "clinical teaching material" rather than as patients (Fein, 1982). There is little opportunity to grow in the I–it relationship for either the "I" or the "it."

In contrast, the I–thou relationship provides opportunities for both parties to grow and develop. The relationship is the opposite of exploitation and selfishness. Each party accepts the other and rejoices in the other's accomplishments and triumphs.

The characteristics described above represent ideals toward which to strive. There are probably very few relationships that conform to the ideal at all times and places. We are not always completely honest in our dealings with a close and intimate friend; we fail to be supportive when it is needed; some of our interactions lack meaningfulness; and we occasionally "use" a friend to satisfy selfish needs. In this vein, it is helpful to consider some of the reasons why you may fail to measure up in your interpersonal relations (Coleman, 1960):

Egocentricity. You see yourself as being at the center of the social world, with others revolving around you. You are so intent on satisfying your own goals and finding your own pleasures that you ignore similar needs in others. In extreme cases, others may refer to you as an egomaniac. People will tend to shy away from you since you appear to lack sensitivity toward them.

Emotional Insulation. In a film titled *The Pawnbroker,* Rod Steiger rendered a chilling portrayal of a person who had insulated himself from all concern for others and their problems. He was thereby enabled to conduct his business without being touched by the human pathos and misery that surrounded him. But he paid dearly for this small comfort. He became like a robot, leading a life that was devoid of feelings and lacking in any deep and sustained human relationship.

Feelings of Inferiority. Individuals who have low self-esteem are characteristically lacking in self-confidence and the willingness to submit to new and different experiences. Their desire to take the "safe route" makes them appear deficient in spontaneity. In some cases, however, they will overcompensate, engaging in boasting and displaying excessive bravado. In either case, they are unwilling to commit themselves to deep and lasting relationships because of personal feelings of inadequacy.

Hostility. On the basis of the mistaken assumption that people work only for their own self-interests, some people are constantly suspicious of the motives of others. This suspicion is readily transformed into hostility, so that they appear to be walking around with a chip on their shoulder. It is difficult, if not impossible, to establish a close relationship with someone who suspects you of being friendly out of some ulterior motive.

Overdependency. Overdependency often accompanies feelings of inferiority. Unsure of one's own adequacy, the individual looks toward others for emotional support and leadership. Such behavior can place a severe burden on a relationship, since the individual appears to be taking more often than giving.

**MARRIAGE AND
THE FAMILY**

How important is marriage to you? If we can judge from a poll of 17,000 students in the class of '83, the answer is "extremely important" (Bachman & Johnston, 1979). In this survey, when the high school students were seniors, they were asked to rate the importance of major life goals. For each goal, they could choose one of four different alternatives: Extremely Important, Quite Important, Somewhat Important, or Not Important. Almost 80 percent of college-bound students selected the first option for marriage—more than for any other goal. Similar results were obtained with non-college-bound students. It is interesting to note that "Strong friendships" was ranked second highest as a life goal by the college-bound students. The results of this aspect of the poll are presented in Table 10.1.

The overwhelming majority of both groups indicated that they expected to marry, with 96 percent saying they planned to have children. Moreover, the majority indicated that it is "very likely" they would remain with the same person for life. Although tolerant of the idea of living together without benefit of marriage, they were far less receptive of deciding "to have and raise a child out of wedlock."

It would therefore appear that, to many young adults, marriage remains a popular institution in spite of many recent assaults against it by the sexual revolution.

Selecting a Marriage Partner

What are some of the factors involved in selecting a mate? Does the rule "similars attract" apply to choosing marriage partners as well as to selecting friends?

TABLE 10.1	THE IMPORTANT THINGS IN LIFE	College (%)	Noncollege (%)
	A good marriage and family life	79	76
	Strong friendships	69	57
	Finding purpose and meaning in my life	66	62
	Finding steady work	65	67
	Being successful in my work	63	52
	Making a contribution to society	23	10
	Having lots of money	16	19
	Being a leader in my community	10	4

Source: Reprinted from *Psychology Today* magazine. Copyright © 1979 American Psychological Association

Apparently, it does (Byrne, 1971). The boy and girl next door frequently do marry. Of course, this may be due in large part to the fact that, in our culture, you do not marry someone you have not met. Most marriages take place betwen individuals who share the same socioeconomic, religious, racial, educational, and ethnic backgrounds. Moreover, they tend to be of approximately the same age, similar levels of intelligence, and are comparable in physical attractiveness (Hill, Rubin, & Peplau, 1976). These findings do not mean that marriages between individuals from different backgrounds are foredoomed to failure. Some of the differences might not be important to either partner. However, if there are differences that are considered significant by at least one partner (e.g., religious, racial, or educational disparities), some open discussion of the differences might wisely be undertaken prior to making a marriage commitment.

It has been argued by some that, although we marry people with similar cultural backgrounds, we are attracted to individuals with complementary personality traits (Winch, 1958, 1963). According to this view, a shy, retiring person is likely to be attracted to someone with opposite traits, such as sociableness and forwardness. However, this view does not receive much research support (Udry, 1966). In truth, individuals with highly incompatible needs might spend an excessive

Eighty percent of 17,000 high school seniors in the class of '83 rated marriage as "extremely important."

© 1981 Kan/Design Conceptions

A survey of 75,000 wives concluded that love could be a solid basis for marriage if it meant couples cared enough for each other to discuss feelings and problems openly and honestly.

© 1976 Joel Gordon

amount of energy pulling against one another, whereas those with similar motives and goals would appear to be more likely to pull together.

Then there is romantic love. This poorly understood but extreme degree of emotional attraction between two individuals is often given as the reason and justification for marriage. "We just cannot live without one another," declare the two lovers fending off the assault by parents, relatives, or friends following their declaration of intent to marry. However, the acute excitement stage of romantic love tends to diminish rapidly after marriage. It is then that many couples learn whether or not they share the more stable and enduring characteristics that will make their marriage work. Indeed, one critic sees marriage based on romantic love as one of the greatest obstacles to a successful marriage. According to this view, individuals drawn together primarily by physical factors tend to ignore those characteristics that make for marital success (De Rougemont, 1949).

The Benefits of Marriage

When two people enter marriage, they encounter interrelationships that are almost totally different from any they have previously experienced with parents, siblings, and friends. Working out these relationships is similar to learning how to walk. They will stumble often and occasionally fall. However, if they persist in their efforts, both partners will continue to grow both emotionally and socially.

In an effective marriage, both individuals feel free to share their ideas with one another. This exchange permits the persons to clarify their own thinking. "Frances, we have a ticklish situation developing at work. Here's the way I propose to handle it. Let me know what you think of my idea. Perhaps you may have a suggestion or two of your own."

There will be a host of decisions to be made involving all aspects of married life—where they will live, whether or not both will be gainfully employed, whether or not to have children and, if so, how many and when. Some of these decisions will be quite complex, involving elements that are linked together as in a chain. To illustrate, the couple may decide that each will pursue a career. Does this mean that they must indefinitely postpone starting a family? Not necessarily. But if they decide to have children, they must also come to grips with the problem of providing a care giver during the hours that they are at work. Should their parents be pressed into service? Should they hire a housekeeper? Or should they place their child in a day-care center? During this decision-making process, they must learn to evaluate the various options in terms of how their choices will affect *us* rather than *me*. If children are added to the scene, they will become part of the "us."

The couple must also learn to allocate each partner's share of the many tasks of marriage. This division of labor becomes especially important when both individuals are employed. Few marriages can survive a husband who sits before the tube cheering for the Steelers to trounce the Chiefs while his working wife is preparing the meals, cleaning the house, washing the dishes and the clothing, corresponding with the folks, keeping financial records, serving as social secretary, and trying to be sexy come bedtime.

There is one technique that may be helpful in forestalling difficulties stemming from an unbalanced division of labor. Compile a list of the many tasks of marriage and have both the husband and wife rate these tasks on a scale of liking. It will often be found that a task abhorred by one partner is enjoyed by another. To illustrate, imagine that Ted and Alice use the following scale to rate the different chores that must be done.

Each rates the tasks as follows:

	Task	Ted	Alice
	Cooking	1	3
1 Enjoy doing	Cleaning house	4	2
2 It's OK	Washing dishes	4	2
3 Don't care for it	Drying dishes	2	3
4 Ugh!	Food shopping	2	4
	Keeping financial records	3	1
	Washing windows	4	4

Today many husbands and wives share responsibility for household chores and the care and raising of children.

Charles Gatewood

From these ratings, it would appear that Ted could do most of the cooking, dry the dishes, and do the food shopping. On the other hand, Alice would probably be willing to clean house, wash the dishes, and keep financial records. Since both detest washing the windows, they could alternate this responsibility or, budget permitting, they could hire someone to do this chore from time to time. The point of this bargaining is to reduce those many irritants and hassles that can rob a marriage of its many positive elements. Each partner recognizes that there are many unexciting tasks to be done and that the burden should not all be placed on the shoulders of one person.

In addition to honing one's skills as a manager and decision maker, marriage provides many opportunities to acquire skills in the fine art of compromise. When an irresistible force is on a collision course with an unmovable object, there will be a mighty explosion unless there is a means of absorbing or deflecting the impact. In seeking a compromise, it is wise to keep the following in mind:

1. It is rare that one side is completely in the right. More frequently both partners have elements of right and wrong on their side.
2. The more strongly you feel on an issue, the more defensively you are likely to react to head off any threat to your feelings, beliefs, or self-esteem. Defensive behavior (projection, rationalization, etc.) distorts our perception of reality and may blind us to the other person's point of view.
3. You should attempt to see things from the other person's perspective. Genuine empathy can prevent the distortions that can arise from viewing everything from a subjective and often biased point of view.
4. Both partners have needs that are pressing for satisfaction. Any "solution" that neglects one partner's needs and ambitions is heading for difficulty.
5. Compromise is not defeat. In compromise, both sides give up something so that greater good can be achieved for all parties concerned. In this day and age, men who cook (the second author of this book can whip up a mean egg custard in the microwave oven), care for the baby, and do chores around the house are more often valued positively than negatively by others. Similarly, a woman is no longer considered unfeminine because she enjoys tinkering around with the family "dream machine."

Making a Marriage Work

Much that has happened during the past century has placed numerous additional strains on marriage. To begin with, we are simply living a much longer time, on the average, than our forebears. To illustrate, at the turn of the century, the life expectancy of a white male was about 48 years; it is now 70 years—an increase of 45 percent. For white females, the increase is 52 percent. It is even more dramatic for nonwhites—almost 100 percent (i.e., double) for males, and nearly 110 percent for females (Runyon, 1981). Part of but far from all of this apparent increase in life span is a statistical artifact, stemming from the reduced percentages of deaths among infants and children. This enormous rise means

With increasing life expectancies, 50-year anniversaries are not uncommon.

© Joel Gordon 1981

that those who remain married will be together twice as many years as those who pledged their vows one century ago. Thus, when present-day newlyweds take the vow to love and honor forever, it turns out that forever is a much longer period of time than it was for our grandparents and great-grandparents. Consequently, there is much more time for things to go wrong in a marriage. It also means that a woman can expect to survive many years beyond the time the last of her children leaves the home. If she has pursued the traditional roles as housewife and mother, she will suddenly have many free hours on her hands. There will be an urge to avoid stagnation—a motivation her husband of many years may not comprehend.

Perhaps of more importance is the fact that the institution of marriage has undergone massive changes during this century. When a couple entered a marriage pact at the turn of the century, both the husband and the wife assumed clearly defined roles. The wife was the homemaker—responsible for bearing and raising the children, preparing the meals, keeping the house, and caring for the needs of her spouse. Very few women competed in the marketplace. Those who did were usually poorly paid and were often regarded with disdain. In contrast, the husband was the wage earner and political figure. He was responsible for providing adequate economic support for the family, defending it in time of war, and voting for political candidates.

Now, in the labor force of people 20 years of age and older, women represent about 4 in every 10 employees. Clearly, with redefined roles come redefined responsibilities. Many of these responsibilities conflict with a woman's former role as chief cook and bottle washer. Inevitably, there is marital discord when the husband's and wife's images of their respective roles are in disagreement. Unless solutions are found, their marriage could well wind up in the divorce courts.

In a *traditional marriage,* the role of the husband and wife are fixed by tradition and the expectations of the couple. In this type of marriage, there is men's work and women's work and never the twain shall meet. These roles developed when women were not part of the work force and didn't openly aspire to compete in a man's world. Moreover, by the time their children left the nest, the women were generally approaching the end of their life span. They looked forward to "taking it easy" and being a doting grandmother. Now, when they leave home, the children often move to distant places where grandmother is only an occasional visitor. And grandmother is still in the prime of her life! What is she to do? Sit in the TV room and suffer chronic indigestion as she gorges herself on the soaps?

An alternative to the traditional marriage is the *equal-partner marriage* (O'Neil & O'Neil, 1972). In this type of marriage, roles are not seen as fixed by tradition and unchanging throughout the life span. Rather they are agreed upon in an interpersonal contract between the husband and wife. However, in recognition of the fact that individuals continue to grow—their needs, values, beliefs, aspirations, and expectations change over time—this contract is subject to renegotiation at any time. To illustrate, when Walter and Anita were married, both had already launched careers. They agreed to share the housework so that each undertook

Because she insisted on the right to nurse her newborn daughter on the set, Lynn Redgrave was replaced in a role for a popular television series. She later gained a role in another series and was allowed to bring her daughter onto the set.

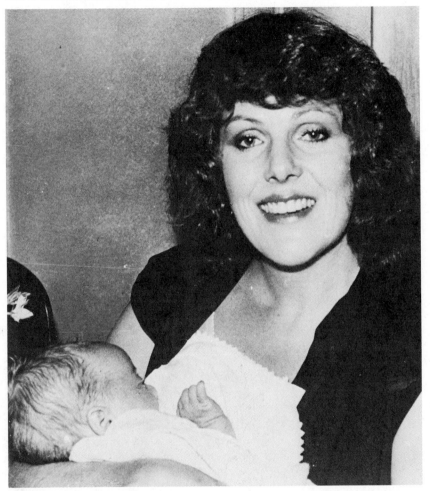

Wide World Photos

tasks that they found agreeable or least disagreeable. Since they planned to start a family immediately, Anita agreed to take maternity leave for a few months shortly before and after the birth of their child. Later, a housekeeper would be hired to care for the child during the day. After a few months of marriage, Anita was given a promotion that would take her out of town for days at a time. Walter agreed to undertake a greater share of the chores when she was away. If the burden became excessive, they would use some of the extra income coming from

Anita's promotion to hire help when needed. Not only did Walter agree, but he pointed out that the expense was tax deductible.

There is more to an equal-partner marriage than contracts concerning the marital roles. Recognizing that people change in many ways after marriage, their agreement permits each partner a large degree of latitude about the directions of personal growth. Some of the features of an equal-partner marriage include: privacy for each individual, frank and honest communication, open companionship, equality, and flexibility of roles.

There are times in most, if not all, marriages in which one of the partners desires private time, an interval during which he or she will be left alone. In a traditional marriage, such a desire may be interpreted by the other partner as a sign of rejection. In an equal-partner marriage, it is recognized as a right whose exercise does not imply rejection or unfavorable regard. A brief furlough can be healthy for everyone.

An equal-partner marriage begins on the premise that communication should be frank and the lines of communication should remain open. The fact that an explicit contract is made prior to marriage sets the tone for the entire marriage. If one partner does something that displeases the other, it is neither buried alive nor does it serve as the occasion for an emotional outburst. The partners sit down, engage in open discussion of their differences, and negotiate new agreements based on their mutual needs and interests.

During all the interplay of marriage, both partners are regarded as equal. When there is a conflict or a problem in a traditional marriage, the woman is expected to do most of the bending. She is expected to accede to her husband's demands in sexual, occupational, social, and political matters. If both are employed and the husband is offered an opportunity in another city, the wife feels obligated to quit her job and move with him. In an equal-partner marriage, the decision is not the husband's to make alone. Both have an equal say in the final decision.

Finally, it is acknowledged that few spouses can be anything and everything to their partners. Each partner should be free to develop significant relationships (not necessarily sexual) with others. The couple need not always appear together at social affairs. Both should feel free not to go if they do not wish to. Carl Rogers refers to close relationships outside of marriage as *satellite relationships* (1977). He notes that these relationships can lead to both pain and personal growth. The pain is caused by the fact that jealousy and mistrust may develop. The growth occurs because the primary marriage relationship does not become "overloaded." Each partner does not feel obligated to meet all of the other's needs. Moreover, since the partners in a marriage are expected to discuss their feelings freely, the improved communication can increase their sense of trust in one another.

Raising a Family

Some have painted marriage as an institution in which happiness begins a steady decline as soon as the honeymoon is over. Others have perceived the opposite—gradual improvement in happiness as the partners learn to improve their accommodation to one another and are better able to fill each other's respective needs. The actual picture appears to be one of ups and downs depending, in large part, on the status of the children in the family.

Marital Happiness

When couples are asked to identify the happiest years of their marriage, they usually point to both the early years—before any children were born—and the later years—after the children have left home (Campbell, 1975). Apparently, the birth of children puts a strain on the marital relationship. This should not be surprising when we consider the changes in lifestyle that the presence of children introduces into a marriage.

Assuming that both partners entered the marriage with mostly positive feelings and attitudes, the period before the first child is born is one of active mutual exploration—emotionally, intellectually, and sexually. As indicated earlier, the newlyweds are learning to make the many adjustments and compromises necessary to mesh their lives together and produce a coherent "us." Their hopes and optimism run high and their vistas often appear unlimited.

The birth of the first child and subsequent children introduces sudden, almost shocklike stresses and strains for which neither parent is usually prepared. Many have been previously exposed to romanticized versions of the joys and utter bliss of parenthood (of which there *are* many) with little indication of the accompanying hardships. In a period of a few days, they may see their freedom of movement sharply abridged. It's not easy to make spur-of-the-moment decisions like, "Let's go to the movies tonight," when arrangements for a babysitter must be made well in advance and impose an additional financial hardship.Then there are the night feedings, endless changing of diapers, sleepless nights when baby is colicky, and disagreements about how to handle a child-rearing problem. The husband may even become jealous of his children when his wife's attention seems to be directed more toward them than him. These years between the birth of the first child and the time at which the last child enters school are usually considered the most stressful and least happy by most parents.

After all the children reach school age, however, there is usually a distinct improvement in companionship, financial concerns, sexual relations, and relations with children (Burr, 1970). When the children finish school and take off on their own, the couple usually enjoys a second honeymoon. This is particularly the case when the marriage was basically sound to begin with. The two partners have the opportunity to become reacquainted with each other as they respond to their newfound freedom and privacy. However, if the foundations of the marriage were shaky—often held together by a joint commitment to the children—the "graduation" of the children may lead to further deterioration and possible dissolution of the marriage.

Working Parents

Many couples who plan to pursue separate careers after marriage raise questions about the advisability of having children. "Is it possible for a child to develop favorably, both emotionally and intellectually, when the parents are missing throughout most of the day?'' The answer to this question depends upon the *quality* of both the care giver and the interactions with the parents during available times. In one study, the personality development of children was compared when: *(a)* the children received care exclusively from their own mothers during the first five years; *(b)* they received substitute care for at least one year under stable conditions (i.e., care by the same individual or individuals); or *(c)* they received at least one year of substitute care under unstable conditions (i.e., frequent changes in those caring for the children (Moore, 1969). Children receiving unstable substitute care evidenced greater insecurity than those cared for by their own mothers or by stable substitutes. No detectable differences were found between those raised by their own mothers and those raised by stable care givers.

A critical factor is establishing favorable attachments between working parents and their children appears to be both the frequency and the quality of their interactions (Etaugh, 1974). It is more important that the interactions, when they occur, be of good quality than that the parents be available on a 24-hour-a-day basis.

Being a Good Parent

Throughout this book, we have made much of the concept of self-esteem. To adjust to the many sudden and unexpected twists and turns in everyday living, we must be in a position to give "our best shot." We cannot do so when we are wrapped in ourselves, engulfed by indecision, and intimidated by the low value we place on ourselves. Rather, when our self-esteem is low, we tend to react defensively to both threats and challenges. Generally speaking, defensive behaviors are mindless and reflexive. They rob us of our flexibility, spontaneity, and creativity in seeking solutions to adjustment problems. With these considerations in mind, we should try to establish a type of physical and emotional environment for our children in which they will achieve competence in many of life's skills and will come to value themselves as individuals. This environment should include the following:

1. Love and Attention.   Earlier we discussed the attachment bonds that develop between each parent and the child. These bonds are strengthened by the quality of the positive interactions that occur between parent and child. During the child's infancy, an effective parent is one who initiates activities that both the parent and the child can enjoy. The fact that one or both parents may be gone much of the time does not preclude the establishment of strong bonds.

The child learns many values from the parents. Children who perceive parental love and attention to be sincere will conclude that they are valued by the parents. What loving parents value must, of itself, be valuable. Thus do children learn a healthy self-esteem.

2. Acceptance of the Child as an Individual.   It is easy to become so involved in the lives of our children that we forget that they are separate and distinct individuals with likes, dislikes, needs, interests, emotional expressions, and goals of their own. Our own self-esteem needs can contaminate the relationship. We may think in terms of what would be good for us rather than what would be good for the child. If it is important that we be known as good and effective parents, we may run roughshod over their individuality, demanding obedience rather then fostering spontaneity. We may glow when people say, "Oh, what a well-behaved child." Only later may we regret the child's timidity and lack of spontaneity.

3. Encouraging Independence.   When we accept the children as individuals, we also want them to develop effective techniques for meeting the demands of everyday living. They must be free to find adjustments—including choice of friends, career decisions—that are uniquely suited to them as individuals. A person who is encouraged to think and act independently will have a greater scope of potential actions than those taught to respond by rote to a fixed set of rules.

4. Clear Parental Expectations and Consistent Discipline. While encouraging children to think and act independently, parents do not abdicate their responsibilities to teach values and to guide children along adaptive lines. Since society cannot function in the absence of standards of behavior, we have an obligation to instruct our children in those values necessary for the survival of a democratic society and for the survival of the individual within that society. Our expectations should be clearly formulated and realistic.

Moreover, there are times that discipline must be administered to every child. The discipline should be consistent and administered in the context of love rather than violence. If punishment is administered, the emphasis should be directed to the act rather than to the individual. The attitude should be, "I am punishing you for what you did rather than for what you are. I still love you and will continue to love you."

CONFLICT

No matter how well two people get along, there will inevitably be differences of opinion that result in open confrontation. Some people believe that fighting is bad and should be avoided at all times. Open confrontation makes them uncomfortable and they actively avoid honest discussions of feelings, disagreements, and annoyances. They see conflict as a sign that the relationship is weakening. When disputes are handled in an immature way with each person destructively trying to hurt the other, the relationship may indeed be in trouble. However, research has shown that when couples are really listening to each other, conflict is an essential ingredient in a healthy intimate relationship (Bach & Wyden, 1968). Frank and open discussions can actually strengthen a relationship by increasing mutual understanding. On the other hand, the absence of open confrontation tends to build resentment, feelings of hostility, and anger, and may ultimately destroy the relationship.

Conflict is an essential ingredient in a healthy, intimate relationship—when a couple really listens to each other.

Jim Whitmer/Nawrocki Stock Photo

How do you fight fair? How do you turn a bitter quarrel into a constructive confrontation? First, forget about winning. When you fight only to win, you may win the battle but lose the war. In other words, your partner may leave the battlefield momentarily defeated but too scarred to care anymore about the relationship. Instead, keep your head and try compromising. Always deal with problems *as they come up.* When resentments are buried, they nurture and grow and inevitably explode. Minor annoyances assume monumental proportions when allowed to fester without relief. However, it is better to avoid a confrontation when one or both partners are tired, ill, or extremely agitated about something else. It is easy to overreact when you are feeling out of sorts. Thus, it is best to schedule confrontations. When something comes up that is particularly meaningful, tell the other person that you would like to discuss the matter as soon as it is convenient. Both partners should be sure to follow through as quickly as possible. Although time is a great healer and can often take the edge off of anger, it is wise not to let too much time pass.

During the encounter, each partner should try to understand the other person's feelings and attitudes. Approached in this way, conflict can be a means of achieving a more satisfactory and fulfilling relationship (Bach & Wyden, 1968). To interact effectively, it is essential to have open and honest communication. In the heat of an argument, many people tend not to listen to what the other person is saying, thus setting the stage for distortions and misunderstandings. Stop to listen carefully to what is being said. Do not assume that the other person will know what you are thinking; explicitly say what you really feel and ask for clarification of points you don't understand. Be aware that anger can blind you and lead you to stray from the issue at hand. Communication can break down when anger causes you to say unkind or destructive things that can hurt the relationship (Bienvenu, 1970).

Although frank and open lines of communication can strengthen a relationship, they can also highlight major areas of disagreement. Once disagreements are out in the open, it may then be apparent that the rift is too great and the best solution is to terminate the relationship.

DIVORCE

Why do some relationships fail to survive? One long-term study provided some interesting insights into why couples split (Hill et al., 1976). As expected, couples who felt more deeply about each other in the beginning of the relationship were not as likely to break up as those who were not as much in love. It is interesting that women's feelings were better predictors of the future course of the relationship than men's feelings. Men seem to fall in love more quickly and women can apparently recognize that something is wrong with the relationship before men do. Living together and having sexual intercourse were unrelated to whether or not the couple eventually broke up. Couples who shared mutual interests, educational aspirations, and were similar in age, intelligence, and physical attractiveness were more likely to stay together. When both parties were equally involved with each other, the couple was less likely to break up than when there was an imbalance in the relationship. Breakups were rarely mutual. Rather, they were usually initiated by the less involved member.

Despite fairy-tale romances, many couples do not live happily ever after. Of those who make it down the aisle, 4 out of 10 end up in the divorce courts (Norton & Glick, 1979). Why are there so many divorces? Some claim it is because marriage is a dying institution, but the statistics do not bear this out. Almost everyone marries at least once and about 80 percent of divorced people eventually remarry.

In the past, couples stuck it out in spite of a deteriorating relationship. They lived together unhappily and the atmosphere was fired with hostility and smoldering resentment. Arguments usually centered on small things because facing up to larger issues was sure to lead to separation or divorce. Staying together became more important than personal happiness. Many couples continued in a hopeless marriage "for the sake of the children," respectability in the community, and because of religious convictions (Goode, 1961).

Today, values have changed from the view that marriage is forever ("for better or worse") to a greater emphasis on personal happiness and satisfaction. In addition, most of the 50 states have changed divorce laws so that it is now relatively easy to obtain a divorce when both parties agree. However, don't be deceived by the ease with which marriages can be ended. Whether a marriage has been good or not, divorce is almost always a difficult and painful experience. After studying people in the throes of divorce or separation, one investigator concluded, "Most separations . . . come about only after a long and anguished process of mutual alienation from which both partners emerge bruised, their morale depleted, their self-esteem low, their ability to function damaged by the varied assaults of the failing marriage" (Weiss, 1975, p. 28).

After the divorce, there is a difficult period of readjustment. The individual must learn to cope with the experience of being on one's own, somehow get back into circulation, and form new attachments. It may take anywhere from one to four years to recover fully from the strain of the breakup (Weiss, 1975). The divorced person may need support from friends and family, from organizations, or from professional counselors.

What about the children of divorce? About 40 to 50 percent of children born in the 1970s will spend some time living in a single-parent family (Hetherington, 1979). By 1990, it is predicted that one out of three 18-year-olds will have experienced the divorce of their parents (Glick, 1979). In a divorce, 9 out of 10 times the mother gets custody of the child so that the father is almost always the absent parent (Lynn, 1974).

Is the two-parent home always the best environment for the growing child? Not necessarily, as one observer notes:

> It is obvious to any clinician that the two-parent system has its own pathology—the two parents may be in serious conflict as to how their parental roles should be performed; one parent may be competent but have his (or her) efforts undermined by the incompetent partner; the children may be caught in a "double bind" or crossfire between the two parents; both parents may be competent but simply unable to work together as an effective team in rearing their children; one parent may be more competent than the other but be inhibited in using this competence by the team pattern inherent in the two-parent system. (LeMasters, 1970, p. 163)

Divorce disrupts everyone's lives. Although many couples stay together because of the children, they unwittingly inflict more harm on the children's psychological health than they would if they had split. In general, the results of studies indicate that damage to a child's personality and social and emotional development is the result of conflict within the home rather than from divorce per se (Raschke & Raschke, 1979). Children from homes full of hostility and conflict, whether intact or not, are usually more unhappy (Bane, 1979).

As two investigators concluded after more than five years of studying families with children that had gone through divorce:

> The conventional wisdom used to be that unhappily married people should remain married "for the good of the children." Today's conventional wisdom holds, with equal vigor, that an unhappy couple might well *divorce* for the good of the children, that an unhappy marriage for the adults is unhappy also for the children; and that divorce that promotes the happiness of the adults will benefit the children as well. . . .

What made the biggest difference for the children was not the divorce itself, but the factors that make for good adjustment and satisfaction in intact families: psychologically healthy parents and children who are involved with one another in appropriate ways. Yet providing these optimal conditions is difficult in the postdivorce family, with its characteristic climate of anger, rejection, and attempts to exclude the absent parent. . . .

Perhaps the most crucial factor influencing a good readjustment was a stable, loving relationship with both parents, between whom friction had largely dissipated, leaving regular, dependable visiting patterns that the parent with custody encouraged. . . .

Except in extreme cases in which a father was clearly abusing children or seriously disturbed, some contact seemed better than none at all. The father's presence kept the child from a worrisome concern with abandonment and total rejection and from the nagging self-doubts that follow such worry. The father's presence, however limited, also diminished the child's vulnerability and aloneness and total dependency on the one parent. . . .

Our other major finding about how important it is for a child to keep a relationship with both original parents points to the need for a concept of greater shared parental responsibility after divorce. In this condition, each parent continues to be responsible for, and genuinely concerned about the well-being of his or her children, and allows the other parent this option as well.[1]

SUMMARY

In this chapter, we looked at marriage and other intimate relationships. More specifically, we examined friendships, marriage and the family, marital conflict, and divorce.

- Well-balanced and healthy personality characteristics appear to be essential for establishing effective interpersonal relationships.

- Personal growth also depends on the quality of the individual's interactions with others.

- Effective interpersonal relationships are characterized by continued growth in honesty, supportiveness, meaningfulness, and selflessness.

- Relationships may fail because of egocentricity, emotional insulation, hostility, and overdependency.

- In spite of the sexual revolution, marriage remains an important goal for most young people. Most expect to get married and have children.

---

[1] Copyright © (Wallerstein, J. S. & Kelley, J. B. "California's Children of Divorce," *Psychology Today*, January 1980, pp. 67–76.

- Marriages tend to take place between individuals who share the same socioeconomic, religious, racial, educational, and ethnic backgrounds. The partners also tend to be the same age, with similar levels of intelligence and physical attractiveness.

- Some of the benefits of marriage include: sharing and clarification of each person's thinking, learning to make complex decisions involving two or more people, learning to allocate each partner's share of the tasks of marriage, honing one's skills as a decision maker, and learning the fine art of compromise.

- The past century has seen many additional strains placed on the marriage contract. These include: the longer life expectancy of each partner, role confusion, and the increased entrance of women into the labor force.

- In view of these changed circumstances, the equal-partner marriage has been advocated. Marital roles are not regarded as fixed and unchangeable at the moment of marriage. They may be renegotiated as circumstances change. Features of equal-partner marriages include: privacy for each individual, frank and honest communication, open companionship, equality, and flexibility of roles.

- Satisfaction from marriage appears to be neither a steady declining or rising curve. Rather, it has many ups and downs.

- Most people report the happiest times of their marriage as coming before the children are born and after the children leave the nest. The most stressful and demanding period appears to come when one or more children are preschoolers.

- Children appear to suffer no personality impairment when both parents work as long, as the substitute care is stable. Working parents may share qualitatively good interactions with their children in spite of limitations in time.

- Being a good parent involves: love and attention, acceptance of the child as an individual, encouraging independence, clear parental expectations, and consistent discipline.

- Effective means of resolving marital conflict include: forgetting about winning, compromise, listening and trying to understand what the other is attempting to communicate, and explicitly saying what you feel.

- About 4 in 10 marriages end up in divorce. The marital breakup is usually initiated by one of the partners—the one least emotionally involved in the marriage.

- Adjustment after divorce is often difficult. The individual must learn to cope with the experience of being on one's own, somehow get back into circulation, and find new attachments.

- Maintaining a hostile and bitter marriage for their sake may inflict more damage on the children than a clean breakup in the relationship.

C H A P T E R 11

HUMAN SEXUALITY

The Language of Sex

Ed and Joan had just finished making love, perhaps for the 800th time since their marriage five years ago.

Ed spoke first. "OK?" he asked.

"OK," she answered.

A deep stillness fell over both of them, disturbed only by the stormy silence of their own private thoughts. "It's not OK," Joan thought. "Not at all. How do I tell him, without shattering his feelings, that I am unsatisfied with his lovemaking? What do I say to him to make him more aware of me, of my needs and my feelings?" She began to weep silently.

"It's not really OK," Ed thought. "It has become almost as routine as taking a glass of water. There's no sense of adventure, no thrill of discovery. The excitement is all gone. How do I tell her without dealing a mortal blow to her ego?"

"I can't go on like this. He takes me to the heights and then drops me like a ton of lead. He's so thoughtful in every other way. Why doesn't he make an effort to understand me when we're making love?"

"I think . . . No, I know we should try something different. But she seems so straight-laced about sex. What do I say to her? How do I communicate my feelings without risk of offending her, of turning her off completely?"

And so the story goes, night after night, week after week, and month after month. Why do Ed and Joan find it almost impossible to talk about sex? Why do *many* people share the same difficulty? It is not a lack of feelings for one another. Ed and Joan are devoted to one another. In many ways, their partnership looks like the ideal marriage, one about which people liked to say, "It was made in heaven." Why had sex become just a little bit like hell?

Although discussion of sexual matters has become much more open in recent years, strong social prohibitions on the subject linger on. Most of our children are taught to conceal their **genitals,** particularly from individuals of the opposite sex. Why is this wrong and shameful? It is easy to conclude that there must be something unsavory about the genitals. Moreover, the genitals are associated with eliminative functions. Therefore, they are dirty. *Even the words used to describe the genitals are, for the most part, considered dirty words.* If not dirty, they are considered crude and even aggressive.

Thus, largely due to cultural inhibitions, we grow up without an adequate vocabulary to describe either sexual organs or sexual acts. The "proper" words are either too clinical or they are not known. To illustrate, years ago, one of the authors was lecturing in class on the mating behavior of rats. A recently

genitals: male and female sexual organs.

295

In a home where parents and children talk to each other about sex, children will develop more positive sexual awareness and not feel that sex is ''dirty'' or something to be ashamed of.

Jim Whitmer/Nawrocki Stock Photo

married student raised his hand and asked, ''What does copulate mean?'' No reply was necessary. The snickering in the class informed him as adequately as a four letter word beginning with the letter ''f.'' How are you to communicate to a loved one your desires, feelings, and attitudes toward sex when most of the words in the vocabulary of sex have distasteful connotations?

Also, many people believe that talk about sex robs it of some of its mystery and all of its spontaneity. These rugged individualists in the sexual frontier assume they know all that is necessary to satisfy a partner or they will learn it in short order. ''You can't learn sex out of a manual,'' they may say. This is certainly true in any general sense. All of us are different in many ways. A "turnon" for one person may be a "turnoff" for another. However, what was left unsaid is that we can learn from a partner. Who knows Joan's sexual needs better than Joan? Who knows better than Ed what turns him on?

There is one further obstacle in the path of candid sexual communication—the risk of self-disclosure. We noted in Chapter 9 that any close or intimate relationship involves a certain degree of self-disclosure. However, revealing your "true self" always involves an element of risk. If the other person does not like what you have revealed about yourself, he or she may ridicule you or even terminate the relationship. Worse yet, if the breakup is hostile and filled with recriminations, the information can conceivably be used against you. So it is with sexual relationships. If Ed tells Joan he would like to vary their sexual intimacy in some specific way, she may be repelled by the idea. "I have been married to you five years and I never dreamed you could be so crude," is one possible outcome of Ed's self-disclosure. On the other hand, couples who genuinely care for and trust each other can enhance their sexual enjoyment by letting each other know what turns them on or off.

One possible start is to seek a vocabulary that is mutually acceptable. Here's how one person handled the challenge:

> Whenever I am with a new person and our relationship has progressed to the point of having sex, I suggest we play a little game where we try to come up with as many different words as we can to name a specific sexual activity or body part. As we play the game, I ask her which words she likes best, often expressing some of my own preferences. Sometimes I discover words I hadn't even heard before. It is a good way to get relaxed and begin talking about sex. Also, it helps in future discussions because we both have a sense of what words to use. (Crooks & Baur, 1980, p. 172)

COMMUNICATING ABOUT SEX

It is one thing to say that we should communicate with our sexual partners about sex; it is another thing to do it. But how do you break the ice? Should you initiate communications in the bedroom or in some neutral zone? On the basis of numerous interviews, one authority suggests that people find it easier to talk about sex "anywhere but bed" (Penney, 1981).

What are some of the techniques to start the ball rolling? Crooks and Baur (1980) suggest the following: Talking about talking; reading and discussing; and using the media as stimulants. Let's take a closer look at each of these suggestions:

1. Talking about Talking. Initially it may be extremely difficult to discuss the specifics of your sexual relationship. Rather, you may find that you are both more comfortable discussing the reasons it is difficult to talk about sexual matters. You may even find it amusing to have a game about the double

Surprisingly, it is easier for most people to discuss their sexual needs and desires in a more impersonal atmosphere.

© Joel Gordon 1980   Peter LeGrand

meanings in the language of sex. See how many different expressions or words you can find that have a sexual connotation in certain situations. Take the word "it" as an example. Delivered with a leer and a suggestive wink of the eye, the sentence "They are doing *it*," leaves little doubt about what they are doing. Similarly, words like dirty, bang, ball, hole, balls, come, make, screw, score, hard, prick, loose, lay, piece, pussy, snatch, and swing may, in certain contexts, take on sexual connotations.

The whole purpose of such discussions is to "come in by the back door," so to speak. The idea is to progress slowly from impersonal and nonthreatening subjects to more intimate feelings and thoughts.

2. Reading and Discussing.   Another way to lead into a discussion of sex that is relatively nonthreatening is to introduce an article or book that is especially interesting or provocative. Many people can openly discuss the intimacies of sexual behavior in the context of what others are doing. Moreover, some of the topics can provide a springboard for introducing personal observations, values, and desires.

3. The Media as Stimulants.   On the recommendation of friends, Joan and Ed went to see the movie *10.* This film depicts the arousal and later disillusionment of a jaded man in midlife crisis by a young bride who scored 11 on a scale of 10. The treatment is both humorous and sexual. Their later discussion of this film set the stage for talking about and later acting out their sexual feelings.

Books, movies, and photographs can often arouse sexual desires and may suggest new techniques that both partners decide to explore. Further, comparing each other's reactions to these materials may provide an impersonal and safe vehicle for communicating the boundaries of acceptable and desired sexual activities.

Now that you have broken the ice, how do you get down to specifics? In other words, how do you go about discovering your partner's needs, desires, likes, and dislikes?

Ask Questions

The most direct way to find out what your partner likes is to ask. But how do you ask? If you phrase your question so that only a yes or no answer is required, that is probably all you will get. For example, when Ed asks Joan, "Did you like the position we used the last time?" she will probably respond with either a yes or a no, leaving little room for further discussion. One of the problems with questions that require only a one-word answer is that they tend to oversimplify an issue that is really more complex. The answers to many sexual questions need to be expanded and qualified. Thus, Joan may have said "Yes" while thinking, "Yes, but I would like to try something new for a change."

The use of open-ended questions is likely to encourage more communication in depth. For example, Ed may have asked, "What are your feelings about different positions?" Joan would now be free to elaborate on her preferences and her feelings. Here are a few open-ended questions suggested by Crooks and Bauer:

1. What things give you the most pleasure when we make love?
2. What aspects of our sexual sharing would you most like to have changed?
3. What parts of your body are most sensitive?
4. What kinds of variations in intercourse positions do you find pleasurable?
5. What is the easiest or most enjoyable way for you to reach orgasm?
6. What are your feelings about oral sex?

(1980), p. 178)

Some people find open-ended questions difficult to answer because they are not sure how to begin their response. This is especially true when they are uncomfortable about discussing either sex in general or specific aspects of sex. For these people, structured questions may be more successful in eliciting the desired information. They may take the form of either-or questions such as, "Do you prefer it when I'm on top or you're on top?" In addition to offering alternatives, the question conveys a sense of concern for the individual's sexual partner. The major drawback to either-or types of questions is that the individual may not like either alternative. If this is the case, it is easy to pose different alternatives.

Self-Disclosure

As we indicated earlier, self-disclosure invites self-disclosure. By disclosing something about your own feelings or attitudes, you also encourage your partner to reply in kind. Moreover, as a result of self-disclosure, you may both find a satisfying form of sexual activity that would not otherwise have been discovered or explored. Such is the case in the following example:

> For the longest time, I was reluctant to bring up the topic of oral sex with my lover. We did about everything else, but this was one area we

avoided both in action and conversation. I personally was both excited and repelled by the prospect of this kind of sex. I didn't have the slightest idea what she felt about it. I was afraid to bring it up for fear she would think I was some kind of pervert. Eventually, I could no longer tolerate not knowing her feeling about what might be incredibly erotic. I brought it up by first talking about my mixed emotions, like feeling that maybe it wasn't natural but at the same time really wanting to try it out. As it turned out she had been having similar feelings but was afraid to bring them up because of how I might react. Afterwards, we laughed about how we had both been afraid to break the ice. Once we could talk freely about our feelings, it was easy to add this form of stimulation to our sex life. (Crooks & Baur, 1980, p. 179)

One of the most difficult things to share with another is your sexual fantasies. Although fantasies are common, most people hesitate to discuss them because they fail to realize that others also have sexual fantasies. Fantasies may be used to stimulate arousal prior to or during sexual activity. Table 11.1 illustrates both the high incidence of and the wide range of sexual fantasies found among a

TABLE 11.1	MARRIED WOMEN'S FANTASIES DURING SEXUAL INTERCOURSE	
		Percentage of Women Reporting Fantasy
	Thoughts of an imaginary romantic lover enter my mind	56
	I relive a previous sexual experience	52
	I enjoy pretending that I am doing something forbidden	50
	I imagine that I am being overpowered or forced to surrender	49
	I am in a different place, like a car, motel, beach, woods	47
	I imagine myself delighting many men	43
	I pretend that I struggle and resist before being aroused to surrender	40
	I imagine that I am observing myself or others having sex	38
	I pretend that I am another irresistibly sexy female	38
	I daydream that I am being made love to by more than one man at a time	36
	My thoughts center about feelings of weakness or helplessness	33
	I see myself as a striptease dancer, harem girl, or other performer	28
	I pretend that I am a whore or a prostitute	25
	I imagine that I am forced to expose my body to a seducer	19
	My fantasies center around urination or defecation	2

Source: E. B. Harlton and J. L. Singer "Women's Fantasies During Sexual Intercourse." Copyright © 1974 by The American Psychological Association. Reprinted by permission of the author.

sample of married women. Sixty-five percent of these women reported having one or more of these fantasies during intercourse with their husbands.

Freedom of Expression

Many couples, like Ed and Joan, want very much to please each other. However, they are suffocated by their own thoughts and are unable to make requests of one another. Often people who have shared an intimate relationship act as if they expect their partner to read their minds. Instead of making explicit their desires, they assume that the other person should know what they are thinking. Frustration, disappointment, and annoyance are often deposited as bitter residues when the other person fails to behave as expected.

If you want something, you must learn to ask for it. You cannot expect the other person to guess what is on your mind. Make your requests as specific as possible since vague requests are confusing and difficult to comply with. Some people find it difficult to openly and unequivocally ask for personal pleasure. But for a sexual relationship to be truly rewarding, both partners must give and receive pleasure. The more guidance you give each other on what makes you feel good, the better the chances for a satisfying and fulfilling experience.

Freedom of expression also includes the right to say no, the right to disclose what you do *not* like, and the right to express criticism. Any criticism should be given for the purpose of improving the quality of the sexual experience and not used as a weapon to hurt, get back at, or otherwise attack your partner. Moreover, nothing is a greater turnoff than critical comparisons, "I liked it better with my first husband."

Criticism is best received when couched in the words of praise. For example, Joan may say to Ed, "I just love the way you massage my body, but could you just use a lighter touch?"

One last word on verbal communication. It is a two-way street. Many people tend not to listen to what others are saying because they are so intent on formulating their own thoughts. Effective communicating requires that each person listen intently to what the other is saying, ask for clarification when necessary, and provide their reactions to what is being said.

Nonverbal Communication

Although there is more sexual freedom today, many people are still inhibited when it comes to talking about sex. They may be more comfortable about communicating their needs, feelings, preferences, and attitudes through the use of gestures, body positioning and movements, and facial expressions. A touch of the hand on your partner's arm can signal your satisfaction and a desire for the stimulation to continue. A gentle push on the hands may suggest that they be moved to a different location. However, such nonverbal modes are not as precise as words and may occasionally be misinterpreted. In the final analysis, there is no adequate substitute for talking.

THE SEXUAL RESPONSE

masturbation: stimulation of one's own genitals to achieve sexual gratification.

clitoris: an extremely sensitive structure of the female external genitals; the principal organ of sexual excitement in the female.

orgasm: the climax of sexual excitement during which sexual tensions are released.

ejaculation: the process whereby semen is suddenly expelled out of the body through the penis during the male's orgasm.

coitus: a technical term for heterosexual intercourse.

Indicate which of the following statements is true or false.

1. **Masturbation** is potentially harmful to the individual.
2. The size of the **clitoris** determines the intensity of the female sexual response.
3. There are two types of **orgasm** in women, vaginal and clitoral.
4. Except for **ejaculation,** the female sexual orgasm appears to be similar to that of the male.
5. The size of the penis is positively related to the ability of the female to achieve orgasm.
6. Sexual intercourse or **coitus** is more taxing for the male than for the female.
7. The only way for both partners to achieve true sexual relief is by simultaneous orgasm.
8. Athletes should not engage in sexual activity before an event since it weakens the individual.
9. Alcohol increases the ability to have satisfactory sexual relationships.
10. Unlike men, discomfort is not experienced by women who are sexually aroused but do not achieve orgasm.

All of these statements are false. Many represent myths that, in prior generations, were held to be true almost without question. Thanks largely to the pioneering efforts of researchers such as Kinsey, Masters and Johnson, and others many of these myths have been dispelled. We now know much about the human sexual response. Much of our knowledge comes from the laboratories of Masters and Johnson (1966). They observed actual sexual behavior and measured the biophysical responses that occur during arousal and orgasm. They noted that sexual responses may be divided into four phases, which they called the "human sexual response cycle." The phases are: *excitement, plateau, orgasm,* and *resolution.* However, physiologically there are no sharp lines of demarcation separating one phase from another. Moreover, there are wide individual differences in terms of the intensity of the responses, the duration of each phase, and the duration of the entire cycle. Although the biological reactions may follow a predictable course, subjective reactions differ considerably from person to person. A description of the biological responses does not do justice to the richness and complexity of the total response. Finally, it should be noted that the response cycle takes place during all forms of sexual activity, whether it be solitary or between two people of the same or different sexes.

Before going further, one word of caution. As a result of learning about the features of the human sexual response, you may be tempted to check them out during your sexual activities. This can turn out to be a wet blanket, as one person reported:

> After learning about the four stages of sexual response in class, I found myself "standing back" and watching my own reactions, wondering if I had passed from excitement into plateau. Also, I began to monitor the responses of my partner, looking for the telltale signs that would tell me

at what point he was. Suddenly I found myself doing clinical observations rather than allowing myself to fully experience the good feelings. It was a real put-off and I had to force myself to stop being the observer and become more of a participant. (Crooks & Baur, 1980, p. 112)

Let's take a closer look at the sexual response of both males and females. (Male and female sexual anatomy are shown in Figure 11.1) There are several features that are essentially the same in both males and females. During the first three phases, both show increases in blood pressure, heart rate, and respiratory rate.

The **excitement phase** can be initiated by a wide variety of stimuli— thoughts, touch, pictures, odors, and so forth. In the male, **erection** is the first observable response. If the stimulus is particularly intense, the penis becomes engorged with blood and rapidly becomes very hard. However, with variations in the stimulation, the penis may alternate between various degrees of erection before a full erection is achieved. There may even be a sex flush—a pink or red rash—that starts under the rib cage and may spread to other parts of the body.

In the female, the nipples become erect and swollen, the clitoris expands, and a fluid is directly secreted from the walls of the vagina (vaginal lubrication). The sex flush is far more common in the female, rapidly spreading to the chest and breasts.

Next is the **plateau phase.** This term is actually rather misleading, since it implies a leveling off. In actuality, there is an enormous surge in sexual energy during this phase. In both male and female, blood pressure and heart rate continue

excitement phase: The first part of the sexual response cycle in which the sexual organs become engorged with blood and there are increases in heart rate, respiration, and muscle tension.

erection: when a sexual organ (penis, clitoris) becomes engorged with blood causing it to become rigid.

plateau phase: the second phase of the sexual response cycle, during which sexual tensions reach a peak.

FIGURE 11.1   FEMALE AND MALE SEXUAL ANATOMY

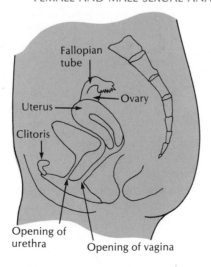
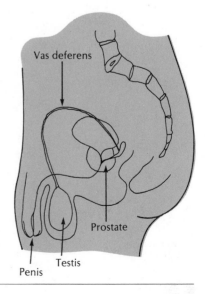

to climb. In the male, the penis and testes enlarge further, and the scrotal sac becomes so congested that the mobility of the testes is sharply reduced. In the female, lubrication is reduced, especially during a prolonged plateau phase, the clitoris shortens in length and retracts from its exposed position, and the breasts become further enlarged as a result of an increased blood supply. The plateau stage is commonly quite brief, lasting from a few seconds up to several minutes. Some individuals report that, by extending the plateau phase, they can enjoy a more intense orgasm. Crooks and Bauer (1980) recommend that couples experiment with each other's plateau phases so as to maximize mutual enjoyment.

orgasm phase: the part of the sexual response cycle during which orgasm occurs.

Orgasm has been described as "the great explosion." This is not surprising when we consider all the events that take place in the body within an extremely short period of time. During the **orgasm phase,** blood pressure, heart rate, and respiratory rate reach their highest levels. In males, orgasm is accompanied by contractions of the penis and ejaculation. Females experience intense contractions in the vaginal area. These contractions (or spasms) gradually taper off. They are similar to the contractions men experience at ejaculation. Other muscles in the body may also tense. In some women, the muscles of the face tense—which explains the contorted appearance of some women's faces at orgasm. However, the subjective feelings are what makes the orgasmic experience so unique. In females, there is a three-stage reaction. During the first, there is a sensation of "suspension" that lasts but a moment. Then there is a feeling of "intense sensual awareness, clitorally oriented, but radiating upward into the pelvis" (Masters & Johnson, 1966, p. 135). Finally, there is pelvic throbbing, centered in the vagina or lower pelvis. Women experience only one type of orgasm, although the primary source of stimulation may be either clitoral or vaginal. Since the outer portion of the vagina is maximally sensitive, the size of the penis is unrelated to female sexual gratification. Indeed, deep penetration can be painful for some women.

In males, orgasm is initiated by a brief period of "inevitability" during which self-control is lost—the individual feels orgasm cannot be prevented. This is followed several seconds later by ejaculation, accompanied by intense pleasure radiating outward from the pelvis to the rest of the body. Typically, the entire process of orgasm takes only a few seconds.

One prominent myth is that both partners should reach orgasm at the same time to maximize the pleasure of both. As a matter of fact, simultaneous orgasms are rare and difficult to achieve. Moreover, by making simultaneous orgasms the focus of a sexual encounter, both partners may be robbed of some of the pleasure and most of the spontaneity of the entire experience.

refractory period: the period of time following orgasm in the male during which sexual arousal is not possible.

It should be noted that orgasm is not always achieved during sexual activities. Some women experience it occasionally and others, never. Both males and females experience discomfort and frustration when they are unable to achieve a climax. On the other hand, approximately 14 to 16 percent of females regularly experience multiple orgasms—two, three, or more orgasms without loss of the excitement of the plateau stage (Kinsey, Pomeroy, Martin, & Gebhard, 1953; Athanasiou, Shaver, & Tavris, 1970). Unlike the female, the male experiences a **refractory period**—a certain period of time must elapse before the male can experience another orgasm.

resolution phase: the final stage of the sexual response cycle during which sexual tensions subside and the body returns to a resting state.

During the **resolution phase,** the various bodily systems involved in the sexual response cycle return to their nonexcited state. Women frequently like to be held, touched, or caressed during this period. The speed with which the male "comes down" depends on the closeness he maintains with his partner. If he withdraws his penis immediately after orgasm, his erection will decrease rapidly. Depending on the individual and the situation, the resolution period may take from minutes up to about two hours.

From the point of view of pleasure and tension relief, the sexual act may be thought of as a means of achieving orgasm. There are many different ways of reaching a sexual climax and many different potential partners. The different methods include vaginal intercourse, anal intercourse **(sodomy),** oral sex, and manual manipulation of the genitalia. Partners may include oneself (masturbation), members of the opposite sex (heterosexual relationship), members of the same sex (homosexual relationship), and animals (bestiality).

sodomy: usually refers to penile-anal intercourse between two males.

ATTITUDES ABOUT SEX

When Kinsey first reported on sexual behavior in the 1940s and 1950s, much of the American public reacted with shocked disbelief. The shock was as much directed at Kinsey's audacity for openly discussing a forbidden topic as it was for the findings he reported. It seems incredible that a book that did not even include a "centerfold" should draw fire from so many different outraged citizens and organizations. Today, hardly an eyebrow is raised when sex surveys are conducted by and reported in popular magazines, and are accompanied by graphic illustrations.

Certainly no one would argue with the observation that times have changed and that there has been a massive upheaval in sexual attitudes and values. What effect have these changes had on what we feel and do about sex? Let's contrast the "traditional" attitudes toward sexual matters with contemporary attitudes.

Traditionally, man was the active partner who initiated the sexual activity; the woman was the passive recipient. The major focus of the sexual relationship was to provide gratification for the male since it was assumed that females didn't derive pleasure from sexual acts. Today, many females have rejected and discarded their roles as docile, unresponsive, and compliant objects of masculine sexuality. Now, both men and women have come to recognize that women have as much capacity to enjoy sex as men. As a result of these changes in attitudes, members of both sexes place a greater emphasis on achieving mutually satisfying sexual experiences. In this respect, it is interesting that the average length of intercourse has increased from less than 2 minutes to about 10 minutes (M. Hunt, 1974). Since a woman generally takes longer than a man to reach a climax, a greater number of females now experience orgasm.

At the time of Kinsey's first publications, the topic of oral-genital sex was mentioned only in hushed whispers behind closed doors. Nevertheless, Kinsey reported that about 60 percent of college educated, 20 percent of high school educated, and 10 percent of grammar school educated couples had experienced oral sex. In a more recent study, the practice was found to be quite widespread

premarital sex: a term commonly used to denote coitus that occurs before marriage.

venereal disease: a condition in which the mode of transmission is almost always through sexual contact.

gonorrhea: a venereal disease in which the mucous membranes become inflamed.

syphilis: a sexually transmitted disease caused by an organism called a spirochete.

sexually transmitted diseases: conditions in which the mode of transmission may be nonsexual as well as sexual.

herpes: blisters on the skin caused by a virus which may be transmitted via sexual contact.

among those surveyed. For example, regardless of educational level, at least 90 percent of married couples under 25 years of age had engaged in oral sex (Hunt, 1974).

Premarital sex also appears to be on the rise. Whereas the traditional view admonished individuals (particularly females) to remain virgins until marriage, peer attitudes today tend to deride celibacy and applaud premarital sexual experimentation. This view is exemplified in the film *Carnal Knowledge.* Arthur Garfunkel complains to Jack Nicholson, "I feel the same way about getting laid as I feel about going to college—I'm being pressured into it."

The change in attitudes about sexual behavior has, for the most part, led to healthier and more enjoyable experiences by diminishing guilt and anxiety. However, the sexual revolution has brought its own share of problems. The increase in sexual activity has driven up the incidence of **venereal disease.** One investigator estimates that approximately 50 percent of young people will contact **gonorrhea** or **syphilis** by the age of 25 (Hyde, 1979).

In addition to conditions that are transmitted exclusively through sexual contact, there are a variety of conditions that may be spread both sexually and nonsexually. These are called by the more general term, **sexually transmitted diseases.** They include conditions such as **herpes,** pubic lice, and genital warts. It is believed that greater public understanding of the prevention and treatment of these diseases will ultimately reduce their prevalence in today's society. There are many health services and clinics that supply free literature, answer questions, and provide names of physicians or clinics that will treat these sexually transmitted conditions at little or no cost. There is even a toll-free help line that can be called 24 hours a day (800/523–1885) called Operation Venus–VD Information. Table 11.2 presents the mode of transmission, symptoms, and treatment of some of the more commonly sexually transmitted diseases.

MASTURBATION

Much of Margo's fantasy life was taken up with thoughts about her relationship with her husband, Harry. They had just celebrated their second year of marriage and she had never experienced a single orgasm during intercourse with Harry. She was sure there was something seriously wrong with her, but she didn't know where to turn for help. Finally, in a fit of desperation, she confided her problem to her best friend, Lisa.

Lisa laughed gently and sympathetically. "Why you poor dear," she said, "Join the club. You're not alone, you know."

"You mean you and Chuck?" she gasped in disbelief.

"Precisely," Lisa answered, "But put that in the past tense."

"Oh, that's great. Then there's hope for me. Could you . . . er . . . tell me what you're doing different?"

"I got in touch with myself and my feelings by masturbating."

Again Margo gasped. She did not know how to react, what to say. She always considered masturbation to be evil, a device of the devil. Yet here was her best friend—married at that—admitting, without hesitation, that she "played with herself." Only the strength of her friendship for Lisa permitted her to continue the conversation.

Lisa was not wrong when she said to Margo, "You're not alone." Approximately 10 percent of sexually active females have never experienced any orgasm, either through self-stimulation or with a sexual partner (Kaplan, 1974; Hite, 1976). One common observation of such women is that many have never engaged in self-stimulation (Kaplan, 1974). Thus, they have deprived themselves of the opportunity to learn about their orgasmic response. This is not the case with males, who are much more likely than females to experiment in early adolescence with self-stimulation techniques. In fact, some individuals, both male and female, continue to masturbate on occasion throughout their lives. To illustrate, in one study it was found that 62 percent of husbands and 68 percent of their wives continued to masturbate after marriage, often as a change of pace (M. Hunt, 1974).

Hunt also accumulated data on the fantasies used by both males and females during masturbation. The results are summarized in Table 11.3.

One final word on masturbation. Even though widely practiced, there is still a widespread belief that it is potentially harmful (Abramson & Mosher, 1975). In reality, there is no basis for the belief that masturbation will produce either physical or psychological damage to the individual. If there is any potential for harm, it arises from the fact that some people think there is something wrong with them because they masturbate and others react with guilt to an act they believe to be sinful.

BIRTH CONTROL

contraceptive methods: techniques used to prevent fertilization and conception.

ovulation: the release of a mature egg from the ovary.

intrauterine devices (IUDs). small plastic coils or loops that are inserted into the uterus for contraception.

It is interesting that the advent of the so-called sexual revolution has been accompanied by many new **contraceptive methods.** To illustrate, prior to the 1960s, the main methods of birth control were total abstinence, partial abstinence based on the woman's **ovulation** cycle, and various mechanical barriers such as the condom and the diaphragm. The wide availability of **intrauterine devices (IUDs)** and the introduction of the pill in the 1960s gave women a greater amount of control over their own sexual lives and reproductive decisions. However, these new methods have been a mixed blessing. Many men have abdicated the responsibility of birth control by simply taking it for granted that the woman is taking care of "that problem." However, a substantial number of women do not practice birth control on a regular basis. Also many couples do not even discuss who is doing what about birth control before jumping into bed. Sharing the responsibility of birth control can promote a better sexual relationship and provide more effective contraceptive results. There are times when it is necessary to use more than one method to ensure contraceptive protection (see Box 11.1).

We shall look at a number of different methods, each with its own advantages and disadvantages in terms of safety, effectiveness, and convenience. Some of the birth-control methods are associated with adverse side effects and increased

TABLE 11.2	COMMON SEXUALLY TRANSMITTED DISEASES (STDs): Mode of transmission, symptoms, and treatment		
STD	*Transmission*	*Symptoms*	*Treatment*
Trichomoniasis	*Trichomonas vaginalis* organism is passed through genital sexual contact; or less frequently by towels, toilet seats, or bathtubs used by an infected person.	White or yellow vaginal discharge that has an unpleasant odor; vulva is sore and irritated.	Metronidazole (Flagyl), a prescription drug.
Moniliasis (yeast infection)	The *Candida ablicans* fungus may accelerate growth when the chemical balance of the vagina is disturbed; it may also be transmitted through sexual interaction.	White, "cheesey" discharge; irritation of vaginal and vulvar tissue.	Vaginal suppositories of Mycostatin or candicidin.
Gonorrhea ("clap")	*Neisseria gonorrhaeae* ("gonococcus") bacteria is spread through genital, oral-genital, or genital-anal contact.	Most common symptoms in men are a cloudy discharge from the penis and burning sensations during urination. If untreated, complications may include inflammation of scrotal skin and swelling at the base of testicle. In women, some green or yellowish discharge is produced. At a later stage, pelvic inflammatory disease may develop.	Penicillin, tetracycline, or erythromycin.
Syphilis	*Treponema pallidum* ("spirochete") is transmitted from open lesions during genital, oral-genital, or genital-anal contact.	*Primary stage:* A painless chancre appears at the site where spirochete entered the body. *Secondary stage:* The chancre disappears and a generalized skin rash develops. *Latent stage:* There may be no observable symptoms. *Tertiary stage:* Heart failure, blindness, mental disturbance, and many other symptoms including death.	Penicillin, tetracycline, or erythromycin.
Nongonococcal urethritis (NGU)	Primary causes are believed to be *chlamydia* and T-strain *mycoplasma* most commonly	Inflammation of the urethral tube. A man has a discharge from the penis and irritation during urination. A woman may have a mild discharge of	Tetracycline or erythromycin.

STD	Transmission	Symptoms	Treatment
	transmitted in coitus. Some NGU may result from allergic reactions or from *Trichomonas* infection.	pus from the vagina, but often shows no symptoms.	
Genital herpes	*Herpes simplex* virus, type 2, appears to be transmitted primarily by vaginal, oral-genital, or anal sexual intercourse.	One or more small, red, painful bumps (papules) appear in genital region, sometimes internally in women or in men experiencing anal intercourse.	Topical treatments may reduce symptoms, but no known cure exists.
Pubic lice ("crabs")	*Phthirus pubis,* or pubic lice, are spread easily through body contact or through shared clothing or bedding.	Persistent itching. Lice are visible and may often be located in pubic hair or other body hair.	Preparations such as A-200 pyrinate or Kwell (gamma benzene).
Genital warts (venereal warts)	Primarily spread through genital, anal, or oral-genital interaction.	Warts are hard and yellow-gray on dry skin areas; soft, pinkish-red, and cauliflower-like on moist areas.	Surface applications of podophyllin; large warts may require surgical removal.

Source: R. Crooks and K. Baur, *Our Sexuality* (Menlo Park, Calif.: Benjamin/Cummings, 1980), p. 341.

TABLE 11.3 MASTURBATION FANTASIES REPORTED IN THE HUNT STUDY

Fantasy	Percentage of Sample Reporting Fantasy	
	Men	Women
Having intercourse with a loved person	75	80
Having intercourse with strangers	47	21
Having sex with more than one person of the opposite sex at the same time	33	18
Doing sexual things you would never do in reality	19	28
Being forced to have sex	10	19
Forcing someone to have sex	13	3
Having sex with someone of the same sex	7	11

Source: M. Hunt, *Sexual Behavior in the 1970s* (Chicago: Playboy Press, 1974), pp. 91–3.

BOX 11.1: USING BACKUP METHODS TO INCREASE CONTRACEPTIVE EFFECTIVENESS

There are a number of circumstances where a couple may need or want to use more than one method to insure effective contraception. Some examples of these circumstances include:

- During the first cycle of birth control.
- For the remainder of the cycle after forgetting to take one or more birth control pills.
- The first month after changing to a new brand of pills.
- During the initial one to three months after IUD insertion.
- When taking antibiotics or aspirin and using an IUD. It is suspected by some sources that aspirin

and antibiotics may lower IUD effectiveness.

- When first learning to use a diaphragm.
- When the couple desires to increase the effectiveness of one method (for instance, using foam and condoms together creates a very effective contraceptive protection).

Abstinence from intercourse and use of condoms, foam, or a diaphragm are possible backup methods which can be combined in many ways with other birth control methods for extra contraceptive protection.

Source: R. Crooks and K. Baur, *Our Sexuality* (Menlo Park, Calif.: Benjamin/Cummings, 1980), p. 489.

---

health risks. However, these dangers should be weighed against the risks of pregnancy and childbirth itself.

Oral Contraceptives

Oral contraceptives, or the pill, as they are commonly called, work by inhibiting ovulation. There are a number of different types of pills that vary in the kind and strength of the hormones they contain. The woman typically begins taking the pill on the fifth day after menstruation begins, continues taking it for 21 days, and then stops for 7 days. Some women prefer to take the kind of oral contraceptives that contains 28 pills—21 hormone pills and 7 inert pills—so that they can stay "in the habit" of taking a pill at the same time every day. When taken as prescribed, the pill is almost 100 percent effective. If a pill is forgotten one day, it should be taken as soon as the omission is realized. If two pills are missed, it is best to use a backup method of contraception.

Because the pill is taken daily apart from the time of sexual activity, none of the spontaneity of sexual activity is sacrificed. Many women consider the pill harmless; however, there are a number of undesirable side effects associated with taking oral contraceptives. For example, the pill has been implicated in the occurrence of blood clots (Seamen & Seamen, 1978). Both surgery and prolonged bed rest involve an increased risk of blood clots. Consequently, the pill should be discontinued whenever possible for at least a month prior to these events. Moreover, there is an increasing danger of circulatory disorders (e.g., high blood pressure and heart attacks) especially for women over 40 years of age who smoke.

Women who have not had children and who have used the pill for seven

There are many variations and types of birth control devices.

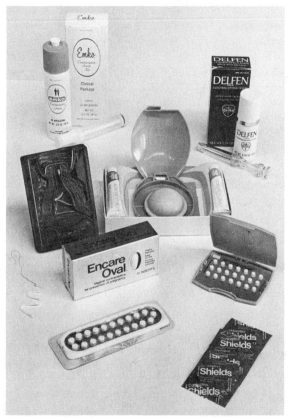

Courtesy Planned Parenthood Association/Chicago Area

years or more sometimes have difficulty conceiving after the pill is discontinued. This condition may be corrected by the use of fertility pills or changes in diet. For example, high-protein diets and various food supplements have been recommended as an initial means of increasing fertility (Seamen & Seamen, 1978). Couples experiencing problems with conception should consult a professional for advice and guidance.

Intrauterine Devices (IUDs)

It is not completely understood how the IUD works. However, it is known that any object placed in the uterus tends to prevent pregnancy. When an IUD is inserted, a thread hangs out of the vagina. This thread assures the woman that the IUD is in place. Although the IUD is more than 95 percent effective, there are some disadvantages. It must be inserted and removed *only* by a professional. Insertion may in itself be uncomfortable with the discomfort lasting for several days. This is especially true for women who have not experienced childbirth. In fact, IUDs are usually not recommended for women who have never been pregnant. Some of the side effects include cramps, pain, backaches, bleeding, and infection. However, the risk of uterine infection can be drastically reduced by using an IUD without a connecting thread (Sparks, Purrier, & Watt, 1981).

Rhythm Method

The rhythm method involves the avoidance of intercourse during the time ovulation is expected to occur. The effectiveness of the method is almost totally dependent on how precisely the time of ovulation can be predicted. One expert recommends the following steps be followed to ensure the most reliable method for determining the "unsafe" period:

1. Keep an accurate record of each menstrual period for at least a year, and at the end of this time determine the shortest and longest cycles.
2. Subtract 18 from the number of days in the shortest cycle, which will give the first unsafe day of the period.
3. Subtract 11 from the number of days in the longest cycle, which will give the day on which the unsafe period ends.

An example will clarify this method. Suppose that over the period of a year the cycles ranged from 26 days to 30 days. Then the unsafe period would be from the 8th day (26 minus 18) to the 19th day (30 minus 11). Wording it another way and again counting the onset of menstruation as day 1, it would be "safe" to have intercourse until day 8 and after day 19. (Pengelley, 1978, pp. 199–200)[1]

There are no associated side effects and the rhythm method is acceptable to those who feel religious constraints. However, the woman must be very committed if this technique is to work, as she must scrupulously keep very accurate records. Stress or illness can upset the cycle and vary the time of ovulation. The rhythm method is only about 80 percent effective and really is only good for the minority of women with very regular menstrual cycles. Finally, strict adherence to this method greatly reduces the amount of time that coitus is safe, which can put inhibiting restraints on the sexual relationship.

Coitus Interruptus (Withdrawal)

This technique, requiring a great deal of control by the male, involves withdrawing the penis from the vagina just before ejaculation. This technique may place a considerable burden on both the male and the female—the male to control

---

[1] Pengelley, E., *Sex and Human Life*, © 1978. Addison-Wesley, Reading, Ma. pp 199–200. Reprinted with permission.

withdrawal, and the female to reach climax before withdrawal. There may be a loss of enjoyment if either or both partners are anxious about withdrawing on time. Withdrawal is commonly used when nothing else is available, even though it is not very effective.

Diaphragm

diaphragm: a birth control device that is inserted into the vagina and used with spermicidal jelly or cream.

A **diaphragm** is a rubber dome with a steel rim that is inserted inside the vagina so that the dome covers the opening into the uterus. Before it is inserted, spermicidal jelly or cream is spread around the rim and over the curved surfaces of the dome. It is inserted up to two hours before intercourse and must stay in place at least 6 additional hours afterward. The diaphragm must be personally fitted by a medical practitioner and refitted if there are any changes in the woman's anatomy, e.g., having a child, an abortion, or a miscarriage. Also a virgin must be refitted after her first coital experience as this may produce some anatomical changes.

This technique was very popular in the 1940s and 1950s, but was largely replaced by the pill. However, adverse publicity concerning possible long-term effects of the pill have brought the diaphragm back into more frequent use. The main disadvantage appears to be the loss of spontaneity since the sexual liaison must be planned in advance.

Foam

Aerosol vaginal contraceptives consist of a white foam that resembles shaving cream. All foams contain a spermicide which kills the sperm, and they should be inserted shortly before intercourse. They are available without a prescription and do not produce any dangerous side effects. However, foams sometimes irritate the genitals and, as with all mechanical devices, spontaneity is sacrificed.

Condoms

condom: a latex or membrane sheath that fits over the penis and is used to prevent conception or infection.

A **condom** is a sheath rolled over the penis which prevents the release of sperm into the vagina. Although some men feel that a condom reduces their sensations, this does not appear likely. There are no side effects, they are easy to use and are generally effective. Moreover, they also serve as an effective protection against venereal disease. But they do require preplanning, thereby robbing the experience of some of its spontaneity. The couple must stop in the midst of sexual excitement so that the condom is in place prior to ejaculation.

Surgical Sterilization

tubal ligation: female sterilization involving cutting the fallopian tubes.

Surgical techniques are available when permanent birth control is desired. In the female a **tubal ligation** is performed involving a small part of each fallopian tube, which is removed and the ends tied, preventing the egg from reaching

vasectomy: surgical sterilization procedure in the male which involves removing a small part of the sperm-carrying tubes and tying the ends.

the uterus or the sperm from reaching the egg. In the male, a **vasectomy** involves removing a small part of the sperm-carrying tubes and tying the ends. This procedure prevents the sperm from reaching the penis and being ejaculated. Surgical techniques are 100 percent effective when properly done.

AGING

Contrary to the traditional view, sexual behavior is not the exclusive province of the young. Sexual urges and the enjoyment of sexual activity do not necessarily cease when people get old (See Box 11.2). The arrival of menopause in women signals the end of reproductive ability, but not sexual desire or capacity. In fact,

---

BOX 11.2: UPSETTING AN OLD TABOO

Her face is lined, her hair white, her hands veined and bony. His features show the years of work, of children brought to adulthood, even of tragedy. Both of them are in their 70s.

But their walk has a snap as they stroll down the street, backs straight. Their eyes sparkle when you talk to them, and they are more ready to smile than to grouse. Almost unconsciously, she grasps his upper arm. And if he thinks nobody is looking, he will let his hand slide slowly down her back.

Shocking? Only to those people who think that sexual activity among the elderly is ridiculous. Yet science is finding that as people get older, the majority seek and need sex as much as, and sometimes more than, young people. In fact, if older people stop having sex, it is mostly because they are physically sick or they have nobody willing to share intimacy with them.

Society at large shames many oldsters for their sexual longings. Dr. Eric Pfeiffer—professor of psychiatry and director of the Sun Coast Gerontology Center, University of South Florida—says that society places "a continuing taboo regarding sexual expression in old age." And this is happening in an era that is open to sex activity at all other ages.

Every survey shows that the vast majority like sex, want to have it, and are sexually active. A 1980 study of 800 men and women over 60—by Drs. Bernard D. Starr and Marcella Bakur Weiner, psychologists at Brooklyn College in New York—revealed that 96 percent like sex and 80 percent still have sexual relations. Of those in their 80s, two out of five still have sex.

Nevertheless, despite the evidence for continuing interest, more and more people abstain from sex in each decade of life. For men, impotence plays a big role—they simply can no longer become aroused. For women, opportunities disappear. Because women live eight years longer than men on the average, they soon outnumber men, which compounds their difficulties. Of every 10 older women, studies show, 6 have no mates; out of every 10 older men, only 2 are unmarried. Men, therefore, have the chance to be much more active sexually than women.

Most experts believe that if there were equal numbers of men and women, women would be the more active sex. "Women's sex drive continues to grow until they reach their 30s and remains the same throughout their lives," says Dr. Carol C. Flax, a New York City sex therapist. "For men, the drive reaches a peak at 19 and then goes down, eventually disappearing for many."

Experts argue over whether to blame the decline in men on social or physical causes. Most agree that many older men who no longer seek sexual activity are in fact sexually potent and have just given up because they cannot perform as they did in their youth. Young men are quickly aroused, remain aroused, and are aroused again quickly. As they grow older, many men believe they have lost potency because events go more slowly. They refuse to adapt.

In general, what you did sexually at 30 governs what you will do at 70. Dr. Mary Calderone—President of the Sex Information and Education Council of the U.S. (SIECUS) and one of the world's leading

BOX 11.2 (concluded)

sexologists—says it is not true that you are born with a certain amount of sex capacity, which you can use up if you are too active in youth. "The more you use it," Calderone says, "the less you lose it—and that's not true of any bank account I've ever heard of." In other words, you can't save it for your old age. Men and women who start sex early and perform frequently do so into their later years.

If a man has an erection in the morning or during sleep, then no matter what his age, he is capable of sexual relations. In many medical centers, sleep laboratories measure sex-organ response during sleep. In the sex act, however, an older man may require more and longer physical stimulation. And it may take longer to achieve climax, a fact often appreciated by his partner.

As with women, older men stop having sex if they lack an interested partner. Both need someone to touch and to love. More than young people, they respond to cuddling, touching, perfumes and words of endearment. If there is someone around who is caring, the physical act follows. Older people are,

in a way, more romantic than younger ones. The elderly seek and value intimacy more.

Many married couples get bored with each other not only sexually but intellectually and emotionally. To keep sex alive, experts say, it is important to find not only new things to do in bed, but new things to think about and to be concerned with.

Society has placed a heavy burden on older people. Sex for them, we say, is unseemly. We have equated sexiness with youth—the body smooth, rounded, and unlined in women; tight, rippling muscles in men. Vigor equals virility. Old women are regarded as intrinsically ugly and unsexy, and old men are seen as repulsive. These attitudes make it all the more difficult for an older person to keep an interest in sex.

Sex for those getting older, the experts declare, is not only right and proper. It may be critical for their mental health. It should not be denied them.

Source: Earl Ubell, "Upsetting an Old Taboo." *Parade,* Nov, 1981. Copyright © 1982 Parade Publications, Inc.

---

the woman's interest in sex may increase because she is no longer concerned about becoming pregnant. Since birth control is no longer an issue, greater spontaneity may be gained. As we have seen, some contraceptive devices require preplanning—a turnoff for some individuals.

With increasing age, vaginal lubrication requires more time before it occurs and men take longer to achieve an erection (Crooks & Baur, 1980). Unless both partners are aware of these normal and natural occurrences, problems may result. The man may fear that he is losing his sexual capability. This fear may trigger such anxiety that the fear ultimately becomes reality. Unaware of the normal process of aging, a woman may interpret the slow rate of response as a sign of waning interest and desire. If properly understood, these changes can have little or no effect on the enjoyment of the sexual experience. There is one further change that may be interpreted as favorable both by the male and his sexual partner. Since an older man can maintain an erection for longer periods of time before orgasm, he has the "prolonged opportunity to enjoy other sensations of sexual response besides ejaculation" (Crooks & Baur, 1980, p. 442).

With aging, there may be losses either in capacity or desire to engage in sexual relations. However, desire is more likely than capacity to fall victim of aging. For those who maintain the desire, Crooks and Baur (1980) recommend the following:

Although there are certain changes in sexual response patterns, there is no real upper-age limit on sexual functioning and enjoyment. A sexless old age is a myth that stems more from psychological and cultural constraints than from physical limitations.

Brent Jones

1. Like all physical expressions, sexual activity may become increasingly fatiguing to the individual who allows his or her physical condition to markedly deteriorate through lack of exercise. Consequently, maintaining a regular program of physical activity (walking, jogging, swimming, and so forth) may enhance erotic abilities in addition to contributing to one's general health.

2. Related to the value of maintaining physical exercise are the known benefits of sexual regularity. Masters and Johnson (1966) maintain that regularity of sexual expression throughout the adult years (whether by masturbation or activity with a partner) is a crucial factor in maintaining satisfactory sexual functioning beyond one's youth and middle age.

3. Overindulgence in food or drink has been frequently linked with declining sexuality. Excessive food intake may become a major problem in older individuals who often slip into a sedentary lifestyle. . . . Moderation in both eating and drinking can indirectly contribute to healthier sexual functioning.

4. The monotony of a repetitious sexual relationship, often exaggerated

after long years of relating to the same individual, may also significantly reduce an older couple's sexual ardor. Perhaps the need for experimentation and variety may become particularly acute at this time. . . . Certainly, not all long-term couples report problems with boredom. For some, who may have grown to understand and adjust to each other's needs over the years, familiarity may breed contentment. (pp. 443–4)

SEXUAL DIFFICULTIES

Over the years of our marriage my sexual desire for my wife has diminished gradually to the point that it is presently almost nonexistent. There have been too many disputes over how we raise the children, too many insensitive comments, too many demands, not enough freedom to be my own person. When I look at her I have to acknowledge that she is a remarkably beautiful woman, just as lovely as the day I was first attracted to her. I certainly feel no physical repulsion to her body. I guess it would be more accurate to say that I simply no longer have sexual feelings for her. One feeling I do have plenty of is hostility. I suspect it is this largely suppressed anger that has been the killer of my sexual interest. I wonder what it would be like if we could go back to the early years of our marriage when there were no children and the conflicts were few and the loving was good. (Crooks & Baur, 1980, p. 280)

In this case example, we are reminded that sexual attraction and excitement may not survive the ups and downs of the marital roller coaster. In an atmosphere charged with hostility and recriminations, this individual has lost all sexual feelings for his wife. Like oil and water, hostility and tender feelings do not mix well. In a marriage devoid of tender feelings, sexual relations can become a burdensome duty rather than an exciting adventure. Hostility and sex make poor bedfellows.

Since the sexual reponse is a complex interaction of biological, cultural, personal, and social factors, it should not surprise us that there are occasional difficulties. Sex is vulnerable to disturbances in any of these areas. To illustrate, if the cultural values you have assimilated hold that oral sex is bad and dirty, it is difficult to clear your mind of such negative thoughts during a sexual encounter. These thoughts may, in turn, interfere with your ability to enjoy the sexual experience. A male may have difficulty achieving and maintaining an erection; a female may be unable to reach a climax. Personal factors may include hostility, boredom, anxiety, or guilt. Indeed, even such common complaints as fatigue and financial worries can wreak havoc with the sexual response.

Only a small proportion of sexual problems involve physical illness, e.g., diabetes, high blood pressure, and the aftereffects of surgery on the prostate glands. Alcohol and other drugs (especially "downers") act on the nervous system as depressants. For example, taken in moderation, alcohol may increase arousal by reducing inhibitions due to fear and guilt. However, excess or chronic alcohol consumption can lead to widespread sexual difficulties in both males and females. To illustrate, women may experience difficulties in arousal and orgasm; men may be unable to obtain an erection. Moreover, heavy drinking leads to general physical deterioration, which affects all aspects of the individual's functioning, including sexual.

Let's take a look at some of the specific sexual difficulties encountered by both men and women.

Male Sexual Difficulties

Most men will experience an occasional failure to get and maintain an erection in spite of his or his partner's efforts. These sporadic disappointments should not be a cause for alarm since, as we have seen, many temporary factors may put a damper on either the individual's ardor or concentration. However, when the individual has usually had satisfying sexual encounters and then experiences a period of chronic **erectile inhibition,** it is time to initiate a thoughtful study of the circumstances under which it occurs. The individual should raise such questions as, "What am I doing that's different?" "Are *we* doing anything different?" "Is something interfering with my ability to concentrate?" At this point, it would be fruitful to initiate discussions with his sexual partner. This is desirable for numerous reasons. Sexual failure of the man may be perceived as humiliating by both partners. The man may feel incompetent and the woman rejected. Moreover, open discussion may not only identify the problem, but may help to alleviate it. One thing is certain. After several consecutive failures, the difficulty may become serious unless it is nipped in the bud. Worry itself can exacerbate the problem. As one observer has noted:

erectile inhibition: a sexual difficulty in which the male is unable to achieve an erection in response to sexual stimulation; sometimes called impotence.

> Regardless of the nature of any particular sexual inadequacy, fears of performance are almost bound to affect both partners adversely. For example, if the male tends to be impotent, he will approach any opportunity for sexual intercourse with the fear that he will fail to obtain an erection, or that if he does he will be unable to retain it long enough to achieve coitus. This fear can be so intense that as such a man approaches a sexual situation, he loses all sense of the pleasure associated with this naturally occurring event, and may even break out in a cold sweat. Thus the fear itself destroys the nature of the sexual situation, and an erection becomes virtually impossible. On the other hand, the female partner of such a man is constantly worried not only on his behalf, but also that she will do something or behave in such a way as to embarrass him or aggravate his problem. Thus the sexual partners turn what should be a pleasurable and natural part of their relationship into a fear-ridden emotional nightmare. (Pengelley, 1978, pp. 104–5)[2]

What should a young man do when he experiences erectile inhibition in all of his initial sexual encounters? With no successful past experiences to fall back upon, he may exaggerate the seriousness of the problem and conclude that he is a sexual dud. Instead of dealing with the reality of his failures, he may avoid

---

[2] Pengelley, E., *Sex and Human Life,* © 1978. Addison-Wesley, Reading, Ma. pp. 104–105. Reprinted wih permission.

any further sexual explorations. He would be well advised at this point to seek professional counseling.

Erectile inhibition is a difficulty in the excitement phase of the sexual response cycle. Problems are also commonly encountered during the orgasm phase. One of the most common is **premature ejaculation.** Premature or rapid ejaculation occurs when a man reaches a climax faster than he or his partner desires. But how fast is too fast? In coitus, if a man ejaculates prior to penetration, we may safely say he has experienced premature ejaculation. But after penetration, it is more difficult to judge. Crooks and Baur (1980) suggest that premature ejaculation is "consistently reaching orgasm so quickly as to either significantly lower subjective enjoyment of the experience and/or to impair one's partner's gratification" (p. 297).

The case example of Mr. and Ms. A illustrates the pervasive effect this problem can have on a couple's total relationship. They have been married 15 years and are experiencing a crisis over their sexual problems.

> Mr. A, a successful restauranteur, is 38. Ms. A, who since marriage has devoted herself to child rearing and managing the home, is 35. She reports that throughout their entire marriage she has been extremely frustrated because sex has "always been hopeless for us." She is now seriously considering leaving her husband.
>
> The difficulty is the husband's rapid ejaculation. Whenever any lovemaking is attempted, Mr. A becomes anxious, moves quickly toward intercourse, and reaches orgasm either immediately upon entering his wife's vagina or within one or two strokes. He then feels humiliated, recognizes his wife's dissatisfaction, and they both lapse into silent suffering. He has severe feelings of inadequacy and guilt, and she experiences a mixture of frustration and resentment toward his "ineptness and lack of concern." Recently they have developed a pattern of avoiding sex, which leaves them both frustrated, but which keeps overt hostility to a minimum.
>
> Mr. A has always been a perfectionist, priding himself on his ability to succeed at anything he sets his mind to. As a child he had always been a "good boy" in a vain effort to please his demanding father. His inability to control his ejaculation is a source of intense shame, and he finds himself unable to talk with his wife about his sexual "failures." Ms. A is highly sexual, easily aroused by foreplay, but has always felt that intercourse is the only "acceptable" way to reach orgasm. Since intercourse with her husband has always been brief, she holds him completely responsible for her sexual frustration. Since she cannot discuss the subject without feeling rage, she usually avoids talking about it. As a result, they have not developed other techniques for pleasing each other, and sex has always been a disaster.
>
> In other areas of their marriage, including rearing of their two children, managing the family restaurant, and socializing with friends, these two are highly compatible. Despite these strong points, however, they are near separation because of the tension produced by their mutual sexual disappointment. (Spitzer, Skodol, Gibbon, & Williams, 1981, p. 108)

Masters and Johnson (1970) devised a method, called the *squeeze technique,* to help men who experience premature ejaculation. With patience and persistence,

premature ejaculation: a sexual difficulty of the male who ejaculates before he or his partner desires.

this method can be mastered by most couples. The couple should position themselves in such a way that the female has easy access to the male's genitals. She should then stimulate the penis to the point of impending orgasm. At that point, she places her thumb on the underside of the erect penis (where the glans penis joins the shaft) and two fingers on the upper side opposite the thumb. She then applies strong pressure for a few seconds until the man loses the desire to ejaculate. The male should guide his partner so that she knows how hard she can squeeze without causing discomfort. This process should be repeated over a period of time (days or even weeks, if necessary). As the man gradually gains control, he will also gain confidence in his ability to change his pattern of premature ejaculation.

Female Sexual Difficulties

We noted earlier that during the excitement phase, vaginal lubrication typically occurs. Failure to lubricate occurs when the female is insufficiently aroused. This difficulty may be due to a variety of different reasons—biological factors, inadequate sexual partner, anger and hostility, or feelings of anxiety and guilt about sex in general or the experience in particular. This lack of lubrication can be a problem during coitus because it irritates both the penis and the vaginal tissues, making the experience unpleasant and painful for both parties. Sometimes this problem can be resolved by taking more time for sexual arousal. Also, the postmenstrual woman who may have a lack of vaginal lubrication may need an artificial lubricant.

A more common sexual difficulty is the inability to achieve orgasm. In some cases, the woman never achieves orgasm regardless of the method of stimulation. In others, she may experience a sexual climax only through self-stimulation. In yet other cases, she may previously have reached orgasm but is now unable to do so. Typically the woman is sexually aroused, lubricates adequately, and finds the experience enjoyable up to the point where orgasm would normally occur. Even when she has an adequate partner, she may still be unable to achieve a climax, as the following case example shows:

> The patient, a 25-year-old female laboratory technician, has been married to a 32-year-old cab driver for five years. The couple has a two-year-old son, and the marriage appears harmonious.
>
> The presenting complaint is the wife's lifelong inability to experience orgasm. She has never achieved orgasm, although during sexual activity she has received what should have been sufficient stimulation. She has tried to masturbate, and on many occasions her husband has manually stimulated her patiently for lengthy periods of time. Although she does not reach climax, she is strongly attracted to her husband, feels erotic pleasure during lovemaking, and lubricates copiously. According to both of them, the husband has no sexual difficulty.
>
> Exploration of her thoughts as she nears orgasm reveals a vague sense of dread of some undefined disaster. More generally, she is anxious about losing control over her emotions, which she normally keeps closely in check.

She is particularly uncomfortable about expressing any anger or hostility. Physical examination reveals no abnormality.[3]

INCREASING SEXUAL SATISFACTION

In the following excerpt from a case example, the woman has been married for four-and-one-half years without ever consummating her marriage:

> She was taught that almost any form of physical expression might be suspect of objectionable sexual connotation. For example, she was prohibited when bathing from looking at her own breasts either directly or from reflection in the mirror for fear that unhealthy sexual thoughts might be stimulated by visual examination of her own body. Discussion with a sibling of such subjects as menstruation, conception, or sexual functioning were taboo. Pronouncements on the subject were made by the father with the mother's full agreement. Her engagement period was restricted to a few chaste, well-chaperoned kisses, for at any sign of sexual interest from her finance, the girl withdrew in confusion.
>
> [She] entered marriage without a single word of advice, warning, or even good cheer from her family relative to marital sexual expression. The only direction offered by her religious adviser relative to sexual behavior was that coital connection was only to be endured if conception was desired. (Masters & Johnson, 1970, p. 254)[4]

In this case example, we see that ignorance is not necessarily bliss and what you don't know can sometimes hurt you. Perhaps the most important principle for improving the quality of sexual intimacy is "know yourself." You and you alone are directly capable of knowing your own values, what pleases you, and what turns you off. In this respect, Crooks and Baur (1980) recommend exploring your own body, exploring your own genitals, and engaging in self-stimulation. Through such explorations, you can experiment with procedures that provide maximum enjoyment. This self-knowledge can then be shared with a partner who, it is to be hoped, has engaged in similar activities of self-discovery.

Once you and your partner have communicated your needs and feelings to one another, you may then engage in activities designed to maximize your shared pleasures. One set of procedures advocated by Masters and Johnson is called **sensate focus.** Although used as a therapy technique with couples who are having sexual difficulties (see Box 11.3), it may also be practiced by any couple wishing to increase sexual sharing and heighten erotic experiences. The couple first finds a quiet place, free of the distractions of daily life, and prepares a setting that suits their shared lifestyles—candlelight for some, music for others. The important point is that both individuals should feel comfortable and at ease within the setting. During a given session, one person takes the role of "giver" and

sensate focus: a technique used to decrease sexual performance fears and to increase sexual pleasure through touching and communicating.

---

[3] R. L. Spitzer, A. E. Skodol, M. Gibbon, and J. B. W. Williams, DSM-III Case Book, Washington, D.C. American Psychiatric Association, 1981, p. 88.

[4] Masters and Johnson, *Human Sexual Inadequacy*. Boston: Little, Brown and Company © 1970, p. 254.

BOX 11.3: SEXUAL THERAPY

For a variety of reasons, some individuals of both sexes are unable to perform one or more of the behaviors required to achieve orgasm. It is illustrative to briefly examine the applications of learning techniques employed by Masters and Johnson to alleviate such sexual dysfunctions as impotence, premature ejaculation, retarded ejaculation, and inorgasmic potential in women (1970; 1974).

To begin with, a husband and wife are treated together. The reason is quite straightforward: sexual intercourse is an intense and intimate personal-social relationship in which the satisfaction of both partners is dependent upon their ability to work together as a team so as to achieve mutual sexual arousal and satisfaction. Indeed, mutual satisfaction is the foundation of the pleasure bond.

During the first few days of the two-week course, the partners are encouraged to spend periods of time in their room, unclothed. They are instructed to touch, fondle, and massage each other. The purpose is to allow each partner to discover the specific body areas which provide maximum sensual pleasure. However, touching the genital regions and the wife's breasts is specifically forbidden during this stage of therapy. The emphasis is completely upon exploration in giving pleasure without the imposition of overt sexual performance pressures that may be anxiety producing to one or both of the partners. In many ways, the procedures are reminiscent of shaping: "Instead of being suggested . . . to go all the way from A to Z sexually on any specific occasion, it is suggested that marital units go from A to B one day, possibly from A to C or D the next . . . ." (1970, p. 205)

The withholding of genital contact during the first few days of therapy serves an additional purpose—by increasing the deprivation level, the incentive value of the reinforcement increases.

In the Masters and Johnson sexual therapy, the period of nongenital contact also serves as encouragement for the dysfunctioning male and his marital partner. In the absence of performance expectations, penile erections occur quite spontaneously during the sensate focus phase of treatment. These spontaneous erections set the stage for manipulative play (teasing technique) with the erective reaction. In sessions lasting up to a half hour, the marital couple engages in slow, nondemanding sexual play during which the male may undergo several erections and losses of erections. Thus, the male gains some measure of control over his erective capacity and the female is sexually stimulated by the opportunity to produce an erection in her partner.

By the time the marital couple is ready for coital experience, they have become quite adept at communicating, often in a nonverbal fashion, their likes and dislikes, pleasures and aversions. They have, in effect, developed a feedback system which selectively rewards and encourages behavior that enhances each other's sexual pleasures. The female, for example, is encouraged to guide the hand of the male to the vaginal area that she wishes to have stimulated, thus obviating clumsy and sometimes painful manipulation.

Throughout all of the therapy period, one theme predominates: the individual should value sexual experiences. Unless each partner is able to internalize a value system that regards sex as pleasurable and desirable, the ability to perform the skills necessary for satisfactory sexual relations will be impaired. In short, the pleasure arising out of the activity is sufficient justification for the activity.

Source: Reprinted with permission from J. S. Wiggins, K. E. Renner, G. L. Clore, R. J. Rose, *Principles of Personality* (Reading, Mass.: Addison-Wesley, 1976), pp. 282–3.

the other is the "receiver." The giver explores and touches different parts of the body of the receiver, initially avoiding the genitalia. The aim is to locate sensual areas of the body and to provide pleasurable stimulation for the partner. Sensate focus does not have as its goal the achievement of orgasm. The goal is for each sexual partner to learn how to please the other and to incorporate this learning into lovemaking activities.

SUMMARY

In this chapter, we took a look at human sexuality, focusing on its role in human adjustment. More specifically, we examined the language of sex, communicating about sex, the sexual response, attitudes about sex, masturbation, birth control, aging, sexual difficulties, and increasing sexual satisfactions.

- Talking about sex does not come easily to most people raised in our culture. Many of the words describing sexual anatomy and activities are either too cold and clinical or they are considered dirty. Moreover, many people believe that to talk about sex is to rob it of its spontaneity. Finally, communicating with others about aspects of your sexuality exposes you to the risk of self-disclosure—your partner may be turned off by what you reveal or may hold it against you.

- In starting discussions of sex, the following suggestions were made: talk about talking, read and discuss, and use the media as stimulants.

- After breaking the ice, you should ask your partner what he or she likes. The use of open-ended rather than direct questions is likely to elicit more information. For those uncomfortable with open-ended questions, structured questions may be more successful, e.g., Do you prefer this position or that? Since self-disclosure invites self-disclosure, its associated risks may be minimized while increasing the probability of learning things that will increase the pleasure and satisfaction of both partners. Freedom of expression is an essential condition that must be satisfied if communicating about one's sexuality is to achieve its purposes.

- The four phases of the sexual response cycle consist of: excitement, plateau, orgasm, and resolution. A number of myths relating to the cycle were discussed in the text.

- Large changes in sexual attitudes and practices have occurred over the past few decades. The traditional attitude about sex placed the male at the center of the stage. He was expected to initiate sexual encounters and satisfying him was the primary goal of sexual relations. Now much greater emphasis is placed on achieving mutually satisfying sexual relationships.

- With the rise in premarital sex has come a sharp increase in the incidence of veneral and sexually transmitted diseases. Toll-free help telephone lines are available on a 24-hour-a-day basis for those needing assistance.

- Masturbation is often depicted as a potentially harmful and depraved practice. Contemporary sexologists, however, consider it a normal activity that can have healthy implications for the individual. It can be a change of pace for married individuals and a means of getting in touch with one's sexuality for those who have had difficulty achieving orgasm.

- Many birth control methods are now available including partial abstinence based on the ovarian cycle, intrauterine devices, oral contraceptives, and spermaticides. Each presents different associated advantages and disadvantages, risks, and religious constraints.

- Contrary to the popular view, sexual urges and the enjoyment of sexual behavior do not necessarily cease when people become old. In many instances, interest in sex will increase after a woman goes through menopause since the risk of pregnancy is eliminated. If individuals are acquainted with the biological changes that typically take place with aging, they are less likely to react with alarm to normal developments in the aging process. There is no physical reason that most people cannot maintain an active sexual life throughout their later years.

- Only a small proportion of sexual difficulties involve physical disorders. Most reflect psychological and cultural factors, such as emotional stress, boredom, and conflicting values. Sexual problems may range from an occasional "failure," which is quite normal, to long periods of sexual inadequacy. Treatment clinics are widely available for couples experiencing sexual difficulties.

- There are means of increasing the pleasures derived from sexual activities. These include: know yourself, communicate this knowledge to your partner, and engage in activities designed to increase the satisfaction of *both* partners. Many individuals can probably benefit from the application of procedures known as sensate focus.

TERMS TO REMEMBER

Genitals	Gonorrhea
Masturbation	Syphilis
Clitoris	Sexually transmitted diseases
Orgasm	Herpes
Ejaculation	Contraceptive methods
Coitus	Ovulation
Excitement phase	Intrauterine devices (IUDs)
Erection	Diaphragm
Plateau phase	Condom
Orgasm phase	Tubal ligation
Refractory period	Vasectomy
Resolution phase	Erectile inhibition
Sodomy	Premature ejaculation
Premarital sex	Sensate focus
Veneral disease	

ABNORMAL BEHAVIOR

Mr. Leonard K, age 55, was referred to the hospital by his family after an episode of reckless promises, extravagant claims, and grandiose commitments. He had usually been a calm and reserved person, but gradually began to show a change in personality. Once a fastidious dresser, he had suddenly surprised his wife by neglecting to shave, wearing suits that had been wrinkled because he slept in them, and refusing to wash. He became more and more expansive, talkative, and occasionally violent. By the time he was committed for treatment, he believed himself to be the state senator, and spoke of his planned travels to "executive emperor" (words he had difficulty in communicating). He was known to stand wherever a crowd was willing to listen and loudly pronounce his views on war, religion, birth control, and nearly any topic that was suggested. (Suinn, 1970, p. 332)

There is little doubt that something is seriously wrong with Leonard. His behavior is abnormal. In this case, it is relatively easy to discern abnormality. However, this is the exception rather than the rule. The reason is that abnormal may be defined in many different ways. The dictionary defines abnormal as "deviating from the normal." This implies that there are standards by which to define normal. If so, what is normal? Each area of human activity has its own set of criteria for arriving at a satisfactory definition. In some fields, these standards are fairly straightforward. To illustrate, years of research in the field of biology have revealed much about the functions of various parts of the body. The distinction between what is normal and what is not is usually quite clear. Unfortunately, this is not the case with psychological functioning. What model of normality should we use against which to judge abnormality? In Chapter 1 we looked at some of the qualities of effective adjustment. Box 12.1 presents some of the characteristics of the "normal" individual.

Note that the normal individual is not always successful, happy, content, kind, considerate, and well loved. In fact, most people have conflicts which they have not resolved; parts of their inner lives they are ashamed to reveal to others. Moreover, how many of us always live up to our own ideals? Even the best among us sometimes procrastinate; we occasionally do things to satisfy ourselves even though we know our actions will hurt or disappoint others. Who among us is entirely free of care and worry?

As we indicated before, there are a variety of ways to define abnormal—legal, adjustment, cultural, or in terms of outstanding symptoms. These definitions frequently conflict with one another. For example, psychological and psychiatric definitions of abnormality often disagree with legal definitions. Indeed, the battle lines in many courtrooms have been drawn in terms of these differences. Recently, many members of Congress called for new standards for judging criminal defen-

---

BOX 12.1: CHARACTERISTICS OF THE "NORMAL" INDIVIDUAL

Attitudes toward self. Emphasizing self-acceptance, adequate self-identity, realistic appraisal of one's assets and liabilities.

Perception of reality. A realistic view of oneself and the surrounding world of people and things.

Integration. Unity of personality, freedom from disabling inner conflicts, good stress tolerance.

Competencies. Development of essential physical, intellectual, emotional, and social skills for coping with life's problems.

Autonomy. Adequate self-reliance, responsibility, and self-direction—together with suffi-

cient independence of social influences.

Growth, self-actualization. Emphasizing trends toward increasing maturity, development of potentialities, and self-fulfillment as a person.

Interpersonal relations. Capacity for forming and maintaining intimate interpersonal relations.

Goal attainment. Does not strive to achieve perfection but sets goals which are realistic and within the individual's capabilities.

Source: *Abnormal Psychology and Modern Life,* 5th Edition by James C. Coleman. Copyright © 1976, 1972, 1964 by Scott, Foresman and Company. Reprinted by permission of the publisher.

---

dants who plead insanity as a defense. The verdict in the trial of John W. Hinckley, Jr. in June of 1982 evoked congressional calls for broad changes in the criminal law under which the assailant of President Reagan was found innocent by reason of insanity.

In some states, defendants are judged legally "insane" only if they are unaware of the consequences of their actions. A mass murderer proclaims, "I shot them because the planets are lining up in the sky. By killing them I saved them from eternal damnation." Since he knew the consequences of his actions (shooting kills), he might be judged legally sane. Mental-health professionals would probably note his chaotic thought processes and argue that he is suffering from a mental disorder.

Members of the mental-health field are in general agreement that you must look at behavior to define abnormal. Various types of behavior are classified as abnormal—the disordered thought processes revealed by the mass murderer's verbalizations, the lack of contact with reality displayed by Leonard's flights of fantasy, or the complete lack of emotionality observed in some patients in a mental-health-care facility. Individuals showing one or more of these signs may be considered abnormal. In addition, individuals who are distressed or extremely uncomfortable with their behavior or feelings may be classified as "abnormal." A case in point is homosexuality. As we shall see later in this chapter (Psychosexual disorders), homosexuality itself is not considered a mental disorder. Only those individuals who are distressed about their homosexuality are considered to be abnormal.

The most comprehensive and widely used system for classifying mental disorders is *The Diagnostic and Statistical Manual of Mental Disorders.* The third edition appeared in 1980 and is usually abbreviated DSM-III. We use the terminology of DSM-III in this book. A major feature of DSM-III is that it avoids labeling *people* as abnormal. Rather it labels *behavior* as abnormal. In the words of the manual:

> A common misconception is that a classification of mental disorders classifies individuals, when actually what are being classified are disorders that individuals have. For this reason, the text of DSM-III avoids the use of such phrases as "a schizophrenic" or "an alcoholic," and instead uses the more accurate, but admittedly more wordy "an individual with Schizophrenia" or "an individual with Alcohol Dependence." (*Diagnostic and Statistical Manual*, 1980, p. 6)

What causes abnormal behavior? For the most part, the answer to this question is, "We still don't know." However, there are a few disorders for which the causes are known. DSM-III refers to them as the "Organic Mental Disorders." These include problems caused by known and verifiable brain disease, such as by drug damage or withdrawal, aging, illness, injuries, and so on. Leonard K was afflicted with one of these disorders. He was diagnosed as suffering from general paresis, a disease of the brain associated with the last stages of syphilis.

Except for the organic disorders, DSM-III is careful to avoid theorizing about the causes of mental problems. The emphasis in the manual is on providing clear descriptive labels for behavioral or psychological patterns that are associated with either a painful symptom or impairment in some areas of everyday behavior. Thus, no matter what the theoretical backgrounds of those using the manual, most will be able to agree on the labels it applies to behavior.

In the new revisions, some terms that have become household words have been removed and others inserted in their place. Among the most important changes is the elimination of the term **neurosis.** Rather than speak of "phobic neuroses" and "anxiety neuroses," we now refer to "phobic disorders" and "anxiety states." This procedure discourages the tendency to refer to people as "neurotics."

neurosis: a term formerly used for emotional disturbances in which maladaptive behavior serves to protect against anxiety.

A Word of Caution

The case of Leonard K shows us that abnormal behavior can be quite bizarre and incomprehensible. This is the aspect of emotional disorders that is played up by the mass media (newspapers, television, radio, and movies). Typically, only the extreme forms of emotionally disturbed behavior are depicted—raving "wild" men and women who are unable to utter a coherent thought, rapists, mass murderers, and so forth. From these accounts, it is easy to generalize that all people suffering mental disorders are dangerous during all moments of their waking lives.

This view is a fiction. In fact, many individuals afflicted with emotional disorders, whether they are hospitalized or not, frequently behave in ways that are indistinguishable from the "normal." There is no sharp border separating normal from abnormal. This is not to deny that there are some individuals who appear to be in a continuous state of upheaval. For them, completing the most routine everyday tasks can seem to present insurmountable barriers.

However, they are not completely alone. At one time or another, all of us have experienced attacks of anxiety, self-doubts, worry, guilt, or shame. Most people have probably engaged in behavior that bordered on the abnormal if not frankly abnormal. The difference between normal and abnormal is so often a matter of degree. The way we view our problems and our success in coping with them may vary by degrees within the normal to abnormal range. As the tides of life wax and wane, how are we to place that survey stake that defines the water's edge?

The same person may change his or her beliefs and attitudes over time and take differing positions on life's issues as circumstances change from day to day, month to month, and year to year. Most of us have had at least one friend or loved one whom we considered the model of adjustment. "Carol is so well adjusted," we say, "nothing seems to phase her." And then one day we find her foundering in a pool of anxiety and in danger of drowning in it. Temporarily, at least, her coping mechanisms have been impaired. However, the opposite can also occur. The tide can move in the opposite direction and conditions change for the better (an improved job situation, resolution of a long-term conflict, or an easing of financial burdens).

One final note of caution. Have you ever heard of students at medical school who discovered that they exhibited the symptoms of almost all the diseases known to medical science? The same thing can happen when learning of mental-health disorders. Because the line between the normal and the abnormal is so thin, it is easy to confuse a relatively common variation in behavior with one that has crossed over that indistinct line into the abnormal. Consequently, you imagine yourself the victim of a psychological disorder. If this happens to you, take note but do not panic. It is a fairly frequent occurrence. However, if the anxiety, worry, or fear persists, you should make an appointment to see a counselor so that you can discuss your concern.

ANXIETY DISORDERS

A college girl was about to sled down a hill in Vermont. As a cold wind hit the hill, she stood holding her chin, looking back at her house in the distance. Her friends heard her mutter something—that she had snow in her boot, or needed the bathroom—some such lie. Then she began to run, looking down at the snow. She couldn't look at the house, it seemed too far away. She started to sweat and her legs went soft. She could not feel her feet, but they were running. Her heart was pounding, her face flushed. She began to panic. She felt as though she were coming apart, as if she had been running forever through the syrupy snow of a nightmare. Six Miltowns rattled against four Valiums in her pocket. The sweat on her body tripped triggers in her brain. The adrenalin signaled the nerves to further panic, "What if I die," she thought. "Oh my God, I'm going crazy." Then she was at the house, the 'safe' place, but she had added more fears to an already long list. (Baumgold, 1977)[1]

anxiety disorders: a group of disorders in which anxiety is the primary disturbance.

This case example dramatically illustrates many of the outstanding features of **anxiety disorders.** This student, M, felt threatened and anxious in a situation that most people would not find dangerous. In fact, the problem with anxiety is that it is difficult to pinpoint the precise trigger for its release. It is a fear reaction to unidentified or unknown stimuli and often takes the form of a premonition that something bad is about to happen.

Persons suffering from anxiety disorders live in a constant state of worry, tension, and vague discomfort. They may have difficulty concentrating or making decisions, or they may suffer acute anxiety attacks—moments of unbearable anxiety, bordering on panic.

Jim Whitmer/Nawrocki Stock Photo

Take the case of M. Her life was so ruled by anxiety that she was almost constantly unhappy. Many situations served as occasions for its arousal. But when she is unable to identify the threat, what coping mechanisms can she use? Thus, rather than coping with threatening situations, M had developed a pattern of avoidance. Her first thought when looking down the hill was, "Run for a safe place." When safe places cannot be found, there are always Miltowns and Valiums.

M's reactions to stress was characterized by rigid clinging to behavior patterns that are maladaptive. Why did she persist in her behavior when it brought her only more misery? The reason is that avoidance behaviors provide instant relief from anxiety. The fact that the relief is only temporary assumes little importance to the individual when the anxiety is both real and immediate. Avoidance behaviors, of course, do not solve the real problem. Indeed, if left unchecked, the fears, anxieties, and imagined threats may generalize to a wide variety of different situations. M developed anxiety reactions to cliffs, planes, and crowds. Later, when married, she could go virtually nowhere unless accompanied by her husband.

In summary, avoidance "solves" the problem of anxiety in the short run. In the long run, however, individuals suffering anxiety disorders persevere in self-defeating behaviors. They often react to threat by resorting to one or more of the defense mechanisms (see Chapter 7), usually in an exaggerated fashion. As we have previously seen, using a defense mechanisms is a good illustration of allowing the tail (defense mechanisms) to wag the dog (the person's life).

Anxiety disorders do not usually require hospitalization—such individuals are not usually dangerous to themselves or to others. However, they can and often do add a great deal of misery to their own lives and to the lives of those to whom they are close. In the ensuing sections, we shall look at a few different types of anxiety disorders. When reading these "textbook" cases, keep the following in mind: In real life, there is rarely a textbook case. Many patients exhibit a combination of different symptoms.

Anxiety States (Anxiety Neuroses)

The 26-year-old wife of a successful lawyer came to a psychiatric clinic with the complaint that she had "the jitters." She said she felt that she was going to pieces. She had fears of being alone, of screaming, of running

---

[1] Source: © 1977 by The New York Times Company. Reprinted by permission.

away, and of committing suicide. These fears were all intensified when she came near an open window. She suffered from constant headaches, fatigue and nervousness, from episodes of abdominal cramps and diarrhea. Twice in the past year there had been "attacks" in which she had become dizzy and had broken out into a cold sweat. Her hands and feet became clammy, her heart pounded, her head seemed tight, she had a lump in her throat and could not get her breath. (Cameron & Magaret, 1951, p. 307)[2]

anxiety state: a disorder characterized by excessive and persistent levels of anxiety.

This case example illustrates many of the features of an **anxiety state.** Its victims are in an almost continuous state of tension or anxiety. They use such words as "being churned up," "jumpy," and "nervous" to describe their feelings. This feeling of being in an almost perpetual stirred-up state—diffuse and without focus—is referred to as "free-floating anxiety." At times, such people will experience an intense anxiety attack in which the levels of anxiety become unbearable, bordering on panic. They also feel a threat which they may ascribe to present environmental circumstances. However, these "threatening" conditions are more a part of the symptoms than they are aspects of the causes. Outside observers will typically fail to perceive threat in situations that arouse an attack in those suffering anxiety states.

Accompanying these attacks are extensive bodily reactions, which may include profuse sweating, heart palpitations, breathing problems, chest pains, dizziness, hot and cold flashes, trembling, diarrhea, lump in the throat, frequent urination, and faintness. Psychological symptoms include a feeling of "loss of control," difficulty in concentrating, inability to make decisions, "a fear of dying, going crazy, or doing something uncontrolled during an attack" (*Diagnostic and Statistical Manual*, 1980, p. 232), and a general feeling of discouragement.

Obsessive-Compulsive Disorders

We have just seen that the anxiety in an anxiety state is free floating, diffuse and without focus. Individuals with this complaint are not afforded the partial protection against anxiety provided by the defense mechanisms. In obsessive-compulsive disorders, the individual develops specific symptoms that provide partial relief from the anxiety. Consider the following case example:

The biggest thing I've got is this obsession which spoils everything I do. If I had the courage I'd kill myself and get rid of the whole lot—it goes on and on, day after day. The obsession governs everything I do from the minute I open my eyes in the morning until I close them at night. It governs what I can touch, and what I can't touch, where I can walk, and where I can't walk. It governs whatever I do. I can touch the ground but I can't touch shoes, can't touch hems of coats, can't use the toilet without

---

[2] Source: Excerpted by permission from Norman Cameron and Ann Magaret: *Behavior Pathology*, p. 307. Copyright © 1951 by Houghton Mifflin Company, renewed 1979 by David Hooke and Gretchen Ann Magaret.

washing my hands and arms half a dozen times—then they must be washed right up the arms. (Marks, 1965, p. 1)

Here we see the pattern of symptoms in an obsessive-compulsive disorder. An **obsession** is a recurring thought or urge that seems to have a will of its own. It continues to intrude on the person's consciousness. The individual described in the above case is obsessed with cleanliness. The obsession is so overpowering that it can dominate a person's cognitive life, leaving little time for other thoughts and fantasies. Obsessions usually give rise to **compulsions** which are repetitive behaviors that suppress the anxiety associated with the recurring and unpleasant thoughts and urges. "The behavior is not an end in itself, but is designed to produce or prevent some future event of situation" (*Dignostic and Statistical Manual*, 1980, p. 235). However, the activity is either excessive or does not have a realistic connection to the event it is designed to prevent.

obsession: a recurring thought or impulse that a person can't stop.

compulsion: ritualistic behavior an individual feels compelled to repeat.

The hand- and arm-washing ritual in the preceding case example should be familiar to those of you who have read Shakespeare's *Macbeth*. Recall Lady Macbeth's obsession with blood on her hands and her compulsion to wash the blood away: "Will all great Neptune's ocean wash the blood clean from my hand?" Her excessive cleaning of her hands will not undo the crime she has committed, neither is it likely to prevent her from committing a similar crime, should the occasion arise.

The outstanding features of obsessive-compulsive disorders are that individuals so afflicted feel they have no control over the thoughts that invade their consciousness. They also recognize the futility of their compulsive acts and derive no pleasure from performing them, but do achieve some relief from tension.

Obsessive thoughts and compulsive deeds are not necessarily indicative of a disorder. They are quite common in times of stress and worry. Surely, at some time or another, you have completed some activity in which you were unsure of the adequacy of your performance. Perhaps you just finished a tough exam. Afterwards you ruminated, "Did I bomb out on it? How did I answer the second part of question five? Did I forget to give all three critical points? I sure hope I did. Well, knock on wood."

A common and usually benign form of obsessive-compulsive behavior is illustrated by the children's rhyme, "Step on a crack and break your mother's back." Generations of children have treaded along the sidewalk with great care so as not to commit this atrocity. The obsession in this example involves thoughts of doing harm to one's mother; the compulsion is to avoid stepping on a crack in the sidewalk. Note the complete lack of any realistic connection between the behavior and the feared future event.

Phobic Disorders

A certain man suffered from a phobia of being grasped from behind, the disturbance appearing in early childhood and persisting to his 55th year. When walking on the street, he found it necessary to look back over his shoulder at intervals to see if he was closely followed. In social gatherings, he arranged to have his chair against the wall. It was impossible for him to enter crowded places or to attend the theater. His other difficulties can readily be inferred. Significantly, he could give absolutely no explanation for the origin of his fear. (Bagby, 1928)

Phobias are exceptionally intense fears of certain situations or objects. The person suffering a **phobic disorder** usually recognizes the exaggerated nature of the fear and understands its irrationality—that no real danger exists. Nevertheless, the debilitating fear persists and the person will avoid the feared object, activity, or situation. Initially, the fear is aroused under rather specific circumstances. As a result, there are almost as many labels attached to phobic fears as there are situations in which they occur. A few are: claustrophobia (fear of enclosed places); agorophobia (fear of the marketplace, i.e., open places); acrophobia (fear of high places); bibliophobia (fear of books); and nyctophobia (fear of night or dark places).

phobic disorder: an anxiety disorder characterized by exceptionally intense and irrational fears of some specific object or situation.

However, the conditions under which the phobic fear was acquired have either been forgotten or repressed. The result is that conscious control over the fear is lost. Consequently, the fear tends to spread to many different situations. The individual may become, both literally and figuratively, a prisoner of his or her fears. This is seen in the above case example. There was hardly any place where he could be completely comfortable; almost nowhere he could go without looking over his shoulders.

How are phobic fears acquired? Some feel that these intense and irrational fears symbolize deep-rooted conflicts. Thus, an unresolved sexual conflict may lead to a fear of snakes. Others feel that most phobic disorders result from classical conditioning—some previously neutral cue or situation that is accidentally paired with a terrifying stimulus or condition acquires the capacity to elicit the fear.

A person suffering acrophobia would be unable to tolerate this view in real life.

Sue Markson

Even if the original conditions of learning the fear are not recalled, the conditioned fear persists and generalizes to other similar circumstances. This appears to be the case with the 55-year-old man in the above example. Let's take a further look at him:

> In his 55th year, he returned to the town in which he had spent his childhood. After inspecting his old home, he went to the corner grocery and found that an old boyhood friend was still behind the counter. He introduced himself and they began to reminisce. Finally, the groceryman said, "I want to tell you something that occurred when you were a boy. You used to go by this store on errands and when you passed you often took a handful of peanuts from the stand in front. One day I saw you coming and hid behind the barrel. Just as you put your hand in the pile of peanuts, I jumped out and grabbed you from behind. You screamed and fell in a faint on the sidewalk." The episode was then vividly recalled for the first time in almost 50 years, and the phobia disappeared after a brief period of readjustment. (Bagby, 1928)

EATING DISORDERS

Gloria is 19 years old. Her friends have all been telling her she looks awful. They call her bones. However, when she looks in the mirror, she is convinced they are lying to her. What she sees is a shamefully bloated and obese girl. No matter what the scale tells her, she weighs 87 pounds, and she is 5 feet 4 inches tall! She wishes people would stop trying to get her to eat more. She's got to lose at least 10 more pounds. . . .

To the casual observer, Gloria appears normal. A bit underweight, perhaps, but the world is full of both underweight and overweight people. In actuality, Gloria is suffering from **anorexia nervosa,** an eating disorder that is potentially life threatening.

anorexia nervosa: a disorder characterized by an extreme loss of body weight secondary to voluntarily limiting food intake.

Perhaps as a result of our society's preoccupation with weight, this disorder is most frequently found among girls who are emerging into adulthood, when concern for physical appearance is paramount. Approximately 4 in 1,000 females between the ages of 12 and 19 will develop this disorder. Anorexia is more than an eating disorder. It involves conflict over the responsibility of emerging adulthood and issues of self-control and self-worth.

Many anorexics, like Gloria, "vigorously defend their gruesome emaciation as not being too thin. They identify with the skeletonlike appearance, actively maintain it, and deny its abnormality" (Bruch, 1978). Because of their phobiclike reaction to food, anorexic individuals have extremely poor nutritional habits. Thus, they typically endanger various bodily systems that malfunction when vital nutrients are lacking in their diets. The mortality rate for anorexics is somewhere between 5 and 15 percent (Liebman, Minuchin, & Baker, 1974). Because of the hazard to both health and life, anorexia is a very serious disorder. In most cases, it is necessary to intervene with counseling and/or medical confinement and treatment.

Betty told herself "I did it again! The second time this week." Lying in her darkened room depressed and disgusted with herself, she recounted the day. She had gone through the line three times at breakfast—first for two sweet rolls, then for a snack of pancakes with double syrup and butter, and a last time for toast and three jellys. After her nine o'clock class, she stopped at the bakery for a whipped cream cake (large) and devoured it in a secluded place near the library. Then instead of going to the lab to prepare for a biology test tomorrow, she went to two carryout places—at each one devouring a couple of burgers, double fries, and triple thick milkshakes. Then back to the dorm where she induced herself to vomit.

bulimia: a disorder characterized by eating binges followed by self-induced purges involving vomiting or laxitives.

Betty has an eating disorder, **bulimia,** also more common among adolescent and young-adult females than males. Typically, the person who is bulimic will eat large quantities of food in a short period of time. The binge, which usually consists of sweets or high-carbohydrate foods which the individual otherwise won't allow herself to eat, is followed by some kind of purging behavior—most commonly self-induced vomiting or using large quantities of laxatives. Unlike anorexics, these people may not be underweight at all. They are aware of but unable to break their binge/purge cycles which are followed by feelings of self-disgust and depression. Counseling and/or medical treatment is needed in most cases to break the recurring cycles.

DISSOCIATIVE DISORDERS

dissociative disorders: disorders which involve some disturbance in memory, usually to escape or avoid anxiety-arousing situations.

psychogenis amnesia: a dissociative disorder which involves the memory loss of important personal information.

fugue: a dissociative disorder in which the individual leaves home, assumes a new identity, and is unable to recall his or her previous identity.

At times, usually under severe stress for which there appears to be no relief in sight, there is a sudden change in the normal functioning of consciousness, self-identity, or motor behavior. Various aspects of the individual's experiences become separated from or dissociated from one another. Collectively, these conditions are known as **dissociative disorders.** If consciousness is altered, the individual is unable to recall certain events in his or her life. This selective loss of personal memory is known as **psychogenic amnesia.** There is no physical or organic reason for the memory failure or other symptoms.

Individuals suffering a loss in self-identity forget who they are. They may even take on a new identity. There may also be motor involvement, such as sudden travel away from the home or place of work. Consider the following case example:

> Steve L had just taken on a challenging new job in a law firm. It had not been going well. One day he disappeared from his apartment and did not report to work. Two weeks later, his parents, having hired a private detective agency, located him working as a dishwasher in a restaurant in a nearby city. He had no recollection of his previous identity and had been drifting from job to job. (Price & Lynn, 1981, p. 154)

Steve is a victim of a dissociative disorder known as a **fugue.** The impaired memory function represents a defense against an anxiety-arousing and ego-threatening situation. Steve has literally escaped the pressures, tension, and fears of failure by abandoning the self under bombardment in favor of a new self who is free of cares.

A rather rare but dramatic form of disorder involving identity is found in the **multiple personality.** In this condition, two or more separate and distinct personalities may exist side by side. At any given time, one of the personalities is dominant. In fiction, we have become acquainted with such personalities in the form of *Dr. Jekyl and Mr. Hyde.* In real life, many of you may be familiar with Billy Milligan, the first person to be found not guilty of major violent crimes by reason of insanity, because he possessed multiple personalities. Billy had 24 different personalities living beneath his skin. In the following excerpt, Billy's therapist, Dr. George Harding decides to inform Billy of the fact that he shares his body with many other people. He introduces Billy to one of the personalities, Arthur.

multiple personality: a dissociative disorder involving the existence of two or more distinct personalities within one individual.

"A part of you is Arthur. Would you like to meet him?"

Billy began to tremble, knees moving so violently that he noticed it and put his hands out to still them. "No. It makes me want to sleep."

"Billy, I think if you tried real hard, you could stay awake when Arthur comes out and talks. You could hear what he says, and then you'd understand what your problem is."

"That's scary."

"Will you trust me?"

Billy nodded.

"All right then. While you're sitting there, Arthur is going to come on the spot and talk to me. You won't go to sleep. You'll hear everything he says, and you'll remember. Just the way some of the others do. You'll be off the spot, but you'll remain conscious.

"What's 'the spot'? You said that last time, but you didn't tell me what it is."

"That's Arthur's explanation of what happens when one of your inner people comes out into the reality and takes over. It's like a big spotlight, and whoever steps on it holds the consciousness. Just close your eyes and you'll see it."

Harding held his breath as Billy closed his eyes.

"I can see it! It's like I'm on a dark stage and the spotlight's shining on me."

"All right now, Billy. If you'll just step to one side, out of the light, I'm sure Arthur will come on and talk to us."

"I'm out of the light," Billy said, and his knees stopped jiggling.

"Arthur, Billy needs to talk to you," Harding said. "I'm sorry to disturb you and call you out, but it's essential to Billy's therapy that he knows about you and the others."

Harding felt his palms moisten. As his patient's eyes opened, the expression changed from Billy's frown to Arthur's heavy-lidded, haughty gaze. And out came the voice he had heard the day before: clipped, upper-class British speech out of a tightly clenched jaw, lips barely moving.

"William, this is Arthur. I want you to know that this is a safe place, and that the people here are trying to help you."

Instantly Billy's facial expression changed, eyes opened wide. He looked around, startled, and asked, "Why didn't I know about you before?"

He switched again to Arthur. "It was my judgment that it would do you no good to know until you were ready. You were very suicidal. We had to wait until the right time before you were told the secret."[3]

SOMATOFORM DISORDERS

"I don't know, Doc, but I think I got something wrong with me again."

"Well, remember last time. We couldn't find anything wrong with any of your organs. I explained that sometimes these things are in the head."

"It's different this time, Doc. Entirely different."

"OK. What is it this time?"

"Well, I have a pain in my stomach, I can't feel any sensations in the toes of my left foot, my heart flutters a lot, and I have difficulty breathing at night."

Following an extensive physical examination and a second opinion, the physician could find no organic basis for Harry's complaints, neither was there any known physiological mechanism that could account for the symptoms. Harry is probably suffering from a **somatoform disorder.** The symptoms do not represent "made up" complaints and are not under the conscious control of the individual. They are really experienced by that person. Telling the person "It's all in your head," provides neither comfort or relief. However, as we can see in the following case example, the symptoms do provide a relief from conflict, pressures, and responsibilities. It is easy to rationalize, "After all, no one can expect sick people to be at their best. And I'm sick."

somatoform disorders: disorders characterized by physical symptoms without a physical basis.

> John M was admitted to a psychiatric hospital following a history of job failure and an unstable family background. He made numerous complaints about his physical health. His concerns began when he experienced a swelling of his glands, which led him to seek help from numerous doctors, all of whom gave him treatments, but no treatment yielded relief. Ultimately, his physical complaints became so severe that he was unable to work.
>
> He is a friendly, pleasant, docile person expressing deep concern about his physical health. He reports that he believes his sex glands are infected, that he has a hernia, suffers from constipation, and has continuing feelings of tightness and pain in his abdomen. While discussing his physical health, he shows deep preoccupation; but later, on another topic, seems relatively indifferent and even cheerful. (Kisker, 1964)[4]

somatization disorder: disorder characterized by numerous physical complaints that have no organic basis.

John is suffering a somatoform disorder known as a **somatization disorder.** His complaints illustrate features that are characteristic of the disorder—preoccupation with health, constant monitoring of the body for signs of unfavora-

---

[3] Source: Daniel Keyes. *The Minds of Billy Milligan.* © 1981 Random House Inc. by permission. 88–89.

[4] Source: Adapted from Kisker, G. W. *The Disorganized Personality.* © 1964 by McGraw-Hill Book Company with permission from the publisher.

ble symptoms, and the rejection of any medical opinion that there is no underlying physical disease. People frequently treat doctor's offices as supermarkets of physical diseases. They shop around hoping they will find what they want—a positive confirmation that they are physically ill.

hypochondriasis: disorder characterized by continued preoccupation with the fear of or belief in having a serious disease.

A somatization disorder is different from **hypochondriasis.** In the latter, the individual interprets normal physical signs and sensations as abnormal. There is an excessive preoccupation with bodily functions, including heartbeat, sweating, or digestive processes, as well as a tendency to overreact to a minor complaint, such as an occasional cough. As with individuals suffering somatization disorders, a considerable amount of "doctor shopping" takes place. The individual with hypochondriasis will fear having a specific disorder (e.g., cancer, heart disease). This is what distinguishes hypochondriasis from the somatization disorders.

SUBSTANCE USE DISORDERS

It has been said that we are a nation of drug users. Indeed, the use of certain substances to alter mood or change behavior has become an integral aspect of the personal and social functioning of many individuals. We ingest caffeine in the form of coffee or soda pop "to give us a lift" (see Box 12.2). Alcohol, when taken in moderation at a social gathering, "takes the edge off," or "helps break the ice." Media messages encourage us to swallow the advertiser's capsules or

---

BOX 12.2: THE GREAT CAFFEINE DEBATE

Over the years critics have linked caffeine to myriad human ills, from stunted growth, diabetes, heart disease, and ulcers to—more recently—cancer, birth defects, and painful lumps in the breast. Each report sets off a round of worry and creates a run on decaffeinated coffee and "uncolas."

Unsettling as the caffeine alarms are, they have failed to sway many Americans, who consume 35 million pounds of the stuff each year. There are also contradictory reports to contend with. On the one hand, the Food and Drug Administration hints that it may strike caffeine from its list of chemicals that by virtue of the long-term use have become known as "generally recognized as safe." On the other hand, the *Harvard Medical School Health Letter* insists "there are no good studies to support the claim of danger in humans."

What exactly are the facts? Is caffeine the villain some say it is?

THE LIFT YOU GET

Caffeine has been providing people in many cultures with a mild lift for centuries, and today it's one of the most widely used psychoactive substances in the world.

In pure crystal form, caffeine is a bitter white powder belonging to the group of chemical compounds called methylxanthines, found naturally in dozens of plants, including coffee beans, tea leaves, and the kola nut—the source of some of the caffeine in cola drinks. In the United States, coffee accounts for most caffeine consumption. A cup contains anywhere from 40 milligrams in instant coffee to 200 mg in a strong drip brew. Other sources include tea, cocoa, and such drugstore products as Anacin, No-Doz, and Dexatrim, with amounts of 5 to 200 mg per serving or dose.

Caffeine is a central nervous system stimulant; it directly affects the cerebral cortex, or "thinking" part of the brain, and the medulla, which regulates the heart and other muscles. Just how caffeine acts as a stimulant was recently discovered at Baltimore's Johns Hopkins University, where Dr. Solomon Snyder and his co-workers found that the substance blocks the brain's ability to use a natural chemical messenger called adenosine. When given to mice, adenosine has

BOX 12.2 *(continued)*

a calming effect. Follow-up doses of caffeine reverse that effect. What the researchers suspect is that caffeine latches onto receptor sites in the brain faster than adenosine.

THE GOOD AND THE BAD

Caffeine boosts blood pressure and pulse rate. It increases the output of adrenaline, stomach acid, and urine. Under caffeine's power, heart muscles contract more forcefully, breathing tubes relax, and nerve responses shift into higher gear. Caffeine raises the basal metabolic rate, the speed at which the body burns calories.

The time it takes for caffeine to work varies, but in most people the peak "wake-up" effect occurs about an hour or less after they ingest it. The effects disappear in less than a day. Incidentally, no amount of coffee will sober a drunk or in any way reverse the depressant effects of alcohol. As the *Harvard Medical School Health Letter* puts it, "Pouring coffee into a drunk will produce nothing more than a drunk full of coffee."

Obviously many people work and feel better with caffeine in their systems. The drug opens coronary arteries, increasing blood flow to the heart. It temporarily reduces muscle fatigue. Studies suggest small amounts even improve driving and typing performance, take the monotony out of repetitions, and sharpen reactions for those driving long distances or using dangerous machinery. Evidence is lacking that caffeine is addictive, but when heavy users quit, withdrawal headaches are common. Too much caffeine causes the jitters (also called coffee nerves), dizziness, insomnia, heart palpitations, shaking, and heart-rhythm changes.

Eventually, some users seem to build up a tolerance. Some can drink coffee frequently during the day and evening, have a cup before bedtime, and sleep undisturbed. Most scientists and coffee drinkers agree, however, that caffeine sabotages sleep, particularly among the elderly, whose tolerance for the drug is generally reduced.

Linking caffeine to more serious disorders is another matter. For one thing, caffeine is consumed in products that may have several other suspect substances in them. Decaffeinated coffee, for instance, is processed with a chemical suspected of being carcinogenic.

Many coffee drinkers also smoke. That complicates the task of researchers trying to size up the relative risks of caffeine and tobacco in such disorders as cancer, heart disease, and premature birth; so does a possible hereditary sensitivity to the substance. Here's what we know and don't know about caffeine, based on recent scientific research.

Birth Defects

In 1976, the Center for Science in the Public Interest, a health advocacy group, petitioned the FDA to require more research and add warning labels on coffee containers. CSPI was concerned because the results of studies by other researchers showed how rats given large amounts of caffeine often bore underweight offspring with missing toes. In September 1980, the FDA warned women about the possible—though not proven—ill effects of caffeine on infants born to mothers who drink coffee during pregnancy.

Tempering the alarm was the reminder by other researchers that drugs that cause defects in experimental animals do not invariably cause similar defects in humans. Going a step further, Harvard researchers analyzed early-pregnancy coffee-drinking habits in more than 12,000 women and found no significant link.

Although it is unlikely that a morning cup of coffee will produce an infant with handicaps or stunt its growth, a committee of the National· Academy of Sciences recommends moderation in caffeine intake during pregnancy.

Behavioral Problems

Coffee's influence on behavior is another story. When Drs. Daniel S. Groisser, Pedro Rosso, and Myron Winick at Columbia University fed pregnant rats either regular or decaffeinated coffee, the newborns of those getting either kind of coffee moved about more but spent less time grooming themselves than the control group of offspring that got no coffee, the researchers reported last spring. (Decaffeinated coffee is not totally caffeine-free.)

BOX 12.2 *(continued)*

Cystic Breast Disease

Several years ago, Dr. John Minton, a surgeon at Ohio State University, suggested that total abstention from caffeine could reduce or eliminate painful, noncancerous lumps in women's breasts. Fifty of sixty-five women under his observation got better after removing coffee, tea, cola, and caffeine-containing drugs from their diets.

When Minton's claims were reported, however, the National Coffee Association and other trade groups disputed their validity. Since then, studies at the Health Services Center of the University of California, San Francisco and data gathered by the Boston Collaborative Drug Surveillance Program have found caffeine and cystic breast disease to be only marginally linked. Writing in the June 1982 *American Journal of Public Health,* scientists at a New York University medical center also said they found no evidence that those with higher levels of coffee consumption are at elevated risk of benign breast disease.

Scientific research aside, many women say they have seen improvement in their condition after giving up caffeine; if cystic disease is a problem, abstaining can't hurt and it might help.

Heart Attacks and Blood Pressure

It's known that drinking two to three cups of coffee a day can temporarily raise blood pressure 10 points and produce transient irregularities in the heartbeat of susceptible individuals. One study went so far as to implicate heavy coffee drinking, defined as six cups a day, in heart attacks, but the Framingham Heart Disease Study and other investigations do not bear this out.

Cancer

A worrisome suggestion that caffeine increases the risk of cancer has been just about buried under an avalanche of criticism. Dr. Brian MacMahon and his co-workers at the Harvard School of Public Health reported in 1981 that coffee drinking was prevalent in 369 pancreatic cancer patients and less so in 644 "controls" with other serious diseases. But other experts quickly pointed out that the controls used in the MacMahon study included patients who for medi-

cal reasons had cut down on their coffee drinking, making them unsuitable for comparison. An earlier university study had found no association between caffeine in ground coffee and pancreatic cancer.

Complications of Pregnancy

A few studies have suggested that women who drink large amounts of coffee have a higher risk of miscarriage, premature birth, stillbirth, or other complications. But whether caffeine or some other factor is to blame is unclear.

WHAT SHOULD YOU DO?

Although the final verdict on caffeine is not in, many Americans aren't waiting to take action. They have already switched to decaffeinated coffee, now 20 percent of the market, or to caffeine-free herbal teas and no-caf soft drinks such as RC 100 and Pepsi Free. Many parents determined to limit their children's sugar intake by reducing their consumption of soft drinks have inadvertently cut out a major source of caffeine.

What should you do about your caffeine intake? Don't be too quick to swallow the scare tactics of makers of caffeine-free soft drinks and other caffeine-free beverages. Many sell both decaffeinated and caffeinated products. Contends the American Council on Science and Health, a nonprofit educational group, "They promote fears of one of their products to sell another," and thus play both ends of the market.

Be wary of sensational headlines. At almost every major scientific meeting, someone reports negatively about caffeine in such a way that the report makes its way into newspapers and onto TV. Such accounts rarely do justice to objectivity.

Ulcer victims and people with high blood pressure or other major risk factors for heart disease might consider reducing or eliminating caffeine as a hedge against what is unknown about the drug's capacity to harm.

For others, caffeine is probably near the bottom of the list of dietary and other health concerns.

capfuls whenever we have difficulty finding sleep. And if our desire is to shed excess pounds without effort, there are diet pills galore that promise to come to our rescue. There are also pills to reduce pain, defeat headaches, and relieve anxiety and tension. In short, you need not do much shopping around to find any number of different substances that promise to cure everything and anything that ails you.

Some psychologists are quick to point out how, through stimulus generalization, we can easily slip from legitimate uses of legal and effective pharmaceuticals to "experimenting with" sniffing, ingesting, or injecting a variety of substances to give us a ride, take us down, or turn on a spiggot of fantastic sensations and perceptions.

substance use disorder. maladaptive behavior associated with the regular use of substances that affect the central nervous system.

Substance use disorders refers specifically to the maladjusted behavior associated with the regular use of various substances. They do not include the organic disorders that describe the acute and chronic effects of these substances on the central nervous system. In the words of DSM-III, "Examples of such

Caffeine and nicotine are mildly addictive drugs. Some people believe they cannot function without their morning cup of coffee. It has been suggested that if caffeine were introduced today, it would not be available without a prescription.

Peter LeGrand

behavioral changes include impairment in social or occupational functioning as a consequence of substance use, inability to control use of or to stop taking the substance, and the development of serious withdrawal symptoms after cessation of or reduction in substance use" (1980, p. 163).

It is useful to distinguish between the nonpathological *use* of various substances and the *abuse* of them (see Box 12.3). Substance abuse is characterized by: a *pattern of pathological use, impairment in social or occupational functioning,* and a *duration* of one month or more. Let's take a closer look at each of these characteristics.

Pattern of Pathological Use. The individual may remain intoxicated throughout the day, be unable to reduce or stop use, continue use even when he or she is aware of a physical disorder that is worsened by the substance, and feel that the substance is needed for normal daily functioning. The person may

---

BOX 12.3 DRUGS

Many people use the terms "drug use" and "drug abuse"interchangeably. These terms really have two different and distinct meanings. When a person drinks a cup of coffee, enjoys an alcoholic drink, inhales the smoke from a cigarette or "joint," or swallows a tranquilizer, he or she is a **drug user.** The person who uses these or other drugs to such an extent that he or she is unable to function without them may be considered a **drug abuser.**

drug user. a person who uses drugs, but not to excess.

drug abuser. a person who uses drugs to excess and is unable to function without them.

Few people would deny that drug abuse (including alcoholism) is one of the most serious problems we face today. Drug abuse itself is unquestionably a symptom of deeper psychological causes. Unfortunately, at the present state of our knowledge, we are better able to describe the effects of drugs on behavior than to specify the underlying causes of drug abuse.

Some drugs are particularly worrisome because their continued use leads to addiction. For example, chronic heroin abusers find that continued use leads to increased **tolerance:** Their bodies not only can stand (tolerate) more of the drug, but actually require greater and greater dosages to achieve the same effect. Before long, they develop a physiological de-

pendence on the drug; this state of physiological dependence is called **addiction.** Should they try to "kick the habit," their bodies will react violently.

tolerance. the body's ability to withstand a given amount of drug and its need for increased dosages of that drug to produce the desired effects.

addiction. physiological dependence on (need for) a drug.

Addiction should be distinguished from **habituation,** which is psychological, rather than physiological, dependence. Withdrawal from habituation is likely to be accompanied by emotional rather than physical distress. People trying to give up cigarettes, for example, are often nervous, tense, and irritable; the physiological symptoms they may have are usually minor.

habituation. psychological dependence on (need for) a drug.

The chemical nature of a drug determines whether continued abuse will lead to addiction or habituation. Drugs such as heroin, morphine, codeine, and the barbiturates are addicting. Habituating drugs include marijuana, cocaine, and the amphetamines.

Source: Haber/Runyon, *Fundamentals of Psychology,* © 1983 p. 266 Addison-Wesley, Reading, MA. Reprinted with permission.

have also experienced complications following episodes of intoxication, e.g., alcoholic blackouts or heroin overdose.

Impairment in Social or Occupational Functioning. Because substance abusers typically fail to meet important obligations to family and friends, their social relationships are usually seriously disturbed. Who wants to be associated with someone who forgets dates, is neglectful of one's feelings, and is sometimes abusive when intoxicated? There may also be legal difficulties stemming from accidents that occurred while the person is intoxicated or by criminal activities engaged in to support the habit.

Since chronic abusers frequently miss work or school and perform poorly when in attendance, they have difficulty sticking to one thing. Their inadequate functioning only adds more fuel to the fire. They seek forgetfulness in intoxication, stimulating experiences in the "rush" of an injection or the bizarre images of a psychedelic drug. In severe cases, their entire lives are dominated by the drug and the need to insure a continued supply. Appealing to their reason with words like, "You're destroying yourself," or "You won't have a friend left in the world," fall on deaf ears.

Duration. The *abuse* of the substance must last one month or more. Although signs of behavioral disturbance need not be present at all times, they should occur with sufficient frequency that a pattern of use, along with social and occupational impairment, is apparent. For example, Jeff's functioning does not seem to be impaired much of the time. However, during the course of one month, he went on several alcoholic binges that resulted in family arguments. (Box 12.4 outlines the phases from purely social drinking to complete alcohol addiction.)

Many of the features of substance abuse can be discerned in the last months of the life of actor/comedian John Belushi:

> They found his nude body in a bungalow in a posh California hotel. The first reports were that the 33-year-old actor had died of natural causes—possibly from choking on food. Then the coroner began the extensive examination of his remains. Within a few days, a new rumor began to spread—narcotics might have been involved.
>
> Close friends and acquaintances of the actor reacted indignantly, "That's nonsense," they would say. "John was not a junkie." The media were filled with such denials. But the coroner's report said otherwise. John Belushi of "Saturday Night Live" and *The Blues Brothers* fame had "speedballed"—injected both a stimulant (cocaine) and a depressant (heroin). Such combinations are extremely dangerous, like going from the lofty peaks of Everest to the depths of the ocean in a few moments of time. In the case of John Belushi, the combination was fatal. His central nervous system was completely disrupted—breathing became irregular and his heart stopped beating.
>
> Afterward, stories began to circulate about how he had appeared in a number of filming sessions "stoned." His poor performance in recent films was attributed to a pattern of drug abuse. His physician was even quoted

BOX 12.4:   PHASES OF ALCOHOL ADDICTION

The phases that most alcoholics follow appear to go from controlled social drinking to complete alcohol addiction. These phases can be summed up as follows.

PREALCOHOLIC PHASES

1. Controlled social, cultural drinking. The first phase is that of controlled social or cultural drinking. It is said that some drinkers become alcoholics with their first drink, but complete loss of control to alcohol usually progresses over a period of 10 to 20 years or longer.

2. Occasional escape from tensions. Just as social drinkers do not become alcoholics overnight, they also have no warning that their drinking has gone beyond that of social or cultural drinking and has progressed to a purposeful drinking—to escape from tensions. About 20 percent of the nation's drinkers fall into this category.

3. Frequent escape drinking. The third phase is entered as innocuously as was the second. As drinkers find that they can temporarily escape the tensions and frustrations of their everyday lives through the use of alcohol, they begin to turn to this escape from real life more often.

During these first three stages, the drinker's tolerance to alcohol steadily increases, but in phase 3 alcohol tolerance takes a sharp upswing and he or she must drink more liquor to achieve the same nirvana that was previously experienced.

EARLY ALCOHOLIC PHASE

4. A progression of drinking takes the escape drinker into the fourth phase, which appears to begin with the occurrence of the first blackout. The blackout is not merely passing out from drinking too much, but is more like temporary amnesia. One may carry on a conversation, move about, even drive a car—but will remember none of these actions later. It has been hypothesized that this phenomenon is due to the drinker's willpower—he or she wishes to remain in control of his or her body to prove the ability to handle the liquor, but the drug effect still overtakes part of the brain so that memory patterns are not established.

The actions of problem drinkers during this phase may be characterized as a progressive preoccupation with alcohol. When social functions are announced, they are more interested in whether drinks are to be served than in who will be attending the function. Before attending social functions, they fortify themselves with alcohol, and at parties they are in continual pursuit of an alcohol supply. These drinkers are far past the social drinking stage. They may begin to drink alone, gulping down the first few drinks to obtain an immediate effect, and their behavior may begin to be embarrassing to others, especially their spouses. Also, during this phase, problem drinkers may develop conscious or unconscious guilt feelings about their drinking and offer "good excuses" for taking a drink. No longer do they brag about their alcohol consumption, but rather tend to underestimate the number of drinks they have consumed. They begin to avoid conversation concerning alcohol altogether.

At this time, changed drinking patterns (drinking at a different time of day, switching to a new alcoholic beverage, using a different mix, etc.) may be used as a means of controlling one's drinking habits, and there may even be periods of total abstinence to prove that alcohol is still on a "take-it-or-leave-it" basis.

TRUE ALCOHOLIC PHASE

5. Again, let it be emphasized that these phases are not definite periods of time made obvious by calendar dates or road signs. Over a period of time, chronic drinkers move from the early alcoholic stage to the true alcoholic phase, in which everything in their being revolves around alcohol. Appearance, home relations, job, and possessions are neglected and begin to deteriorate. Family members change their habits to avoid confrontations with the alcoholic, and as a result of this, deep resentment and self-pity are manifested in the alcoholic. He or she may go through extended periods of constant drinking for consolation.

It is during this phase that the drinker can no longer stop after one drink. It has been suggested that perhaps by this time the alcoholic's first drink of the day or evening affects those cortical cells that control

BOX 12.4 *(continued)*

drinking judgment, and thus he or she cannot stop after one drink.

6. The sixth phase is ushered in by regular morning drinking, drinking that usually continues throughout the day. The alcoholic is now in danger of withdrawal symptoms if alcohol is not kept in his or her system at all times.

This phase is often represented by the comic figure who hides bottles all over the house and office. But at this point, the alcoholic is really a tragic figure, who neglects proper nutrition and whose family life deteriorates to the point of complete disruption. Alcohol is the alcoholic's purpose for living; he or she has become totally addicted to the drug.

7. The last phase of alcoholism is one in which social, medical, and psychological help must be given to the alcoholic or death will occur. By this time, he or she may have severe liver damage and possible brain-tissue damage.

In this or the previous stage, the alcoholic is most likely to experience the DTs, or delirium tremens. This reaction is characterized by delirium, muscle tremor, confusion, and hallucinations of delusions (mainly visual, such as moving animals, but tactile hallucinations may occur that cause alcoholics to feel that small animals or bugs are crawling on their skin). DTs do not generally occur until the alcoholic has been in the last two phases of alcoholism for several years, and at the onset of DTs the alcoholic may hallucinate only occasionally, but the symptoms gradually increase in duration and intensity. The psychotic episode lasts from two days to two weeks, frequently terminating in a long, deep sleep. In about 10 percent of the cases, death occurs, mainly due to pneumonia, complete renal shutdown, or cardiac arrest.

During any one of these phases, alcoholics may change their drinking pattern to one of partial or complete abstinence. It is believed that once chronic drinkers can no longer control their drinking, that is, can no longer stop at one or two drinks, they cannot return to a social drinking status, but must become totally abstinent. Alcoholics Anonymous calls for this complete abstinence, and it has been the most effective agency in the nation in helping alcoholics recover.

Source: D. Dusek and D. A. Girdano, *Drugs: A Factual Account,* 3rd ed., © 1980, Addison-Wesley Publishing Company. 57–59. Reprinted with permission.

---

as having warned the actor of his allergy to cocaine and the danger that it could someday lead to an arrest in his ability to breathe. Characteristic of the chronic drug abuser, he failed to heed the warning.

PSYCHOSEXUAL DISORDERS

Murray/Mary, aged 26, had the appearance and behavior of a not unattractive woman. She was heavily made up, batted her long eyelashes, wore a skirt short enough to show off her legs, and had noticeable breasts. Her only masculine features were a slightly roughened face, broad shoulders, and a deep voice. Physical examination revealed normal male characteristics, except for breast development and diminished beard growth due to estrogen therapy.

As a child, Murray/Mary had dressed like a girl, played like a girl, and fantasized about "really" being a girl. Her mother and grandmother collaborated in this and enjoyed giving her permanents, clothing, and jewelry. Her childhood playmates were girls, and she had no interest in boys' games like "ball or bat or dumb marbles." She always went to the ladies' rest room and never learned to urinate while standing; the thought of holding her penis to urinate was repulsive to her. . . .

After divorcing her 6-foot, 4-inch husband, the woman on the left had a sex-change operation and became the man we see on the right.

Before

After

United Press International Photo

She was considered a "sissy" at school, but had no particular troubles until puberty. In the sixth grade, the teachers began to insist that she play with boys. In the masculine role, she felt awkward and frightened around boys. As a girl, however, she adored the boys and their company and attention and had a "crush" on a boy in the seventh grade. Boys frequently teased her and called her "queer"; however, she strongly repudiated homosexuality. . . .

She remembers being ecstatic when a man first whistled at her, and the first time she was kissed she was "in heaven" . . . she had passed successfully as a woman, both vocationally and socially. . . . She dates men and likes to be petted and cuddled, but she avoids sexual intimacy. She regrets that, despite sex-reassignment surgery, she will be unable to bear a child by the man she loves. She persists in her efforts to become a "full woman." (Sabalis, Frances, Appenzeller, & Moseley, 1974, p. 907)[5]

---

[5] Source: R. F. Sabalis, A. Frances, S. N. Appenzeller, and W. B. Moseley, in *The American Journal of Psychiatry*, vol. 131:8, pp. 907, 1974. Copyright © 1974, The American Psychiatric Association.

In this case example, we see one of the most puzzling but intriguing of the psychosexual disorders—transsexualism. In this disorder, there is a persistent sense of discomfort and conflict between one's biological sex and one's gender identity (a person's self-concept as a male or female). As one observer remarked about male transsexuals, he "feels himself to be a woman trapped in a man's body" (Benjamin, 1966, p. 16). Over 2,000 people have gone through sex-change operations in an attempt to make their bodies more in tune with their minds.

Although gender identity disorders have received much publicity, they are relatively rare. They comprise one of several categories included in the psychosexual disorders.

ego-dystonic homosexuality. a disorder in which sexual orientation is a persistent source of distress and conflict.

The psychosexual disorders are a mixed bag, ranging from various unconvential sexual behaviors to a variety of sexual adjustment problems or dysfunctions. Some of the psychosexual dysfunctions were discussed in Chapter 11. Included in this category is one of the most controversial disorders—**ego-dystonic homosexuality.** Is homosexuality a mental disorder? The arguments for and against this issue have generated much heat but little light. There are those who consider homosexuality to be an abnormal behavior resulting from pathological flaws in the individual's development. Others argue that homosexuality is merely a different, but normal means of sexual expression. After many years of conflict over the inclusion of homosexuality as a mental disorder, a compromise was finally reached. DSM-III states explicitly that "homosexuality itself is not considered a mental disorder." The category ego-dystonic homosexuality includes only those homosexuals who are distressed and in conflict about their sexual orientation. Thus, an individual who has adjusted to, and is comfortable with, his or her sexual orientation is not included in this category.

PERSONALITY DISORDERS

Most people would agree that flexibility is one of the attributes of healthy functioning. To be able to adapt one's behavior and attitudes to ever-changing situations and circumstances is certainly a sign of effective adjustment. There are some people who are not able to do so. Their inflexibility and rigidity lead to significant impairments in everyday functioning. Sometimes personality patterns such as these are deeply ingrained.

personality disorders. deeply ingrained maladaptive patterns of behavior.

Personality traits are persistent and "enduring patterns of perceiving, relating to, and thinking about the environment and oneself, and are exhibited in a wide range of important social and personal contexts. It is only when *personality traits* are inflexible and maladaptive and cause either significant impairment in social or occupational functioning or subjective distress that they constitute **personality disorders"** (DSM-III, 1980, p. 305).

The Antisocial Personality

In most of the disorders we have looked at so far, the individual is uncomfortable, anxious, or emotionally upset about his or her condition. Indeed, in most

antisocial personality. a personality disorder characterized by the absence of anxiety and the inability to learn from experience.

of these disorders, a tight rein is kept on anxiety. In contrast, the person with an **antisocial personality** doesn't experience the extremes of anxiety and thus has built no adequate defenses against it. Sometimes called a sociopath or psychopath, the antisocial personality is characterized by an inability to form deep and lasting interpersonal attachments or loyalties. Such persons appear to have no sense of responsibility and are callous and given to immediate pleasures. Their lack of ethical or moral values frequently gets them into trouble with society. Sometimes they do experience personal distress. They may feel tense, depressed, and have problems tolerating boredom. They may believe that other people are hostile toward them. Often, they are correct in this belief. However, they rarely display bizarre distortions in their mental processes.

Some people with antisocial personalities are fairly successful. These individuals are usually quite charming and captivating. They know all the "right" things to say and do. But they have no scruples. They will take advantage of anyone at any time. They will stop at almost nothing to get what they want.

Most antisocial personalities are not successful. They cannot hold jobs and frequently encounter difficulty with the law. The prisons are filled with these unsuccessful delinquents and criminals. In the more extreme cases, they may commit the most shocking crimes with no apparent sense of guilt.

In the following case history, note the early onset of this disorder, the inability to profit from previous mistakes, and the continuation of this pattern in adulthood.

Louis was considered by his family always to have been an "angry child." He simply would not mind. "Father would spank him and put him in a corner, but he would come out and do the same thing again and get spanked again."

Louis was particularly fatalistic in his attitude toward his problems when he came to the clinic at age 15. He was aware of his lack of impulse control but had little hope of gaining control through his parents' way of "handling" him. He could envision only further antisocial behavior and eventual destruction of himself. He was unable to identify with a father whom he saw as passive and ineffectual but potentially destructive.

Louis was one of the older subjects seen in the follow-up. At 28, he was an unemployed truck driver. He had been fired for physically attacking his boss, an attack which he felt was justified because the boss was "unfair" to him. He had been discharged from military service a few years earlier as "incapable of adapting to military life."

His relationship to his family was still a hostile, dependent one. He and his father argued constantly. "Sometimes I don't talk to dad or mom at all for weeks at a time." His relationship with peers is equally poor. He described much rowdy, antisocial behavior with a gang of fellows who rode motorcycles in a group. "I used to get so smacked when I was out with them that the guys would put me on my cycle and head me toward my house." He is proud of his marksmanship with a gun. "I keep a pistol and it's loaded. Dad ordered me to get rid of it, but I wouldn't."

He was referred for psychiatric help after acting out while in the military service and again more recently. He dismissed these therapeutic contacts with the statement: "I was told that I am an angry person and I've decided that I really am."

The consistent, unchanging course of Louis' antisocial behavior seems singularly unrelated to any internal process of learning from experience, let alone to internal anxiety. He does become depressed and pessimistic over his belief that his hostility will lead, eventually, to his destruction. (Cass & Thomas, 1979, p. 175)

SEVERE DISORDERS: AFFECTIVE AND SCHIZOPHRENIC

psychoses: severe mental disorders characterized by withdrawal from reality, disordered thought processes, and personality disorganization.

delusion: an unshakable belief despite contrary evidence. Common delusions are delusions of grandeur (the belief that one is a very important person) and delusions of persecution ("they're out to get me").

In most of the disorders we have discussed so far, the individual is rarely so disturbed that hospitalization is required. However, the behavior of some individuals is so bizarre that they simply cannot function adequately and often must be committed to hospitals for treatment. The most severe forms of mental disorders—formerly known as the **psychoses**—are characterized by a major loss of contact with reality, disordered thought processes, and personality disorganization.

Such individuals often have **delusions**—false beliefs that are contrary to the facts. A severely disturbed man may believe he is Superman. He will not change this belief even though he cannot fly. Such persons may have *hallucinations*—sensory experiences in the absence of a stimulus, the most common of which is hearing voices. These voices may advise them or insult them. Usually the person answers, even engaging in running conversations with these imaginary voices.

See how many of these characteristics you can identify in the following letter written by a patient to one of her male physicians.

Dear Dr._____

"My Plan," or as mother used to call you, "The Little Plant," or else one little Plant for I was the other Plant, called "Tant." Will you please see that I am taken out of this hospital and returned to the equity court so I can prove to the court who I am and thereby help establish my identity to the world. Possibly you do not remember or care to remember that you married me May 21, 1882, while you were in England and that I made you by that marriage the Prince of Wales, as I was born Albert Edward, Prince of Wales, I am feminine absolutely, not a double person or a hermaphrodite, so please know I am England's feminine king—the king who is a king.

Your first duty is to me, and if you do not intend to do the right thing, helping me to get out of here, stop the thefts of clothing, money, jewelry, papers, letters, etc., etc.; you will please let me know so I can make some absolute change and further demand of the nations my release.

1874 Building was to have been a palace for my mother, father, myself and you, that is, if you are the one I married—so why not get busy and furnish it up as such when I go abroad. Make my trips (our trips?) short and return to America on important matters and have the right place to hold court. You and Dr. Black can take me to the equity court where I prove up my individuality and this must be done.

Sincerely,
"Tant"

Queen of Scotland, Empress of the World, Empress of China, Empress of Russia, Queen of Denmark, Empress of India, Maharajahess of Durban, "Papal authority" as a Protestant. (Noyes & Kolb, 1963, p. 338)

Some theorists believe that these types of conditions are truly distinct and fundamentally different from all other forms of mental disorders. Others argue that psychotic conditions are merely an exaggerated or more intense form of anxiety disorder. According to this latter view, individuals suffering anxiety disorders build castles in the air and those with severe disorders live in them.

What causes a person to be so disturbed that contact with reality is severely impaired? With the exception of certain conditions that can be attributed to known physiological factors, there is still much controversy surrounding the question of causes. Many theorists believe that biological and/or genetic factors play a role in all forms of mental distress. Studies of biochemical abnormalities in the brain have prompted many investigators to pursue this lead. Others suggest that we look at the interaction between biological, biochemical, and psychological forces.

Some theorists argue that if you cannot find a physiological cause, then environmental factors must be at fault. They believe that early childhood experiences are crucial in the development of severely disturbed behavior. Case histories such as the following are used to bolster their argument:

As we began to learn about the family background, it became clear that the patient conducted his hospital life in the same autocratic, pompous, and captious manner in which the father had governed the parental household. [The father] was an ingenious and successful foreign-born manufacturer, but at home he ruled his roost like an Eastern potentate, a role for which he also claimed divine sanction and inspiration via a special mystical cult that he shared only with a very few special friends. The patient would permit only a chosen few of the staff into his sanctum, just as the father had secluded himself in his bedroom during most of the time that he spent at home, with only his wife and the children's governess permitted to enter and attend to his needs. [The father], successful inventor and merchant, would sit there in his underclothes reading religious books by the hour. The entire household participated in the religious rites, the mother sharing his beliefs completely and continuing to do so even after his death, which according to the cult meant continuing life in a different form; the widow did not dare to disavow his teachings, because she believed he would know of it. More than imitation and caricaturization of the father's behavior was involved. Both the patient and his only sister were emotionally deprived children who were isolated from the parents and from the surrounding community because the family milieu was so aberrant."[6]

What about stress? We have already seen that unusually stressful circumstances can have a disruptive effect on a person's emotional and physical health. But not all people are equally vulnerable to the effects of stress. Some people are able to endure sustained stress while others cannot seem to tolerate even mild

---

[6] Reprinted by permission of the publisher from *Family Dynamics and Origins of Schizophrenia*, 1960: pp. 337–38. © 1960 The American Psychiatric Society, Inc.

Severe and prolonged stress can precipitate a psychotic episode.

Historical Pictures Service, Inc.

levels of stress. Can stress precipitate a psychotic episode? Some theorists believe that all people have a breaking point and point to case examples such as the following to illustrate the effects of sudden catastrophe:

> An unmarried woman of 37 entered a psychiatric hospital in a state of extreme agitation, weeping, moaning, and wringing her hands. From her cousins who accompanied her, it was learned that the close-knit rural family to which the patient belonged had been recently and abruptly dissolved. The patient's brother, to whom she was strongly attached, had been killed in an accident, and shortly afterward, the patient's aged father and her ailing mother died within a week's time. (Cameron & Magaret, 1951, p. 257)[7]

Although causes are still in dispute, all would agree that individuals with psychotic disorders are severely disabled and represent a major social and medical problem. In the following sections we shall look at psychotic mood disturbances (classified as major affective disorders) and the most common psychotic disorder—schizophrenia.

---

[7] Source: Excerpted by permission from Norman Cameron and Ann Magaret: *Behavior Pathology*, p. 257. Copyright © 1951 by Houghton Mifflin Company, renewed 1979 by David Hooke and Gretchen Ann Magaret.

Major Affective Disorders

Most people have experienced times when they feel on top of the world and other times when they feel blue and unhappy. These shifts in mood are fairly common and of no great concern. However, in some people these changes are striking and dramatic. Generally the mood changes involve either a highly elated (manic) or a severely depressed state, and are **major affective disorders.** There is a marked disturbance in mood in which one emotion predominates and colors the entire psychic life. The mania and depression do not always go together, however—mania, depresion, and normal behavior can occur in cycles. In fact, three types of major affective disorders are described in DSM-III. In the *manic episode* the manic state predominates, although there may be underlying depression. In the *major depressive episode* a mood of deep depression prevails. Finally, the *mixed bipolar disorder* involves both manic and major depressive episodes intermixed or rapidly alternating every few days.

major affective disorders: psychosis and related thought disturbances characterized by severe disturbances of feeling or mood.

In the depressed state, the person feels profoundly sad and hopeless. Severely depressed individuals lose all pleasure in their usual activities, show no interest in anything, and lack energy for even the simplest task. Depression is not an uncommon experience (see section on Depression in Chapter 5). Most people have times when they feel unhappy or down in the dumps. A period of grieving or depression is expected when a loved one dies or a person experiences a major crisis or disappointment. Indeed, depression at these times is fairly common and probably serves to help the person adjust to these circumstances. These normal feelings of depression usually disappear after a reasonable period of time. However, in a major depressive episode, the depression is prolonged and extremely intense.

In contrast, a person experiencing a manic episode is highly agitated, excessively cheerful, and unusually grandiose. The individual is generally hyperactive, sociable, and extroverted—to the point of being outrageous. According to DSM-III,

> Almost invariably there is increased sociability, which includes efforts to renew old acquaintances and calling friends at all hours of the night. The intrusive, domineering, and demanding nature of these interactions is not recognized by the individual. Frequently, expansiveness, unwarranted optimism, grandiosity, and lack of judgment lead to such activities as buying sprees, reckless driving, foolish business investments, and sexual behavior unusual for the individual. Often the activities have a disorganized, flamboyant, or bizarre quality, for example, dressing in colorful or strange garments, wearing excessive, poorly applied makeup, or distributing candy, money, or advice to passing strangers (*Diagnostic and Statistical Manual,* 1980, p. 206).

At the height of a manic episode, the person may run wildly about the room, gesturing dramatically, and yelling incoherent and meaningless words. Sometimes, the person gets irritated, especially when someone tries to intervene. The following example illustrates the elation, hyperactivity, and boundless energy of a person experiencing a manic episode.

Alan C was a 43-year-old unmarried computer programmer who had led a relatively quiet life until two weeks before. After a short absence

Why did John Hinckley shoot President Reagan? What motivations underlie this kind of behavior?

Courtesy of the National Broadcasting Company, Inc.

for illness, Alan returned to work exhibiting mild hypomanic behaviors. Others in the office noticed that he was unusually happy and energetic, greeting everyone at work. A few days later, during the lunch hour, Alan bought a huge cake and insisted that his fellow workers eat some of it. At first, everyone was amused by his antics. But two colleagues working with him on a special project became increasingly irritated, because Alan failed to devote any time to the project. He merely insisted that he would finish his part in a few days. On the day the manager decided to inform Alan of his colleagues' concern, Alan exhibited delirious manic behaviors. When he came to work, he immediately jumped on top of a desk and yelled, "Listen, listen! We are not working on the most important aspects of our data! I know since I've debugged my mind. Erase, reprogram, you know what I mean. We've got to examine the total picture based on the input!" Alan then proceeded to spout profanities and address obscene remarks to several of the secretaries. Onlookers thought that he must have taken drugs. Attempts to calm him down brought angry and vicious denunciations. The manager who had been summoned also failed to calm Alan. Finally, he threatened to fire Alan. At this point, Alan called the manager an incompetent fool and stated that he could not be fired. His speech was so rapid and disjointed that it was difficult to understand him. Alan then picked up a chair and said he was going to smash the computers. Several co-workers grabbed him and held him to the floor. Alan was yelling so loudly that his voice was quite hoarse, but he continued to shout and struggle. Two police officers were called and had to handcuff him to restrain his movements. Within hours, he was taken to a psychiatric hospital for observation.[8]

As we shall see in Chapter 13, many people who suffer from the major affective disorders can take certain drugs and function quite well in everyday life.

---

[8] Source: D. Sue, D. W. Sue and S. Sue, *Understanding Abnormal Behavior.* Copyright © 1981, Houghton Mifflin Company, used by permission.

Schizophrenic Disorders

About half the patients in mental hospitals are diagnosed as schizophrenic. What is schizophrenia? In spite of thousands of studies, schizophrenia is still an enigma. Scientists cannot even agree on whether schizophrenia is a single disorder or a group of similarly appearing disorders with different underlying causes.

There are certain common symptoms among those patients classified as schizophrenic. However, there are some very big differences in the kinds of behavior observed. It is these differences in behavior that allow us to identify the different types of schizophrenia. Let's look at one of these types, paranoid schizophrenia.

A.B., a physician, 38 years of age, was admitted in 1937 to a public hospital for mental disease following his arrest for disturbing the peace. Specifically, he had frightened his neighbors by hurling objects at imaginary people who, he said, were tormenting him, by beating the air with ropes, and by breaking glass in the apartment that he and his wife occupied.

*   *   *   *   *

Soon after completing his internship, trouble developed between the young physician and the chief resident. The former was compelled to resign but secured appointment in another hospital and completed an internship. . . . For some reason not stated in the history, but presumably because of beginning mental disease, the patient gave up his practice and became a medical officer in a Civilian Conservation Camp. He soon began to complain that the commanding officer was "against" him. He made frequent applications of cocaine to his nasal mucous membrane, not, he said, because he was a cocaine addict but in order to neutralize the effects of chloral hydrate, which was being sprayed upon him. After a few months he was released from his camp appointment. He then began practice in another city, but as he believed that the spraying of chloral hydrate continued there, he remained but two months and then returned to his original place of practice. He met with little success, as the same ideas of persecution persisted. According to his history, too, "He became forgetful and neglected his cases. He had lapses of memory and seemed to be preoccupied with his own thoughts."

As the patient's mental disorder progressed, he developed a great wealth of delusions. He stated that he was "the link between the living and the dead," that he was a "universal medium," that a certain physician called on him by mental telepathy for added strength and skill in surgical operations. He believed that someone was hiding in a trunk in his house and so he fired several bullets into the trunk. He accused his brother of spraying him with chloral hydrate from the third floor of his house. He therefore sat behind a closed door waiting for his brother, and upon hearing a noise, shot through the door. He grew a beard because his face, he said, was being changed in subtle ways by outside influences, adding that if he wore a beard, his true identity would not be known. Following his admission to the hospital, he often spent long hours in his room where he could be heard pacing the floor, moaning, or making a noise like a dog, striking his head with his fist, or pounding the wall. When asked the reason for his behavior, he explained that he was suffering tortures because people abused their powers of mental telepathy and were directing those powers toward him. (Noyes & Kolb, 1963, pp. 348–9)

In this example, we see many of the symptoms that characterize paranoid schizophrenia. The patient had delusions of persecution—imaginary people were tormenting him, his commanding officer was against him. See if you can identify other delusions of persecution in his case history. He also had delusions of grandeur (e.g., a certain physician called on him for added strength and skill). Generally the delusions and hallucinations of a paranoid schizophrenic are illogical and fragmented.

A paranoid schizophrenic is potentially dangerous. When a situation is perceived as threatening, the paranoid schizophrenic may strike out at the source of "danger." Find examples of this type of behavior in A.B.'s case. Many people believe that Sirhan Sirhan, the assassin of Robert F. Kennedy, was a paranoid schizophrenic who was haunted by the delusion that he was the "savior of the people."

SUMMARY

- The word abnormal means "deviating from the normal." Many different approaches to the definition of abnormal behavior are commonly used. We use the terminology of the *Diagnostic and Statistical Manual of Mental Disorders* (DSM-III) for the classification of various mental disorders.

- We still don't know what causes abnormal behavior. Moreover, there is no distinct border separating normal from abnormal. Sometimes an abnormal person behaves quite normally; in contrast, normal people sometimes do abnormal things.

- Anxiety disorders are characterized by excessive and persistent levels of anxiety. The person is almost continually unhappy, uncomfortable, and distressed in seemingly nonthreatening situations. Behaviors are developed to escape and avoid the anxiety rather than to cope with it.

- Anxiety disorders include anxiety states, obsessive-compulsive disorders, and phobic disorders.

- Individuals suffering dissociative disorders experience disturbances in memory including amnesia and fugue states.

- Somatoform disorders are characterized by physical complaints which are not "made up" but have no organic basis. Included in this category are somatization disorders in which the indivdiual is preoccupied with health and constantly checking the body for signs of sickness.

- Substance use disorders involve maladaptive behavior associated with the regular use of various substances such as alcohol, caffeine, and narcotics.

- There are many diverse categories included in the psychosexual disorders. They include problems with gender identity such as transsexualism, a variety of unconventional sexual behaviors, and various sexual adjustment problems. Ego-dystonic homosexuality is a category reserved only for those homosexuals who are distressed and in conflict about their sexual orientation.

- The antisocial personality is one type of personality disorder. Antisocial personalities fail to learn from past mistakes or experiences. They often have difficulty assuming adult responsibilities and frequently find themselves in trouble with the law.

- In the severe disorders, the individual is unable to function in society. The affected person loses contact with reality and shows disordered thought processes and personality disorganization.

- Major affective disorders involve profound disturbances in mood, either a highly agitated or severely depressed state.

- Schizophrenia is the most common of the severe disorders. Different behaviors are associated with different types of schizophrenic disorders.

TERMS TO REMEMBER

Neurosis	Hypochondriasis
Anxiety disorders	Substance use disorder
Anxiety state	Drug user
Obsession	Drug abuser
Compulsion	Tolerance
Phobic disorder	Addiction
Anorexia nervosa	Habituation
Bulimia	Ego-dystonic homosexuality
Dissociative disorders	Personality disorders
Psychogenic amnesia	Antisocial personality
Fugue	Psychoses
Multiple personality	Delusion
Somatoform disorders	Major affective disorders
Somatization disorder	

C H A P T E R 13

TECHNIQUES OF COUNSELING

AND THERAPY

Why Counseling and Therapy?

Carlos is 19 years old and is entering his second year in college. He has not yet declared a major because he is still uncertain what career he should pursue. He is quite unsettled by the indecision and he is sure it is interfering with his academic performance.

Virginia is 40 years of age, recently divorced, and returning to college after a lapse of 20 years. Since she was always good in mathematics and liked activities "where one and one always equals two," she is pursuing a major in computer programming. However, her life is pervaded with doubts, anxieties, and unanswered questions. Can she hack it after all these years? Does she have the discipline necessary to complete assignments? What about her arrangements with her exhusband? Will he be good to his word or will he skip out? What about the children? How badly will they suffer from a week here, a weekend there, a summer somewhere else? These questions invaded her sleeping hours so that she felt drained of energy most of the time. One question dominated all the rest: "Am I going crazy?"

Mrs. C just couldn't stop washing. Twenty-five to thirty times a day, she had to wash her hands. Her morning shower lasted two or more hours. Moreover, every member of her body had to be washed in a precise sequence. If she forgot where she was, she had to start all over again. Her husband, George, had to get up at 5 A.M. morning after morning and help her keep track of where she was in sequence. If he overslept, there was no guarantee that the bathroom would be available for his use by 7 A.M. Mrs. C also had a hang-up about underwear. They could only be worn once and never washed. Thousands of pieces were scattered throughout the house. George decried the fact that he had hundreds of dollars invested in once-worn underwear.[1]

A few months back, Roger was on top of the world. He and his wife owned their own home, the bills were all paid, and the union had negotiated a contract that gave him a 12 percent annual increase over each of the coming three years. With both he and his wife working, their combined income was impressive. He was even beginning to contemplate that little summer retreat snuggled back in the nearby forest. And then, blue Monday. Over the weekend, his employer had announced the closing of the mines because "Lowered quality of ore combined with rising costs made it economically unsound to continue operations." In a moment, Roger's home had lost most of its value since the town in which he lived had never diversified. It drew 90 percent of its economic vitality, either directly or indirectly, from the operation of the mine and the smelter. Roger sank into a depressed state.

---

[1] Adapted from J. O. Prochaska, *Systems of Psychotherapy: A Transtheoretical Analysis* (Homewood, Ill.: Dorsey Press, 1979), with permission.

What do these people have in common? Several things. Although not always obvious on the surface, all of their lives are in turmoil. Until Carlos resolves his career plans, much of his efforts involve aimless wanderings from course to course. Lacking the focus to give meaning to the rest of his daily activities, he is listless, emotionally flat.

Virginia, on the other hand, is the victim of one of the hallmarks of our times—divorce that casts a shadow on broken families and fractured human relationships. Half way through the biblical four-score years of her life span, she must try to assemble all the pieces, set new goals, and change the entire direction of her life.

Mrs. C is the victim of a crippling obsessive-compulsive disorder. Almost nothing else in her life matters other than keeping her body clean and undefiled. She is literally in a prison without bars, but a prison just the same.

Roger's turmoil arises from circumstances beyond his control. There was no hint of the mine's closing; no way to plan in advance for the sudden financial crisis. Nevertheless, like the others, his emotions seemed to be in a perpetual churned-up state and he couldn't get his mind off his problems.

Besides their turmoil, all four of these people share one other characteristic in common: all are in need of some form of guidance, and all could probably

Although close friends and loved ones can often provide the emotional support needed to help an individual during troubled times, sometimes a visit to a professional is warranted.

© Joel Gordon 1980

benefit from professional counseling or psychotherapy. A common misconception is that professional help should be reserved only for those with severe mental disorders. The fact of the matter is that about 1 out of 10 people now living will seek professisonal help sometime in their life. The reason for the high proportion is that *any* of life's many crises might better be handled with professional assistance. This help need not require prolonged and intensive psychotherapeutic sessions. Some difficulties can be cleared up in one or two visits. The amount of time depends on such considerations as the severity of the problem, the individual's coping resources, and the quality of environmental supports. The importance of environmental supports cannot be overestimated. An abused child may receive the finest of therapeutic care but, if he or she is thrown back into the situation in which the abuse occurs, the therapy may be of as little use as an umbrella during a tornado.

How do you know if you should seek professional help? There is no simple and universal answer to this question. However, there are a few considerations to keep in mind.

1. Compare the severity of your emotional discomfort to physical ailments you have experienced in the past. If your unhappiness, anxiety, tension, or depression were a physical disorder, is it sufficiently severe that you would make an appointment to see your family doctor? If it is comparable in discomfort, a visit to a mental-health professional is in order.
2. Have you noted significant changes in some aspects of your behavior? For example, do you "fly off the handle" at the slightest provocation? Has the quality of your work deteriorated? Do you have difficulty concentrating because your thoughts are constantly directed elsewhere? Do you find it difficult to make it through the day without drugs or alcohol? Have your relationships with others gone downhill? An affirmative answer to one or more of these questions might warrant a visit to a professional.
3. Do your friends or relatives tell you that you need some help? Perhaps they are noticing something of which you are unaware. Recall the defense mechanisms—their main objective is to block awareness of those aspects of ourselves which, if known, would damage our self-esteem. Other people may simply be seeing through our defenses since they are able to view us in a more objective and factual light.
4. Persistent suicidal thoughts and urges are a red flag. If they occur, you should seek professional help without delay.

Once you decide you want therapy or counseling, what do you do? Where do you go? There are a variety of avenues for you to explore. If you are a college student, there may be a counseling center or mental-health facility right on campus that provides assistance to students who have emotional problems. Generally these centers are staffed by mental-health professionals and personnel whose training is especially geared to prepare them for the special kinds of problems encountered by college students. If you are experiencing difficulties and feel that it's time for outside help, you should not hesitate to utilize these services. One study

After a worker answers a "hotline" call at a crisis center, he contacts the appropriate response center and verifies the location on the map.

John Thoeming

found that those students who used campus counseling services were most likely to complete college in four years and least likely to drop out because of low grades (Frank & Kirk, 1975). It seems that students who use the college services to help them deal with problems that interfere with their ability to study, take exams, or otherwise function in college fare better because of this experience. If your college or university does not provide psychological services on campus, the chances are they can refer you to sources of help off campus.

The Community Mental Health Act of 1963 provided funds to make psychological services more accessible to individual communities. Since the passage of this legislation, most communities now have mental-health centers which provide therapy and counseling directly or can refer clients to outside therapists. In addition, crisis centers (hot lines) have been established to deal with acute and urgent psychological problems such as depression or anxiety usually associated with some specific event or situation. Crisis intervention in such emergency situations as threatened suicide, rape, drug overdose, or a family split can often help to reduce symptoms or at least bring the situation under control.

One of the best ways to find a therapist is to use your telephone directory. You will find listings of most of the mental-health facilities available locally, as well as independent private practitioners in counseling, psychology, and psychiatry (see Box 13.1). Since psychiatrists have a medical degree, they are usually listed under "physicians."

There are other potential resources for finding a therapist. You might check with your psychology professor, minister, priest, or rabbi, or other friends who

---

BOX 13.1: PERSONNEL IN PSYCHOTHERAPY PROFESSIONAL

Clinical Psychologist

Ph.D. in psychology with both research and clinical skill specialization. One-year internship in a psychiatric hospital or mental-health center. Or Psy.D. in psychology (a professional degree with more clinical than research specialization) plus one-year internship in a psychiatric hospital or mental health center.

Counseling Psychologist

Ph.D. in psychology plus internship in a marital or student counseling setting; normally, the counseling psychologist deals with adjustment problems not involving mental disorder.

Psychiatrist

M.D. degree with internship plus residency training (usually three years) in a psychiatric hospital or mental-health facility.

Psychoanalyst

M.D. or Ph.D. degree plus intensive training in theory and practice of psychoanalysis.

Psychiatric Social Worker

B.A., M.S.W., or Ph.D. degree with specialized clinical training in mental-health settings.

Psychiatric Nurse

R.N. in nursing plus specialized training in care and treatment of psychiatric patients. M.A. and Ph.D. in psychiatric nursing is possible.

Occupational Therapist

B.S. in occupational therapy plus internship training with physically or psychologically handicapped, helping them make the most of their resources.

PARAPROFESSIONAL

Community Mental Health Worker

Capable person with limited professional training who works under professional direction (especially crisis intervention).

Alcohol or Drug-Abuse Counselor

Limited professional training but trained in the evaluation and management of alcohol- and drug-addicted persons.

Pastoral Counselor

Ministerial background plus training in psychology. Internship in mental-health facility as a chaplain.

In both mental health clinics and hospitals, personnel from several fields may function as an interdisciplinary team in therapy—for example, a psychiatrist, a clinical psychologist, a social worker, a psychiatric nurse, and an occupational therapist may work together.

Source: *Abnormal Psychology and Modern Life,* 6th edition by James C. Coleman, James N. Butcher and Robert C. Carson. Copyright © 1980 Scott, Foresman and Company. Reprinted by permission.

---

have participated in personal counseling or therapy. In addition, you can check with the local Psychological Association for referrals and information about the credentials of a psychotherapist.

If cost is a consideration, you should first find out whether psychological services will be reimbursed by your insurance. Community mental-health centers and many private practitioners charge on an "ability to pay" scale. Generally, fees will be higher for psychiatrists than for psychologists or counselors. Finally, group therapy is considerably less expensive than individual therapy since the therapist's fee is "shared" by several people.

COUNSELING AND PSYCHOTHERAPY

Counseling psychology and psychotherapy overlap to a large extent. Both are concerned with helping the individual overcome some adjustment problem that is sufficiently serious to incapacitate the individual to varying degrees. However, the functions of the counselor include a broader range of activities. Indeed, five basic functions have been identified: individual counseling, assessment of the individual and the environment, program development and consultation, research, and supervision (Osipow, Walsh, & Tosi, 1980).

In performing the individual counseling function, the counselor has three broad areas of responsibility: (1) Educational counseling in which the focus is to improve a student's efficiency of scholastic performance and to assist in the choice of schools and courses of study. (2) Career counseling in which the student makes vocational choices and plans a curriculum appropriate to these choices. (3) Personal adjustment counseling in which an attempt is made to identify emotionally laden situations and behavior that interfere with the individual's efforts to achieve his or her objectives. It should be noted that all three areas of concern overlap to some extent. For example, Carlos may be having difficulty finding a career objective because personal problems interfere with his ability to perform well in courses related to vocational fields that interest him. An effective counselor attempts to deal with the whole individual rather than some segmented part that "is in difficulty."

psychotherapy: The use of psychological methods to treat emotional disturbances.

Psychotherapy is the treatment of mental disorders by psychological methods. The underlying assumption of psychotherapy is that the individual's beliefs, past experiences, expectations, and coping strategies have all played a part in the development of the disorder. Psychotherapists believe that people can change, that they can learn more adaptive ways of perceiving and coping with their environment. Although practiced by professionals, psychotherapy is an experience most of us are familiar with:

> Everyone who tries to console a despondent friend [or] calm down a panicky child in a sense practices psychotherapy. He tries by psychological means to restore the disturbed emotional equilibrium of another person. Even these commonsense, everyday methods are based on the understanding of the nature of the disturbance, although on an intuitive and not a scientific understanding . . . Methodological psychotherapy to a large degree is nothing but a systematic, conscious application of methods by which we influence our fellow men in our daily life. (Alexander, 1946)

In this chapter, we shall concentrate on personal adjustment counseling, the area in which the boundaries between counseling and psychotherapy are often obscure. Indeed, we shall not even attempt to make a distinction between the methods used by counselors and psychotherapists since both professions derive their procedures from a common pool of individual therapies including psychoanalytic, humanistic, rational, and behavioral therapies.

Complicating the discussion is the fact that more than 130 different therapies have been identified (Parloff, 1976). This sounds somewhat more formidable than it is. In many, the differences are more theoretical than actual. Indeed, their similarities often outweigh their differences. They all share a common goal: to bring about changes in behavior. Although differing in particulars, most share the following characteristics in common. They try to:

Provide a setting in which the patients or clients feel free to reveal their innermost thoughts and feelings.

Furnish some opportunity for emotional release.

Bring about cognitive changes in the individual (better understanding of their own motives and feelings and improved comprehension of their relationship with significant people in their lives).

Encourage the individual to talk, the so-called talk therapies.

Bring about an improvement in the individual's self-esteem.

medical therapy: the use of medical methods to treat emotional disturbances.

When psychological methods are used, we refer to the treatment as *psychotherapy*. When medical methods are used, the treatment is called **medical therapy.** Since all forms of therapy overlap to varying degrees, they should not be regarded as separate and distinct entities.

The differences among therapies include the following:

The emphasis on treating the symptoms or searching for root causes of disorders.

The extent to which the therapist controls the course of therapy.

The emphasis on achieving "insight" into one's personal problems as opposed to changing behaviors whether or not the patient understands his or her problem.

INDIVIDUAL THERAPIES

Psychotherapy may be administered to individuals in which the patient and therapist are one on one. There are also some therapies in which a number of patients are treated together and in which the interaction among patients is considered an essential aspect of the treatment. In this section, we shall look at four widely practiced forms of individual therapy: psychoanalysis, client-centered therapy, rational-emotive therapy, and behavior therapy.

Psychoanalysis

Let us return for a moment to the case of Mrs. C. Recall that she was obsessed with thoughts of dirt and filth. To relieve the anxiety associated with her fear of unsanitary conditions, she developed a washing and bathing compulsion. However, this was but the tip of the iceberg.

At the time she was observed, Mrs. C was 47 years old and had six children: Arlene, 17; Barry, 15; Charles, 13; Debra, 11; Ellen, 9; and Frederick, 7. Clues to her compulsive tendencies can be found in the preceding sentence. Can you find them?

Note that her children were named in alphabetical order and were spaced a nice and orderly two years apart. It may or may not be significant that she stopped having children when she got to the first letter of her husband's name, George. One might speculate on her dilemma had his name begun with the letter Z. In any event, we might imagine that such a woman would value orderliness. This was the case. As previously noted, she washed 25 to 30 times a day, took at least two hours for her morning shower, and refused to recycle underwear.

Indeed, so driven was she for the need for orderliness, she lost interest in her personal appearance, often walking about the house bare from the waist up. This was a cause of acute embarrassment to her teenage sons. In addition, she stopped buying new clothes for herself and never set her hair, in spite of prolonged daily scrubbings. The overall effect of her constant washing of her body and hair gave her an "appearance that was like a combination of a prune and a boiled lobster with the frizzies" (Prochaska, 1979, p. 20).

Mrs. C came from a strict, authoritarian home dominated by a father who, at 6 feet 4 inches tall and 250 pounds, looked like lineman for a professional football team. Neither Mrs. C nor her sisters were granted any freedom of expression. She was not permitted any display or even mild disagreement. After each date, she was subjected to the humiliation of having to account for what she had done down to the last detail. To add coals to the fire, her mother was like a broken record, repeating the theme that sex is disgusting and that she must keep herself clean and disease-free. After marriage, Mrs. C engaged in sexual relations with her husband only to satisfy him. During the past two years, she had had intercourse only twice.

Mrs. C's compulsive concern with cleanliness was apparently triggered by a siege of illness in the family. One daughter contracted pinworms while the rest of the family was bedridden with the Asian flu. Her physician cautioned her to keep the household linens and bedsheets completely sanitary to prevent the spread of the pinworm infestation. However, even after the family recovered, the need to keep things clean persisted.

Let us now examine this case from the psychoanalytic perspective. Recall that, during the critical stages of psychosexual development, a person may experience conflicts that are not successfully resolved. These may then be repressed but they continue to operate at the unconscious level. A severe psychological trauma at a later date may precipitate a regression to one of the earlier psychosexual stages. It would not be surprising to learn that Mrs. C failed to resolve conflicts at the anal stage of development. It is almost certain that her parents demanded that she control her bowels and not permit herself to become messy. This control was probably generalized to almost all aspects of her emotional life, including the expression of aggression or even tender feelings. Her excessive zeal for personal cleanliness was undoubtedly a defense against such anal pleasures as being dirty and openly expressing impulses.

We previously noted that anxiety is one of the consequences of harboring thoughts, feelings, and impulses associated with unresolved conflicts. A way must be found to reduce or ward off the psychological pain associated with this anxiety. A person without effective coping mechanisms—as must have surely been the case with Mrs. C—has little choice but to unconsciously adopt one or more defenses. One way to achieve forgetfulness is to repress unacceptable urges. However, although repression provides some relief from the acute phase of the anxiety, it does not remove the anxiety but buries it alive.

Moreover, people often develop symptoms as a way of dealing with anxiety, e.g., phobic fears, obsessive thoughts, compulsive acts. However, repression conceals the original source of the anxiety from them. Thus, they remain unaware of underlying conflicts. In Mrs. C's case, she felt an overwhelming and inexplicable urge to remain clean and to avoid anything she regarded as dirty, including sex. But how can you deal effectively with situations you do not comprehend? If your car doesn't start and you know nothing about its ignition and combustion system, how likely are you to correct the fault?

psychoanalysis: therapy approach based on psychoanalytic theories. The psychoanalyst endeavors to help the client gain insight into unconscious impulses, thoughts, and conflict.

Psychoanalysis sets up as a therapeutic goal improved self-understanding on the part of the patient. An effort would be made to bring Mrs. C's submerged (repressed) impulses and thoughts to the surface so that she understands why she behaves as she does and she can subsequently exercise some control over the changes she makes in her life. Let's look at some psychoanalytic techniques.

Free association: a psychoanalytic tool in which clients, made as relaxed as possible, are encouraged to report all thoughts and feelings as they occur.

"Just relax and tell me anything that comes to your mind." These are familiar words to someone undergoing psychoanalytic therapy. while seated in a comfortable chair or lying on a couch, the patient is asked to use **free association**— say anything that comes to mind. There are no restrictions on what the patients may say. They are free to choose any subject, but they are required to report all thoughts that go through their minds and any feelings accompanying these thoughts. They are discouraged from constructing a logical and coherent narrative, but rather encouraged to report spontaneously all thoughts as they occur. During this time, the therapist often sits out of the patient's direct line of sight so as to minimize distracting stimuli.

The psychoanalyst wishes the patient to achieve a state of relaxation similar to the one we experience just before falling to sleep. During these periods, our minds are often flooded with disconnected thoughts, feelings, and desires. Psychoanalysts feel that our vigil over our thoughts is relaxed during such periods. Thus, it is possible to gain relatively direct entry to the unconscious. However, layers upon layers of defenses do not peel off in a moment. Revelations typically take place gradually over a number of sessions of free association. In time, the patients will achieve insight into the conflicts that have been pushed into their unconscious.

Psychoanalytic therapy is in itself a struggle. As much as Mrs. C might want to be helped, she does not relinquish her defenses willingly. She will continue to fight for protection against anxiety-arousing thoughts and impulses. As she

The psychoanalyst interprets the patient's report of his feelings, thoughts, and wishes that come to mind in the relaxed environment of the therapy situation.

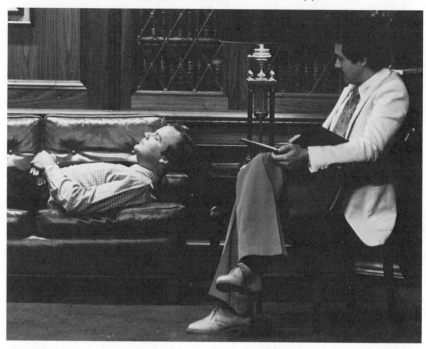

John Thoeming

probes even deeper into her unconscious, "dangerous" thematic material begins to emerge during the course of free association. She may resist further encroachments into the unconscious and suddenly shut up tighter than a clam, talk excessively about an unrelated topic, or deny a statement she made on a previous occasion. To illustrate, when told to lie on the couch and say whatever came into her mind, Mrs. C became anxious. She would begin to talk about her obsessions rather than to free associate. **Resistance** may express itself in many different ways—being late for an appointment, forgetting it altogether, or even discontinuing therapy.

As previously noted, the reason for assuming a relaxed position during therapy is that resistance is lessened. However, in the view of psychoanalysis, controls over unconscious impulses are presumed to be least during sleep. This is the reason that psychoanalysts have historically directed much attention to the content of dreams. Certain thoughts, wishes, and urges that are unacceptable to the waking individual manage to find their way into dreams.

This does not mean that all controls are relaxed during dreams. Materials

resistance: in psychoanalysis, the tendency to resist or avoid anxiety-arousing material.

that remain threatening to the individual will come out in disguised or symbolic form. If you look only at the manifest content—the thematic material as it appears to the dreamer—you may miss the hidden meaning of the dream altogether. However, the actual meaning of the dream—its latent content—represents repressed content striving for expression. Dream analysis consists of an attempt to reveal unconscious conflicts and unacceptable urges by the study of the symbols as they appear in our dreams. The following excerpt from the 48th hour of psychoanalytic therapy of a 28-year-old unmarried male shows the disguised form that repressed impulses may take in dreams:

CLIENT: I had another of these dreams last night. I woke up in a sweat and was frightened almost to death.

THERAPIST: Tell me about it.

CLIENT: It's pretty much the same thing, I was driving a big truck along a dark country road at night. I saw a woman walking along it ahead of me, and I could have avoided her easily. But [*great agitation*] I didn't seem to want to! I just held the truck to the curve of the road on the right side, and I hit her! I hit her! And it was awful! I stopped and went around to her, and she was still alive but dying fast, and she was terribly battered!

THERAPIST: Tell me about the woman. Just say whatever comes to mind now. Think about the woman and just say whatever occurs to you.

CLIENT: Well, she was nobody I've ever known. She seemed small and sort of helpless. She was just walking along the road. It's not always the same woman in these dreams, but they're usually little old ladies like this one. She had dark hair and was terribly, terribly disfigured after the truck hit her. Mother's hair is almost snow white now, but this woman was dark. I've never known anybody like her. [*pause*]

THERAPIST: It seems important to you not to know who this woman was. Go on.

CLIENT: But I don't know who she was! She was just a little old woman on a dark country road. It was horrible! The accident messed her up so dreadfully! I felt nauseated and revolted by all the mess as well as by the horror of what I had done. But—and this is very strange—I didn't feel any remorse in the dream, I don't think. I was terrified and sick at the sight but not really sorry. I think that's what wakes me up. I'm not really sorry.

THERAPIST: Almost as if you were glad to have got rid of this little old lady. Go on. Just say whatever comes to mind.

CLIENT: [*After a long pause*] I guess the horror of the sight is that she was so messy and bloody. Mother, the only older woman that I know really well, is always so neat and clean and well taken care of. This woman in the dream seemed, I don't know, evil somehow in spite of her being so helpless.

THERAPIST: Your mother is quite a burden on you at times isn't she?

CLIENT: Why, no! How can you say that? She's a wonderful person, and I'm glad to do what I can for her. She means more to me than anybody else.

THERAPIST: These things are pretty painful to think about at times, but I'm pretty impressed by your knowing only your mother as a helpless little old lady and your dreaming so repeatedly about killing just such a person. And *you* are the one who dreams it! (Shaffer & Shoben, 1956, pp. 516–7)[2]

Have you ever awakened during the course of a dream and thought, "I'm going to fix that dream in my mind so that I can recall it in the morning"? Even as you rehearse it in your mind, some of the details begin to slip away. The next morning you may not remember the dream or even the fact that you had a dream. One possible reason is that, once awake, our defenses begin to filter out the material that is objectionable. For this reason, the authors keep a pen and pencil on their bedstand so that some of the details can be jotted down. Other people we know keep a portable cassette tape recorder at their bedside.

During psychoanalysis, many complex relationships develop between the patient and the therapist. The therapist is often responded to emotionally as some adult figure who played a significant role in the patient's childhood. This unconscious process is known as **transference.** The patient may, at times, respond to a therapist *as if* he or she was a mother figure, a father figure, a sibling, or a spouse. Without understanding the reason, patients frequently alternate between attitudes of love and hate toward the therapist. The interpretation of this transference relationship may provide valuable insights into sources of earlier conflicts and emotions.

transference: a psychoanalytic term for the tendency of clients to project or transfer onto the therapist the emotional attitudes they felt toward other significant figures, such as parents or siblings.

Traditional psychoanalysis is usually expensive, long-term, and time-consuming, sometimes requiring as many as five sessions a week over many years. There have been numerous efforts in recent years to shorten the time requirements.

Client-Centered Therapy

Psychoanalysis takes the historical approach to the understanding of mental disorders. It assumes that the way we are now represents the totality of our experiences, from the moment we are born until the present. Further, it assumes that the only way to bring about permanent changes in the individual's mental well-being is to probe into that person's past experiences. Like a surgeon trying to remove an obstruction deep in the folds of the body, psychoanalysis tries to penetrate tissues of self-deception to reveal the root causes of conflicts. In so doing, psychoanalysts are often cast in the role of demigods. They frequently provide interpretations of the patient's behavior, verbalizations, and dreams. Moreover, while providing the opportunity to express emotions freely, intellectual rather than emotional considerations tend to dominate a psychoanalytic session.

---

[2] Laurance Frederic Shaffer and Edward Joseph Shoben, Jr. *The Psychology of Adjustment*, Second Edition, pp. 516–7. Copyright © 1956 by Houghton Mifflin Company. Used by permission.

Indeed, some have questioned the advisability of psychoanalytic therapy for those who are either inarticulate or of limited intelligence.

client-centered therapy: a nondirective form of therapy concerned primarily with the current adjustment of the individual.

In some ways, **client-centered therapy** is at the opposite pole. It is far less interested in the past history of the clients than it is in their present functioning. The emphasis turns away from, "Show me what happened in your past" to "Tell me what bothers you right now." Consequently, very little time is devoted to searching for underlying causes. Efforts are directed at improving the *current* level of adjustment of the individual. Further, client-centered therapy stresses the emotional rather than the intellectual growth of the individual. These features are evident in the following excerpt from a session with an 18-year-old boy. In his previous statements during the session, the client has said, "I don't want to be inferior in anything. . . . I try to cover the inferiority up as much as possible." The excerpt begins near the end of the interview.

CLIENT: Yes, but you can never destroy the things you're inferior in. They always remain where everybody can see 'em, right on the surface. No matter how well you can talk, no matter how well you can dance, no matter how good a time you are to the persons who are with you, you certainly can't wear a veil.

THERAPIST: M-hm. It's *looks* again, isn't it?

CLIENT: Yeah. I wish I was like my brother. He's dark, just as the rest of the family is. Me—I'm light—puny. He's heavier built than I am, too. Guess I was just made up of odds and ends. I'm too darn light. I don't like my face. I don't like my eyebrows and my eyes. Bloodshot, little cow eyes. I hate my pimple chin and I detest the way my face is lopsided. One side is so much different from the other. One side, the chin bones stick out further and the jaw bones are more pronounced. My mouth isn't right. Even when I smile, I don't smile the way other people do. I tried and I can't. When other people smile, their mouths go up—mine goes down. It's me; backward in everything. I'm clumsy as the devil.

THERAPIST: You feel sort of sorry for yourself, isn't that right?

CLIENT: Yes, self-pity, that's me. Sure I know I pity myself, but I got something to pity. If there were two of me I would punch myself right in the nose just for the fun of it.

THERAPIST: M-hm.

CLIENT: Sometimes I get so disgusted with myself!

THERAPIST: Sometimes you feel somewhat ashamed of yourself for pointing out all of those physical inadequacies, right?

CLIENT: Yes, I know I should forget them—yeah, forget them—I should think of something else. And that's—I hate myself because I'm not sure. That's just another thing I can hate myself for.

THERAPIST: You're sort of in a dilemma because you can't like yourself, and yet you dislike the fact that you don't like yourself.

CLIENT: M-hm. I know it isn't natural for a person not to like himself. In fact, most people are in love with themselves. They don't know quite so much of themselves. I've known people like that.

THERAPIST: M-hm.

CLIENT: But not me. [*pause*] I don't see how anybody loves me, even Mom. Maybe it's just maternal love. They can't help it, poor things. [*pause*]

THERAPIST: You feel so worthless you wonder how anyone would think much of you.

CLIENT: Yeah. But I'm not gonna worry about it. I've just gotta make up for it, that's all. I've just gotta forget it. And try to compensate for it.

THERAPIST: M-hm. [*pause*]

CLIENT: I've always tried to compensate for it. Everything I did in high school was to compensate for it.

THERAPIST: M-hm. You've never had much reason to think that people really cared about you, is that right?

CLIENT: That's right. Oh, if you only knew how they—

THERAPIST: M-hm.

CLIENT: Everything anyone ever said or ever did they were just trying to get something out of me. Or else they were. . . .

THERAPIST: It sort of made you feel inadequate not having the security of having people show that they cared a lot for you.

CLIENT: That's right.

THERAPIST: M-hm.

CLIENT: No one ever did. . . .[3]

A therapist and client interact during a client-centered therapy session.

Mike Jaeggi

Carl Rogers is to client-centered therapy what Sigmund Freud was to psychoanalysis. Both formulated theories of personality that formed the basis for treating people with mental disorders. Both use essentially "talk therapy" to bring about change in the individual's behaviors, emotional life, thoughts, and attitudes.

However, their approaches to life reveal basic differences that express themselves in the psychotherapeutic session. Freud saw us essentially as hapless victims of primitive, instinctual forces over which we have little direct control. Critics have argued that during much of psychoanalytic therapy, both the patient and the therapist wallow about in primordial ooze—exposing the seamy side of human nature in hopes of effecting change.

In contrast, Rogers and his followers present a basically optimistic approach to life. They do not regard the people seeking their help as "sick." Indeed, rather than being referred to as patients, they are called clients. They believe that people are essentially good and will choose constructive patterns in life given the opportunity. Thus, when not torn by conflicts, they will become productive and healthy human beings.

[3] Source: William U. Snyder, *Casebook of Non-Directive Counseling*. Copyright © 1947, Houghton Mifflin Company, used by permission.

The therapeutic atmosphere is also quite different. The psychoanalyst is often the dominant force during an analytic session, providing interpretations and becoming, at times, an object of love and, at other times, a hate object. In client-centered therapy, the therapist purposely assumes a low profile. It is the client who has center stage.

The environment is warm, friendly, supportive, and nonthreatening. Rogers believes that such an environment allows clients to accept aspects of themselves that they previously viewed negatively.

phenomenal self: a concept proposed by Rogers; the way individuals view themselves.

ideal self: a concept proposed by Rogers; the way the individual would like to be.

A key distinction is made between two selves—the **phenomenal self** (the way individuals view themselves) and the **ideal self** (the way they would like to be). The two selves are frequently at variance. All of us probably have experienced moments when we have done something that makes us feel ashamed or guilty. We may say such things to ourselves as "You idiot, why did you behave so badly toward Margo? Why can't you be the type of person I know you are?" When the two views of ourself are characteristically in conflict, we become unhappy or maladjusted. The well-adjusted person shows less of a disparity (Butler & Haigh, 1954).

Let's return to the case of Mrs. C and consider how she might be regarded by a client-centered therapist. To begin with, her adjustment was complicated by the enormous gap between the way she felt she must be to be worthy and the way her family wanted her to be. Her grooming habits—her frequent washing, her emphasis on cleanliness, and her denial of sexuality—were her unique way of saying, "Look at me. I am clean and without disease. I am worthy of your love and respect."

She saw herself as dirty and she wanted to be clean. But she perceived her family as making an impossible demand on her. They wanted her to stop washing! Only if she did so would they accept her and love her. But this is catch-22. Her self-esteem was threatened. If she did what was necessary to make her family happy, she would regard herself as unworthy. However, by continuing her preoccupation with cleanliness, she was in danger of losing their love.

According to client-centered therapy, caring is the basic issue rather than whether or not Mrs. C continues to wash and scrub, scrub and wash. It is vital that she experience the acceptance and esteem of another person who genuinely cares for her in spite of her "faults."

According to Rogers, constructive personality change in the client depends on three fundamental attitudes of the therapist: (1) genuineness in the relationship, (2) acceptance of the client, and (3) an accurate understanding of the client's phenomenal world. These attitudes are more significant than the orientation, amount of training, and the techniques of the therapist (Rogers, 1969).

Rational-Emotive Therapy

Although living a continent apart—Ellen on the east coast and Jeffrey on the west—they were joined for a moment by a common reversal in fortunes. Both had worked hard at their jobs with an advertising agency, lining up new accounts while going out of their way to maintain constructive relationships with existing accounts. When a new and important position opened up at their respective agencies, everyone assumed that they had the inside line. They seemed to have everything going for them. They were bright, industrious, sociable, and charismatic. Visiting clients would seek them out whenever the clients were in town.

Both they and their friends were shocked when their respective companies passed them up and hired an outsider to fill the new position. The immediate reaction of the two of them was the same—fury, a deep sense of loss, and despair. The self-esteem of both of them was at low ebb.

Their immediate reaction was as far as the similarity went. Jeffrey was unable to turn his hostility outward. His sense of being wronged churned inside of him like stew simmering in a kettle. He directed the full force of his fury at himself. "See what good it did you to break your back for the company? I really wanted this more than anything else in the world. I tried. God knows I tried. There must be something wrong with me. I guess I don't have what it takes." The more he thought, the deeper into despair and depression he sank.

Ellen was a study in contrast. She recovered with astonishing rapidity from her emotional down. "Damnit," she said to herself, "I have given this company the best of everything I have. I know I have done a better-than-average job and I deserved the promotion. But I refuse to let this thing derail me from my ambitions. I am continuing to learn on the job. I am getting better every day. It's just a matter of time and patience. Another opportunity will come and, when it does, I'll be there to grab it."

rational-emotive therapy: therapeutic approach that directs clients to change irrational beliefs and behavior.

These contrasting reactions to misfortune serve well to introduce some of the basic concepts of **rational-emotive therapy.** Albert Ellis, its founder, agrees with the psychoanalytic position that irrational forces underlie mental disorders. However, he sees digging in depth into a person's past as an exercise in futility. So what if patients gain insight into why they are thinking and behaving as they do? Will this knowledge, in and of itself, turn things around for them? "No," is Ellis' answer. He had observed many patients with remarkable insights into their past who seemed unchanged by this knowledge. They continued to drown in pools of unhappiness; they continued to make trouble for themselves.

According to Ellis, free association on the couch is far too passive to force the behavioral changes necessary for effective adjustment. Patients have many false beliefs and erroneous reasoning processes that cannot remain unchallenged. These must be vigorously challenged so that patients are forced to repudiate irrational ideas, beliefs, and assumptions. A rational-emotive therapist would not permit Jeffrey to lie on a couch and free associate on why he feels he is a failure. He would be challenged to prove he is a failure and poorly suited for his chosen vocation.

The first three letters of the alphabet can be used to summarize the rational-emotive theory of personality. First are the *A*ctivating Events, such as an outbreak of disease in a family or failure to gain an expected and well-deserved promotion. These events activate the *B*elief Systems which are involved in the processing and interpretation of the activating events. These beliefs may be either rational (rB) or irrational (iB). A rational belief activated by the failure to be promoted could be, "It's a great disappointment but life must go on. In the meantime I'll continue to give my utmost and I'll continue to grow. My efforts will someday pay off." On the reverse side of the coin, an irrational belief might consist of nonproductive and counterproductive thoughts such as, "I am a failure. All my efforts were to no avail. I should find a different line of work."

The *C*onsequences of the Activating Events well be emotionally healthy and productive if processed through a rational belief system. True, there may be an immediate sense of grief, disappointment, sadness, and other negative emotional reactions. However, the healthy orientation of the person's life will increase that individual's determination to change whatever can be changed.

What happens when the Activating Event is processed through an irrational belief system? The Consequences are continued misery, poor productivity, and useless, self-defeating behaviors. Box 13.2 summarizes 12 irrational ideas that Ellis believes are common to this culture.

BOX 13.2 TWELVE "IRRATIONAL" IDEAS

You might find it interesting to see which of these beliefs you have entertained at one time or another in your life. Since such ideas are so much a part of many people's thinking, it would not be at all unusual to agree with a number of the beliefs listed below.

1. The idea that you must, yes, must have sincere love and approval almost all the time from all the people you find significant.

2. The idea that you must prove yourself thoroughly competent, adequate, and achieving; or that you must at least have real competence or talent at something important.

3. The idea that people who harm you or commit misdeeds rate as generally bad, wicked, or villainous individuals, and that you should severely blame, damn, and punish them for their sins.

4. The idea that life proves awful, terrible, horrible, or catastrophic when things do not go the way you would like them to go.

5. The idea that emotional misery comes from external pressures and that you have little ability to control your feelings or rid yourself of depression and hostility.

6. The idea that if something seems dangerous or fearsome, you must become terribly occupied with and upset about it.

7. The idea that you will find it easier to avoid facing many of life's difficulties and self-responsibilities than to undertake some rewarding forms of self-discipline.

8. The idea that your past remains all-important and that, because something once strongly influenced your life, it has to keep determining your feelings and behavior today.

9. The idea that people and things should turn out better than they do and that you have to view it as awful and horrible if you do not quickly find good solutions to life's hassles.

10. The idea that you can achieve happiness by inertia and inaction or by passively and uncommittedly "enjoying yourself."

11. The idea that you must have a high degree of order or certainty to feel comfortable, or that you need some supernatural power on which to rely.

12. The idea that you give yourself a global rating as a human and that your general worth and self-acceptance depend upon the goodness of your performance and the degree that people approve of you.

Source: Adapted from Albert Ellis and Russell Grieger, *Handbook of Rational-Emotive Therapy*, pp. 12–13. Copyright © 1977 by Springer Publishing Company, Inc., New York. Used by permission.

In Ellis' view, many therapies devote too much time and effort to the Activating Event. To illustrate, psychoanalysis searches into the deepest layers of the individual's history. But the past is past. It cannot be changed. Knowledge of past events may provide some insights, but insights do not in and of themselves change irrational beliefs. Other therapies direct their attention to the other end of the scale, the Consequences. People are encouraged to openly discuss and express their emotions—tell all about their feelings when they are depressed, anxious, fearful, jealous, or angry. However, expressing emotions leaves the Belief System untouched. It does not change irrational beliefs, although it may make people with irrational beliefs feel better for a while. Behavior is also a Consequence. Getting people to change their behaviors without corresponding alterations in their belief structure, will not produce permanent gains.

Rather, rational-emotive therapy goes right to the core of the Belief System, directing its attention and energies to analysis and understanding of, and attack upon the irrational belief structure of the client. To illustrate, what irrational beliefs in Mrs. C's system would be subject to challenge during the course of therapy? Certainly the belief that she must be without fault or blemish—free of disease, dirt, and unclean desires—to be loved. What about the pinworm episode? Are the consequences of pinworms sufficiently severe that they must be treated as a major disaster? Above all, the belief must be attacked that her carelessness had contributed to her family's earlier episode of flu and pinworms. It should be noted that rational-emotive therapy is not as easy as ABC. Irrational beliefs are protected by strong defensive mechanisms and "reasoning" under the guise of rationality. Irrational beliefs do not die easily.

Behavior Therapy

behavior therapy: psychotherapeutic approach which employs classical conditioning and operant learning techniques in an attempt to eliminate or modify problem behavior, addressing itself primarily to the client's overt behavior, as opposed to thoughts, feelings, or other cognitive processes (American Psychological Association, 1982).

Behavior therapy is the application of the principles of both classical and operant conditioning to the modification of maladaptive behavior. The attention of the behavior therapist is directed at the behavior rather than the underlying causes. Thus, like client-centered therapy and rational-emotive therapy, it does not focus on the past and gaining insights from the history of the individual. The advocates of behavior therapy have a different way of looking at behavioral disorders. To illustrate, its adherents do not regard disorders as the end product of complex unconscious conflicts, disparities between the phenomenal and ideal selves, or irrational beliefs. Behavior therapists simply regard behavioral disorders as a collection of bad habits. Since all habits (good and bad) are learned, they can also be unlearned.

Let's again look at Mrs. C, this time from the point of view of the behavioral therapist. Behavioral therapists would *not* look to unconscious processes, such as unsatisfied anal impulses, for an explanation of her aversion to dirt, disease, and sex. They would argue that she had been trained to avoid unclean situations through conditioning and/or modeling. Thus, for understanding, they would look at her prior training and at those who served as models for her behavior. Significant persons in her life (such as her mother and father) punished her or threatened

Desensitization therapy begins by teaching clients to relax as they are taken through a series of graduated exercises from least to most stressful. The client has her index finger raised to signal that she is visualizing the anxiety-provoking situation.

Courtesy Joseph Wolpe

to do so if she engaged in unclean behavior. They also rewarded her for avoiding situations that were dirty. The result was behavior that was merely an exaggerated form of activities that gained parental approval. Thus, she avoided washing or even handling once-worn underwear as well as the "messy" jobs of cooking or engaging in sex. Moreover, her mother was also an excellent model from whom she could learn to be anxious in the presence of dirt and sexual stimuli. Mrs. C learned all too well from that model.

The behavioral treatment of Mrs. C must focus on disassociating her anxiety from stimuli she regarded as dirty. For example, she might be taught to relax in the presence of "forbidden" stimuli. Only then would she be free to acquire different and adaptive behaviors in the presence of these stimuli.

The techniques employed in behavior therapy are based on the principles of conditioning discussed in Chapter 2. They include extinction, desensitization, modeling, use of positive reinforcement, and use of aversive conditioning.

All of us experience certain situations or events that arouse greater amounts of discomfort or emotionality than we find in other circumstances. We could probably construct a hierarchy in which we listed stimuli in order, from those that produce the least emotionality or discomfort to those that produce the most. In *desensitization therapy,* each patient first learns to relax. When this behavior is acquired, they are told to imagine a situation which is low on their hierarchy (least discomfort producing). If they are successful in relaxing while imagining this situation, they are asked to imagine the next higher item in the hierarchy. When a stimulus produces tension, they are told to stop and concentrate on relaxing again. These procedures gradually lead the patients through a series of increasingly emotion-arousing stimuli until they are able to tolerate the situation that is highest on their list.

In the following example, desensitization therapy was used with a college student who was absolutely terrified of examinations.

> He first made up a hierarchy of circumstances which he felt produced fear responses. He was then instructed in relaxation of muscle groups. The lowest item on his anxiety hierarchy list, being asked a question by his kid brother, was then presented while the patient was relaxing. When it was evident that this situation was well tolerated, the next item on the list was evoked, and so on. Within a month, the student reported being able to undertake examinations with only a modicum of tension. The patient returned, however, during final examinations with a recurrence of his paralyzing fear. Retraining continued with an emphasis on generalizing the relaxation responses to a wider variety of evaluational situations. Excellent progress has been noted and the student has recently been notified of his acceptability for graduate admissions. (Suinn, 1970, p. 242)

GROUP AND ALTERNATIVE THERAPIES

About nine people file into a room slowly, tentatively. Each has seen only one other person in the room: the therapist, a week earlier, in a diagnostic interview. Some appear reluctant, some enthusiastic, but all have come to this first meeting with at least the willingness to go along with the therapist's belief that the group could be useful to them. They sit in a circle, quiet and expectant. Their posture reveals a bit of anxiety. What will go on here? What can go on here? What will the therapist do? Several in the group have had previous psychotherapy. One woman begins the interaction by describing her current predicament and the disappointments she experienced in previous treatments. Others chime in. Sympathetic offerings of similar tales of woe are heard from various people in the room. From time to time the therapist comments, pointing out the expectations of the various group members. People are beginning to get to know one another. Each of the people is attending for a different reason, but they all share some similar concerns. Will the group members accept me? Are there other people in this room with similar problems and concerns? Will I be really understood? Can I take risks with these people? After the first session, all of the group members have had an opportunity to express why they came and what their expectations are for future meetings. This is but one of many different types of groups. But for this group, for these people, group therapy begins. Adapted from Lieberman, 1975)

group therapy: psychotherapy in which several people are treated at the same time.

Many emotional problems involve interpersonal relations. People often have difficulty communicating and interacting with others. **Group therapy** provides an opportunity to work out these problems in a setting which is more like the real world than the protected atmosphere of individual therapy. Individuals can try out new ways of relating to others; they can practice and improve their social skills. Indeed, group treatment is especially useful for treating social difficulties such as forming and maintaining personal relations (Parloff & Dies, 1977). Moreover, group members may help each other by providing support and encouragement. For some people, just knowing that they're not alone in their struggle to meet life's challenges, that other people have problems too, can be both a relief and a push toward change and growth.

Group treatment was a necessary outgrowth of the increased demand for psychological services accompanied by a severe shortage of trained therapists to treat people individually. In the group situation, several people are treated at one time. There are a variety of group treatment approaches, including groups organized to combat specific problems such as alcoholism, drugs, or divorce. Virtually all types of therapy are represented in the group treatment spectrum. Some groups represent an extension of traditional psychotherapeutic techniques, whereas others completely depart from these procedures. Some groups have experienced professional leaders while others have no leader at all.

One variation of the conventional talking techniques involves the use of psychodrama in which the individual acts out conflicts and feelings in a simulated real-life setting. For example, suppose a young man is disturbed about his relationship with his family. He might act out a typical family fight in which other group members play the roles of his parents, brothers, and sisters. Then he might switch and play the role of another member of the family. Often this *role reversal* helps the individual to empathize with and better understand the conflicts from another person's point of view. Psychodrama provides the opportunity to resolve conflicts, try out solutions to problems, and gain greater awareness of one's self and others.

There are a wide variety of therapeutic avenues the emotionally distressed

A group therapy session.

Sue Markson

can explore. Help is offered in homes, businesses, weekend retreats, over the radio or television, and even in your neighborhood bookstore. Even those who don't really feel distressed can find help to guide them toward greater self-fulfillment. Moreover, clients are no longer limited to just talking. They can scream, run around nude, stay up for days, or touch and feel their way to greater openness and trust.

encounter group: a group of people who meet with the goal of expressing feelings openly and honestly.

One popular form of group therapy is the **encounter group** in which members are encouraged to recognize and express their feelings openly and honestly. Treatment is seen as an intense emotional experience and may include a great deal of touching, kissing, yelling, and even crying. The goal is to shed the masks worn in public and present the "true" self. Emphasis is placed on activities and conversations that encourage people to respond with open displays of emotion, hostility, affection, approval, or criticism. It is assumed that people will grow in positive directions when freed of artificial barriers erected against seeing the true self. Members are encouraged to tear down facades and defenses in encounters that can be brutally frank.

The effects of encounter groups are still somewhat controversial. Some individuals report gains in openness, honesty, and empathy after participation (Rogers, 1970). Most findings, however, have been lukewarm. The changes that occur are often not so great or long lasting as proponents would like to believe. In fact, the experience may even be destructive (Hartley, Roback, & Abramowitz, 1976). An unstable individual guided by an inexperienced leader may feel threatened and suffer harmful psychological consequences when defenses are withdrawn (Yalom & Lieberman, 1971). Moreover, many critics feel that encounter group interactions are too superficial, especially if problems are deep-rooted. The openness that is encouraged during group meetings may not carry over into everyday life. The impersonal atmosphere of school or work usually doesn't encourage openness and trust.

In one study of encounter groups, 200 students were randomly assigned to 17 different groups representing 10 different styles of therapy. Control group members did not participate in any of the groups. Assessments were made six months and one year after participation. Generally, the results were not encouraging—about one third showed some positive gains, one third were adversely affected by the experience, and one third showed no changes. Those students who participated in the encounter group experience seemed no better or worse off than the control subjects (Lieberman, Yalom, & Miles, 1973).

Much of the benefit or cost of encounter group experiences seem to depend, to a large extent, on the leader. Leaders that are seen as warm, skilled at interpreting experiences, and not too pushy in encouraging participation and giving orders are the most helpful (Lieberman et al., 1973).

Although there are many variations of the group treatment experience, let us look at one which has received considerable attention. Erhard Seminars Training (EST) were begun in 1971 by Jack Rosenberg, a former used car salesman who changed his name to Werner Erhard. Seminars are held in various public facilities for 60 hours over two weekends. A variety of techniques are utilized, ranging from aggressive confrontation to exercises in relaxation and trust. The avowed goal of EST is to accept oneself. Once participants have done so, they have "gotten IT." IT costs about $350 whether or not you get it. What is IT? One participant described the conclusion of an EST seminar:

> At the end of the training, the trainer asks if people "got it." One group of people say they got it; they are applauded. Then another group says they weren't sure they got it; the trainer talks to them and they all say they got it. One group says they definitely didn't get it. He talks to all but one, and finally this last person says he didn't get it, and the trainer says, "Well, you got it, 'cause there's nothing to get" and they turn the whole thing into a joke. (Gordon, 1976, pp. 298–9)

Some of the critics of EST suggest that the experience may do more harm than good, especially for those with poor self-esteem and a low tolerance for group criticism (Kirsch & Glass, 1977). Some people cannot handle the confrontations and find it threatening to have their defenses attacked and torn down. There have been some reports of psychotic breakdowns in people with no previous history of mental disorder after completing EST training (Glass, Kirsch, & Parris, 1977). Since EST and other alternative forms of treatment may be threatening to certain types of personalities, applicants should be carefully screened for signs of instability or severe emotional disturbance.

What about self-help books? Can they help to reduce emotional stress, make you happier, and lead you toward greater self-fulfillment? The advertisements for many of these books certainly promise answers to any and all problems. There are some who believe that self-help literature can be valuable especially in improving interpersonal relations, reducing tension, and increasing self-esteem. However, most professionals caution against relying solely on self-help books as psychological counselors.

The stresses and strains of daily life produce a certain amount of anxiety, depression, and discomfort as a normal part of everyday living. Self-help books may suggest that these emotions are maladaptive. Perfectly well-adjusted people may get the false impression that they are not coping well if they experience these normal emotions. Moreover, severely disturbed individuals may delay getting much needed professional help if they believe these books can help solve their problems (Bevcar, 1978).

Family Therapy

Traditionally, therapists have focused exclusively on the individual, apart from his or her surroundings. However, in recent years, many therapists have begun to acknowledge the importance of the individual's social context. New mental-health techniques have evolved which place a greater emphasis on the importance of family relationships to the mental health of the individual. A whole new form of therapy, known as family therapy, has begun to attract a wide variety of practitioners.

One of the leaders in family therapy describes the differences between individual and family therapy:

> A therapist oriented to individual therapy still tends to see the individual as the site of pathology and to gather only the data that can be obtained from or about the individual. For instance, an adolescent boy might be referred to therapy because he is shy and daydreams in class. He is a loner, with difficulty relating to his peers. A therapist who operates in individual sessions would explore the boy's thoughts and feelings about his present life and the people in it, the historical development of his conflict with parents and siblings, and the compulsive intrusion of this conflict into extrafamilial, seemingly unrelated situations. He would establish contact with the family and the school, but to understand the boy and the boy's relationship with his family, he would rely mainly on the content of the boy's communication and on transferential phenomena. An internal cognitive-affective rearrangement is regarded as the necessary step to facilitate improvement of the presenting problem. . . . If the same boy were referred to a family therapist, the therapist would explore his interactions within significant life contexts. In family interviews, the therapist would observe the relationship of the boy and his mother, with its mingled closeness and hostility. He might see that when the boy talks in the presence of his parents, he rarely addresses his father, or that when he does talk to his father, he tends to do so through his mother, who translates and explains her son to her husband. He might notice that other siblings seem more spontaneous, interrupt the parents, and talk to the father and mother alike. Thus, the therapist does not have to depend on the boy's descriptions of his father, mother, and siblings to postulate the introjection of the familial figures. The family members are present, demonstrating behavior in relation to the boy that can be operationally described. The broader focus and the greater flexibility opened to the therapist enhance the possibilities for therapeutic intervention. The therapist is not restricted to the family interaction as internalized by the boy, but can himself experience the way in which the family members support and qualify each other. He then develops a transactional theory to explain the phenomena he is observing. He can also be in touch with the boy's school, since the presenting problem is related to school performance, and the theories and techniques of family therapy lend themselves readily to work with the individual in contexts other than the family.
>
> Thus, the family therapist does not conceive of an "essential" personality, remaining unchanged throughout the vicissitudes of different contexts and circumstances. He sees the boy as a member of different social contexts, acting and reacting within them. His concept of the site of pathology is much broader, and so are the possibilities for intervention.[4]

---

[4] Source: Reprinted by permission of the publishers from *Families and Family Therapy*, by Salvador Minuchin, Cambridge, Mass.: Harvard University Press, copyright © 1974 by the President and Fellows of Harvard College.

**MEDICAL
THERAPIES**

psychosurgery: a
controversial technique
for treating emotional
disturbances by cutting
or destroying parts of the
brain.

There are a number of techniques used for treating mental disorders which do not involve psychological methods. Some involve altering the chemistry or structure of the body. These techniques are either used alone or in conjunction with various psychotherapeutic methods.

Of all the medical therapies, the most controversial is **psychosurgery**—surgery done on the brain to treat mental disturbances. When first introduced, psychosurgery was used fairly often. But then some discouraging findings dampened the enthusiasm for this drastic and irreversible procedure. Some patients emerged from the operation little more than "vegetables," and some experienced irreversible side effects such as impaired intellectual functioning (Valenstein, 1973). Consequently, psychosurgery is now used only occasionally and usually as a last resort.

A less dramatic, but still controversial form of medical therapy involves passing an electric current through the brain for just a fraction of a second and is known

A patient being prepared for ECT.

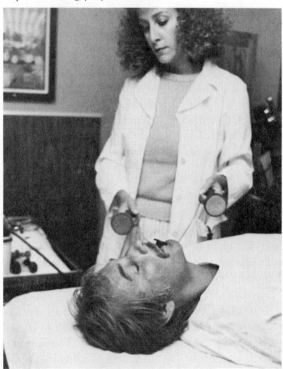

Sue Markson

electroconvulsive (electroshock) therapy (ECT): a type of medical therapy in which an electric current is passed through the brain.

as **electroconvulsive (electroshock) therapy (ECT).** Patients treated with ECT go into a brief convulsion and then lapse into unconsciousness for a short time. When they wake up, they are often confused and may suffer some memory loss for a while. Some people are left with a permanent memory loss (Squire, et al., 1981). We don't know why ECT works, when it does, but it appears to be effective for treating depression, especially severe depression (Scovern & Kilmann, 1980). Because of its fast action, it may even be the treatment of choice for a depressed patient considered to be at risk for suicide.

Perhaps the most promising of all the medical therapies is **chemotherapy** which involves the use of drugs to treat mental disorders.

chemotherapy: a therapeutic technique involving the treatment of disorders through the use of drugs.

Sometimes tension and anxiety levels are so high that normal functioning is impaired. **Minor tranquilizers** such as Valium, Miltown, and Librium are commonly used to alleviate such feelings. However, there are often undesirable side effects to these drugs, and sudden withdrawal can be harmful. Consequently, tranquilizers should be used with care and only under medical advice.

minor tranquilizers: drugs used to produce relaxation and reduce anxiety and tension.

A number of drugs, known as **antidepressants,** have proved to be effective in treating depression. Indeed, a review of studies of 6,000 patients found that four widely used antidepressants led to improvement in approximately 65 percent of the cases (Wechsler, Grosser, & Greenblatt, 1965).

antidepressants: drugs used to counteract depression.

The most dramatic effects of chemotherapy have been found with the **antipsychotic drugs.** These drugs, also known as the major tranquilizers, brought radical changes to the treatment of schizophrenia. First introduced in the 1950s, a drug called chlorpromazine reduced such symptoms as delusions, hallucinations, and disordered thinking. Schizophrenic patients showed increased rates of improvement and the proportion in mental hospitals sharply declined. Within a few years of its discovery, chlorpromazine and other antipsychotic drugs were being used as the primary form of treatment for psychotic individuals, particularly schizophrenics. Many schizophrenic patients are now able to leave the hospital and return to society to lead reasonably normal lives.

antipsychotic drugs: drugs that alleviate psychotic symptoms, making patients more manageable and amenable to other forms of treatment.

DOES THERAPY WORK?

One of the harshest critics of psychotherapy, Hans Eysenck (1952), startled everyone when he concluded that psychotherapy was no more helpful than the mere passage of time. He surveyed the research literature on therapy and found that about two thirds of the people seemed to improve whether or not they received any formal treatment.

Eysenck's findings were vehemently challenged and attacked. His methods and choice of sample were severely criticized. Nonetheless, his work served as a catalyst to stimulate much research on the assessment of therapy. It also helped to focus on the inherent difficulties of obtaining convincing evidence that therapy is effective. There is relatively little carefully controlled research in this area because of a variety of problems. For one, therapy is often a long, complicated procedure. The experience may be extremely variable and thus resistant to a precise description. Also, how "success" is defined can be a tricky problem. How do you determine whether a client has improved and, if so, to what extent?

In the most careful studies, judges rate participants before and after therapy, without knowing whether or not the patient has received any treatment. In general, the research findings show that various therapeutic techniques are not as successful as their supporters would like to believe. However, although therapy doesn't help everybody, on the whole there are modest but positive gains (Bergin & Suinn, 1975; Smith & Glass, 1977). In some cases though, therapy may actually be harmful. One study (Bergin, 1971) found deterioration that could be attributed to therapy in about 5 percent of the cases investigated.

Is one method better than another? Advocates of the various "schools" of therapy often claim high rates of success for their techniques, but there is little evidence to support these claims. Indeed, the superiority of one form of therapy over another has not yet been effectively demonstrated.

In one study, 90 outpatients were randomly assigned for four months to one of three groups—short-term psychoanalytic therapy, behavior therapy, or minimal treatment. The clients were generally anxious, depressed, or otherwise distressed. None was severely disturbed. The therapists were prominent and experienced. Independent judges who did not know to which group the client was assigned made extremely comprehensive assessments both before and after treatment. On the average, all three groups showed some improvement—which shows that time itself can sometimes heal emotional wounds. However, clients in the two treatment groups improved more than those with minimal treatment. Behavioral and psychoanalytic approaches appeared equally effective (Sloane, Staples, Cristol, Yorkston, & Whipple, 1975).

A therapist will often draw on a variety of schools or techniques as they seem appropriate and thus tailor the therapy to meet the needs of the client. Many therapists no longer rely on one particular method; they choose whatever technique seems most promising in each case.

A number of studies have shown that the personal characteristics of therapists are more important than the techniques they use (Gomes-Schwartz, Hadley, & Strupp, 1978). Those therapists able to develop warm, close relationships and a strong trusting bond between themselves and their clients are usually most effective.

In one study, clients were treated either by highly experienced therapists or by college professors who had demonstrated the ability to form warm and understanding relationships. The professors were drawn from such diverse fields as English, history, and mathematics. Participants in both groups improved equally (Gomes-Schwartz et al., 1978).

What about the client? Do some people benefit more than others from the therapy experience? The evidence seems to indicate that clients who are intelligent and highly motivated are likely to make the best use of therapy (Luborsky et al., 1971). The nature of the problem is important, too. The less serious problems show the greatest improvements. A person with a minor adjustment problem, of fairly recent origin, stands a better chance in therapy than those with severe and long-standing maladjustments (Gomes-Schwartz et al., 1978). For example, the antisocial personality is extremely resistant to therapy. These people do not seem to profit or learn from past mistakes and don't experience the anxiety that other disturbed people are so eager to escape.

Thus it seems that a sincere desire to change and rid oneself of maladaptive behavior is one of the keys to success in therapy. Further, likelihood of success is increased if one believes that the treatment will help, sees the therapist as warm and understanding, and is doing his or her best to proceed in ways that will provide relief.

SUMMARY

- About 1 person in 10 will seek professional help at some point in life. Several factors that might affect one's decision to seek help are: severity of discomfort; significant negative changes in various aspects of behavior; other people suggesting help is needed; and persistent suicidal thoughts. A variety of community or college psychological services are available.

- Psychological and psychotherapeutic counseling overlap to a large extent, particularly in the area of personal adjustment counseling. Psychotherapy refers to treatment through psychological methods; medical treatment methods are called medical therapy.

- Four types of individual therapies were discussed: psychoanalysis, client-centered therapy, rational-emotive therapy, and behavior therapy.

- Psychoanalysis attempts to have the client gain insight into maladaptive behavior by uncovering repressed impulses and conflicts through such techniques as free association and dream analysis.

- Client-centered therapy stresses the here-and-now adjustment of the individual with a special emphasis on emotional growth.

- In rational-emotive therapy, the individual is challenged to abandon irrational beliefs and behaviors.

- Behavior therapy uses the principles of conditioning to help clients change behavior.

- A variety of techniques have been developed for the simultaneous treatment of several people. Many groups are merely extensions of traditional psychotherapeutic techniques, while others represent a departure from the conventional methods.

- Medical therapies include psychosurgery, electroshock therapy, and chemotherapy. These methods may be used alone or in conjunction with various psychotherapeutic techniques.

- It is difficult to assess the effectiveness of therapy. The evidence seems to indicate that individuals do benefit from the various therapeutic techniques; however, no one technique has yet proved superior over the others. The most important factors for successful therapy appear to be the personal characteristics of the therapist and his or her ability to establish a strong trusting bond with the patient.

TERMS TO REMEMBER

Psychotherapy	Behavior therapy
Medical therapy	Group therapy
Psychoanalysis	Encounter group
Free association	Psychosurgery
Resistance	Electroconvulsive (electroshock) therapy (ECT)
Transference	
Client-centered therapy	Chemotherapy
Phenomenal self	Minor tranquilizers
Ideal self	Antidepressants
Rational-emotive therapy	Antipsychotic drugs

GLOSSARY

Achievement motive: The desire to do well and succeed.

Addiction: Physiological dependence on (need for) a drug.

Affiliation: The need to be with others and to form attachments to them.

Aggression: Physical or verbal attack intended to harm or injure. Whereas anger is an emotion, aggression is behavior. Anger does not always lead to aggressive behavior and aggression does not always stem from anger.

Altruism: The act of helping others without expectation of personal gain.

Ambivalent: Mixed feelings, both positive and negative, toward a person, an object, or a situation.

Amniocentesis: The surgical procedure used to obtain fluid from a pregnant woman. This fluid is then analyzed to determine whether there are genetic abnormalities in the fetus.

Androgyny: The ability to integrate both "masculine" and "feminine" characteristics as the situation requires.

Anorexia nervosa: A disorder characterized by an extreme loss of body weight secondary to voluntarily limiting food intake.

Antidepressants: Drugs used to counteract depression.

Antipsychotic drugs: Drugs that alleviate psychotic symptoms, making patients more manageable and amenable to other forms of treatment.

Antisocial personality: A personality disorder characterized by the absence of anxiety and the inability to learn from experience.

Anxiety: Vague unpleasant feeling; a premonition that something bad will happen.

Anxiety disorders: A group of disorders in which anxiety is the primary disturbance.

Anxiety states: A disorder characterized by excessive and persistent levels of anxiety.

Assertiveness: Standing up for your rights without violating the rights of others.

Assertiveness training: Training in the social skills required to be able to refuse requests; to express both positive and negative feelings; to initiate, engage in, and terminate conversation; and to make personal requests without suffering from excessive stress. (APA, 1982)

Attribution theory: A theory concerned with the rules we use to make judgments about the causes of behavior.

Autonomic nervous system (ANS): The part of the nervous system which regulates the heart, stomach, intestines, genitals, blood vessels, and other internal organs. The ANS controls such reactions as trembling, pulse rate, blood pressure, and perspiration.

Behavior therapy: Psychotherapeutic approach which employs classical conditioning and operant learning techniques in an attempt to eliminate or modify problem behavior, addressing itself primarily to the client's overt behavior, as opposed to thoughts, feelings, or other cognitive processes (APA, 1982).

Biofeedback: A technique which allows the individual to monitor and control his or her own internal bodily functions.

Biological drives: Motives that arise from the physiological state of the organism, e.g., hunger.

Blunted affect: When the feeling or experience of emotion is dulled or deadened.

Bulimia: A disorder characterized by eating binges followed by self-induced purges involving vomiting or laxitives.

Castration anxiety: In Freudian theory, a boy's fear that his father will castrate him in retaliation for his oedipal desires.

Catastrophizing: Exaggerating the importance or significance of a situation; blowing up a problem into a major disaster.

Central nervous system: The brain and spinal cord.

Chemotherapy: A therapeutic technique involving the treatment of disorders through the use of drugs.

Classical conditioning: A form of learning in which a formerly neutral stimulus, through repeated pairings with a stimulus that elicits a response, acquires the capacity to elicit the response made to the original stimulus.

Client-centered therapy: A nondirective form of therapy concerned primarily with the current adjustment of the individual.

Climacteric: The time of life associated with various glandular and bodily changes in men.

Clitoris: An extremely sensitive structure of the female external genitals; the principal organ of sexual excitement in the female.

Cognitions: An individual's thoughts, ideas, and knowledge.

Coitus: A technical term for heterosexual intercourse.

Compulsion: Ritualistic behavior an individual feels compelled to repeat.

Concentration: Focusing complete attention on the situation at hand.

Concrete operational stage: In Piaget's theory, the final stage of cognitive development during which the child develops the ability to deal with abstract relationships.

Conditional positive regard: Acceptance of the value of a person based on the acceptability of that person's behavior.

Conditioned response: In classical conditioning, the learned response to a previously neutral stimulus.

Conditioned stimulus: In classical conditioning, the neutral stimulus after it has acquired the capacity to elicit the conditioned response.

Condom: A latex or membrane sheath that fits over the penis and is used to prevent conception or infection.

Conflict: The simultaneous arousal of two or more incompatible motives.

Conservation: The concept that certain properties (e.g., quantity, volume) of objects remain the same in spite of alterations in their appearance.

Contraceptive methods: Techniques used to prevent fertilization and conception.

Coping mechanisms: Those behaviors and thoughts that deal directly with the causes of strain.

Critical period: A time of maximum readiness for the development of a particular skill or behavior.

Defense mechanisms: Devices used to alleviate or avoid anxiety associated with strain.

Delusion: An unshakable belief despite contrary evidence. Common delusions are delusions of grandeur (the belief that one is a very important person) and delusions of persecution ("they're out to get me").

Denial: A defense mechanism in which one simply denies an unpleasant reality.

Desensitization: A technique for reducing anxiety by systematically pairing relaxation with the anxiety-arousing situation.

Diaphragm: A birth control device that is inserted into the vagina and used with spermicidal jelly or cream.

Discrimination: Learning to respond in a different manner to similar stimuli.

Displacement: A defense mechanism in which unacceptable impulses are redirected to something or someone other than the original source.

Dissociative disorders: Disorders which involve some disturbance in memory, usually to escape or avoid anxiety-arousing situations.

Drug abuser: A person who uses drugs to excess and is unable to function without them.

Drug user: A person who uses drugs, but not to excess.

Egocentrism: The inability to see things from any perspective except one's own.

Ego-dystonic homosexuality: A disorder in which sexual orientation is a persistent source of distress and conflict.

Ejaculation: The process whereby semen is suddenly expelled out of the body through the penis during the male's orgasm.

Electra complex: In Freudian theory, a young girl's unconscious sexual desires for her father.

Electroconvulsive (electroshock) therapy (ECT): A type of medical therapy in which an electric current is passed through the brain.

Electroencephalograph (EEG): An instrument used to record the electrical activity of the brain.

Embryonic period: Human development from the time of implantation to about the eighth week after conception.

Emotion: Complex state involving physiological reactions, situational factors, cognitions, feelings, and behavior.

Empathy: The ability to see things from another person's perspective.

Encounter group: A group of people who meet with the goal of expressing feelings openly and honestly.

Epinephrine: A hormone produced by the adrenal glands that activates the body during times of emotion or stress.

Erectile inhibition: A sexual difficulty in which the male is unable to achieve an erection in response to sexual stimulation, sometimes called impotence.

Erection: When a sexual organ (penis, clitoris) becomes engorged with blood, causing it to become rigid.

Erogenous zones: Sensitive areas of the body that become the centers of sexual pleasure.

Eustress: According to Selye, "good" stress that is beneficial to the individual.

Excitatory nucleus: A group of neurons that activate the behavior for which it is responsible. For example, activation of the excitatory nucleus for eating leads to increased eating.

Excitement phase: The first part of the sexual response cycle in which the sexual organs become engorged with blood, and there are increases in heart rate, respiration, and muscle tension.

Expectancy: Anticipating or predicting an outcome based on past experiences.

Experimental extinction: The reduction in response strength that occurs in classical conditioning when the conditioned stimulus is repeatedly presented *without* the unconditioned stimulus.

Fetus: The unborn infant from about the end of the second month after conception until birth.

Fixation: In Freudian theory, arrested development at a particular psychosexual stage.

Formal operational stage: In Piaget's theory, the final stage of cognitive development during which the child develops the ability to deal with abstract relationships.

Frame of reference: One's unique standard of beliefs and attitudes by which one evaluates events and situations.

Free association: A psychoanalytic tool in which clients, made as relaxed as possible, are encouraged to report all thoughts and feelings as they occur.

Free-floating anxiety: Anxiety that is diffuse and without focus.

Frustration: A blocking or thwarting of goal-directed activities.

Fugue: A dissociative disorder in which the individual leaves home, assumes a new identity, and is unable to recall his or her previous identity.

Genitals: Male and female sexual organs.

Gonorrhea: A venereal disease in which the mucous membranes become inflamed.

Group therapy: Psychotherapy in which several people are treated at the same time.

Habituation: Psychological dependence on (need for) a drug.

Hallucination: Imaginary sensation such as seeing, hearing, or feeling things that do not exist.

Herpes: Blisters on the skin caused by a virus which may be transmitted via sexual contact.

Hypochondriasis: Disorder characterized by numerous physical complaints that have no organic basis.

Hypotheses: Proposed explanations of the relationships between events or variables that can be examined in the light of relevant evidence.

Ideal self: A concept proposed by Rogers; the way the individual would like to be.

Inhibitory nucleus: A group of neurons that suppress or curb the behavior for which it is responsible. For example, activation of the inhibitory nucleus for eating leads to decreased eating.

Internal communications: Thoughts that create stress. They may occur so quickly that we are often unaware of them. However, they may influence our behavior by interacting with the environmental situation.

Internalize: To incorporate the norms and values of society into one's internal system of values.

Interpersonal relations: Relationships involving two or more people.

Intrauterine devices (IUDs): Small plastic coils or loops that are inserted into the uterus for contraception.

Isolation: A defense mechanism in which one separates conflicting thoughts or impulses by putting them into separate "compartments."

Learned helplessness: The belief that one's actions are ineffective and have little to do with the outcome.

Lipostat: A mechanism in the hypothalamus that sets the amount of fat the organism needs for maintenance.

Major affective disorders: Psychosis and related thought disturbances characterized by severe disturbances of feeling or mood.

Maladaptive behavior: Behavior that fails to conform to the requirements of the situation.

Masturbation: Stimulation of one's own genitals to achieve sexual gratification.

Maturation: Developmental changes that follow a genetically preprogrammed growth process.

Medical therapy: The use of medical methods to treat emotional disturbances.

Menopause: The period in a woman's life when menstruation ceases.

Minor tranquilizers: Drugs used to produce relaxation and reduce anxiety and tension.

Motivation: A general term referring to the forces that determine the arousal and direction of goal-seeking behavior.

Multiple personality: A dissociative disorder involving the existence of two or more distinct personalities within one individual.

Mystification: A form of miscommunication in which either one or both parties are hiding true feelings or intention from the other.

Negative reinforcer: An event that increases the probability of a response that precedes it by virtue of its removal.

Neurosis: A term formerly used for emotional disturbances in which maladaptive behavior serves to protect against anxiety.

Neurotransmitter: Chemical substance that transmits messages between nerve cells.

Norepinephrine: A hormone produced by the adrenal glands that leads to the physiological changes associated with anger.

Object permanence: The recognition that an object continues to exist even though it is out of sight.

Objectivity: Giving facts as they are without a bias toward either side.

Obsession: A recurring thought or impulse that a person can't stop.

Oedipus complex: In Freudian theory, a young boy's unconscious sexual desires for his mother.

Operant conditioning: A form of learning that occurs whenever the consequences following a response increase or decrease the probability that the response will occur again.

Orgasm: The climax of sexual excitement during which sexual tensions are released.

Orgasm phase: The part of the sexual response cycle during which orgasm occurs.

Ovulation: The release of a mature egg from the ovary.

Parallaction: A form of noncommunication in which conversations parallel one another without interacting.

Penis envy: In Freudian theory, the female's unconscious feelings of jealousy because she doesn't have a penis.

Personality disorders: Deeply ingrained maladaptive patterns of behavior.

Phenomenal field: The sum total of one's experiences, both conscious and unconscious, that defines personal reality.

Phenomenal self: A concept proposed by Rogers; the way individuals view themselves.

Phobia: An irrational and intense fear of people, objects, or events in which the danger is exaggerated.

Phobic disorder: An anxiety disorder characterized by exceptionally intense and irrational fears of some specific object or situation.

Placebo: An inactive substance given in place of a drug in an experiment.

Plateau phase: The second phase of the sexual response cycle during which sexual tensions reach a peak.

Pleasure principle: The tendency to seek immediate gratification of basic needs.

Positive reinforcer: An event that increases the probability of a response that precedes.

Premarital sex: A term commonly used to denote coitus that occurs before marriage.

Preoperational stage: In Piaget's theory of cognitive development, the stage in which language begins to dominate cognitive development.

Progressive relaxation: A method of achieving deep relaxation by alternately tensing and relaxing different muscle groups.

Projection: A defense mechanism in which individuals attribute their own unacceptable impulses or feelings to others.

Psychoanalysis: Therapy approach based on psychoanalytic theories. The psychoanalyst endeavors to help the client gain insight into unconscious impulses, thoughts, and conflicts.

Psychogenic amnesia: A dissociative disorder which involves the memory loss of important personal information.

Psychoses: Severe mental disorders characterized by withdrawal from reality, disordered thought processes, and personality disorganization.

Psychosomatic disorders: Physical symptoms which are aggravated by emotional factors and may involve any of the organ systems controlled by the autonomic nervous system.

Psychosurgery: A controversial technique for treating emotional disturbances by cutting or destroying parts of the brain.

Psychotherapy: The use of psychological methods to treat emotional disturbances.

Rapid eye movement (REM):   Rapid movements of the eye that occur during sleep. When subjects are awakened during stage 1 REM, they generally report that they have been dreaming.

Rational-emotive therapy: Therapeutic approach that directs clients to change irrational beliefs and behavior.

Rationalization: A defense mechanism in which the individual represses underlying motives and invents plausible and acceptable reasons to justify behavior.

Reaction formation: A defense mechanism in which anxiety-arousing impulses are controlled by acting in the opposite way.

Reality principle: Adapting the demands of the id to the realities of the environment.

Refractory period: The period of time following orgasm in the male during which sexual arousal is not possible.

Regress: Return to behaviors characteristic of an earlier stage of development.

Reinforcement: A stimulus that increases the strength of a response that precedes it.

Repression: A defense mechanism in which anxiety-arousing thoughts or desires are automatically ejected from consciousness.

Resistance: In psychoanalysis, the tendency to resist or avoid anxiety-arousing material.

Resolution phase: The final stage of the sexual response cycle during which sexual tensions subside and the body returns to a resting state.

Self (self-concept):   An internal perception of one's competencies, virtues, and feelings of value.

Self-actualization: Maslow's name for the individual's need to strive toward realizing his or her fullest potential in accord with the highest ideals of humanity.

Self-disclosure: The act of openly and honestly revealing certain aspects of oneself to others.

Self-esteem: The way in which we feel about ourselves; self-respect.

Sensate focus: A technique used to decrease sexual performance fears and to increase sexual pleasure through touching and communicating.

Sensitive period: The period of time during which a particular skill or behavior is likely to develop.

Sensory adaptation: The tendency to adjust to a stimulus and stop responding after a time.

Sensory deprivation: An extreme reduction in stimulation.

Sensory-motor stage: According to Piaget, the first stage of cognitive development during which the child comes to know the world through sensory and motor experiences.

Sensory overload: An extreme excess of stimulation.

Sex roles: Social expectations about how men and women are supposed to behave simply because of their sex.

Sexually transmitted diseases: Conditions in which the mode of transmission may be nonsexual as well as sexual.

Social learning: A form of learning that occurs as a result of observing models.

Social self: The self as defined by the ways in which others react to us.

Sodomy: Usually refers to penile-anal intercourse between two males.

Somatization disorder: Disorder characterized by numerous preoccupations with the fear or belief of having a serious disease.

Somatoform disorders: Disorders characterized by physical symptoms without a physical basis.

Spontaneous recovery: The rebound of a previously extinguished learned response following a rest period.

Stimulus generalization: When we have learned to make a response to one stimulus, we tend to make the same response to similar stimuli.

Stimulus needs: The tendency to seek certain kinds of stimulation. No underlying physiological bases have been discovered for this tendency.

Strain: Intense and sometimes harmful tension produced by physical or psychological conditions in life.

Stress: Conflicts, pressures and other external situations or circumstances that impinge upon the organism.

Sublimation: The substitution of alternative or secondary goals for those that are denied.

Substance use disorder: Maladaptive behavior associated with the regular use of substances that affect the central nervous system.

Suppression: Consciously inhibiting thoughts and reactions to events that cause strain.

Syphilis: A venereal disease.

Tolerance: The body's ability to withstand a given amount of drug and its need for increased dosages of that drug to produce the desired effects.

Transference: A psychoanalytic term for the tendency of clients to project or transfer onto the therapist the emotional attitudes they felt toward other significant figures, such as parents or siblings.

Tubal ligation: Female sterilization by cutting the fallopian tubes.

Unconditional positive regard: Rogers' term for acceptance of the value of a person regardless of their behavior.

Unconditioned response: In classical conditioning, any response that is elicited automatically by the unconditioned stimulus.

Unconditioned stimulus: In classical conditioning, a stimulus that automatically elicits a particular response.

Underachievers: People with low levels of achievement motivation whose performance does not live up to their ability.

Vasectomy: Surgical sterilization procedure in the male which involves removing a small part of the sperm-carrying tubes and tying the ends.

Venereal disease: A condition in which the mode of transmission is almost always through sexual contact.

Zygote: Product of the union of an ovum and a sperm; the fertilized egg.

BIBLIOGRAPHY

Abramson, P. R., & Mosher, D. L. Development of a measure of negative attitudes toward masturbation. *Journal of Consulting and Clinical Psychology*, 1975, *43*, 485–490.

Adams, D. B., & Michels, P. J. History-taking: The subleties of body language. *Diagnosis*, December 1981, pp. 37–39.

Ainsworth, M. D. S. The development of infant-mother attachment. In B. Caldwell & H. Ricciuti (Eds.), *Review of child development research* (Vol. 3). Chicago: University of Chicago Press, 1973.

Ajzen, I. Effects of information on interpersonal attraction: Similarity versus affective value. *Journal of Personality and Social Psychology*, 1974, *29*, 374–380.

Aleksandrowicz, M. K. The effect of pain-relieving drugs administered during labor and delivery on the behavior of the newborn: A review. *Merrill-Palmer Quarterly*, 1974, *20*, 2.

Alexander, F. Individual psychotherapy. *Psychosomatic Medicine*, 1946, *8*, 110–115.

Alexander, J. F. Defensive and supportive communications in normal and deviant families. *Journal of Consulting and Clinical Psychology*, 1973, *40*(2), 223–231.

Altman, I., & Taylor, D. *Social penetration: The development of interpersonal relationships.* New York: Holt, Rinehart & Winston, 1973.

Ambrose, J. A. The concept of a critical period in the development of social responsiveness. In B. M. Foss (Ed.), *Determinants of infant behavior* (Vol. 2). New York: John Wiley & Sons, 1963.

Antonovsky, A. *Health, stress and coping.* San Francisco: Jossey-Bass, 1979.

Argyle, M. *Bodily communication.* New York: International Universities Press, 1975.

Athanasiou, R., Shaver, P., & Tavris, C. Sex. *Psychology Today,* July 1970, pp. 39–52.

Atkinson, J. W. *An introduction to motivation.* New York: Van Nostrand Reinhold, 1964.

Atkinson, J. W., & Litwin, G. H. Achievement motive and test anxiety conceived as a motive to approach success and to avoid failure. *Journal of Abnormal and Social Psychology,* 1960, *60,* 52–63.

Ayllon, T., & Michael, J. The psychiatric nurse as a behavioral engineer. *Journal of the Experimental Analysis of Behavior,* 1959, *2,* 323–334.

Ax, A. The physiological differentiation between fear and danger in humans. *Psychosomatic Medicine, 15,* 433–442, 1953.

Bach, G., & Wyden, P. *The intimate enemy: How to fight fair in love and marriage.* New York: William Morrow, 1968.

Bachman, J. G., & Johnston, L. D. The freshmen, 1979. *Psychology Today,* September 1979, pp. 79–87.

Bagby, E. *Psychology of personality.* New York: Henry Holt, 1928; also in Whittaker, J. O. *Introduction to psychology* (2nd ed.). Philadelphia: W. B. Saunders, 1970.

Balagura, S. *Hunger: A biopsychological analysis.* New York: Basic Books, 1973.

Baltes, P. B., & Schaie, K. W. On the plasticity of intelligence in adulthood and old age: Where Horn and Donaldson fail. *American Psychologist,* 1976, *31,* 720–25.

Bandura, A. The role of modeling processes in personality development, in W. W. Hartup & N. L. Smothergill (Eds.), *The young child.* Washington: National Association for the Education of Young Children, 1967.

Bandura, A. *Social learning theory.* Englewood Cliffs, N.J.: Prentice-Hall, 1979.

Bandura, A., Blanchard, E. B., & Ritter, B. Relative efficacy of desensitization and modeling approaches for inducing behavioral, affective, and attitudinal changes. *Journal of Personality and Social Psychology,* 1969, *13,* 173–179.

Bane, M. J. Marital disruption and the lives of children. In G. Levinger & O. C. Moles (Eds.), *Divorce and separation: Context, causes, and consequences.* New York: Basic Books, 1979.

Barchas, J. D., Akil, H., Elliot, G. R., Holman, R. B., & Watson, S. J. Behavioral neurochemistry: Neuroregulators and behavioral states. *Science,* 1978, *200,* 964–973.

Barnett, R. C., & Baruch, G. K. Women in the middle years: A critique of research and theory. *Psychology of Women Quarterly,* 1978, *3,* 187–197.

Bateson, G. Minimal requirements for a theory of schizophrenia. *Archives of General Psychiatry,* 1960, *2,* 477–491.

Baumgold, J. Agoraphobia: Life ruled by panic. *New York Times Magazine,* December 4, 1977, p. 46.

Baxton, W. H., Heron, W., & Scott, T. H. Effects of decreased variation in the sensory environment. *Canadian Journal of Psychology*, 1954, *8*, 70–76.

Beck, A. T. *Cognitive therapy and the emotional disorders*. New York: International Universities Press, 1976.

Beck, A. T., & Greenberg, R. L. "Coping With Depression." Institute for Rational Living, Inc., 1974.

Beck, A. T., & Young, J. E. College blues. *Psychology Today*, September 1978, pp. 80–92.

Bem, S. The measurement of psychological androgyny. *Journal of Counseling and Consulting Psychology*, 1974, *42*, 155–162.

Bem, S., & Lenney, E. Sex-typing and the avoidance of cross-sex behavior. *Journal of Personality and Social Psychology*, 1976, *33*, 48–54.

Benjamin, H. *The transsexual phenomenon*. New York: Julien Press, 1966.

Berger, R. The sleep and dream cycle. In A. Kales (Ed.), *Sleep: Physiology and pathology*. Philadelphia: J. B. Lippincott, 1969.

Bergin, A. E. The evaluation of therapatic outcomes. In A. E. Bergin & S. L. Garfield (Eds.) *Handbook of psychotherapy and behavior change: An empirical analysis* New York: John Wiley & Sons, 1971.

Bergin, A. E., & Suinn, R. M. Individual psychotherapy and behavior therapy. *Annual Review of Psychology*, 1975, *26*.

Berscheid, E., & Walster, E. Physical attractiveness. In L. Berkowitz (Ed.), *Advances in experimental social psychology* (Vol. 7). New York: Academic Press, 1974.

Bevcar, R. J. Self-help books: Some ethical questions. *Personnel and Guidance Journal*, 1978, *56*, 160–162.

Bienvenu, M. Measurement of marital communication. *Family Coordinator*, 1970, *19*, 26–31.

Birren, J. E., Kinney, D. K., Schaie, K. W., & Woodruff, D. S. *Developmental psychology: A life-span approach*. Boston: Houghton Mifflin, 1981.

Bleecker, E. R., & Engel, B. T. Learned control of ventricular rate in patients with atrial fibrillation. *Psychosomatic Medicine*, 1973, *35*, 161–175.

Blehar, M. C., Lieberman, A. F., & Ainsworth, M. D. Early face-to-face interaction and its relation to later infant-mother attachment. *Child development*, 1977, *48*, 182–194.

Bremer, J. *Asexualization.* New York: Macmillan, 1959.

Broverman, I. K., Vogel, S. R., Broverman, D. M., Clarkson, F. E., Rosenkrantz, P. S. Sex-role stereotypes: A current appraisal. *Journal of Social Issues*, 1972, *28*, 59–78.

Brown, R. W. *Social psychology*. New York: Free Press, 1965.

Bruch, H. Obesity and anorexia nervosa. *Psychosomatics*, 1978, *19*, 208–221.

Buber, M. *I and thou*. New York: Charles Scribner's Sons, 1970.

Burr, W. Satisfaction with various aspects of marriage over the life cycle. *Journal of Marriage and the Family*, 1970, *32*(1), 29–37.

Butler, J. M., & Haigh, G. V. Changes in the relation between self-concepts and ideal concepts upon client-centered counseling. In C. R. Roger & R. F. Dymond (Eds.), *Psychotherapy and personality change*. Chicago: University of Chicago Press, 1954.

Byrne, D. *The attraction paradigm*. New York: Academic Press, 1971.

Byrne, D., Baskett, G. D., & Hodges, L. Behavioral indicators of interpersonal attraction. *Journal of Applied Social Psychology*, 1971, *1*, 137–149.

Cameron, N., & Magaret, A. *Behavioral pathology*. Boston: Houghton Mifflin, 1951.

Campbell, A. The American way of mating: Marriage si; children only maybe. *Psychology Today*, May 1975, pp. 37–43.

Cannon, W. B. *Bodily changes in pain, hunger, fear and rage* (2nd ed.). New York: Appleton-Century-Crofts, 1929.

Cartwright, R. D. *A primer on sleep and dreaming*. Reading, Mass.: Addison-Wesley Publishing, 1978.

Cass, L. K., & Thomas, C. B. *Childhood pathology and later adjustment: The question of prediction*. New York: John Wiley & Sons, 1979.

Chess, S., Thomas, A., & Birch, H. G. *Your child is a person*. New York: Viking Press, 1965.

Clifford, M., & Walster, E. The effect of physical attractiveness on teacher expectation. *Sociology of Education*, 1973, *46*, 248.

Coleman, J. C. *Personality dynamics and effective behavior*. Glenview, Ill.: Scott, Foresman, 1960.

Coleman, J. C. *Abnormal psychology and modern life* (5th ed.). Glenview, Ill.: Scott, Foresman, 1976.

Coleman, J. C., Butcher, J. N., and Carson, R. C. *Abnormal psychology and modern life*. 6th ed. Glenview, Ill.: Scott, Foresman, 1980.

Costa, P. T., Jr., & McCrae, R. R. Still stable after all these years: Personality as a key to some issues in aging. In P. B. Bales & O. G. Brim (Eds.), *Life-span development and behavior* (Vol. 3). New York: Academic Press, 1980.

Cox, F. D. *Human intimacy*. St. Paul, Minn.: West Publishing, 1979.

Crain, L. S. Neonatal screening: An overview. *Continuing Education*, February 1982, pp. 53–54, 56–57, 63.

Crooks, R., & Baur, K. *Our sexuality*. Menlo Park, Calif.: Benjamin/Cummings Publishing, 1980.

Deci, E. L. Intrinsic motivation and personality. In E. Staub (Ed.), *Personality: Basic aspects and current research*. Englewood Cliffs, N.J.: Prentice-Hall, 1980.

Dennis, W. Causes of retardation among institutional children: Iran. *Journal of Genetic Psychology*, 1960, *96*, 47–59.

De Rougemont, D. The crisis of the modern couple. In R. N. Anshen (Ed.), *The family: Its function and destiny.* New York: Harper & Row, 1949.

Diagnostic and Statistical Manual of Mental Disorders (DSM-III) (3rd ed.). Washington, D.C.: American Psychiatric Association, 1980.

Dion, K., Berscheid, E., & Walster, E. What is beautiful is good. *Journal of Personality and Social Psychology,* 1972, *24,* 285–290.

Dohrenwend, B. P. & Dohrenwend, B. S. Social and cultural influences on psychopathology. *Annual Review of Psychology,* 1974, *25,* 417–452.

Dorfman, R., & Shipley, T. *Androgens: Biochemistry, physiology, and clinical significance.* New York: John Wiley & Sons, 1956.

Dunbar, F. *Psychosomatic diagnosis.* New York: Harper & Row, 1943.

Dunlap, K. *Habits: Their making and unmaking.* New York: Liveright, 1932.

Ehrlich, H., & Graeven, D. Reciprocal self-disclosure in a dyad. *Journal of Experimental Social Psychology,* 1971, *7,* 389–400.

Eibl-Eibesfeldt, I. Strategies of social interaction. In R. Plutchik and H. Kellerman (Eds.), *Emotion: Theory, research, and experience.* New York: Academic Press, 1980, 57–80.

Ekman, P. The universal smile: Face muscles talk every language. *Psychology Today,* September 1975.

Ekman, P., Sorenson, E. R., & Friesen, W. V. Pan-cultural elements in facial displays of emotion. *Science,* 1969, *164,* 86–88.

Ellison, G. D. Animal models of psychopathology: The low-norepinephrine and low-serotonin rat. *American Psychologist,* 1977, *32,* 1036–1045.

Elmadjian, F. Excretion and metabolism of epinephrine. *Pharmacological Review,* 1959, *11,* 409–415.

Engler, B. *Personality theories: An introduction.* Boston: Houghton Mifflin, 1979.

Etaugh, C. Effects of maternal employment on children: A review of recent research. *Merrill-Palmer Quarterly,* 1974, *20,* 71–98.

Eysenck, H. J. The effects of psychotherapy: an evaluation. *Journal of Consulting Psychology,* 1952, *16,* 319–324.

Farberow, N. L., & Litman, R. E. *A comprehensive suicide prevention program. Suicide Prevention Center of Los Angeles, 1958–1969* (HEW, NIMH Grants No. MH14946 & MH00128). Los Angeles, HEW, NIMH, 1970.

Feather, N. Positive and negative reactions to male and female success and failure in relation to the perceived status and sex-typed appropriateness of occupations. *Journal of Personality and Social Psychology,* 1975, *31*(3), 536–548.

Fein, R. What is wrong with the language of medicine? *The New England Journal of Medicine,* 1982, *306*(14), 863–864.

Ferster, C. B. A functional analysis of depression. *American Psychologist,* 1973, *28,* 857–870.

Fieve, R. R. *Moodswing: The third revolution in psychiatry.* New York: Bantam, 1975.

Firestone, I. J., Kaplan, K., & Russell, J. C. Anxiety, fear and affiliation with similar-state versus dissimilar-state others: Misery sometimes loves nonmiserable company. *Journal of Personality and Social Psychology,* 1973, *26,* 409–414.

Fisher, W. A., & Byrne, D. Too close for comfort: Sex differences in response to invasions of personal space. *Journal of Personality and Social Psychology,* 1975, *32,* 15–21.

Fleck, S. Family dynamics and origin of schizophrenia. *Psychosomatic Medicine,* 1960, *22,* 337–339.

Ford, C., & Beach, F. *Patterns of sexual behavior.* New York: Harper & Row, 1951.

Fraiberg, S. *Insights from the blind: Developmental studies of blind children.* New York: Basic Books, 1976.

Frank, A. C. & Kirk, B. A. Differences in outcomes for users and nonusers of university counseling and psychiatric services: A 5-year accountability study. *Journal of Consulting Psychology,* 1975, *22,* 252–258.

Freud, A. *The Ego and the Mechanisms of Defense* (C. Baines, trans.). New York: International Universities Press, 1946.

Freud, S. *The Psychopathology of Everyday Life* (3rd ed.). New York: MacMillan, 1915.

Friedman, M., & Rosenman, R. *Type A.* New York: Alfred A. Knopf, 1974.

Fuller, G. D. Current status of biofeedback in clinical practice. *American Psychologist,* 1978, *33*(1), 39–48.

Garwood, S. G., et al. Beauty is only "name" deep: The effect of first-name on ratings of physical attraction. *Journal of Applied Social Psychology,* 1980, *10*(5), pp. 431–435.

Glass, D. C. Stress, competition, and heart attacks. *Psychology Today,* 1976, pp. 56–59.

Glass, L. L., Kirsch, M. A., & Parris, J. N. Psychiatric disturbances associated with Erhard Seminars Training: I. Report of cases. *American Journal of Psychiatry,* 1977, *134,* 245–247.

Glick, P. C. Children of divorced parents in demographic perspective. *Journal of Social Issues,* 1979, *35*(4), 170–182.

Gomes-Schwartz, B., Hadley, S. W., & Strupp, H. H. Individual psychotherapy and behavior therapy. *Annual Review of Psychology,* 1978, *29,* 435–471.

Goode, W. J. Family disorganization. In R. K. Merton & R. A. Nisbet (Eds.), *Contemporary social problems.* New York: Harcourt Brace Jovanovich, 1961.

Goodenough, F. *Anger in young children.* University of Minnesota Institute of Child Welfare Monographs, No. 9. 1975. Reprint of 1931 edition.

Gordon, S. *Lonely in America.* New York: Simon & Schuster, 1976.

Gould, R. Growth toward self–tolerance. *Psychology Today,* February 1975.

Grasha, A. F. *Practical applications of psychology*. Cambridge, Mass.: Winthrop Publishers, 1978.

Gray, J. A. Anxiety. *Human Nature*, 1978, *1*, 38–45.

Guze, S. R. Early recognition of depression. *Hospital Practice*, September 1981, pp. 87–89.

Haber, A., & Runyon, R. P. *Fundamentals of psychology* (3rd ed.). Reading, Mass.: Addison-Wesley Publishing, 1983.

Hall, E. T. Proxemics. *Current Anthropology*, 1968, *9*, 83–107.

Hamilton, D., & Bishop, G. Attitudinal and behavioral effects of initial integration of white suburban neighborhoods. *Journal of Social Issues*, 1976, *32*, 47–67.

Hamilton, J. Demonstrable ability of penile erection in castrate men with markedly low titers of urinary androgen. *Proceedings of the Society of Experimental Biology and Medicine*, 1943, *54*, 309.

Hariton, E. B., & Singer, J. L. Women's fantasies during sexual intercourse: Normative and theoretical implications. *Journal of Consulting and Clinical Psychology*, 1974, *42*, 313–322.

Harrison, J. Warning: The male sex role may be dangerous to your health. *Journal of Social Issues*, 1978, *34*, 65–86.

Hartley, D., Roback, H. B., & Abramowitz, S. I. Deterioration effects in encounter groups. *American Psychologist*, 1976, *31*, 247–255.

Hartmann, E., Baekeland, F., & Zwilling, G. Psychological differences between long and short sleepers. *Archives of General Psychiatry*, 1972, *26*, 463–468.

Hetherington, E. M. "Divorce: A child's perspective." *American Psychologist*, 1979, *34*, 851–859.

Hill, C. T., Rubin, Z., & Peplau, L. A. Break-ups before marriage: The end of 103 affairs. *Journal of Social Issues*, 1976, *32*, 147–158.

Hite, S. *The Hite Report: A nationwide survey on female sexuality*. New York: Macmillan, 1976.

Hochberg, J. *Perception* (2nd ed.). Englewood Cliffs, N.J.: Prentice-Hall, 1978.

Hoffman, L. W., & Nye, F. I. (Eds.). *Working mothers: an evaluative review of the consequences for wife, husband, and child*. San Francisco: Jossey-Bass, 1974.

Hohmann, G. W. Some effects of spinal cord lesions on experienced emotional feelings. *Psychophysiology*, 1966, *3*, 143–156.

Holmes, T. H., & Rahe, R. H. The social readjustment rating scale. *Journal of Psychosomatic Research*, 1967, *11*, 213–218.

Holroyd, K., Andrasik, F., & Westbrook, K. Cognitive control of tension headache. *Cognitive Therapy and Research*, 1977, *1*, 121–133.

Horner, M. S. Toward an understanding of achievement-related conflicts in women. *Journal of Social Issues*, 1972, *28*, 157–175.

Hunt, J. McV. Psychological development: early experience. *Annual Review of Psychology*, 1979, *30*, 103–143.

Hunt, J. McV., Mohandessi, K., Ghodssi, M., & Akiyama, M. The psychological development of orphanage-reared infants: Interventions with outcomes (Tehran). *Genet. Psychol. Monogr.*, 1976, *94*, 177–226.

Hunt, M. *Sexual behavior in the 1970s.* Chicago: Playboy Press, 1974.

Hyde, J. S. *Understanding human sexuality.* New York: McGraw-Hill, 1979.

Isaacson, R. L. Relation between n-Achievement, test anxiety, and curricular choices. *Journal of Abnormal and Social Psychology*, 1964, *68*, 447–452.

Jacobson, E. *Progressive Relaxation.* Chicago: University of Chicago Press, 1938.

James, W. What is an emotion? *Mind*, 1884, 9.

Janda, L., O'Grady, K., & Capps, C. Fear of success in males and females in sex-linked occupations. *Sex Roles*, 1978, *4*(1), 43–50.

Janis, I. L., & Feshback, S. "Effects of fear-arousing communications." *Journal of Abnormal and Social Psychology*, 1953, *48*, 78–92.

Janis, I. L., & King, B. T. The influence of role playing on attitude change. *Journal of Abnormal and Social Psychology*, 1954, *99*, 211–218.

Johnson, D. W. *Reaching out: Interpersonal effectiveness and self-actualization.* Englewood Cliffs, N.J.: Prentice-Hall, 1972.

Kahn, M. The physiology of catharsis. *Journal of Personality and Social Psychology*, 1966, *3*, 278–86.

Kales, A., Caldwell, A., Preston, T., Healey, S., & Kales, J. Personality patterns in insomnia. *Archives of General Psychiatry*, 1976, *33*, 1128–1134.

Kales, A., & Kales, J. Recent advances in the diagnosis and treatment of sleep disorders. In D. Usdin (Ed.), *Sleep. Research and Clinical Practice.* New York: Brunner/Mazel, 1973.

Kaplan, H. *The new sex therapy: Active treatment of sexual dysfunction.* New York: Breunner/Mazel, 1974.

Kaplan, H. S., & Sager, C. J. Sexual patterns at different ages. *Medical Aspects of Human Sexuality*, 1971, *5*(6), 10–23.

Kelley, H. H., & Michela, J. L. Attribution theory and research. *Annual Review of Psychology*, 1980, *31*, 457–501.

Kinsey, A., Pomeroy, W., & Martin, C. *Sexual Behavior in the Human Male.* Philadelphia: W. B. Saunders, 1948.

Kinsey, A., Pomeroy, W., Martin, C., & Gebhard, P. *Sexual behavior in the human female.* Philadelphia: W. B. Saunders, 1953.

Kirsch, M. A., & Glass, L. L. Psychiatric disturbances associated with Erhard Seminars Training. *American Journal of Psychiatry*, 1977, *134*, 1254–1258.

Kisker, G. W. *The disorganized personality.* New York: McGraw-Hill, 1964.

Kobasa, S. C. Stressful life events, personality and health: An inquiry into hardiness. *Journal of Personality and Social Psychology*, 1979, *37*, 1–11.

Kobasa, S. C., & Maddi, S. R. Existential personality theory. In R. Corsini (Ed.), *Current Personality Theory.* Itasca, Ill.: F. E. Peacock Publishers, 1977.

Kobasa, S. C., Maddi, S. R., & Courington, S. Personality and constitution as mediators in the stress-illness relationship. *Journal of Health and Social Behavior,* 1981, 368–378.

Kobasa, S. C., Maddi, S. R., & Puccetti, M. C. Personality and exercise as buffers in the stress-illness relationship. *Journal of Behavioral Medicine,* 1982, *5,* 391–404.

Kohlberg, L. The development of children's orientations toward a moral order: I. Sequence in the development of moral thought. *Vita Humana,* 1963, *6,* 11–33.

Kohlberg, L. *The meaning and measurement of moral development.* Heinz Werner Memorial Lecture, 1980.

Korman, A. K., Greenhaus, J. H. and Badin, I. J. Personal attitudes and motivation. *Annual Review of Psychology,* 1977, *28,* 175–196.

Krisher, H. P., Darley, S. A., & Darley, J. M. "Fear-provoking recommendations, intentions to take preventive actions, and actual preventive action." *Journal of Personality and Social Psychology,* 1973, *26,* 301–308.

Kroeber, T. C. The coping functions of ego mechanisms. In R. W. White (Ed.), *The study of lives.* New York: Atherton Press, 1973.

Landreth, C. *Early childhood: Behavior and learning.* New York: Alfred A. Knopf, 1967.

Lanzetta, J. T., Cartwright–Smith, J., & Kleck, R. E. Effects of nonverbal dissimulation on emotional experience and autonomic arousal. *Journal of Personality and Social Psychology,* 1976. *33,* 354–370.

Laumann, E. O. Friends of urban men: An assessment of accuracy in reporting their socioeconomic attributes, mutual choice, and attitude agreement. *Sociometry,* 1969, *32,* 54–69.

Lazarus, R., interviewed by Goleman D. Positive denial: A case for not facing reality. *Psychology Today,* 1979.

Lee, J. A. The styles of loving. *Psychology Today,* October 1974, pp. 43–51.

Leff, M. J., Roatch, J. F., & Bunney, W. E., Jr. Environmental factors preceding the onset of severe depression. *Psychiatry,* 1970, *33,* 298–311.

LeMasters, E. E. *Parents in Modern America,* rev. ed. Homewood; Ill.: Dorsey Press, 1974.

Lepper, M. R., & Greene, D. (Eds.). *The hidden costs of reward: New perspectives on the psychology of motivation.* Hillsdale, N.J.: Erlbaum, 1978.

Lepper, M. R., Greene, D., & Nisbett, R. E. Undermining children's intrinsic interest with extrinsic reward: A test of the "overjustification" hypothesis. *Journal of Personality and Social Psychology,* 1973, *28,* 129–137.

Levenstein, P. The mother–child home program. In *The preschool in action,* (2nd Ed.) Ed. M. C. Day and R. K. Parker, Boston: Allyn & Bacon, 1976.

Levenstein, P. The mother-child home program. In M. C. Day & R. K. Parker (Eds.), *The preschool in action* (2nd ed.). Boston: Allyn & Bacon, 1976.

Leventhal, H., & Singer, R. Affect arousal and positioning of recommendation in persuasive communications. *Journal of Personality and Social Psychology,* 1966, *4,* 143–146.

Levinson, D. J. with Darrow, C. N., Klein, E. B., Levinson, M. H., & McKee, B. *The seasons of a man's life.* New York: Alfred A. Knopf, 1978.

Lewin K. *A dynamic theory of personality.* New York: McGraw-Hill, 1935.

Lewinsohn, P. M. The behavioral study and treatment of depression. In M. Hersen, R. M. Eisler, & P. M. Miller (Eds.), *Progress in behavior modification* (Vol. 1). New York: Academic Press, 1975.

Liberman, R. P. & Raskin, D. E. "Depression: A Behavioral Formulation." *Archives of General Psychiatry,* 1971, *24,* 515–523.

Lieberman, M. A. Group methods. In F. H. Kanfer & A. P. Goldstein (Eds.), *Helping people change.* Elmsford, N.Y.: Pergamon Press, 1975.

Lieberman, M. A., Yalom, I. D., & Miles, M. *Encounter groups: First facts.* New York: Basic Books, 1973.

Liebert, R. M., Poulos, R. W., & Strauss, G. *Developmental Psychology.* Englewood Cliffs, N.J.: Prentice-Hall, 1974.

Liebman, R., Minuchin, S., & Baker, L. An integrated treatment program for anorexia nervosa. *American Journal of Psychiatry,* 1974, *131,* 432–436.

Lowenthal, M. F., & Chiriboga, D. Transition to the empty nest. *Archives of General Psychiatry,* 1972, *26,* 8–14.

Luborsky, L., et al. Factors influencing the outcome of psychotherapy: A review of quantitative research. *Psychological Bulletin,* 1971, *75,* 145–185.

Luchins, A. S. Primacy–recency in impression formation. In C. I. Hovland (Ed.), *The order of presentation in persuasion.* New Haven, Conn.: Yale University Press, 1957.

Luft, J. *Of human interaction.* Palo Alto, Calif.: National Press Books, 1969.

Luft, J. *Group processes: An introduction to group dynamics.* Palo Alto, Calif.: National Press Books, 1970.

Lynn, D. *The father: His role in child development.* Monterey, Calif.: Brooks/Cole Publishing, 1974.

Maddi, S. R. Personal communication. 1983.

Marks, J. M. *Patterns in meaning in psychiatric patients.* London: Oxford University Press, 1965.

Maslach, C. Negative emotional biasing of unexplained arousal. *Journal of Personality and Social Psychology,* 1979, *37,* 359–369.

Maslow, A. H. *Motivation and personality,* 2d. ed. New York: Harper & Row, 1970.

Maslow, A. H. *Toward a psychology of being.* Princeton: Van Nostrand, 1962.

Masters, W., & Johnson, V. *Human sexual response*. Boston: Little, Brown, 1966.

Masters, W., & Johnson, V. *Human sexual inadequacy*. Boston: Little, Brown, 1970.

McCaul, K. D., Solomon, S., & Holmes, D. S. Effects of paced respiration and expectations on physiological and psychological responses to threat. *Journal of Personality and Social Psychology*, 1979, *37*, 564–571.

McClelland, D. C. Business drive and national achievement. *Harvard Business Review*, July-August 1962, pp. 99–112.

McCroskey, J. C., Larson, C. E., & Knapp, M. L. *Introduction to interpersonal communication*. Englewood Cliffs, N.J.: Prentice-Hall, 1971.

McGinley, H., LeFevre, R., & McGinley, P. The influence of a communicator's body position on opinion change in others. *Journal of Personality and Social Psychology*, 1975, *31*, 686–690.

Meichenbaum, D. *Cognitive behavior modification*. New York: Plenum Press, 1977.

Meichenbaum, D. Toward a cognitive theory of self control. In G. Schwartz, and D. Shapiro (Eds.), *Consciousness and self-regulation: Advances in research*. New York: Plenum Press, 1976.

Meichenbaum, D., & Turk, D. The cognitive-behavioral management of anxiety, anger and pain. In P. O. Davidson (Ed.), *The behavioral management of anxiety, depression, and pain*. New York: Brunner/Mazel, 1976.

Mendels, J. *Concepts of depression*. New York: John Wiley & Sons, 1970.

Middlebrook, P. N. *Social psychology and modern life*. New York: Alfred A. Knopf, 1980, 1982.

Milgram, S. Behavioral study of obedience. *Journal of Abnormal and Social Psychology*, 1963, *67*, 371–378.

Milgram, S. Liberating effects of group pressure. *Journal of Personality and Social Psychology*, 1965, *1*, 127–134.

Milgram, S. *Texture of everyday urban experience*. Lecture given at the University of California, Berkeley, January 20, 1977.

Miller, N. E. Experimental studies of conflict. In J. McV. Hunt (Ed.), *Personality and the behavior disorders* (Vol. I). New York: Ronald Press, 1944.

Miller, N. E. Postscript. In D. Singh & C. T. Morgan (Eds.), *Current status of physiological psychology: Readings*. Monterey, Calif.: Brooks/Cole Publishing, 1972.

Miller, N. Summary and conclusions. In H. Gerard, & N. Miller, *School desegregation*. New York: Plenum Press, 1975.

Miller, N. E., Behavioral medicine: Symbiosis between laboratory and clinic. *Annual Review of Psychology*, 1983, *34*, 1–31.

Mischel, W. *Personality and assessment*. New York: John Wiley & Sons, 1968.

Montagu, A. *The nature of human aggression*. New York: Oxford University Press, 1976.

Moody, S., & Graham, V. Why? *Sunday Sun Times,* November 26, 1978, pp. 8–10.

Moore, T. Stress in normal childhood. *Human Relations,* 1969, *22,* 235–250.

Mueller, C., & Donnerstein, E. The effects of humor–induced arousal upon aggressive behavior. *Journal of Research in Personality,* 1977, *11,* 73–82.

Musante, G. J. The dietary rehabilitation clinic: Evaluative report of a behavioral and dietary treatment of obesity. *Behav. Ther.,* 1976, *7,* 198–204.

Muson, H. Getting the phone's number. *Psychology Today,* April 1982, pp. 42–49.

Nathan, P. E., & Harris, S. L. *Psychopathology and society* (2nd ed.). New York: McGraw-Hill, 1975.

Navarick, D. J. *Principles of learning: From laboratory to field.* Reading, Mass.: Addison-Wesley, 1979.

Neugarten, B. L. Adaptation and the life cycle. *Journal of Geriatric Psychiatry,* 1970, *4.*

Neugarten, B. L. Grow old along with me. *Psychology Today,* December 1971.

Neugarten, B. L. interviewed by E. Hall. Acting one's age: New rules for old. *Psychology Today,* April 1980.

Newman, B. M., & Newman, P. R. *Development through life: A psychosocial approach* (2nd ed.). Homewood, Ill.: Dorsey Press, 1979.

Norton, A. J., & Glick, P. C. Marital instability in America: Past, present, and future. In G. Levinger, & O. C. Moles (Eds.), *Divorce and separation.* New York: Basic Books, 1979.

Novaca, R. A treatment program for the management of anger through cognitive and relaxation controls. Unpublished doctoral dissertation, Indiana Unversity, Bloomington, Indiana, 1974.

Novack, D., & Lerner, M. Rejection as a consequence of perceived similarity. *Journal of Personality and Social Psychology,* 1968, *9,* 147–152.

Novaco, R. W. *Anger control: The development and evaluation of an experimental treatment.* Lexington, Mass.: Lexington Books, 1975.

Novaco, R. W. Stress inoculation: A cognitive therapy for anger and its application to a case of depression. *Journal of Consulting Clinical Psychology,* 1977a, *45,* 600–608.

Novaco, R. W. A stress inoculation approach to anger management in the training of law enforcement officers. *American Journal of Community Psychology,* 1977b, *5,* 327–346.

Noyes, A. P., & Kolb, L. C. *Modern clinical psychiatry.* Philadelphia: W. B. Saunders, 1963.

O'Neill, N., & O'Neill, G. *Open marriage: A new lifestyle for couples.* New York: Evans, 1972.

Osipow, S. H., Walsh, W. B., & Tosi, D. J. *A survey of counseling methods.* Homewood, Ill.: Dorsey Press, 1980.

Papalia, D. E. The status of several conservation abilities across the life span. *Human Development*, 1972, *15*, 229–243.

Parloff, M. B. Shopping for the right therapy. *Saturday Review*, February 21, 1976.

Parloff, M. B., & Dies, R. R. Group psychotherapy outcome research 1966–1975. *International Journal of Group Psychotherapy*, 1977, *27*, 281–319.

Parmelee, A. H., & Haber, A. Who is the risk infant? *Clinical Obstetrics and Gynecology*, 1973, *16*, 376–387.

Paul, G. L. Physiological effects of relaxation training and hypnotic suggestion. *Journal of Abnormal Psychology*, 1969, *74*, 425–437.

Pelletier, K. R. *Mind as healer, mind as slayer.* New York: Dell, 1977.

Pempus, E., Sawaya, C., & Cooper, R. E. *"Don't fence me in": Personal space depends on architectural enclosure.* Paper presented to the American Psychological Association, Chicago, 1975.

Pengelley, E. *Sex and human life.* Reading, Mass.: Addison-Wesley, 1979.

Penney, A. *How to make love to a man.* New York: Clarkson N. Potter, 1981.

Peplau, L. Impact of fear of success and sex-role attitudes on women's competitive achievement. *Journal of Personality and Social Psychology*, 1976, *34*, 561–568.

Phillip, A. E., & Clay, E. L. Psychiatric symptoms and personality traits in patients suffering from gastrointestinal illness. *Journal of Psychosomatic Research*, 1972, *16*, 47–51.

Piaget, J. *The moral judgment of the child.* New York: Free Press, 1948.

Piaget, J. *The origins of intelligence in children.* New York: International Universities Press, 1952.

Piaget, J. Intellectual evolution from adolescence to adulthood. *Human Development*, 1972, *15*, 1–12.

Plutchik, R. *Emotion: A psychoevolutionary synthesis.* New York: Harper & Row, 1980.

Price, R. H., & Lynn, S. J. *Abnormal psychology in the human context.* Homewood Ill.: Dorsey Press, 1981.

Prochaska, J. O. *Systems of psychotherapy: A transtheoretical analysis.* Homewood Ill: Dorsey Press, 1979.

Publication Manual (2nd. ed.). Washington D.C.: American Psychological Association, 1974.

Rakel, R. E. et al., Interpret every nonverbal cue. *Patient Care*, September 15, 1981, pp. 106–119.

Raschke, H. J., & Raschke, V. J. Family conflict and children's self-concepts: A comparison of intact and single-parent families. *Journal of Marriage and the Family*, 1979, *41*, 367–374.

Rees, L. The importance of psychological, allergic, and infective factors in childhood asthma. *Journal of Psychosomatic Research*, 1964, *7*, 253–262.

Rest, J. R. The hierarchial nature of moral judgment: The study of patterns of comprehension and preference with moral stages. *Journal of Personality,* 1974, *41,* 92–93.

Retardation: 'fragile X' accounts for only 25% of chromosomes' dangling tips. *Medical World News,* March 1, 1982, p. 31.

Reykowski, J. Social motivation. *Annual Review of Psychology,* 1982, *33,* 123–154.

Rogers, C. R. *Carl Rogers on personal power.* New York: Delacorte, 1977.

Rogers, C. *Carl Rogers on encounter groups.* New York: Harper & Row, 1970.

Rogers, C. *Client-centered therapy.* Boston: Houghton Mifflin, 1951.

Rogers, C. A theory of therapy, personality and interpersonal relationships as developed in the client-centered framework. In S. Koch (Ed.), *Psychology: A study of a science* (Vol. 3). New York: McGraw-Hill, 1959.

Rogers, C. *On becoming a person.* Boston: Houghton Mifflin, 1961.

Rogers, C. The therapeutic relationship: Recent theory and research. In I. G. Sarason, (Ed.), *Contemporary Research in Personality.* Princeton, N.J.: Van Nostrand, 1969.

Rosenman, R. H., Brand, R. J., Jenkins, C. D., Friedman, M., Straus, R., & Wurm, M. Coronary heart disease in the Western Collaborative Group Study: Final follow-up experience of 8 1/2 years. *Journal of the American Medical Association,* 1975, *233,* 872–877.

Rubin, K. H., Attewell, P. W., Tierney, M. C., & Tumolo, P. Development of spatial egocentrism and conservation across the life span. *Developmental Psychology,* 1973, *9,* 432.

Rubin, Z. Measurement of romantic love. *Journal of Personality and Social Psychology,* 1970, *16,* 270.

Runyon, R. P. *How numbers lie: A consumer's guide to the fine art of numerical deception.* Lexington, Mass.: Lewis Publishing, 1981.

Sabalis, R. F., Frances, A., Appenzeller, S. N., & Moseley, W. B. The three sisters: Transsexual male siblings. *American Journal of Psychiatry,* 1974, *131,* 907–909.

Scanlon, J. W. & Alper, M. H. *Perinatal pharmacology and evaluation of the newborn.* Boston: Little, Brown, 1974.

Schacter, S. The interaction of cognitive and physiological determinants of emotional state. In L. Berkowitz, (Ed.), *Advances in Experimental Social Psychology* (Vol. 1). New York: Academic Press, 1964.

Schachter, S. *The psychology of affiliation.* Stanford, Calif.: Stanford University Press, 1959.

Schachter, S. *Emotion, obesity and crime.* New York: Academic Press, 1971.

Schachter, S., & Rodin, J. *Obese humans and rats.* Potomac, Md.: Lawrence Earlbaum, 1974.

Schacter, S., & Singer, J. E. Cognitive, social and physiological determinants of emotional state. *Psychological Review,* 1962, *69,* 379–399.

Schanche, D. A. The emotional aftermath of "the largest tornado ever." *Today's Health,* 1974, *52;* 16–19; 61; 63–64.

Schreiber, F. R. *Sybil.* New York: Warren Books, 1974.

Schurenberg, E. Sheepish smiles don't hide embarrassment. *Psychology Today,* November, 1981, p. 29.

Schutz, W. C. *Joy.* New York: Grove Press, 1967.

Sclafani, A. Appetite and hunger in experimental obesity syndrome. In D. Novin, W. Wyrwicka, & G. Bray, (Eds.), *Hunger: Basic mechanisms and clinical implications.* New York: Raven Press, 1976.

Sclafani, A., & Kluge, L. Food motivation and body weight—Level I. Hypothalamic hyperphagic rats: A dual lipostat model of hunger and appetite. *Journal of Comparative and Physiological Psychology,* 1974, *86,* 28–46.

Scovern, A., & Kilmann, P. R. Status of electroconvulsive therapy: Review of the outcome literature. *Psychological Bulletin,* 1980, *87,* 260–303.

Scrimshaw, N. S. Early malnutrition and central nervous system function. *Merrill Palmer Quarterly,* 1969, *15,* 375–388.

Seamen, B., & Seamen, G. *Women and the crisis in sex hormones.* New York: Bantam, 1978.

Seligman, M. E. P. *Helplessness.* San Francisco: W. H. Freeman, 1975.

Selye, H. *The stress of life.* New York: McGraw-Hill, 1978.

Shaffer, L. F., & Shoben, E. J. *The psychology of adjustment* (2nd ed.). Boston: Houghton Mifflin, 1956.

Sheehy, G. *Passages: Predictable crises from adult life.* New York: E. P. Dutton, 1976.

Sheehy, G. *Path finders.* New York: William Morrow, 1981.

Singer, R. D., & Singer, A. *Psychological development in children.* Philadelphia: W. B. Saunders, 1969.

Skeels, H. M. Adult status of children with contrasting early life experiences. *Monographs of the Society for Research in Child Development,* 1966, *31*(3).

Sloane, R. B., Staples, F. R., Cristol, A. H., Yorkston, N. J., & Whipple, K. *Psychotherapy versus behavior therapy.* Cambridge, Mass.: Harvard University Press, 1975.

Smith, M. L., & Glass, G. V. Meta-analysis of psychotherapy outcome studies. *American Psychologist,* 1977, *32,* 752–760.

Smith, S. & Lewty, W. Perceptual isolation using a silent room. *Lancet,* 1959, *1,* 342–345.

Snyder, W. U. *Casebook of non-directive counseling.* Boston: Houghton Mifflin, 1947.

Sorlie, P., Gordon, J., & Kennell, W. B. Body build and mortality: The Framingham study. *Journal of the American Medical Association*, May 9, 1980.

Sparks, R. A., Purrier, B. G., & Watt, P. J. Does a tailed IUD facilitate uterine infection? *Modern Medicine*, September 1981, pp. 154–155.

Spence, J. T., Helmreich, R., & Stapp, J. Ratings of self and peer on sex-role attributes and their relation to self-esteem and conceptions of masculinity and femininity. *Journal of Personality and Social Psychology*, 1975, *32*, 29–39.

Spielberger, C. D. Conceptual and methodological issues in anxiety research. In C. D. Spielberger (Ed.), *Anxiety: Current trends in theory and research* (Vol. II). New York: Academic Press, 1972.

Spitz, R. A. Hospitalization: An inquiry into the genesis of psychiatric conditions in early childhood. In R. A. Eissler, et al. (Eds.), *The psychoanalytic study of the child* (Vol. 1). New York: International Universities Press, 1945.

Spitzer, R. L., Skodol, A. E., Gibbon, M., & Williams, J. B. W. *DSM-III case book*. Washington D.C.: American Psychiatric Association, 1981.

Squire, L. R. et al. *Archives of General Psychiatry*, 1981, *38*.

Star, S., Williams, R., Jr., and Stouffer, S. Negro infantry platoons in white companies. In H. Proshansky, and B. Seidenberg, (Eds.), *Basic studies in social psychology*. New York: Holt, Rinehart & Winston, 1965.

Stewart, A. How women cope with stress—contrasting styles. *Psychology Today*, 1978, p. 116.

Strelau, J. *A regulative theory of temperament*. University of Warsaw, 1980.

Strupp, H. H., & Hadley, S. W. Specific versus nonspecific factors in psychotherapy: A controlled study of outcome. *Archives of General Psychiatry*, 1979, *36*, 1125–1136.

Sue, D., Sue, D. W., & Sue, S. *Understanding abnormal behavior*. Boston: Houghton Mifflin, 1981.

Suinn, R. M. *Fundamentals of behavior pathology*. New York: John Wiley & Sons, 1970.

Sullivan, K., & Sullivan, A. Adolescent-parent separation. *Developmental Psychology*, 1980, *16*, 93–99.

Taylor, S., & Mettee, D. When similarity breeds contempt. *Journal of Personality and Social Psychology*, 1972, *20*, 75–81.

Tavris, C., & Jayaratne, T. E. How happy is your marriage? What 75,000 wives say about their most intimate relationship. *Redbook*, June 1976, pp. 90–92; 132; 134.

Teichman, Y. Emotional arousal and affiliation. *Journal of Experimental Social Psychology*, 1973, *9*, 591–605.

Thesaurus of psychological index terms (3rd ed.). Washington, D.C.: American Psychological Association, 1982.

Thomas, D. W., & Mayer, J. The search for the secret of fat. *Psychology Today,* ·September 1973, pp. 74–79.

Timson, J. Is coffee safe to drink? *Human Nature,* December 1978.

Ubell, E. Upsetting an old taboo. *Parade,* November 1, 1981, pp. 4–5.

Udry, J. R. *The social context of marriage.* Philadelphia: J. B. Lippincott, 1966.

U.S. News & World Report, January 15, 1979, p. 67.

Vaillant, G. *Adaptation to life.* Boston: Little, Brown, 1977.

Valenstein, E. S. *Brain control.* New York: John Wiley & Sons, 1973.

Van Buren, A. *The Best of Dear Abby.* New York: Andrews and McMeel, Inc., 1981.

Van Gelder, L., & Carmichael, C. But what about our sons. *MS Magazine,* October 1975.

Wallerstein, J. S., & Kelly, J. B. California's children of divorce. *Psychology Today,* January 1980, pp. 67–76.

Walster, E., & Walster, G. W. *A new look at love.* Reading Mass.: Addison-Wesley Publishing, 1978.

Wechsler, H., Grosser, G. H., & Greenblatt, M. Research evaluating anti-depressant medications on hospitalized mental patients: a survey of published reports during a 5-year period. *Journal of Nervous and Mental Disease,* 1965, *141,* 231–239.

Weideger, P. *Menstruation and menopause: The physiology, the psychology, the myth and the reality.* New York: Alfred A. Knopf, 1976.

Weiner, B., Frieze, I., Kukla, A., Reed, L., Rest, S., & Rosenbaum, R. M. *Perceiving the causes of success and failure.* General Learning Corporation, 1971.

Weiss, J. M., Glazer, H. I., and Pohorecky, L. A. Neurotransmitters and helplessness: A chemical bridge to depression. *Psychology Today,* 1974, pp. 58–65.

Weiss, R. S. *Marital separation.* New York: Basic Books, 1975.

Wells, G., & Harvey, J. Do people use consensus information in making causal attributions? *Journal of Personality and Social Psychology,* 1977, *35,* 279–293.

White, B. L. Critical influences in the origins of competence. *Merrill-Palmer Quarterly,* 1975, *21,* 243–266.

White, B. L., & Watts, J. C. *Experience and environment* (Vol. 1). Englewood Cliffs, N.J.: Prentice-Hall, 1973.

White, M. Interpersonal distance as affected by room size, status, and sex. *Journal of Social Psychology,* 1975, *95,* 241–249.

Whittaker, J. O. *Introduction to psychology* (2nd ed.). Philadelphia: W. B. Saunders, 1970.

Winch, R. F. *Mate selection: A study of complementary needs.* New York: Harper & Row, 1958.

Winch, R. F. *The modern family* (Rev. ed.). New York: Holt, Rinehart & Winston, 1963.

Winterbottom, M. R. The relation of childhood training in independence to achievement motivation (Doctoral dissertation, University of Michigan, 1953). *University Microfilms,* No. 5113.

Wirtenberg, T., & Nakamura, C. Education: Barrier or boon to changing occupational roles of women. *Journal of Social Issues,* 1976, *32,* 165–179.

Wolf, S., & Wolff, H. G. *Human gastric functions.* New York: Oxford University Press, 1947.

Wolpe, J., & Lazarus, A. A. *Behavior therapy techniques.* Elmsford N.Y.: Pergamon Press, 1966.

Worchel, S., & Cooper, J. *Understanding social psychology* (Rev. ed.). Homewood Ill.: Dorsey Press, 1979.

World Almanac and Book of Facts. New York: Newspaper Enterprise Association, 1980.

Yalom, I., & Lieberman, M. A study of encounter group casualties. *Archives of General Psychiatry,* 1971, *25,* 16–30.

Yang, R. K., Zweig, A. R., Douthitt, T. C., & Federman, E. J. Successive relationships between maternal attitudes during pregnancy, analgesic medication during labor and delivery, and newborn behavior. *Developmental Psychology,* 1976, *12*(1), 6–14.

Yarrow, L. J. Separation from parents in early childhood. In M. L. Hoffman, & L. W. Hoffman (Eds.), *Review of child development research* (Vol. 1). New York: Russell Sage Foundation, 1964.

Yarrow, L. J. The development of focused relationships during infancy. In J. Hellmuth (Ed.), *Exceptional infant.* Special Child Publications, 1967.

Zaludek, G. M. How to cope with male menopause. *Science Digest,* February 1976, pp. 74–79.

Zillman, D. Excitation transfer in communication-mediated aggressive behavior. *Journal of Experimental Social Psychology,* 1971, *7,* 419–434.

Zillman, D., Johnson, R. C., & Day, K. D. Attribution of apparent arousal and proficiency of recovery from sympathetic activation affecting excitation transfer to aggressive behavior. *Journal of Experimental Social Psychology,* 1974, *10,* 503–515.

Zimbardo, P. G. *Shyness.* Reading, Mass.: Addison-Wesley Publishing, 1977.

Zimmerman, B. J., & Dialessi, F. Modeling influences on children's creative behavior. *Journal of Educational Psychology,* 1973, *65,* 127–134.

Zuckerman, M. *Manual and research report for the Sensation-Seeking Scale (SSS).* University of Delaware, Newark, Delaware, April 1972.

INDEX

This book has been set VideoComp in 10 and 9 point Renaissance, leaded 2 points. Chapter numbers are 24 point Renaissance and chapter titles are 16 point Renaissance bold. The overall type area is 36 by 47½ picas.